NEWCOMER'S HANDBOOK

For Moving To and Living In

Seattle

Including Bellevue, Redmond, Everett, and Tacoma

2nd Edition

FIRST BOOKS

6750 SW Franklin
Portland, OR 9722?
503-968-6777
www.firstbooks.cor

D0210261

Authors: Monica Fischer, Amy Bellamy
Series Editor: Bernadette Duperron
Publisher: Jeremy Solomon
Design: Erin Johnson
Maps provided by Jim Miller/fennana design
Transit map courtesy of MetroTransit

ISBN 0-912301-51-1
ISSN 1540-7098

Printed in the USA on recycled paper.

Published by First Books, 6750 SW Franklin Street, Portland, OR 97223, 503-968-6777.

TABLE OF CONTENTS

CONTENTS

Apartment finding tips, rental publications, listing services, roommate services; leases; rent and eviction control; renter's/homeowner's insurance; house hunting tips, real estate agencies, mortgages

CONTENTS

WELCOME TO SEATTLE, ONE OF THE MOST LIVABLE URBAN AREAS in the world! No doubt you've heard about the rain, but there's a lot more to the "Emerald City" than that. Part of the Pacific Northwest, Seattle is one of the most beautiful and lush regions in the United States. On a clear day, from atop every one of Seattle's many hills, you can view snow-capped mountains, including majestic Mount Rainier to the southeast, crystal-clear lakes, or the magnificent Puget Sound.

Don't be daunted by the rumors you've heard about Seattle and rain. While it's certainly true that the city has its share of rainy days, much of Seattle's rain is really a fine mist or drizzle. Often a day that starts off cloudy becomes bright and sunny by afternoon. Winters are wet but mild, averaging about five inches of rain per month from November to January, with temperatures seldom falling below the low to mid-30s. Summers are comfortably warm, typically in the mid-70s. Spring and fall are cool but often sunny, and you'll enjoy some of the most spectacular views during these seasons, with snowy mountains set against a backdrop of radiantly clear, sunlit blue sky. Surprisingly, some residents prefer the cooler days, and as summer ends will tell you that they're relieved to be done with the weeks of "hot" temperatures. Most appreciate the rain, understanding that it is an indispensable factor in creating some of the wonderful characteristics of this area, such as the abundant green expanses, colorful rhododendrons, and plentiful lakes and waterways.

Situated between two bodies of water and two mountain ranges, Seattle has stunning vistas that can be enjoyed throughout the city. To the west is the Puget Sound, an inland saltwater sea that connects to the Pacific Ocean. The Sound is what makes Washington immediately recognizable on every map of the United States, creating the Olympic Peninsula. Running along the middle of the peninsula are the Olympic Mountains (the "Olympics"), which are surrounded by forests and small logging towns.

From Seattle, one can see the Olympics clearly, and recognize The Brothers, a twin-peaked mountain in the center of the range.

East of the city lies Lake Washington, 22 miles long and part of a system of lakes in the Seattle area that were formed by glaciers. Other lakes within the city include Lake Union, just north of downtown and connected by man-made channels to Lake Washington and Puget Sound, as well as Green Lake, Haller Lake, and Bitter Lake, all located in the north end of the city. All of these lakes are fed by mountain streams created by melting snow in the Cascades, a volcanic mountain range that runs the length of the state and separates Western and Eastern Washington. Mount Rainier is part of the Cascade Range, as are many smaller mountains that can be seen from vantage points throughout the city.

All of these natural wonders contribute to the abundant recreational opportunities that make Seattle a favorite of outdoor enthusiasts. From early spring to late summer, residents hike and camp in both the Cascades and the Olympics. There is water-skiing in nearby lakes, kayaking on the Sound, and fishing along the many rivers and streams. More intrepid adventurers travel to the eastern side of the Cascades for rock-climbing and bouldering, or head into the mountains for challenging mountain-climbing on Mount Rainier, Mount Baker, Mount Adams, or The Brothers. In the winter several popular ski resorts in the Cascades offer downhill skiing, snowboarding, and cross-country skiing. Those resorts on Snoqualmie Pass are just an hour drive from Seattle on I-90; others are slightly farther away on Mount Baker, Stevens Pass, and Mount Rainier.

ALL OF THESE NATURAL WONDERS CONTRIBUTE TO THE ABUNDANT RECREATIONAL OPPORTUNITIES THAT MAKE SEATTLE A FAVORITE OF OUTDOOR ENTHUSIASTS.

In addition to the mild weather and the natural beauty of the area, Seattle and its surrounding communities also share a dynamic economy. Just ten minutes east of Seattle lies the city of Bellevue, home to the world's richest man, Bill Gates, and just ten minutes east of Bellevue lies the town of Redmond, home to Gates' company, Microsoft. Other national giants headquartered here include Amazon.com, Eddie Bauer, Starbucks, and REI.

In the 1990s, according to the 2000 census, the booming economy and beautiful surroundings brought thousands of newcomers to Seattle. King, Snohomish, Kitsap, and Pierce counties, which make up the Seattle metropolitan area, added over a half a million people for a total of 3.3 million. Seattle proper grew nine percent, adding 47,000 people. While the pace of growth has slowed, a million more newcomers are expected in the next 25 to 30 years.

To accommodate the influx, city townhouses and condominiums have slowly replaced single-family houses with large yards. While some Seattle homes are still affordable for middle-income and first-time homebuyers, housing prices have continued their relentless upward march. With the increased demand for housing, some formerly overlooked Seattle neighborhoods, like South Park, Beacon Hill, and the Central District, are now being revitalized, with old homes remodeled and new houses built in these areas. Other newcomers are opting for homes outside the city limits.

Seattle entered the national spotlight in the 1990s, making espresso (Starbucks), "grunge" music (Nirvana, Pearl Jam), microbrews (Red Hook), and software (Microsoft), a daily part of US culture. In recent years, the city's residents have added fine dining and baseball to their list of favorite leisure pursuits. Economic prosperity and explosive growth have generated a wealth of highly rated new restaurants, and an improved Seattle Mariners team has drawn scores of fans to the new Safeco Field baseball stadium. In addition, Seattle has a thriving and nationally recognized performing arts community, including the Seattle Symphony, the Seattle Opera, and the Pacific Northwest Ballet, as well as several theatrical companies including Intiman, the Seattle Repertory Theater, and A Contemporary Theater.

As newcomers soon learn, conversations here, which used to revolve primarily around microbrews, coffee, computers, and the weather, now lament the traffic. According to a report from the Puget Sound Regional Council, the area's residents currently spend about 130,000 hours per day stuck in traffic delays, and it predicts that number could jump to one million hours per day unless improvements are made. In spring 2002, the Texas Transportation Institute's annual study of 75 urban areas listed Seattle as the fifth most traffic congested city in the country, following Los Angeles, San Francisco, Chicago, and D.C. Your daily commute is an extremely important factor to consider when choosing a place to live here, especially if your route includes either of the two bridges. Highway 520 and Interstate 90 run along bridges that span Lake Washington, connecting Seattle with the Eastside communities, which include Bellevue, Kirkland, Issaquah, Renton, Redmond, and Woodinville. Both bridges create traffic bottlenecks during rush hour. On the bright side, the views of Lake Washington and Mount Rainier from the bridge decks are amazing!

As Seattle continues to grow, another point of concern for new and old residents alike is personal safety. In the past several years, Seattle's crime rates have remained level or have declined, due in part to the area's economic prosperity and strong community involvement. Exceptions, however, are auto thefts and car prowls—car break-ins and burglary—that are a serious problem throughout the state and continue to plague residents despite efforts by local police agencies. No matter which neighborhood you choose, take precautions to avoid becoming a target: lock your car and remove valuables, and park in well-lighted areas. As in any major city, be sure to take reasonable precautions when in unfamiliar surroundings. Keep money and other possessions out of sight, and avoid exploring new neighborhoods after dark. (For more tips on keeping safe in Seattle, see the **Safety** section in **Getting Settled**.)

WHAT TO BRING

- **A detailed map**; although most of Seattle proper is on a straightforward grid, many of the major streets don't follow the rules. You can purchase a handy laminated *Rand McNally* fold-out map or the comprehensive *Thomas Brothers Map Guide* from First Books (www.firstbooks.com), publisher of this *Newcomer's Handbook®*.
- **A car**; public transportation (buses, monorail, ferries) is available, but it can be time consuming to explore the city without a car. Buses stop at nearly every block, and transferring buses can cause long delays. If a car is not possible, expect to spend some time getting used to the bus routes and schedules, and don't try to travel around at night by bus without checking the schedule beforehand; many buses stop running or change routes early in the evening.
- **An umbrella or rain hat**; most likely it will be raining when you arrive. Also bring a lightweight but warm jacket. Temperatures and weather conditions can vary sharply during the day, going from sunny and warm to cold and rainy within a few minutes. However, after you've been here a while, you may find yourself adopting the local disdain for umbrellas and a relaxed attitude about getting wet (it's a fact of life).
- **A cell phone**; which is convenient for contacting potential landlords from the road. If you plan to search the classifieds for your new abode, get a jump on the competition by picking up the Sunday edition of *The Seattle Times/Seattle Post-Intelligencer* on Friday night. The paper is available at most grocery and convenience stores.
- **A good attitude and a smile**; while most people in Seattle are friendly and outgoing, you'll notice a layer of reticence when meeting strangers. With a little patience and a calm demeanor you'll be able to get help from just about anybody in Seattle. So stop in, have a café latte, and stay for a while or forever. Welcome to Seattle, a wonderful place to live!

SEATTLE WAS FOUNDED ON ITS PRESENT SITE IN FEBRUARY 1852, four months after the first party of white settlers landed the schooner Exact on Alki Point, in what is now known as West Seattle. This group, known as the Denny Party, included Arthur Denny and his family, his brother David, as well as the Lows, the Bells, the Borens, and the Terrys. Many of the city streets are named after these founders of Seattle. In early 1852 Denny, Low, and Boren set out in a canoe to find a more sheltered area for their settlement. They crossed Elliott Bay and, measuring the depth of the bay using a piece of rope and a horseshoe, chose a harbor for their new city (Seattle) just west of what is now Pioneer Square.

Seattle is named for Chief Sealth, a Salish Indian. Dr. David "Doc" Maynard, who arrived in 1852 and started Seattle's first store and hospital, was instrumental in naming the city. Maynard was a friend of Chief Sealth's and suggested Seattle as a more easily pronounced version of the Chief's name. Maynard thought the original name for the settlement, Duwamps, a derivative of the name for one of the Indian tribes that lived around Elliott Bay, the Duwampish or Duwamish, might not attract visitors or new settlers to the area. The other nearby tribe, the Salish or Suquamish, lived between the Bay and what is now Lake Washington. There may have been additional tribes in the Seattle area, but because Native Americans around the Puget Sound were a loose-knit group, it is not clear how many separate tribes were here originally. What is clear, however, is that all of the area tribes were jointly represented by Chief Sealth. These tribes remained in the area until 1855 when, after some minor skirmishes between the settlers and the Indians, they were relocated to the Suquamish Indian Reservation across Puget Sound. Chief Sealth's farewell speech is an oft-quoted piece of Seattle history, and an inspiring reminder of the great Native American leader.

Henry Yesler, another of Seattle's most prominent and influential citizens, arrived in the fall of 1852, soon after Doc Maynard. Yesler was a tight-fisted businessman who, in 1853, built a sawmill, cookhouse, and a meeting hall, all firsts for the new city. The sawmill initially received its supply of lumber from the heavily wooded hills east of the settlement, areas that are now a part of the city. The trees were pushed to the mill down a slick wooden slipway, built into the side of a hill in downtown Seattle. The term "skid road" or "skid row," coined for this innovative contrivance, quickly became synonymous with the run down streets and rowdy behavior of the mill workers who lived in that area.

On June 6, 1889, near what is now 1st Avenue and Madison Street, a glue pot caught fire in a carpenter's workshop, starting the Great Seattle Fire. Coming after an unusual early summer drought, the fire quickly burned down every building within a 60-acre area. Soon after the fire, city officials passed an ordinance requiring that new buildings be constructed of bricks or stone. The buildings destroyed in the fire were swiftly rebuilt under these new regulations. Surprisingly, the result of the fire was a strengthened city economy, as the rebuilding projects provided much needed business to local bricklayers and builders. The sawmill was not adversely affected because demand for lumber was still great in California, and most of what was produced at Yesler's mill was shipped to San Francisco. However, the fire and subsequent renovations did have one strange consequence. The city, taking advantage of the opportunity to correct some of the drainage problems that had plagued downtown, constructed streets at a level 12 feet higher than they had been before the fire. However, some merchants rebuilt businesses at their original level, leading to sharp inclines between the city-owned streets and the privately owned sidewalks. Eventually the city put in new sidewalks at the higher street level, and the first floors of these downtown buildings became basements and open spaces. For many years these spaces were used as an underground mall, housing legitimate businesses; they later became infamous as opium dens, brothels, and moonshine establishments. Today, the Seattle Underground Tour is a popular tourist attraction that takes visitors through some of the original labyrinthine tunnels under downtown.

During the late 1800s, gold was discovered in several nearby locations, including the Fraser River in British Columbia, Boise and Coeur d'Alene in Idaho, and the Sultan and Skagit rivers in Washington. Though gold was never present in Seattle itself, the city served many of these locations as a supplier of prospecting goods. In 1877, the Seattle & Walla Walla Railroad was constructed to transport coal (which had replaced lumber as the city's major export) from Renton to Seattle. Then in 1893, the Great Northern Railroad placed its western terminus in Seattle, and the Northern Pacific Railroad Co. bought land in Seattle, extending its western route from Tacoma to Seattle. These events nicely positioned the manufacturers and merchants of Seattle who were able to reap immense profits during

Canada's Klondike gold rush. The rush, which officially began in the summer of 1897 when the steamer Portland docked in Seattle carrying "a ton of gold," brought prospectors through Seattle, many of whom geared up for their expeditions here. Seattle also benefited from the gold rush by opening its first assay office, establishing the city as a regional financial center as well as a port and manufacturing city.

By the 20th century, Seattle was a prosperous city with both an expanding population and business community. The need for more space inspired the Denny Regrade project, which began in 1907. Originally, in addition to First Hill, Capitol Hill, and Queen Anne Hill, there was another hill located at the north end of the city center, known as Denny Hill. The hill (actually a bluff overlooking Elliott Bay) prevented easy expansion of the downtown, standing, as it did, 190 feet above the level of nearby Pioneer Square. In 1898 some of the western side of the hill had been carted away to fill in around Western Avenue and Alaskan Way. In 1907, the project of regrading the entire hill began in earnest, primarily funded by private property owners. The dirt was hauled away and dumped into Elliott Bay, creating much of the current Seattle waterfront as well as the land that connects Downtown with the Duwamish River neighborhoods. Completed in 1931, the Denny Regrade is now the site of much of downtown, including the Belltown neighborhood.

DURING THE LATE 1800s, GOLD WAS DISCOVERED IN SEVERAL NEARBY LOCATIONS, INCLUDING THE FRASER RIVER IN BRITISH COLUMBIA, BOISE AND COEUR D'ALENE IN IDAHO, AND THE SULTAN AND SKAGIT RIVERS IN WASHINGTON.

The Seattle population has increased steadily since the early 1900s and the city has spread out, enveloping many communities that were originally suburbs. When Seattle hosted the World's Fair in 1962, it built a 74-acre campus that featured the Space Needle and the International Fountain. Today, this site known as Seattle Center, is home to 21 arts, science, and sports organizations, including Key Arena, the Seattle Opera, and the Pacific Science Center, as well as the monorail to downtown.

Since the 1980s the area has been regularly ranked as one of America's most livable cities, and the resulting influx of newcomers has added to an already growing population. Washington's natural resources have so far provided for such basic needs as water and electricity, and, until recently, the size of the city has provided for plenty of open space and housing, as well as a pleasant small-town culture. Today, much of that is changing as Seattle braces for additional population growth, and expansion issues such as adequate public transportation and affordable in-city housing.

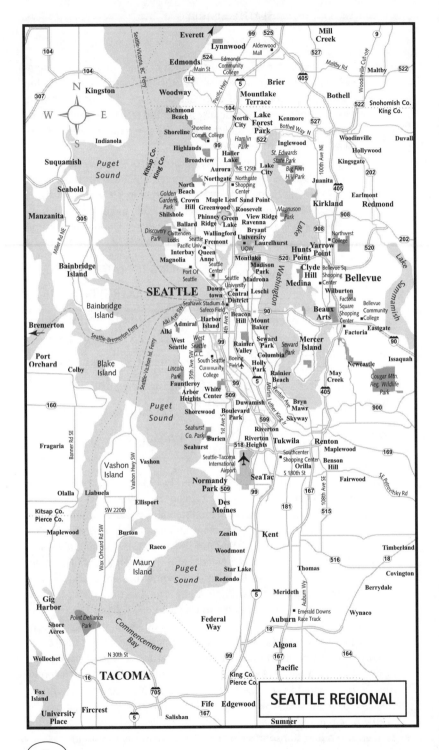

SEATTLE REGIONAL

EFORE GOING INTO THE NEIGHBORHOOD PROFILES, WE HAVE provided tips for getting around Seattle and the Eastside, and then metro-wide county information, which should prove helpful as you begin your search for a home.

SEATTLE ADDRESS LOCATOR

While most Seattle streets stick to a grid pattern, running east-west or north-south, others meander seemingly aimlessly through several neighborhoods. The information here will give you a good starting point for finding your way around the city, but a map or street atlas is highly recommended. The guidelines below apply only to streets within Seattle proper, or immediately north or south of the city limits. Other suburbs and communities use different methods for assigning addresses. The *Thomas Guide for Metropolitan Puget Sound* covers the Seattle metropolitan area, as well as cities in King, Pierce, and Snohomish counties. You can get one at a bookstore or office supply outlet, or order online at www.firstbooks.com.

The **center of the Seattle grid** is at 1st and Yesler. Street names outside downtown are provided with a North, East, South, West, NE, NW, SE, SW location tag. The tag indicates location relative to the center. Downtown streets have no location tag, and run northwest-southeast (parallel to the shore of Elliott Bay) or northeast-southwest. Outside the downtown area, most Seattle streets run north-south or east-west. Street and house numbers increase as you move away from downtown.

North-south streets are called "avenues" with the location tag at the end; for instance, 24th Avenue NW or 32nd Avenue South. Roads that run east-west are "streets" with the location tag at the beginning; for instance, NE 49th Street or SW Spokane Street. Most avenues in the city are numbered. South of the Lake Washington Ship Canal (which bisects the city north of downtown, and connects Lake Washington and Lake Union to the Puget Sound), most streets have names rather than numbers, such as Union Street or East Aloha Street. North of the ship canal streets are numbered. Location tags are assigned as follows:

North of Denny Way, as far as the Lake Washington Ship Canal, streets are labeled:
- **West** if they are located west of 1st Avenue North, in Magnolia and parts of Queen Anne.
- **North** if they are located directly north of downtown, on Queen Anne and around Lake Union or between 1st Avenue North and Eastlake Avenue East.
- **East** if they are located east of Lake Union, in Eastlake and Montlake.

North of the Lake Washington Ship Canal, streets are labeled:
- **NW** if they are located north of the ship canal and west of 1st Avenue NW, in Ballard and Broadview.
- **North** if they are directly north of downtown between 1st Avenue NW and 1st Avenue NE, in Phinney Ridge, Green Lake, Wallingford, and Northgate.
- **NE** if they are north of the ship canal and east of 1st Avenue NE, in Lake City, the University District and Sand Point.

South of Yesler Way, all streets are labeled:
- **South** if they are located south of downtown and east of 1st Avenue South, in Rainier Valley, Mount Baker and Beacon Hill.
- **SW** if they are located southwest of downtown and west of 1st Avenue South, in West Seattle.

Between the Lake Washington Ship Canal and Yesler Way, and east of Lake Union, all east-west running streets are labeled *East,* including those in Madrona, Leschi, the Central District, Capitol Hill, and Madison Park. However, north-south streets in this area have no location tags.

Several main thoroughfares don't follow all of the above rules. For example:
- **Martin Luther King Jr. Way:** "MLK" begins at Madison Street at the north end of the Central Area, and runs south through the Central Area, Madrona, Leschi, Beacon Hill, Mount Baker and Rainier Valley.
- **Boren Avenue/Rainier Avenue South:** Boren Avenue runs northwest-southeast over First Hill. South of Jackson Street, Boren Avenue becomes Rainier Avenue South, and continues southeast through the south end of the Central Area and into the Rainier Valley.

- **Madison Street**: One of the city's most convenient streets, Madison Street runs east from downtown, through First Hill and Capitol Hill, and along the north end of the Central Area to Madison Park on Lake Washington.

Useful highways within Seattle are listed below. Be careful of these "thoroughfares" at rush hour:

- **Interstate 5**: I-5 runs north-south through the city and is the most commonly used thoroughfare in Seattle.
- **Interstate 90**: I-90 begins at Safeco Field in downtown Seattle and runs east. The I-90 bridge is the only roadway to Mercer Island, and has more lanes in either direction than the Highway 520 bridge to the north.
- **Highway 520**: a state highway connecting I-5 (at the north end of Capitol Hill) with the Eastside communities of Bellevue, Kirkland and Redmond, the 520 bridge is always packed during rush hour.
- **Highway 99**: running parallel to, but west of, I-5 through Seattle, Highway 99 begins as Aurora Avenue in the north end, where it is a major thoroughfare lined with strip malls, inexpensive hotels and other businesses. Crossing the Lake Washington Ship Canal into the city, Highway 99 runs through the Battery Street Tunnel and becomes the Alaskan Way Viaduct, a large stacked highway along the waterfront. South of the waterfront, Highway 99 becomes East Marginal Way South and eventually Pacific Highway.
- **Highway 522**: commonly known as Lake City Way NE, Highway 522 begins at NE 75th Street, runs northeast through the Lake City neighborhood to Lake Washington, and eventually turns into Bothell Way NE at the north end of the lake.
- **West Seattle Freeway**: the West Seattle Freeway connects both I-5 (at Beacon Hill) and Highway 99 with the West Seattle peninsula.

GETTING AROUND THE EASTSIDE

There are two highways that transport travelers from Seattle to the Eastside via a pair of floating bridges: Interstate 90, via the I-90 bridge, and Highway 520, via the Evergreen Floating Bridge. Interstate 90 brushes up against the Mount Baker neighborhood, crosses Lake Washington to Mercer Island, and passes through Bellevue, Issaquah and Snoqualmie before crossing the Cascade Mountains into Eastern Washington. Highway 520 begins in Montlake north of downtown Seattle, crosses Lake Washington and passes through Bellevue and Kirkland before its end in Redmond.

Interstate 405 runs north-south from Renton in the south to Lynnwood in the north, and is commonly used as a connector to either I-90 or Highway 520, as well as other less traveled roads on the Eastside. Other primary thoroughfares include the Redmond-Fall City Road (Highway 202), which connects Kirkland, Redmond, Fall City, Snoqualmie and North Bend; Highway 522 runs from Bothell to Monroe and passes through Woodinville.

It's no secret that traffic in the Seattle area is a challenge. The Eastside is no exception. Dramatic growth over the last decade has flooded the community's streets and highways with commuters. There are ways to avoid the rush hour headache, however. If your employer offers flexible hours, consider working outside the standard 8 a.m. to 5 p.m. You may want to carpool with your co-workers. The diamond (carpool) lanes offer quicker commutes and relief from stop-and-go traffic. See the **Transportation** chapter for information on Metro Transit carpool programs. King County, which encompasses the Eastside, offers a comprehensive online commuting resource called "My Commute," complete with traffic cams and flow maps, at www.metrokc.gov/kcdot/mycommute. If you must drive to the city during rush hour, there isn't much you can do but grin and bear it.

SEATTLE AREA COUNTIES

KING COUNTY

KING COUNTY IS ONE OF THE LARGEST COUNTIES IN THE UNITED States, covering more than 2,200 square miles and serving 1.5 million residents. The county stretches from Bothell and Shoreline in the north to Enumclaw in the south. Bordered by Puget Sound to the west, the county includes tiny Vashon Island. The county's eastern border abuts the Cedar and Green River watersheds, as well as the Alpine Lakes Wilderness.

Cities served by King County include, from north to south: **Bothell, Shoreline, Woodinville, Duvall**, Skykomish, **Redmond, Kirkland**, Carnation, **Bellevue, Seattle**, Sammamish, **Mercer Island, Snoqualmie, Issaquah**, North Bend, **Renton, Burien, Tukwila**, SeaTac, **Des Moines, Kent**, Maple Valley, **Federal Way**, Black Diamond, Auburn, Enumclaw.

Outside the cities, the county provides services to regions that lie in "unincorporated King County." In addition to what is available to all county residents, like courts, public health, and property tax appraisals, the county may also provide additional local services, like land-use regulation, emergency management, and county parks.

County Executive: elected to a four-year term by county voters; King County Courthouse, 516 Third Avenue, Room 400, Seattle, 206-296-4040, www.metrokc.gov/exec

County Council: the Metropolitan King County Council consists of 13 members who represent geographic districts throughout the county; King County Courthouse, 516 Third Avenue, Room 1200, Seattle, 206-296-1000, www.metrokc.gov/mkcc

County Map: www.metrokc.gov/images

Government: King County Courthouse, 516 Third Avenue, Seattle, 206-296-0100, www.metrokc.gov

Libraries: the King County Library System is the third-largest circulating library in the United States, with 41 libraries and a traveling library center; 960 Newport Way NW, Issaquah, 425-369-3200, www.kcls.org

Sheriff: King County Sheriff's Office, 516 Third Avenue, Room W-116, Seattle, 206-296-4155, www.metrokc.gov/sheriff

Online: www.metrokc.gov

KITSAP COUNTY

Kitsap County is located on Kitsap Peninsula, across the Puget Sound from Seattle. One of the state's smallest counties, it is bordered by Hood Canal on the west, Puget Sound on the east, and Mason and Pierce counties to the south. The county seat is located in the town of Port Orchard. Because of the distance, it is fairly unusual for residents of Kitsap County to commute to jobs in Seattle. For that reason, only **Bainbridge Island**, which has begun to lure many residents away from the city, has been profiled.

County Board of Commissioners: one commissioner is elected from each of three districts; 614 Division Street, Port Orchard, 360-337-7146, www.kitsapgov.com/boc

County Clerk: an elected official who serves as the county's administrative and financial officer; 614 Division Street, Room 202, Port Orchard, 360-337-7164, www.kitsapgov.com/clerk

Government: 614 Division Street, Port Orchard, 360-337-7150, www.kitsapgov.com

Libraries: the Kitsap Regional Library System includes nine community branches, a bookmobile and outreach services; 1301 Sylvan Way, Bremerton, 360-405-9119, www.krl.org

Sheriff: Kitsap County Sheriff's Office, 614 Division Street, Port Orchard, 360-337-7101, www.kitsapgov.com/sheriff

Online: www.kitsapgov.com

PIERCE COUNTY

South of King County is Pierce County, a region of 1,790 square miles with a population of about 713,000. The county's primary city is **Tacoma**. The northern border of Pierce County is located just south of Federal Way, and a bit north of Tacoma, about a 40-minute drive from Seattle mid-day or in the evening, and well over an hour during rush hour. For that reason, few commuters make the trek from Tacoma to Seattle each day, although more

Seattleites have moved to Pierce County in recent years as they seek lower home prices.

Outside of Tacoma, Pierce County is a mix of rural communities and new housing developments. The county is also home to Fort Lewis, which consists of 87,000 acres that house and/or employ 19,000 soldiers and 5,000 civilians.

County Council: consists of seven members who are elected in their respective districts; 930 Tacoma Avenue South, Tacoma, 253-798-7777, www.co.pierce.wa.us

County Executive: elected official serves as the chief executive officer of the county; 930 Tacoma Avenue South, Tacoma, 253-798-7477, www.co.pierce.wa.us

Government: 930 Tacoma Avenue South, Tacoma, 253-798-7272, www.co.pierce.wa.us

Libraries: the Pierce County Library System includes 20 neighborhood branches and two bookmobiles; 3005 112th Street East, Tacoma, 253-536-6500, www.pcl.lib.wa.us

Sheriff: 930 Tacoma Avenue South, Tacoma, 253-798-7530, www.co.pierce.wa.us

Online: www.co.pierce.wa.us

SNOHOMISH COUNTY

Snohomish County is located north of King County. It covers just under 3,000 square miles and borders the Puget Sound to the west, Chelan County to the east, and Skagit County to the north. At its southern boundary is **Bothell**, which straddles the border of King and Snohomish counties. Other Snohomish County cities are **Edmonds, Mountlake Terrace, Lynnwood,** and **Everett,** which has served as the county seat since 1897.

Between 1990 and 2000, Snohomish County grew by about 30%, to just over 606,000 residents. According to the Puget Sound Regional Council, the population forecast for Snohomish County is 706,959 for the year 2010 and 833,661 for the year 2020.

County Council: the five members of the council are elected to four-year terms; 3000 Rockefeller, Everett, 425-388-3494, www.co.snohomish.wa.us/council

County Executive: elected to a four-year term; 3000 Rockefeller, Everett, 425-388-3460, www.co.snohomish.wa.us/executiv

Government: 3000 Rockefeller, Everett, 425-388-3411, www.co.snohomish.wa.us

Libraries: the Sno-Isle Regional Library System serves more than half a million residents in Snohomish and Island counties through 20 community libraries, four outreach vans and a bookmobile; 7312 35th Avenue NE, Marysville, 360-651-7000, www.sno-isle.org

Sheriff: the Snohomish County Sheriff is elected to a four-year term; 3000 Rockefeller, Everett, 425-388-3393, www.co.snohomish.wa.us/sheriff

Online: www.co.snohomish.wa.us

SEATTLE NEIGHBORHOODS

As with many large and growing US cities, most of Seattle's neighborhoods began as small communities located outside the city limits. As Seattle expanded over the years, the city annexed many of these small mill towns and commerce centers. While the old village names survive as neighborhood monikers, so do many of the original neighborhood names. A good example of this can be seen in Ballard, where residents may refer to their homes as being in Shilshole, North Beach, Sunset Hill, Blue Ridge, or Crown Hill, all of which are located in the larger neighborhood of Ballard.

As you explore Seattle, you may notice certain repeating housing styles. Most Seattle neighborhoods have only gradually grown denser and more urban, so it is common to see several types of houses on a single residential city block. Victorians dating from the late 1800s, with their turreted front rooms and ornamented rooflines, are in most downtown neighborhoods, sitting alongside Craftsman style bungalows, Tudors, Colonials, and Northwest Moderns.

The Northwest Modern or "Classic Box" style of architecture is one of the most plentiful, introduced in Seattle around the turn of the 20th century and instantly popular with local architects and builders. Also known as the "Capitol Hill Box" because of the number of these houses in the Capitol Hill neighborhood, this style was still being built in Seattle as late as the 1940s. Classic Box houses are large, two-story, four-square structures with symmetrical windows, front porches, hardwood floors and high ceilings. The slope of the Classic Box roof starts above the entire square of the second story, so that the upstairs rooms are often the same in size and number as those below. Bungalows were introduced in Seattle in the early 1900s, appearing in the architectural pattern books that were a mainstay of local builders. In particular, the Arts-and-Crafts and Craftsman style bungalows were popular in the city. Unlike the Classic Box, the bungalow is characterized by a sloped second story roof, usually with one or two front gables and bracketed roof overhangs. These homes typically have three to four large bedrooms, oak or fir floors, and original built-in cabinetry.

Elaborate and symmetrical Colonials and Dutch Colonials, often referred to as "barn houses" for their distinctive shape, were built throughout Seattle in the decades between the two world wars. Tudors, recognizable for their steep roofs, arched doorways, and leaded windows, dot Seattle neighborhoods, as do simple Cape Cod cottages. Some north Seattle neighborhoods contain examples of the ranch house, also called ramblers. Built in the 1940s and 1950s and related to the Prairie School style created by Frank Lloyd Wright, these are sprawling single-story brick houses with giant picture windows. Olympic Manor, in the north end of Ballard, is built almost entirely in this style.

Seattleites are proud of where they live, a fact exemplified by the large number of community centers and organizations, neighborhood newspapers, and bustling corner coffee shops. Seattle's **Department of Neighborhoods**, 206-684-0464, www.cityofseattle.net/don, runs the neighborhood service centers (listed after each profile), and administers neighborhood-matching funds for local projects. Community newspapers, usually free, provide valuable information about local issues, upcoming events, and activities. Every neighborhood in Seattle has at least one coffeehouse or espresso stand, which is often a good place to start your exploration of a particular area. See the neighborhood resources that follow each neighborhood profile for information about organizations, publications, post offices, nearest emergency hospitals, and public transportation routes. (Note: only bus routes that begin or end in a neighborhood are listed under that profile. Check with Metro Transit, 206-553-3000, www.transit.metrokc.gov, for specifics on routes running through your neighborhood.)

Unlike many other major cities, Seattle's neighborhoods do not have official borders. Those listed in this book reflect widely accepted neighborhood boundaries, many of which are guided by simple geography. For instance, many of Seattle's neighborhoods sit atop a single hill, separated by a miniature "valley" from the next neighborhood. The following neighborhood profiles are only those located within the city limits. Other communities, such as Bellevue, Redmond, Everett, and Renton are not a part of the city, but may interest newcomers; you will find these and others profiled in the **Surrounding Communities** section.

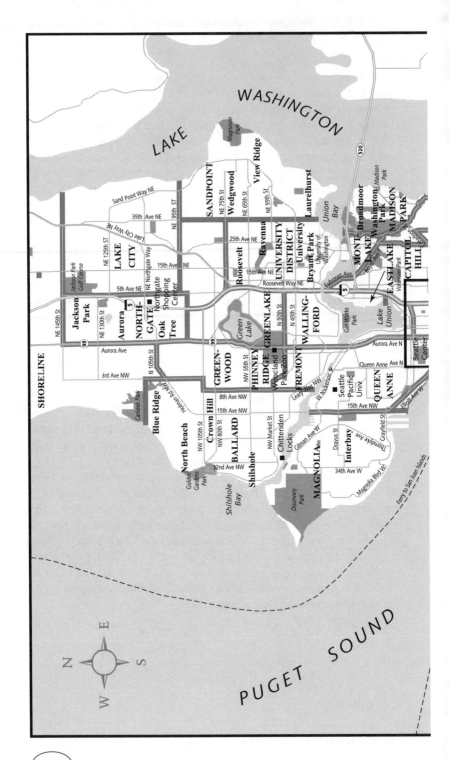

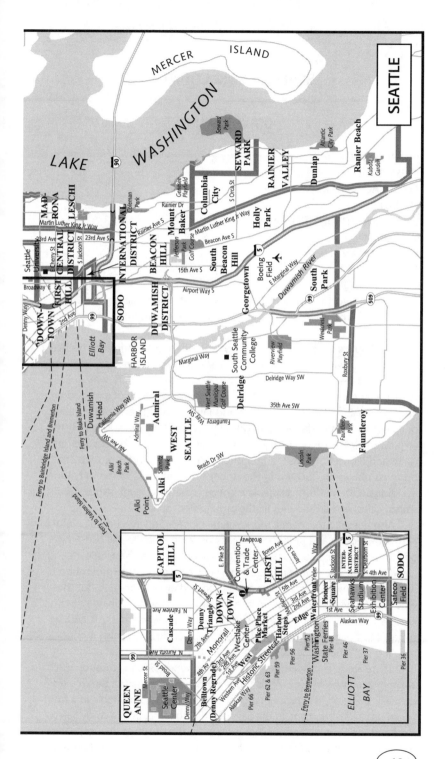

SEATTLE

MERCER ISLAND

LAKE WASHINGTON

90

MAD-RONA
Martin Luther King Jr Way
LESCHI
CENTRAL DISTRICT
23rd Ave
23rd Ave S
Seattle University
Cherry St
S Jackson St
Broadway E
FIRST HILL
DOWN-TOWN
Denny Way
2nd Ave
99
Elliott Bay

INTERNATIONAL DISTRICT
SODO
DUWAMISH DISTRICT
HARBOR ISLAND

BEACON HILL
Rainier Ave S
Rainier Dr
Mount Baker
Beacon Ave S
15th Ave S
South Beacon Hill
Airport Way S
Marginal Way
South Seattle Community College
Riverview Playfield
Marginal Way

Coleman Park
Jefferson Park Golf Course

Seward Park
SEWARD PARK
RAINIER VALLEY
Dunlap
Ranier Beach
Atlantic City Park
Kubota Garden

Genesee Playfield
Columbia City
S Orca St
Holly Park
Martin Luther King Jr Way
Georgetown
Boeing Field
E Marginal Way
99
Duwamish River
South Park
5
509

Roxbury St

Admiral Way
California Way SW
Admiral
WEST SEATTLE
Alki Ave SW
Duwamish Head
Alki Beach Park
Schmitz Park
Alki Point
Alki

West Seattle Municipal Golf Course
Delridge
Delridge Way SW
35th Ave SW
Beach Dr SW
Lincoln Park
Fauntleroy Way SW
Fauntleroy Park
Fauntleroy

Westcrest Park

Ferry to Bainbridge Island and Bremerton
Ferry to Blake Island
Ferry to Vashon Island

QUEEN ANNE
Seattle Center
Mercer St
Broad St
Denny Way
99
N. Aurora Ave
N. Fairview Ave
Cascade
Denny Way
Denny Triangle
7th Ave
Belltown (Denny Regrade)
4th Av
3rd Ave
2nd Ave
1st Ave
Western Ave
Alaskan Way
Monorail
Westlake Center
Stewart St
E Pike St
Boren Ave
Jame St
Way
Broadway
CAPITOL HILL
5
Convention & Trade Center
FIRST HILL
S Jackson St
James St
5th Ave
3rd Ave
2nd Ave
1st Ave
S Dearborn St
S. 4th Ave
5
INTER-NATIONAL DISTRICT
SODO
DOWN-TOWN
Pike Place Market
Harbor Steps
West
Historic Streetcar
Yesler
Pioneer Square
Seahawks Stadium
Exhibition Center
Safeco Field
Addison St
Edge
Waterfront
Washington State Ferries
Pier 48
Ferry to Bremerton
Pier 52
Pier 56
Pier 59
Pier 62 & 63
Pier 66
Pier 46
Pier 37
Pier 36
Alaskan Way
ELLIOTT BAY

19

SEATTLE—KING COUNTY

DOWNTOWN

PIONEER SQUARE
WEST EDGE
PIKE PLACE MARKET
HARBOR STEPS
BELLTOWN (DENNY REGRADE)
WATERFRONT
DENNY TRIANGLE
CASCADE

Boundaries: North: Denny Way, Mercer Street; **West:** Elliott Bay; **South:** South Royal Brougham Way, South Jackson Street; **East:** Interstate 5

Pioneer Square is perhaps the best-known and most historic of all districts in the Downtown area. Located near the site of Henry Yesler's saw mill and the original "skid road" (now Yesler Way), Pioneer Square was quickly rebuilt after the Great Seattle Fire of 1889 destroyed much of early Seattle. The Pioneer Building at 1st Avenue and James Street is one of the oldest buildings in Seattle, designed in 1889 by architect Elmer H. Fisher, at the request of Henry Yesler. Today, the brothels and gambling dens are long gone and Pioneer Square is a flourishing business and retail district. Small business offices are located in the upper floors of most of the old stone buildings. Oriental rug sellers, kite shops, sporting goods stores, bookstores, cafes, and art galleries fill the ground floor spaces.

Also home to a dynamic music scene, Pioneer Square's bars fill nightly with music-lovers and party-goers. Many of Seattle's influential bands have played in area clubs, such as the Central Saloon. Both the New Orleans and Larry's feature fine blues and jazz musicians; the Fenix Underground hosts rock and alternative bands. Joint cover is offered on the weekends for those who want to visit several bars in one evening. Fat Tuesday, Seattle's Mardi Gras celebration, fills the district with revelers for a week of music and festivities (and occasional violent clashes). Pioneer Square is also a popular meeting place before Seattle sporting events.

There are several apartment buildings in Pioneer Square, most of which are converted warehouses. While this is a busy, exciting part of the city, residentially speaking, it's most appropriate for residents comfortable in a fast-paced urban environment. In the days of the Kingdome, before costly Safeco Field and the new football stadium were built, this area was an inexpensive part of the city in which to live, and as a result several homeless shelters were placed here. Today, intermingled with expensive new developments and refurbished high-tech office spaces, these residences for the down and out remain. In less prosperous times, Pioneer Square was home to numerous artists' residences and work spaces, but many artists were squeezed out by rising rents. In early 2000, the Washington Shoe Building, which once housed five floors of galleries and artists' studios, closed its doors. The building is being transformed into an office block with a posh, top-floor penthouse. Many of the displaced residents moved south to Georgetown. Others are pinning their hopes on a proposed development at South Washington Street and Prefontaine Place South, near the County Courthouse. Minneapolis-based Artspace Projects and the Pioneer Square Community Development Organization hope to buy the Tashiro and Kaplan buildings, and create 50 units exclusively for artist housing and work space.

In September of 2001, the Downtown Seattle Association and then Mayor Paul Schell christened the new **West Edge** neighborhood, an area bordered by Lenora Street to the north, Cherry Street to the south, Second Avenue to the east, and Western Avenue to the west. Essentially a marketing tool to attract more diners and shoppers, most residents continue to use more familiar downtown neighborhood names, like Pike Place and Harbor Steps, when referring to this general area.

Established in 1907, the **Pike Place Market** is Seattle's most beloved Downtown landmark. City dwellers come here first with their out-of-town guests to see the fish-throwers at the seafood stands, sample teas at Market Spice, or listen to talented street musicians. Many Seattle residents frequent Pike Place weekly for fresh fruits and vegetables, fish and shellfish, teas and coffees, and baked goods.

Local farmers who wanted to sell their produce without the involvement of middlemen organized the market. Gradually fish and meat were added to the available goods, then bakeries and cafes moved in, soon followed by folks selling jewelry, pottery, honey, flowers, kites, and coffees. Today, you can find just about anything at the Market, from the best local tomatoes and homemade jams to kitchen wares and furniture. Many of these products are sold in shops in the blocks around the Market itself, or in the Corner Market Building, designed in 1912, and located at the corner of 1st Avenue and Pike Street. A few blocks south of Pike Place is the magnificent Seattle Art Museum with its notable "A Hammering Man" sculpture facing the waterfront.

A short stroll from Pike Place Market is **Harbor Steps**, one of Seattle's newest neighborhoods and a perfect example of Downtown's ongoing revitalization. Whereas many Seattle communities were named for their proximity to water (Green Lake, Eastlake), Harbor Steps was named for a wide outdoor staircase that climbs from Western Avenue, near the waterfront, to First Avenue at University Street. The Harbor Steps Apartments, www.harborsteps.com, opened in 1992 and now houses about 1,200 residents, with rents ranging from $1,000 to $5,000 per month. The complex's two high-rise towers feature private balconies and expansive glass windows, offering residents sublime views of the sound and mountains. According to the property's marketing director, residents range from young singles to retired couples, empty nesters, and executives moving here from around the world. The small, upscale community is also home to Harbor Steps Park, the Inn at Harbor Steps, and a selection of upscale restaurants, boutiques, and galleries.

Located north of the Pike Place Market and centered around 2nd Avenue and Bell Street, **Belltown** is a part of the Denny Regrade, a section of Downtown created when Denny Hill was flattened in the early 1900s. The earth of the original steep bluff that stood in this area was carted off and dumped into Elliott Bay, creating part of what is now the Waterfront area. Like Pioneer Square, the Belltown district is a hub for Seattle's nightlife and music scene. The Crocodile Cafe on 2nd Avenue is a great club for new and local bands; the Moore Theater, also on 2nd Avenue, is an historic concert hall designed in 1907 by Seattle architect Edwin W. Houghton.

For most of the 1970s and '80s, Belltown was best known for its wandering homeless, drug dealers, and panhandlers, but as 2000 approached, *Sunset Magazine* declared it the "newest belle of the ball," and compared it to New York's Upper West Side. According to 2000 US Census data, in the 1990s Belltown, along with Denny Regrade, was one of Seattle's fastest growing neighborhoods. The combined communities grew by 6,000 residents, and the number of housing units in the neighborhood jumped by nearly 2,000 units, to 7,760. Over one thousand more units were under construction at the turn of the century, halfway to the city's goal of adding 6,500 new units to the area by 2014. However, much to the dismay of area developers, by the fall of 2001 the vacancy rate in Belltown was high, about nine percent. According to a December 2001 *Seattle Post Intelligencer* article, in response to the region's economic downturn the vacancy rate is expected to get worse before it gets better. This is good news for would-be-renters who can expect lower rental rates in Belltown and other downtown Seattle neighborhoods.

High-rise condominiums facing Elliott Bay and the Olympic Mountains are on 1st Avenue, south of Pike Place Market. These amenity-rich units, with high-speed internet access, parking garages, free cable, and fitness centers, command premium rents. At Site 17, www.site17.com, for instance, renters enjoy the use of private balconies, a fitness center, rooftop deck and community room with large-screen television, and pay from $995 to $2,000 each month. Condos are also pricey in trendy Belltown. *The Seattle Times* reports that at The Ellington, a 312-unit complex at First Avenue and Broad Street, condos run from $158,000 to $800,000. The units boast gas fireplaces, six telephone lines, and views of Downtown and Elliott Bay.

Only a few blocks east there are more affordable studios and one-bed-rooms in buildings dating from the early 1900s. North of Pike Place, there is an assortment of apartments and low-income housing units. Like much of downtown, home and personal security issues may make Belltown an unsuit-able choice for some newcomers. People interested in living Downtown should become familiar and comfortable with the area before choosing a home here. (See the end of this profile for more on safety concerns.)

The Seattle **Waterfront**, facing Elliott Bay and the craggy snow-capped Olympic Mountains, is another lively and exciting neighborhood in Downtown. Though one of the most touristy areas of Seattle the Waterfront has many attractions for city residents. Fine restaurants featur-ing fresh local seafood and superior views line the piers, as do many more casual eateries and several ice cream stands. A short walk from Pike Place down the market steps ends at Pier 62/63, where the "Summer Nights at the Pier" concert series combines internationally known musicians with incredible summer sunsets over the Olympics. Seafaring residents tie up their boats next to the pier to listen to the concerts for free.

In the past few years the city's Downtown retail district has expanded, enticing shoppers back from the suburban malls. Seattle-based Nordstrom, still the dominant player in the Downtown shopping scene, moved several years ago to the spacious and remodeled Frederick & Nelson building, and the posh Pacific Place mall attracted Coach, Tiffany & Co., and J. Crew. Nike Town, FAO Schwartz, and Kenneth Cole added stores on 6th Avenue, and Adidas and Anthropologie are newcomers to 5th Avenue. The Four Seasons Olympic Hotel, on the original site of the University of Washington, offers visi-tors lavish accommodations close to the City Center and Rainier Square shops.

Bounded by Denny Way, Interstate 5 and 5th Avenue, the often-over-looked **Denny Triangle** neighborhood is experiencing a renaissance, simi-lar to the 1990s redevelopment of the Belltown and Denny Regrade neighborhoods. Development plans here include a large number of new housing units; in fact, the city's comprehensive plan for the area estimates a 450% increase by 2014, to about 5,000 units. This increase in available housing is particularly noteworthy in Denny Triangle where, for years, the only recognizable landmarks were the Greyhound Bus Station and the ven-erable Camlin Hotel. The area already is home to multi-use high-rises with offices, condos, apartments, and hotels. Major new projects in the 143-acre slice of land include the 25-story Nordstrom headquarters at 7th Avenue and Olive Way, the 31-story Metropolitan Tower Apartments, bordered by Virginia Street and Seventh and Westlake avenues, and the federal court-house. Also new to the area, the Cornish College of the Arts of Capitol Hill is creating a campus in three buildings in the vicinity of Denny Way, Terry Avenue, and Virginia Street. As in Belltown, rents here are expected to con-tinue to rise, but the Denny Triangle Neighborhood Association says housing will be aimed at all income levels. The Nordstrom-Clise development, for instance, includes 65 units of affordable housing.

Finally, northeast of Downtown, at the south end of Lake Union, the **Cascade** neighborhood, which was once primarily industrial, is enjoying the benefits of the city's plan to triple the number of residents over the next 20 years. New apartments and low-income housing units have been built in the blocks east of Fairview Avenue. In late 2000, the Low Income Housing Institute, with help from *The Seattle Times*, Fred Hutchinson Cancer Research Center, and various financial institutions, developed the Lakeview Apartments at the intersection of Harrison Street and Minor Avenue North. Sophisticated Federal style brick buildings on Eastlake Avenue also offer affordable apartments and low-income housing opportunities. The REI flagship store near I-5 has increased commercial interest here, and the Cascade P-Patch community garden at Minor Avenue North and Thomas Street, and Cascade Children's Park, temper the industrial feel of the neighborhood.

A cautionary note, Seattle's downtown core is a varied and lively area; a mix of modern condominiums and apartments, artists' lofts, and homeless shelters amidst busy shopping and nightlife districts. Such an urban mix is a far cry from more traditional secluded neighborhoods, and is something to consider when examining the livability of the area. A recent *Seattle Post-Intelligencer* article reported that, while Seattle has one of the lowest violent crime rates for a US city of its size, violent crimes in 2001 were highest in Seattle's downtown core: the Pioneer Square, International District, Georgetown, Denny Regrade, Duwamish and Belltown neighborhoods. And, in other parts of Seattle burglaries and car prowls continue to be a problem. (See **Safety and Crime** in **Getting Settled** for more information.)

Web Site: www.cityofseattle.net
Area Code: 206
Zip Codes: 98121, 98101, 98104, 98109, 98134
Post Office: Main Office Station, 301 Union Street, 800-275-8777, www.usps.com
Libraries: Central Library, 1000 4th Avenue, 206-386-4636, www.spl.lib.wa.us; Washington Talking Book ad Braille Library, 2021 9th Avenue, 206-615-0400, 206-615-0419 (TTY), www.spl.lib.wa.us
Public Schools: Seattle Public Schools, P.O. Box 19116, Seattle, WA 98109-1116, 206-298-7000, www.seattleschools.org
Police: West Precinct, 610 3rd Avenue, 206-684-8917, www.cityofseattle.net/police
Emergency Hospital: Harborview Medical Center, 325 9th Avenue, 206-731-3074, www.washington.edu/medical/hmc
Community Resources: Downtown Neighborhood Service Center, 820 Virginia Avenue, 206-233-8560, www.cityofseattle.net; Downtown

Seattle Association, 500 Union Street, 206-623-0340, www.down-townseattle.com

Public Transportation: Metro Transit, 206-553-3000, www.transit.metrokc.gov

1: Downtown/Belltown/Queen Anne
5: Downtown/Fremont/Greenwood/Northgate/Shoreline
10: Capitol Hill/Downtown
11: Madison Park/First Hill/Downtown
12: Capitol Hill/First Hill/Downtown
13: Downtown/Belltown/Queen Anne
14: Downtown/International District/Central District/Mount Baker
15: Downtown/Queen Anne/Interbay/Ballard/Crown Hill/Blue Ridge
16: Downtown/Queen Anne/Wallingford/Green Lake/Northgate
17: Downtown/Ballard/Sunset Hill/Loyal Heights
18: Downtown/Queen Anne/Interbay/Ballard/Loyal Heights/North Beach
19: Downtown/Belltown/Magnolia
20: Downtown/Delridge/White Center/Shorewood
21: Downtown/SODO/West Seattle
22: Downtown/SODO/West Seattle/White Center
24: Downtown/Belltown/Magnolia
25: Downtown/Eastlake/Montlake/University District/Laurelhurst
26: Downtown/Fremont/Wallingford/Green Lake
27: Downtown/Central District/Leschi
28: Downtown/Fremont/Ballard/Whittier Heights/Broadview
33: Downtown/Belltown/Magnolia
35: Downtown/SODO/West Seattle
36: Downtown/Beacon Hill/Rainier Beach
37: Downtown/Harbor Island/West Seattle
39: Downtown/SODO/Beacon Hill/Seward Park/Rainier Beach/Southcenter
41: Downtown/Northgate
42: Downtown/Rainier Beach
43: Downtown/Capitol Hill/Montlake/University District
54: Downtown/West Seattle/White Center
55: Downtown/West Seattle
56: Downtown/SODO/West Seattle
57: Downtown/SODO/West Seattle
64: Downtown/Greenlake/Ravenna/Wedgwood/Lake City
66: Downtown/Eastlake/University District/Maple Leaf/Northgate
70: Downtown/Eastlake/University District
71: Downtown/Eastlake/University District/Ravenna/View Ridge/Wedgwood
72: Downtown/Eastlake/University District/Maple Leaf/Lake City

73: Downtown/Eastlake/University District/Green Lake/Maple Leaf/
Jackson Park

74: Downtown/University District/Ravenna/Sand Point

76: Downtown/Green Lake/Ravenna/Wedgwood

77: Downtown/Maple Leaf/Jackson Park

79: Downtown/University District/Maple Leaf/Lake City

81: (Night Owl) Downtown/Queen Anne/Ballard/Loyal Heights

82: (Night Owl) Downtown/Queen Anne/Fremont/Wallingford/Green
Lake/Greenwood

83: (Night Owl) Downtown/Eastlake/University District/Maple Leaf/Ravenna

84: (Night Owl) Downtown/First Hill/Madrona/Madison Park

85: Downtown/SODO/West Seattle/White Center/Delridge

INTERNATIONAL DISTRICT

Boundaries: North: South Jackson Street; **West**: 4th Avenue South; **South**:
South Dearborn Street; **East**: Rainier Avenue South

Also known as Chinatown, the International District was originally home to
immigrant Chinese men who, in the late 1800s, provided an inexpensive
source of labor for the railroad, fish, and lumber industries. In the early
1900s, the center of the neighborhood shifted from the waterfront to its
present location, just east of the new football stadium. By then, Japanese
immigrants had also moved to the area, and Filipino families soon followed.
Today, a blend of Asian influences flavors the International District, with
residents of Chinese, Japanese, Filipino, and Vietnamese descent sharing
one bustling community.

The International District is located conveniently close to downtown,
Pioneer Square, and the Central District, and I-5 passes right through the
neighborhood. But, until recently, the appearance of Asian characters in
shop windows was the only indication to visitors that they had come to a
culturally diverse and distinct community. The neighborhood lacked a
definitive entrance, like the ornamental gates of San Francisco's
Chinatown. International District leaders hope the creation of 11 vividly
colored dragon lamp post sculptures at various street corners will charm
visitors into shopping and dining here, and will help the International
District maintain its Asian identity in the shadow of Safeco Field and the
Seahawk's football stadium.

Visitors frequent the area primarily for its Asian cuisine, with dozens of
restaurants specializing in traditional Chinese, Japanese, and Vietnamese
dishes. Herb stores, groceries and bakeries line South King Street and sur-

rounding side streets, and the king of all Asian markets, Uwajimaya, anchors the neighborhood at 600 Fifth Avenue South. The $15 million expansion and redevelopment of Uwajimaya doubled the size of the old store, and added 176 apartments and several restaurants. Rents range from just under $1,000 to about $2,000 per month The huge complex serves as a bridge between the community's ancient culture and contemporary development.

The heart of the International District is the site of the old Chinatown, which lies between 4th Avenue South and I-5. The main thoroughfare is Jackson Street, although many of the historic buildings and businesses are a few blocks off Jackson. Chinatown is peppered with historic hotels, many of which have been converted into low-income housing and affordable apartments for senior citizens. There are also apartments and condominiums available for middle-income families and young professionals, similar to the units at the Uwajimaya Village Apartments. On the east side of I-5, a stretch of the International District known as "Little Vietnam" or "Little Saigon" is centered around the intersection of 12th Avenue and Jackson Street. Here you'll find an inviting selection of Vietnamese groceries and tasty take-out restaurants.

There have been a handful of highly publicized crimes in the International District in recent years, but such violent incidents are uncommon. Crime rates here are comparable to the rest of downtown.

While most residents in the International District are of Asian or Pacific Island descent, others live here as well. An interest in downtown living seems to be attracting younger residents to a community that in recent decades had a median age in the mid-50s. According to 2000 US Census figures, the International District grew by more than 25% during the 1990s.

Web Site: www.cityofseattle.net
Area Code: 206
Zip Codes: 98134, 98144, 98104
Post Office: International Station, 414 6th Avenue South, 800-275-8777, www.usps.com
Library: Central Library, 1000 4th Avenue, 206-386-4636, www.spl.lib.wa.us
Public Schools: Seattle Public Schools, P.O. Box 19116, Seattle, WA 98109-1116, 206-298-7000, www.seattleschools.org
Police: West Precinct, 610 3rd Avenue, 206-684-8917, www.cityofseattle.net/police
Emergency Hospital: Harborview Medical Center, 325 9th Avenue, 206-731-3074, www.washington.edu/medical/hmc
Community Resources: Downtown Neighborhood Service Center, 820 Virginia Avenue, 206-233-8560, www.cityofseattle.net; Chinatown/International District Business Improvement Area, 409 Maynard

Avenue South, 206-382-1197, www.seattlechinatown.org; Jackson Place P-Patch, 16th Avenue South and South Weller Street, 206-684-0264, www.cityofseattle.net/don/ppatch
Public Transportation: Metro Transit, 206-553-3000, www.transit.metrokc.gov

FIRST HILL

Boundaries: North: East Pike Street; **West**: I-5; **South**: Yesler Way; **East**: 12th Avenue East

First Hill, commonly referred to as "Pill Hill" because of the concentration of hospitals, clinics, and medical offices in the area, lies directly east of downtown. Seattle's elite originally settled in First Hill in the mid-1800s as the city expanded beyond the downtown boundary. Later, many affluent First Hill residents moved to more distant neighborhoods, such as Madison Park and Laurelhurst. Only a few of the early homes remain, including the Tudoresque Stimson-Green Mansion built in 1898. Other remaining structures not supplanted by medical office buildings, schools, hospitals, and hotels, serve as private clubs and reception halls.

The main commercial street on First Hill is Madison Street, with an assortment of cafes, delis, hotels, and pharmacies that serve hospital and office personnel, patients, and nearby residents. The Sorrento Hotel on Madison Street is an exquisite brick building, constructed in 1907 and designed by well-known Seattle architect Harlan Thomas, designer of the 1929 Harborview Medical Center. Harborview, a few blocks south of Madison Street on First Hill, serves as the premier emergency care center in the Seattle area.

There are few single-family houses on First Hill except for those in the area south of Harborview, which tends to be noisy due to ambulance sirens and the nearby freeway. Most First Hill residents live in apartments or condominiums facing downtown to the west or Capitol Hill to the north. On the west side of First Hill, an assortment of apartment buildings bordering I-5 offer views of downtown and Elliott Bay. Although freeway noise can be distracting in these residences, there is a nice mix of high- and low-end apartments, and many downtown professionals and doctors choose to live in the area for convenience. Elegant brick apartment buildings from the early 1900s are tucked along side streets, offering secured entrances and pleasant surroundings. These buildings are only a few minutes walk from downtown. Also, check the north end of First Hill for a selection of brick or stucco apartment buildings that date from the late 1920s.

As with nearby Capitol Hill, First Hill plays an important role in Seattle's Catholic community. Two influential Catholic schools are located here:

Seattle University, a private Jesuit college on Broadway, and O'Dea Catholic High School near Madison Street.

Web Site: www.cityofseattle.net
Area Code: 206
Zip Codes: 98101, 98104
Post Office: Main Office Station, 301 Union Street, 800-275-8777, www.usps.com
Library: Central Library, 1000 4th Avenue, 206-386-4636, www.spl. lib.wa.us
Public Schools: Seattle Public Schools, P.O. Box 19116, Seattle, WA 98109-1116, 206-298-7000, www.seattleschools.org
Police: East Precinct, 1519 12th Avenue, 206-684-4300, www.cityofseattle.net/police
Emergency Hospital: Harborview Medical Center, 325 9th Avenue, 206-731-3074, www.washington.edu/medical/hmc
Community Resources: Yesler Community Center, 835 Yesler Way, 206-386-1245
Public Transportation: Metro Transit, 206-553-3000, www.transit. metrokc.gov

CAPITOL HILL

Boundaries: North: Fuhrman Avenue East; **West:** I-5; **South:** East Pike Street; **East:** 23rd/24th Avenue East

Vibrant and diverse, Capitol Hill is one of Seattle's best-loved neighborhoods, where affordable rents, off-beat retailers and ethnic eateries lure a rainbow of residents. It is both the center of Seattle's large gay community and a neighborhood of traditional Catholic families. At the north end, there is St. Mark's Cathedral and the Episcopal Archdiocese; at the south end is Neighbor's, a cavernous gay dance club.

Broadway is the main street of Capitol Hill. Running the length of the hill it serves as the center of the community's commercial district. It is the place to go for lively dining or take-out; boisterous, young residents fill innumerable restaurants and bars nightly, and on summer evenings the street rings with voices late into the night. In addition to the local eateries, there are many businesses on Broadway that cater to a youthful clientele, including tattoo and body piercing shops, second-hand clothing and record stores, costume jewelers, bead shops, head shops, and gay/lesbian bookstores.

East Pike Street and East Pine Street, south of Broadway's retail core, are the center of Capitol Hill's nightlife. The area has an assortment of smoky bars, pool halls, dance clubs, and restaurants, though in the past few years this slightly seedy district has become a bit more refined. On East Pike Street, a collection of trendy boutiques has sprung up. A large grocery and shopping complex, featuring a QFC grocery, a Burger King, and a Great Clips hair salon takes up the corner of East Pike Street and Broadway.

Fifteenth Avenue East, five blocks east of Broadway, is another Capitol Hill retail district. This area is understated and stylish but also funky and quaint, with mod boutiques, swank eateries, and cozy pubs. Fifteenth Avenue East caters to a slightly older crowd, attracting hip baby boomers and comfortably domestic gays and lesbians. The mood here is laid-back and placid, an agreeable alternative to the constant bustle of Broadway.

To the north, Capitol Hill is filled with lovely, albeit expensive, houses, most with enchanting views. To examine the stunning vistas yourself, climb to the top of the old water tower in Volunteer Park. Homes on the eastern slope of Capitol Hill have views of the Cascades or Lake Washington; a few even offer a glimpse of Mount Rainier from a top story window. On the west side, residences look out over Lake Union, the Fremont Bridge, and the Olympic Mountains. Homes in Capitol Hill, particularly at the north end, are large and fashionable. While many are Colonials, Dutch Colonials, Victorian or Federal style houses, the most common type of home in this area is the Northwest Modern, or "Capitol Hill Box House."

In addition to the water tower, Volunteer Park features the Seattle Asian Art Museum, a charming old water reservoir, a delightful glass conservatory, and an outdoor amphitheater for summer concerts.Homes around Volunteer Park include some of the most formal and ornate mansions in Seattle. Many are old Victorian or Federal style houses, while others are stately versions of the Northwest Modern style. Though a few homes have become unobtrusive bed and breakfasts, most are still occupied by wealthy Seattle families. Many of Capitol Hill's affluent Catholic residents live in the area and attend church at the beautiful St. Joseph's Catholic Church. Others attend St. Patrick's, at the far north end of Capitol Hill, near Roanoke Park.

South of East Aloha Street, apartments are more common and houses are smaller. Federal style brick buildings abound in this area, subdivided into small but classic apartments, with hardwood floors and coved ceilings. Most people who live near Broadway are renters, although there are houses tucked away on the side streets that lead back toward Volunteer Park. West of Broadway, almost all of the available residences are apartments or condominiums, with many large modern apartment complexes built over I-5 and offering views of downtown and the Olympic Mountains. Rents are relatively high in this area, although many studio apartments are available. Despite its dense population, the charm of this neighborhood is that it is one of the few Seattle areas where you can walk anywhere you might need to go. In fact, having a car can be a disadvantage here, where parking is a challenge. In addition, several bus routes connect Capitol Hill with downtown and the University District, the major hubs of the Metro bus system.

East of Broadway, residences are a haphazard mix of houses, duplexes, and apartment buildings. Homes tend to be smaller and less ornate than those on north Capitol Hill but the styles are similar—primarily Northwest Moderns, Colonials, and Victorians. Many houses here are available as single-family or multiple tenant rentals. Apartments in this area are generally less expensive than those on the west side of the hill, depending on the building and location. East of 15th Avenue East and south of East John Street, houses and apartments are even less expensive, particularly south of the radio towers and close to the Central District. Residents here tend to be young, a mix of artists, musicians, and college students from Seattle Central Community College or Seattle University.

Web Site: www.cityofseattle.net
Area Code: 206
Zip Codes: 98102, 98112, 98122
Post Office: Broadway Station, 101 Broadway, 800-275-8777, www.usps.com
Library: Henry Library, 425 Harvard Avenue East, 206-684-4715, www.spl.lib.wa.us
Public Schools: Seattle Public Schools, P.O. Box 19116, Seattle, WA 98109-1116, 206-298-7000, www.seattleschools.org
Police: East Precinct, 1519 12th Avenue, 206-684-4300, www.cityofseattle.net/police
Emergency Hospital: Swedish Medical Center, 747 Broadway, 206-386-6000, www.swedish.org
Community Resources: Capitol Hill Neighborhood Service Center, 501 19th Avenue East, 206-684-4574; Capitol Hill Youth Center, 509 10th Avenue East, 206-329-7912; Miller Community Center, 330 19th Avenue East, 206-684-4753; Capitol Hill P-Patch, 1010 East Thomas Street, 206-684-0264, www.cityofseattle.net/don/ppatch
Public Transportation: Metro Transit, 206-553-3000, www.transit.metrokc.qov
    10: Capitol Hill/Downtown
    12: Capitol Hill/First Hill/Downtown
    14: Capitol Hill/Downtown/International District/Central District/Mount Baker
    60: Capitol Hill/First Hill/Beacon Hill/Georgetown/White Center

EASTLAKE

Boundaries: **North**: Lake Washington Ship Canal; **West**: Lake Union; **South**: East Galer Street; **East**: I-5

Just north of downtown, on the east side of Lake Union, lies the aptly named Eastlake neighborhood. Long thought of as simply an easy shortcut to downtown, Eastlake has blossomed into a charming close-knit community. Along Eastlake Avenue East are most of the retail shops and restaurants of the neighborhood, including the original Red Robin Burger & Spirits Emporium, the first of a successful local restaurant chain. Rows of houseboats share the shore of Lake Union with marine repair shops, dry docks, and National Oceanic and Atmospheric Administration (NOAA) ships. To explore the appealing houseboats in Eastlake, begin at Pete's Grocery, located at the base of East Lynn Street then work north or south along the shore. While the houseboats vary widely in size and luxury, all share in the daily spectacle of sailboats and seaplanes on Lake Union, and the annual Independence Day fireworks display and Christmas Ship Parade.

More traditional housing is abundant in Eastlake as well. The neighborhood has an interesting mix of apartments, condominiums, duplexes, and single-family homes. Large 1970s style apartment buildings dot the area and offer fairly inexpensive rentals, many with views of Lake Union. More traditional brick Federal style buildings offer both apartments and condominiums. Homes in Eastlake range from turn-of-the-century Victorians to simple Northwest Moderns. Eastlake has boomed in recent years as both a commercial and residential area, and the result has been extensive new construction throughout the area. New townhouses and apartments can be found in the few blocks between Eastlake Avenue and the lake, and along Franklin Avenue East.

At the north end of Fairview Avenue, along the edge of Lake Union, are the last vestiges of the old Eastlake community. Here quaint and slightly run-down summer cottages face the lake shore. This is the site of the Eastlake P-Patch community garden, which, like the community gardens in the International District and on Capitol Hill, is a quiet treasure for those who live here. Unfortunately, what makes this area quaint—the small number of houses—also makes it difficult to find a place to live.

Eastlake is nice. It's well located with easy access to downtown and the 520 bridge, and it's friendly. Prospective neighbors might include university students in rental housing and apartment complexes along busy Boylston Avenue East; young professionals who rent and buy homes and condominiums along Franklin Avenue East, East Roanoke Street and East Lynn Street; and well-to-do baby boomers who live west of Eastlake Avenue

East, close to Lake Union. In addition, many older lifelong Eastlake residents still live in this community. While, like much of Seattle, rents here continue to rise, Eastlake is still affordable for most middle-income families. A recent report from Dupre + Scott Apartment Advisors, www.dsaa.com, noted that the average rent for an apartment in the Eastlake neighborhood is about 35% lower than the average rent for an apartment downtown.

Web Sites: www.cityofseattle.net, www.eastlake.oo.net
Area Code: 206
Zip Codes: 98102
Post Office: Broadway Station, 101 Broadway, 800-275-8777, www.usps.com
Library: Henry Library, 425 Harvard Avenue East, 206-684-4715, www.spl.lib.wa.us
Public Schools: Seattle Public Schools, P.O. Box 19116, Seattle, WA 98109-1116, 206-298-7000, www.seattleschools.org
Police: West Precinct, 610 3rd Avenue, 206-684-8917, www.cityofseattle. net/police
Emergency Hospital: Harborview Medical Center, 325 9th Avenue, 206-731-3074, www.washington.edu/medical/hmc
Community Resources: Montlake Community Center, 1618 East Calhoun Street, 206-684-4736; Eastlake Community Council, 117 East Louisa Street, www.eastlake.oo.net; Floating Homes Association, 2329 Fairview Avenue East, 206-325-1132
Public Transportation: Metro Transit, 206-553-3000, www.transit. metrokc.gov

QUEEN ANNE

INTERBAY
LOWER QUEEN ANNE
WESTLAKE

Boundaries: North: Lake Washington Ship Canal; **West**: 15th Avenue West, Elliott Avenue West; **South**: Denny Way; **East**: Lake Union, Aurora Avenue North (Highway 99)

Situated on a hill towering 457 feet over downtown and Elliott Bay, Queen Anne is one of the oldest and loveliest residential areas in the city. In the 1890s, streetcar lines from downtown brought affluent residents up the south slope of the hill to their grand mansions. Since its origin, the Queen Anne neighborhood has flourished, remaining an idyllic residential area only minutes from downtown. Queen Anne Avenue North is the main commercial street, and is where residents gather for morning coffee and brunch in picturesque cafes, meet for lunch or dinner at quaint local pubs and restaurants, or shop in the upscale boutiques, specialty bakeries, and small bookstores.

Surrounding the shopping district, modest Colonials and simple bungalows are home to a mix of students, artists, professionals, and families. In addition, formal Northwest Moderns and Tudors are home to retired folks who have lived on the hill for many years. The most affordable houses and apartments are those without a view. This is a pleasant area, with well-maintained houses surrounded by lovely lawns and beautiful nearby parks. The playground at John Hay Elementary School, east of Queen Anne Avenue North, is the site of weekend basketball games; a block west of this main thoroughfare, city ball-parks are host to softball games on lazy summer afternoons.

The southwest corner of Queen Anne remains an enclave for affluent and longtime residents. The homes in this area are lavish; many glimpsed only through breaks in landscaped hedges. West Highland Drive, offering unbelievable views of downtown, Elliott Bay, Mount Rainier, and the Olympic Mountains, is lined with many of the hill's original Queen Anne-style houses. In the blocks north of West Highland Drive, homes are less expensive but still well maintained. Most are modest Four Square or Queen Anne-style houses; a few are Craftsman-style bungalows. To see the merits of this neighborhood, walk or drive to Kerry Park, located on the south side of West Highland Drive. From this vantage point, the downtown cityscape and the shipping activities of Elliott Bay seem an arm's length away; in the distance, Mount Rainier towers over the city. The park is a favorite of nearby residents, who come after dark to admire the brilliant lights of downtown or to watch fireworks over the bay on Independence Day.

East of Queen Anne Avenue North, a variety of large and expensive homes share a lovely view of downtown and Mount Rainier. Many are elaborate Elizabethans and Colonials; others are large unadorned contemporary homes. Residents include a mix of wealthy entrepreneurs, foreign diplomats, and affluent professionals. In addition to breathtaking glimpses of Mount Rainier and downtown, the east side of the hill offers views of azure Lake Union and Capitol Hill. Many 1950s apartment buildings cling to this side of the hill, offering affordable rentals for young professionals. In addition, several houses and apartment buildings in the area have been remodeled and made into condominiums. Many of the people living in this corner of Queen Anne are middle-income professionals who work downtown. A word of advice: this is not the neighborhood to live in if your job is on the Eastside. Commuting from Queen Anne to the Eastside can take as much as an hour during peak travel times.

The north and west sides of Queen Anne Hill are the best locations for reasonably priced rentals in the neighborhood. The west side of Queen Anne, including **Interbay,** a light industrial strip between Queen Anne and Magnolia, offers affordable rental apartments in modest brick and large contemporary buildings as well as rental houses and duplexes, mostly converted bungalows. Many students and faculty live in Queen Anne because Seattle Pacific University (SPU) is located at the base of the hill to the north. Around the SPU campus are numerous rentals, including unpretentious apartment buildings, modest houses, tiny houseboats, and renovated storefronts.

Apartments are also plentiful in the **Lower Queen Anne** area, which surrounds the Seattle Center, site of the Space Needle. Built for the 1962 World's Fair, the 74-acre Seattle Center is a combination amusement park and community center. Among its many attractions are the Pacific Science Center, Opera House, Pacific Northwest Ballet, Seattle Repertory Theater, Intiman Theater, and Key Arena, where the Seattle Sonics and Seattle Storm play. Every summer, Seattle Center is the site for Bumbershoot, a music and arts festival, as well as the Northwest Folk Life Festival and the Bite of Seattle (See **A Seattle Year** for more details about these and other annual events). The Lower Queen Anne area includes retail and residential districts to the north and west. Small ethnic restaurants are located along Roy Street north of the Seattle Center, and aromatic cafes, scrumptious bakeries, old-fashioned diners, and upscale restaurants cluster around Queen Anne Avenue North. Apartment buildings of all styles fill this area, from small brick buildings on Roy Street to enormous contemporary buildings along Queen Anne Avenue North.

Finally, the **Westlake** area, located at the eastern base of the hill, is a commercial district that runs along the west side of Lake Union. Westlake Avenue is lined with upscale view restaurants, private marinas, and marine shops, a combination common in Seattle's waterfront areas. A few houseboats, including the one featured in the movie "Sleepless in Seattle," are moored here.

Though rents can vary greatly depending on which Queen Anne neighborhood you choose, Dupre + Scott Apartment Advisors recently estimated that the average rent in this area is about 30% lower than the average rent downtown. For buyers, Queen Anne remains one of the priciest neighborhoods in Seattle. Home and condominium prices continue to rise, as they have since the late 1990s.

Web Site: www.cityofseattle.net
Area Code: 206
Zip Codes: 98109, 98119
Post Office: Queen Anne Station, 415 1st Avenue North, 800-275-8777,
   www.usps.com

Library: Queen Anne Library, 400 West Garfield Street, 206-386-4227, www.spl.lib.wa.us

Public Schools: Seattle Public Schools, P.O. Box 19116, Seattle, WA 98109-1116, 206-298-7000, www.seattleschools.org

Police: West Precinct, 610 3rd Avenue, 206-684-8917, www.cityofseattle. net/police

Emergency Hospital: Harborview Medical Center, 325 9th Avenue, 206-731-3074, www.washington.edu/medical/hmc

Community Resources: Queen Anne Community Center, 1901 1st Avenue West, 206-386-4240; Queen Anne Help Line, P.O. Box 9697, 206-282-1540; Queen Anne/Magnolia Neighborhood Service Center, 521 2nd Avenue West, 206-684-4812, www.cityofseattle.net

Public Transportation: Metro Transit, 206-553-3000, www.transit. metrokc.gov

1: Downtown/Belltown/Queen Anne

2: Madrona/Central District/First Hill/Downtown/Belltown/Queen Anne

3: Madrona/Central District/First Hill/Downtown/Belltown/Queen Anne

4: Judkins Park/Central District/First Hill/Downtown/Belltown/Queen Anne

8: Rainier Valley/Capitol Hill/Queen Anne

13: Downtown/Belltown/Queen Anne

45: Queen Anne/Wallingford/University District

MAGNOLIA

Boundaries: **North**: Lake Washington Ship Canal; **West**: Puget Sound; **South**: Elliott Bay; **East**: 15th Avenue West

Just west of Queen Anne is the neighborhood of Magnolia, which like Queen Anne, is both a landmark Seattle hill and a community. Rumor has it that the hill was originally named for the distinctive Madrona trees that line the bluff, which a visiting sailor mistakenly identified as magnolias. In any case, the name stuck and now designates a charming neighborhood, which, despite its proximity to downtown, is truly a residential community. It has an interesting mix of homes, mainly Northwest Moderns, Craftsman style bungalows, and brick Tudors—many with views of the beautiful Puget Sound and craggy Olympic Mountains to the west, or of the downtown skyline and busy Elliott Bay to the southeast.

There are a few commercial centers on the hill that collectively serve just about every need imaginable, from medical prescriptions to pet grooming. There's even a cobbler shop for shoe repair. The heart of Magnolia is "the Village," a collection of restaurants, shops, and banks that spill over McGraw Street between 32nd and 34th avenues. Families gather here for Halloween trick-or-treating and in the summer for a children's parade. Professionals line up at one of the two coffeehouses each morning before work, or meet friends at the local pub at the end of the day. Szmania's, a critically acclaimed restaurant, is located in the Village, along with a handful of small family-friendly eateries. A marina at the south end of Magnolia is also home to several popular restaurants, which share a spectacular panorama of Elliott Bay and downtown.

Because of the extraordinary views and the easy commute to downtown, homes in Magnolia are fairly expensive. Along "the bluff," which traces the west edge of Magnolia from south to north, is where you'll find especially lavish homes. More modestly sized and priced homes are located at the north end of the hill and in the middle valley where there is little or no view. Here homeowners tend to be a mix of young families, established professionals or senior citizens; many are longtime residents.

Renters in Magnolia represent all levels of income and occupations. Because Magnolia is not conveniently located to I-5, apartments here rent for slightly less than the Seattle average, even those with water or city views. This is particularly true for the larger, two-bedroom apartments; studio rents are comparable to other neighborhoods. You'll find many apartment buildings located at the north end of the hill, facing Ballard.

Nearby, on the Lake Washington Ship Canal, the Fisherman's Terminal is an energetic hub with constant activity from the fishing vessels that dock there. Just off West Emerson Street, part of the Fisherman's Terminal was transformed into a small shopping and dining destination, featuring Chinook's restaurant and the Bay Café, a nautical-theme gallery and gift store, and the Highliner Tavern. Continue on this route and you'll find Discovery Park and the Hiram Chittenden Locks. The locks, which separate the Lake Washington Ship Canal from the Puget Sound, offer an easy route for foot and bicycle traffic between Magnolia and Ballard. Discovery Park, in the northwest corner of Magnolia, is Seattle's largest and most verdant park, consisting of 534 acres of meadows, forest, and beach, with clay cliffs and seven miles of nature trails. The nearby West Point Lighthouse was built on the northwest point of the beach in 1881 and is still a popular attraction, although the attraction is now somewhat diminished by the close proximity of the West Point Sewage Treatment Plant.

Although Magnolia is not technically a peninsula, access to the hill is limited to Dravus Street, Nickerson Street, and the Magnolia Bridge. When the bridge is closed, as it has been twice in the last few years due to mudslides and an earthquake, the commute to and from Magnolia lengthens considerably. Interbay, the semi-industrial area between Magnolia and Queen Anne, effectively cuts off Magnolia from the main thoroughfare of 15th Avenue West (Elliott Avenue), so only those three streets serve as overpasses into the neighborhood. Still, Magnolia is actually quite convenient to downtown and the surrounding neighborhoods, although getting to I-5 can be difficult.

Web Site: www.cityofseattle.net
Area Code: 206
Zip Codes: 98199
Post Office: Magnolia Station, 3211 West McGraw Street, 800-275-8777, www.usps.com
Library: Magnolia Library, 2801 34th Avenue West, 206-386-4225, www.spl.lib.wa.us
Public Schools: Seattle Public Schools, P.O. Box 19116, Seattle, WA 98109-1116, 206-298-7000, www.seattleschools.org
Police: West Precinct, 610 3rd Avenue, 206-684-8917, www.cityofseattle.net/police
Emergency Hospital: Swedish Medical Center Ballard, 5300 Tallman Avenue NW, 206-781-6341, www.swedish.org
Community Resources: Queen Anne/Magnolia Neighborhood Service Center, 521 2nd Avenue West, 206-684-4812, www.cityofseattle.net; Magnolia Community Center, 2550 34th Avenue NW, 206-386-4235; Magnolia Community Club, 206-283-1188; Magnolia Help Line, 3213 West Wheeler, 206-284-5631
Public Transportation: Metro Transit, 206-553-3000, www.transit.metrokc.gov
   19: Downtown/Belltown/Queen Anne/Magnolia
   24: Downtown/Belltown/Queen Anne/Magnolia
   31: Magnolia/Queen Anne/Fremont/Wallingford/University District
   33: Downtown/Belltown/Queen Anne/Magnolia

BALLARD

SHILSHOLE
CROWN HILL
NORTH BEACH
BLUE RIDGE

Boundaries: **North**: NW 110th Street; **West**: Puget Sound; **South**: Lake Washington Ship Canal; **East**: 3rd Avenue NW

Home to about 50,000, Ballard is a quaint and delightful neighborhood located just 15 minutes north of downtown. Originally a town made up of workers for the local Stimson Mill, Seattle annexed it in 1906 after a dead horse in the town's drinking water forced residents to turn to the city for a new water supply. In the early 1900s, Scandinavian immigrants settled in Ballard, attracted to the abundant fish in the Puget Sound. Although currently commercial salmon fishing in the Sound is restricted to local Native American tribes, Ballard remains home to many professional fishermen who catch pollack, halibut, cod, and salmon along the coast of Alaska. Off-season, from the Ballard Bridge and homes in the south end of the neighborhood, are views of the colorful fishing vessels harbored at Fisherman's Terminal and along the Lake Washington Ship Canal. To learn about the boating and fishing history of Ballard, visit the Hiram Chittenden Locks and Fish Ladder, located at the west end of NW Market Street (just as the street becomes Seaview Avenue NW).

Ballard is well known as a tight-knit Scandinavian community, celebrating its heritage by hosting yearly festivals for Santa Lucia (a Swedish saint honored during the Christmas Season), and for Syettende Mai (May 17, Norway's Constitution Day). During these celebrations, Ballard's main street, NW Market Street, is roped off from traffic and gaily decorated, and everyone is welcome to attend the festivities. Northwest Market Street is the retail section of the original town, lined with quaint Scandinavian bakeries, delis, and restaurants, as well as modern hobby shops, record stores, ethnic eateries, and a new, locally owned movie theatre. The Nordic Heritage Museum at 3014 NW 67th Street offers a fascinating glimpse at the Scandinavian culture that pervades the neighborhood. In contrast, one very un-Scandinavian restaurant on NW Market Street is the popular Lombardi's, famous for good Italian food, and host of an annual garlic festival. Samples from this lively event include such delicacies as garlic ice cream and garlic martinis. A welcome addition to the Market Street dining scene is the Market Street Urban Grill, 1755 NW Market, which is already becoming a neighborhood favorite.

Another major street in Ballard is 15th Avenue NW, which begins at the Ballard Bridge and runs north through the neighborhood. It's lined with a variety of small businesses, appliance and auto repair shops, fast-food restaurants, dry cleaners, pet shops, and antique malls. The streets off this main thoroughfare, however, are largely residential. Typically you'll find modest 1950s bungalows, brick Tudors, and simple wood-frame houses lining quiet streets. Many of these homes have views of the Olympic Mountains to the west; others overlook the boating activity along the Lake Washington Ship Canal. All homes in Ballard have easy access to downtown but, because of the longer distance to I-5, they are often less expensive than comparable houses elsewhere in the city.

In recent years, a number of hip bars, restaurants, shops, and galleries have opened in the two blocks of Ballard Avenue just south of Market Street. Newcomers like Bad Albert's Tap & Grill and The Old Town Ale House present live jazz, blues, and alternative rock to complement the rockabilly and roots rock offered for years at the Tractor Tavern. This small slice of Ballard is also home to the locally famous bar and eatery Hattie's Hat. Though often smoke-filled, Hattie's Hat offers great comfort food and stiff, spicy Bloody Marys. Grapes, a wine and cheese merchant, Madame K's Pizza, and Taco Del Mar are also located on Ballard Avenue.

East of 32nd Avenue NW, the **Shilshole** section of Ballard offers modest brick Tudors and Arts-and-Crafts style homes with a panorama of Bainbridge Island, Puget Sound, and the Olympics. Shilshole is best known throughout the city for the seafood restaurants that line Seaview Avenue NW, like Ray's Boathouse and Anthony's Homeport, and for Golden Gardens Park. On summer evenings, visitors to the park watch in awe as the sun dips behind the Olympic Mountains. The park also attracts Seattle residents for summer picnics, swimming, and volleyball, as well as the occasional after-dark campfire. Golden Gardens is also home to one of Seattle Parks and Recreation's seven off-leash dog areas.

Rental homes are available throughout Ballard, particularly south of NW 65th Street, and apartment buildings line 24th Avenue NW, offering reasonable rents for studios and one- or two-bedroom units. Modest condominiums are available near NW Market Street; more plush condos can be found in the Shilshole area along the waterfront. Public transportation is readily available in Ballard. Several bus routes run to downtown along 15th Avenue NW and 24th Avenue NW, and there are regular routes to Wallingford and the University District that run along NW Market Street and NW 85th Street.

One of Seattle's 12 "official" hills, **Crown Hill** begins where 15th Avenue NW meets NW 85th Street, at an intersection dominated by Safeway and QFC grocery stores. The neighborhood stretches north along 15th Avenue NW, then curves east along Holman Road. Though at first glance Crown Hill appears to be simply an accumulation of fast food outlets, auto body shops, and adult entertainment venues, the community does have its share of hidden treasures, like the Library Café and Crown Hill Hardware, which has been here for more than 80 years. Crown Hill's residential clusters are quiet, with well-tended yards and a mixture of brick Tudors and ramblers. Homes are still mostly affordable here, particularly north of NW 85th Street.

Elegant homes with views of the Puget Sound and the Olympic Mountains are situated on the northern and western hillsides of Ballard. Many of the homes in the **North Beach** area, north of NW 85th Street, are sprawling 1950s ranch houses with exquisitely landscaped yards. Other more recent additions to the neighborhood include elaborate colonials, immaculate brick Tudor cottages, and contemporary designs from the 1960s and '70s. Homes in this area have a front-row seat for breathtaking sunsets over the Olympic Mountains. In the summer months, residents watch weekend sailboat races on the sound; during the winter holidays, colorfully lighted ships follow the shoreline as part of the annual Christmas Ship Parade.

The *Seattle Post-Intelligencer* referred to the hillside community of **Blue Ridge** as one of the least known and most isolated neighborhoods in the city. Located on Puget Sound, north of Northwest 100th Street and south of Carkeek Park, Blue Ridge was developed during the Depression by William Boeing for some of his airplane company executives. Entirely residential, with less than 500 homes, the community features a club, swimming pool, tennis courts, playfields, and a private beach. Blue Ridge is a covenant community, which means there are rules and restrictions that residents are required to follow. For instance, there may be guidelines for landscaping or improvements that homeowners can make to their properties. Small homes that might have sold for $200,000 in Greenlake in the late 1990s went for about $300,000 in Blue Ridge—tack on another $200,000 for a view. Larger homes, like those originally built by William Boeing, go for seven figures.

Despite the pricier accommodations of Blue Ridge, homes in Ballard generally are still affordable, especially compared to nearby neighborhoods like Queen Anne and Magnolia. Renters may also find Ballard to their liking. According to Dupre + Scott Apartment Advisors, rents run about a third less than those downtown or in Belltown.

While Ballard used to be known as a Nordic community, today people of many cultural backgrounds call it home. In addition to fishermen, Ballard is home to local merchants, teachers, public servants, and a flourishing senior-citizen community. Shilshole and North Beach attract affluent professionals and wealthy retirees. Despite its proximity to downtown, Ballard has retained its village appeal and offers residents a close-knit community and convenient location.

Web Sites: www.cityofseattle.net, www.inballard.com

Area Code: 206

Zip Codes: 98107, 98117, 98103

Post Office: Ballard Station, 5706 17th Avenue NW, 800-275-8777, www.usps.com

Library: Ballard Library, 5711 24th Avenue NW, 206-684-4089, www.spl.lib.wa.us

Public Schools: Seattle Public Schools, P.O. Box 19116, Seattle, WA 98109-1116, 206-298-7000, www.seattleschools.org

Police: North Precinct, 10049 College Way North, 206-684-0850, www.cityofseattle.net/police

Emergency Hospital: Swedish Medical Center Ballard, 5300 Tallman Avenue NW, 206-781-6341, www.swedish.org

Community Resources: Ballard Community Center, 6020 28th Avenue NW, 206-684-4093, www.ci.seattle.wa.us/parks; Ballard Neighborhood Service Center, 2305 NW Market Street, 206-684-4060, www.cityofseattle. net; Ballard Pool, 1471 NW 67th Street, 206-684-4094, www.cityofseattle. net/parks; Loyal Heights Community Center, 2101 NW 77th Street, 206-684-4052, www.ci.seattle.wa.us/parks

Public Transportation: Metro Transit, 206-553-3000, www.transit. metrokc.gov

15: Downtown/Queen Anne/Interbay/Ballard/Crown Hill/Blue Ridge
17: Downtown/Westlake/Queen Anne/Ballard/Sunset Hill/Loyal Heights
18: Downtown/Queen Anne/Interbay/Ballard/Loyal Heights/North Beach
44: Shilshole/Ballard/Wallingford/University District/Montlake
46: Shilshole/Ballard/Fremont/Wallingford/University District
48: Loyal Heights/Crown Hill/Greenwood/Ravenna/University District/ Montlake/Central District/Columbia City/Rainier Beach
75: Ballard/Crown Hill/Northgate/Lake City/Sand Point/University District
81: (Night Owl) Downtown/Queen Anne/Ballard/Loyal Heights

PHINNEY RIDGE/GREENWOOD

Boundaries: **North**: Holman Road NW, North 105th Street; **West**: 8th Avenue NW, 3rd Avenue NW; **South**: North 50th Street; **East**: Aurora Avenue North (Highway 99)

The Phinney Ridge and Greenwood neighborhoods are located north of Fremont, between Ballard and Green Lake. The central feature of Phinney Ridge is the Woodland Park Zoo, located southwest of Green Lake across Aurora Avenue North. If visiting, be sure to walk through the fabulous rose garden at its 50th Street entrance. Phinney Ridge, a neighborhood known for its ever-present population of young families, is a perennial favorite of lower-middle-income, white collar professionals—teachers, public servants, non-profit organization employees, etc., creating a neighborhood reputation of liberal political views and strong community involvement. However, in more recent years, the neighborhood has become popular with more affluent professionals, and housing prices have risen accordingly.

Most Phinney Ridge residents live in Northwest Moderns or Craftsman bungalows on the west side of the hill, sharing lovely views of Ballard, the Puget Sound, and the Olympic Mountains. Apartment buildings line Phinney Avenue North along the ridge of the hill, although they taper off north of the zoo as retail shops and restaurants become more prevalent. Just north of NW 65th Street, Phinney Avenue North jogs over to become a stretch of Greenwood Avenue North and the true commercial district begins. Here the

Red Mill Burger Company serves delicious burgers to people from all over Seattle; on summer evenings the line to the counter commonly stretches out the door and along the sidewalk. On Sunday mornings, another popular destination is Mae's Phinney Ridge Café at 65th Street, where hungry Seattle residents also fill the sidewalk during the brunch hour—you know you've found it by the large Holsteins painted on the bright green walls of the café. This area also offers a fun selection of ethnic and vegetarian restaurants, cozy pubs, funky coffeehouses, card and gift shops.

The main intersection of the Greenwood neighborhood is NW 85th Street and Greenwood Avenue NW. Commercial buildings include banks, antique stores, old-fashioned diners, and well-stocked pubs, as well as the Greenwood Senior Center and the Greenwood Library. Heavy traffic on NW 85th Street keeps this area from being a walkable shopping district, but generally it's comfortable and pleasant. South of NW 85th Street, the Phinney Ridge and Greenwood neighborhoods are almost identical, with roomy bungalows and Northwest Modern homes on either side of the Greenwood Avenue NW retail core. North of NW 85th Street is a collection of more modest homes. Apartment seekers will find a selection of new apartment buildings along NW 85th Street, particularly in the few blocks just west of Aurora, and apartments circa 1970 line Greenwood Avenue NW, north of NW 90th Street. Affordable cottages, modern split-level homes, and duplexes can be found tucked away from the main streets of Greenwood Avenue North and 8th Avenue NW. Both Greenwood and Phinney Ridge are comfortable middle-class neighborhoods and many of the residents here are young professionals and their families.

Several blocks of both Greenwood and Phinney Ridge are situated close to Aurora Avenue North, a busy state highway and commercial district; prospective residents should consider this when looking at homes in the few blocks closest to Aurora Avenue North.

Web Sites: www.cityofseattle.net, www.phinneycenter.org
Area Code: 206
Zip Codes: 98103, 98107, 98117
Post Office: Greenwood Station, 8306 Greenwood Avenue North, 800-275-8777, www.usps.com
Library: Greenwood Library, 8016 Greenwood Avenue N, 206-684-4086, www.spl.lib.wa.us
Public Schools: Seattle Public Schools, P.O. Box 19116, Seattle, WA 98109-1116, 206-298-7000, www.seattleschools.org
Police: North Precinct, 10049 College Way North, 206-684-0850, www.cityofseattle.net/police
Emergency Hospital: Swedish Medical Center Ballard, 5300 Tallman Avenue NW, 206-781-6341, www.swedish.org

Community Resources: Greenwood Neighborhood Service Center, 8515 Greenwood Avenue North, 206-684-4096, www.cityofseattle.net; Greenwood Senior Center, 525 North 85th Street, 206-461-7841; Phinney Neighborhood Association, 6532 Phinney Avenue North, 206-783-2244

Public Transportation: Metro Transit, 206-553-3000, www.transit.metrokc.gov

82: (Night Owl) Downtown/Queen Anne/Fremont/Wallingford/Green Lake/Greenwood

---

FREMONT

Boundaries: **North**: North 46th Street/North Market Street; **East**: Stone Way North; **West**: 8th Avenue NW; **South**: Lake Washington Ship Canal and Fremont Bridge

Ten minutes north of downtown and across from the Lake Washington Ship Canal lies the picturesque Fremont district, a small Seattle neighborhood with its central core at the intersection of Fremont Avenue North, North 35th Street, and Fremont Place North, one block north of the Fremont Bridge. From here it is less than a five-minute walk to two of Seattle's most beloved sculptures, "Waiting for the Interurban" and the "Fremont Troll," as well as Seattle's most controversial statue, Emil Venkov's "Lenin," which was originally displayed in communist Slovakia in 1988.

The self-proclaimed "Center of the Universe," Fremont charms even the most cynical of Seattle residents with its mixture of inviting shops and events. It is the home of the original Red Hook Brewery, as well as several other microbreweries and pubs. There are art galleries galore, vintage clothing and "junk" stores, barber shops, and tattoo parlors. On the weekends, Seattle residents flock to the district for brunch and shopping, or for coffee and dessert at The Still Life Coffeehouse on North 35th Street. At night, Fremont's pubs overflow with a friendly and diverse crowd of locals. This area is still miraculously free of tourists, despite its proximity to downtown.

During the summer, the neighborhood hosts the Fremont Sunday Market, where residents and visitors can buy goods from local artists and artisans. Also popular is the Puget Consumers Co-op on North 34th Street, a refreshing alternative to the corporate mega-grocers. One weekend in June is devoted to the summer solstice, and includes the annual Solstice Parade and Fremont Fair. On summer Saturday evenings, a parking lot doubles as the site for the Fremont Outdoor Cinema. Moviegoers bring their own chairs to watch the flick, which is projected on the wall of a building bordering the lot.

The area is primarily residential, with a combination of artists, students, and young professionals calling Fremont home, though the last five years have seen rapid commercial growth here. The Quadrant Lake Union Center, located just east of the Fremont Bridge is home to Adobe Systems, and Getty Images plans to inhabit the Park View Building just west of the bridge. Despite the new construction, the neighborhood has maintained its delicate balance of bohemian culture and middle class comfort. It is a close-knit community, popular among low and middle-income families and fortunately still affordable for first-time homeowners.

If you'd like to rent in Fremont, your best bet is to drive, bicycle, or walk through the area looking for "For Rent" signs in windows. There is plentiful rental property here, both apartments and houses, but available units are generally snapped up before being advertised in the local newspapers. Fremont's shopping district contains some rental space, especially in the few blocks north of Fremont Place North, but don't limit your search to that area. To the east of Fremont Avenue, and across or under Aurora Avenue, there are many affordable housing opportunities. Aurora can be fairly noisy during high traffic times, so if you're sensitive to that, try to visit nearby rentals on a weekday, around 5 p.m. to experience the noise level first-hand.

A few blocks north of Fremont's shopping district is NW 39th Avenue, which is lined with large apartment buildings built during the 1950s and '60s. Since this area is along one of the main routes between Ballard, downtown, and the University District, it can be a little noisy during high traffic times. You'll find a more traditional residential area of 1920s Craftsman style bungalows between NW 39th and NW 46th streets, and east of Fremont Avenue North. As with most Seattle neighborhoods near a university or college, the best time for renting is late April through early June, when students are making plans to head home for the summer. Fremont is 20 to 25 minutes by car or bus from the University of Washington, and a 5 to 15 minute walk from Seattle Pacific University, which is just across the Fremont Bridge on the north side of the Queen Anne neighborhood.

Web Sites: www.cityofseattle.net, www.fremont.com
Area Code: 206
Zip Codes: 98103, 98107
Post Office: Wallingford Station, 1329 North 47th Street, 800-275-8777, www.usps.com
Library: Fremont Library, 731 North 35th Street, 206-684-4084, www.spl.lib.wa.us
Public Schools: Seattle Public Schools, P.O. Box 19116, Seattle, WA 98109-1116, 206-298-7000, www.seattleschools.org

Police: North Precinct, 10049 College Way North, 206-684-0850, www.cityofseattle.net/police

Emergency Hospital: Swedish Medical Center Ballard, 5300 Tallman Avenue NW, 206-781-6341, www.swedish.org

Community Resources: Fremont Neighborhood Council, 206-781-6624; Fremont Neighborhood Service Center, 908 North 34th Street, 206-684-4054, www.cityofseattle.net; Fremont Public Association Community Resource Center, 1501 North 45th Street, 206-694-6700, www.fremontpublic.org

WALLINGFORD

Boundaries: North: Northeast 50th Street; **West**: Aurora Avenue North (Highway 99); **South**: Lake Washington Ship Canal; **East**: I-5

A symbol of a bygone era, the old gasworks at the north end of Lake Union marks the tip of the Wallingford neighborhood. In the early 1900s, when the plant was still operational, Wallingford was a hub of industrial activity. Now the neighborhood is predominantly residential, and the old plant is a beloved Seattle landmark and popular public park. Gasworks Park is a favorite for kite-flying enthusiasts because of steady winds off the lake, and for bicyclists who meet to ride the Burke-Gilman trail along Lake Union and Lake Washington. In addition, Gasworks Park is the site of one of Seattle's annual Independence Day fireworks displays. Although the fireworks can be seen from anywhere around the lake, attendees here have the added benefit of watching the fireworks to the accompaniment of the Seattle Symphony.

Despite its proximity to downtown, Wallingford exudes a quiet charm. On summer evenings, couples stroll down tree-lined streets and visit with neighbors. On Sundays, people crowd into local restaurants for brunch or catch a matinee at the Guild 45th Theater. Like nearby Fremont, Wallingford is aesthetically pleasing and community focused. Elegant Wallingford Center, an old school that was remodeled in the 1980s to become an upscale condominium and retail shopping center, is considered the crown jewel of the area. Nearby, the 45th Street Community Clinic shares a remodeled fire station with the Wallingford branch of the Seattle Public Library. Northeast 45th Street, connecting Fremont and Ballard to the University District, offers a pleasant assortment of ethnic restaurants, travel and used bookstores, and funky boutiques.

North of Gasworks Park, on the south slope of the hill, beautifully restored homes look out over the park and the downtown skyline. Many of the Victorian and Colonial houses here were built in the early 1900s.

Northwest Moderns and Craftsman bungalows were added during the 1920s. Homeowners in this area tend to be young professionals, although rental opportunities attract students from the nearby UW and Seattle Pacific University. Streets here are quiet; churches and old schools dot the area, as do corner grocery stores and coffeehouses. Spectacular views of Lake Union and downtown, as well as modestly sized homes, have attracted many middle-income families to this area. That trend is changing slowly, however, as higher real estate prices have made this neighborhood less affordable for single-income families.

North of 45th Street and close to I-5, modest and more affordable homes can be found. Most are bungalows similar to those in the south end of the neighborhood, without the panoramic views of Lake Union and downtown but occasionally with views of the tips of the Cascades to the east. The area population includes young professionals and students residing in a mix of rentals and owner-occupied houses. There are few true apartment buildings in the blocks between 45th Street and Green Lake, but they become more common as one heads toward I-5 and the University District.

Wallingford is well located for those commuting to either downtown or the Eastside. Aurora Avenue North (Highway 99) runs parallel to Stone Way, just a few blocks into the Fremont neighborhood. This is generally an excellent route into downtown, and even to West Seattle or the Sea-Tac Airport. Savvy Eastside commuters take a shortcut along Lake Union to bypass I-5 and catch up with Highway 520 at the Montlake entrance.

Web Sites: www.cityofseattle.net, www.wallingford.org
Area Code: 206
Zip Codes: 98103, 98105
Post Office: Wallingford Station, 1329 North 47th Street, 800-275-8777, www.usps.com
Library: Wallingford Library, 1501 North 45th Street, 206-684-4088, www.spl.lib.wa.us
Public Schools: Seattle Public Schools, P.O. Box 19116, Seattle, WA 98109-1116, 206-298-7000, www.seattleschools.org
Police: North Precinct, 10049 College Way North, 206-684-0850, www.cityofseattle.net/police
Emergency Hospital: University of Washington Medical Center, 1959 NE Pacific Street, 206-598-3300, www.washington.edu/medical/uwmc
Community Resources: Wallingford Boys and Girls Club, 503 North 50th Street, 206-547-2133; Wallingford Community Council, 2100-A North 45th Street, 206-632-4759, www.wallingford.org; Wallingford Senior Center, 4649 Sunnyside North, 206-461-7825

GREEN LAKE

MAPLE LEAF

Boundaries: North: NE 110th Street; **West**: Aurora Avenue North (Highway 99); **South**: North 50th Street; **East**: I-5

In the late 1800s trolleys connected Green Lake to downtown, creating a popular recreation spot for Seattle residents. An amusement park was opened on the west side of the lake and Woodland Park Zoo was developed at the south end. In the early 1900s, the city of Seattle annexed Green Lake and its surrounding lands, designating them a public space. Today, Green Lake is one of Seattle's most popular public parks. It is surrounded by a three-mile paved walkway that attracts bicyclists, in-line skaters, runners, and walkers. During the summer, fields at the east side of the lake fill with volleyball teams; basketball courts offer informal but competitive pick-up games; and in-line skaters play hockey in a drained wading pool. At the south end of the lake, Woodland Park has baseball and soccer fields, lighted tennis courts, and a running track.

North and east of Green Lake, cozy coffee shops, fragrant bakeries, sporting goods and bike shops provide services for visitors and residents. Most are located near the intersection of Ravenna Avenue and Green Lake Way, or a few minutes north at Green Lake Way and 80th Street. Beautiful Northwest Modern and Tudor style homes line Green Lake Way, facing the lake. Even though there is heavy traffic along this main thoroughfare, the view of the lake and the popularity of the area keep up the value of these homes. Original neighborhood houses still exist, although the distance from these houses to the lake shore increased when the lake was partially drained in the early 1900s.

The neighborhood's charm and immediate accessibility to the park make Green Lake a high demand area, which is reflected in its real estate prices. The Northwest Multiple Listing Service reports that from February 2001 to February 2002, the average home price rose by more than 11%. As in other neighborhoods, however, the market has slowed, with sales decreasing 25% during the same period.

Homes just off the lake are the most expensive; many are elegant Colonial style mansions with views of the lake and even of the Olympic Mountains. Recent construction has increased the number of condominiums and townhouses east of the lake, although the area remains primarily a mix of detached houses and apartments. More modest Northwest Modern and Craftsman style homes line idyllic residential streets in the blocks southeast of Green Lake, bordering the Wallingford neighborhood. These homes have the advantage of proximity to Green Lake without the inconvenience of heavy traffic or summer parking problems. Northwest and west of the lake, particularly across Aurora Avenue North near the Phinney Ridge neighborhood, modest and affordable Craftsman style bungalows and Cape Cod style cottages line steep, quiet streets. There are few rentals available in this area, but prices for homes are often much lower than those closer in to the lake. Unpretentious yet comfortable homes may be found north of 80th Street. While many of these areas seem far from the lake, most are merely a few minutes' walk away. Green Lake is one of the few Seattle neighborhoods where many residents walk to do their errands. The area around the lake is flat rather than hilly and the heavy traffic in the area makes walking a pleasant alternative to driving.

While most houses around Green Lake are detached bungalows, ramblers, or duplexes, there are many options for those who would like to rent in the Green Lake area. On the southeast and east sides of the lake, particularly near Ravenna Boulevard, there are several apartment buildings and condominiums. Most are contemporary high-rise complexes; others are smaller Federal or 1950s style apartment buildings. Many are a few blocks off the lake, surrounded by houses or other similar apartment buildings. In the smaller buildings, apartments are not often advertised in local newspapers, so prospective tenants should visit the area periodically looking for rental signs. For the best deals, try the area in the spring, when University of Washington students vacate for the summer. Dupre + Scott Apartment Advisors estimates that average monthly rent in Greenlake/Wallingford is nearly 30% lower than downtown.

The Green Lake neighborhood is predominately middle-income. Southeast of the lake and across Aurora Avenue (Highway 99) to the west, couples and young families keep that part of the neighborhood hopping. These two areas have been growing rapidly as housing prices increase in the more affluent blocks north and east of Green Lake. According to the *Seattle Post-Intelligencer*, the city's Office of Management and Planning estimates that by the year 2014, the number of existing households in the Green Lake area will grow to 1,839 households—an increase of 400 since 1997, and a climb in density from 13.4 households per gross acre to 17.2.

Just north of Green Lake is the **Maple Leaf** neighborhood, recognizable by its blue water tower decorated with enormous white maple leaves. It is a neighborhood of quiet streets and modest but well maintained homes. Most houses in the area are brick Tudors or contemporary split-levels, with small landscaped yards. Perched on a hill over I-5, many homes have views of the Olympics or Mount Rainier. Compared to other desirable neighborhoods in Seattle, housing prices in Maple Leaf are surprisingly affordable considering the neighborhood's proximity to Green Lake and I-5. A *Seattle Times* computer analysis in 2000 showed that Maple Leaf had a median sales price about 17% less than Green Lake's.

Web Site: www.cityofseattle.net

Area Code: 206

Zip Code: 98103

Post Office: Wedgwood Station, 7724 35th Avenue NE, 800-275-8777, www.usps.com

Library: Green Lake Library, 7364 East Green Lake Drive North, 206-684-7547, www.spl.lib.wa.us

Public Schools: Seattle Public Schools, P.O. Box 19116, Seattle, WA 98109-1116, 206-298-7000, www.seattleschools.org

Police: North Precinct, 10049 College Way North, 206-684-0850, www.cityofseattle.net/police

Emergency Hospital: Northwest Hospital, 1550 North 115th Street, 206-364-0500, www.nwhospital.org

Neighborhood Organizations: Green Lake Community Center, 7201 East Green Lake Drive North, 206-684-0780, www.cityofseattle.net/parks; Green Lake Community Council, P.O. Box 31536, Seattle, WA 98103; Maple Leaf Community Council, P.O. Box 75595, Seattle, WA 98125, www.ci.seattle.wa.us

Public Transportation: Metro Transit, 206-553-3000, www.transit.metrokc.gov

26: Downtown/Fremont/Wallingford/Green Lake

UNIVERSITY DISTRICT

ROOSEVELT
RAVENNA
UNIVERSITY PARK
BRYANT

Boundaries: **North**: NE 75th Street; **West**: I-5; **South**: Lake Washington Ship Canal; **East**: NE 35th Street, Union Bay

In 1861, the University of Washington was founded on the present-day site of the Four Seasons Olympic Hotel in downtown Seattle. Four Grecian pillars, all that remain of the original building, can now be seen on a small piece of land near the Paramount Theater (at the intersection of Pike Street and Boren Avenue). The university moved to its present location near Union Bay in 1895, intent upon shaking off its reputation as an elementary and high school—the UW graduated its first university student in 1876, but continued accepting pre-college students as late as 1897. Two influential Seattle citizens, Arthur Denny and Daniel Bagley, were instrumental in bringing the college to Seattle. Denny persuaded the legislature to grant Seattle the rights to the territorial university and donated 10 acres of his own property as the original site. Bagley had convinced Denny that the college would be more of an asset to the city than the other available alternatives: the state capitol, prison, or customs house. Asa Mercer, the university's first president and teacher, is best known today as the man who went east and recruited single women to move to Seattle when it was still a primarily male logging community. His substantial academic and advisory contributions to the fledgling college are largely overlooked. In 1909, the Alaska-Yukon-Pacific Exposition was held on campus, marking a turning point for the young university. Originally intended to celebrate the 10th anniversary of the Klondike Gold Rush, the event was held two years late but drew nearly four million visitors to the area. As a result of the exposition, the university received several new permanent buildings and gained national attention. Since then, annual enrollment has reached the 35,000 mark and the university has gained a reputation as a premier medical research institution. While some critics claim that the university gives special preference to its graduate and research programs, particularly the sciences over the humanities, it remains an affordable way to receive a high quality undergraduate education.

Students, staff, and faculty of the university buzz about the campus and fill area coffeehouses at all hours of the day. On campus, be sure to visit the Burke Museum for, among other attractions, its marvelous exhibits on local Native American tribes, and the Graduate Reading Room, a beautiful cathedral-shaped room in the Suzzallo Library. For a look at one of Seattle's natural wonders, stop at "Frosh Pond" for a fabulous view of Mount Rainier over the Guggenheim Fountain.

In addition to its solid academic reputation, the University of Washington is nationally recognized for its football program. The Huskies routinely attract sold-out crowds for home games, even during disastrous seasons. Wealthy UW graduates and football fans are generous supporters of the program, and regularly generate more interest in the team than the current university students. The UW crew and basketball teams (particularly the women's) also receive local attention, although they are overshadowed by the fervent devotion of Husky football fans. All of the UW sports facilities are on the shore of Union Bay, an inlet of Lake Washington, along Montlake Avenue. Parking is scarce and traffic problems are common on football Saturdays; at other times two large parking lots north of the stadium are sufficient. City regulations benefit those who live near the stadium by assigning parking stickers and by limiting parking on most streets to neighborhood residents. Some lucky football fans come to the games by boat, tying up at the east side of the UW stadium. Others take advantage of the additional buses added to local routes on game days. For the fitness and environmentally minded, you can bike or walk to the games via the Burke-Gilman trail.

Locals and students refer to the university as the UW (pronounced "U-Dub") and to the area around it as the "U-District." Although the campus is the geographic focal point of the area, the center of the community is "the Ave." (University Way), running just a block west of the campus. A tad run down, it's a great place to see movies, buy books and CDs, play video games, or eat at a variety of ethnic restaurants. Along the Ave., plans are underway to add landscaping, create wider sidewalks, and to improve the street surface. The Ave. is also a central location for bus service to the University District and other parts of the city, with routes to neighborhoods throughout the north end of Seattle and to downtown and Capitol Hill. Just south of NE 45th Street on the Ave., the University Bookstore carries an array of books, gifts, and art supplies, as well as required materials for UW classes. During the school year, the Ave. is a favorite student hangout. In the summer it is the site for the University District Street Fair, which takes over several blocks of the street for an entire weekend.

As one would expect, the University District is primarily a neighborhood of young people (the median age is 22). Residents include undergraduate and graduate students and university faculty members, as well as young professionals, scholars, and artists. Some families own homes in the northeast corner of the district near Ravenna Boulevard, but over 90% of U-District residents are renters. Just north of campus, 17th Avenue NE, a tree-lined avenue known informally as "Greek Row," is bordered by beautiful colonial-style mansions. Many of these buildings, as well as those in the blocks east of 17th Avenue NE, have been converted into fraternities, sororities, and rooming houses. The north end of this area is popular with graduate students and visiting faculty, as well as long-time neighborhood residents.

West of campus you'll find apartment buildings and shared houses galore. Close to the campus there are several brick apartment buildings, offering small studios or one-bedrooms with hardwood floors and occasional views. Modern accommodations, built in the 1980s, are located near I-5 and offer multiple bedroom apartments. Other rental opportunities are available near the University Village Mall, at the northeast corner of the UW campus. The mall includes a Starbucks and national chain stores such as The Gap, Eddie Bauer, Banana Republic, and Pottery Barn. Apartment buildings and townhouses line NE 22nd Street, and other rentals are tucked into the base of the hill behind the retail stores and strip malls that line NE 25th Street. The most affordable options here are rooms for rent in group houses—these are often listed in local papers such as *The Stranger* and *The*

Seattle Weekly, and in the UW student paper *The Daily*. Rental houses are also readily available, particularly north of 50th Avenue NE. The best time for finding rentals of any kind is at the end of the school year when students head home for the summer. Many rentals are not listed in local papers, so it is generally a good idea to roam the neighborhood looking for "For Rent" signs. Additionally, the University of Washington Student Housing Affairs provides information to students and non-students alike about off-campus opportunities. Visit them in Room G20 of the Husky Union Building or call 206-543-9887.

The Roosevelt and Ravenna neighborhoods, located north of the University District, traditionally attract UW graduate students, faculty, and staff. In recent decades, professionals willing to commute to downtown or the Eastside have also moved to these areas. The center of the **Roosevelt** neighborhood is a small retail district based around the intersection of Roosevelt Avenue NE and NE 65th Street, which boasts several small ethnic restaurants, coffee shops, and bookstores. On the first Wednesday of every month, motorcycle enthusiasts flock to Teddy's Bar, lining the street with bikes of all makes and models. Despite this "biker bar" tradition, the Roosevelt neighborhood is a tranquil residential community. Most houses in the Roosevelt District are Arts-and-Crafts style bungalows and Tudor-style cottages. There are a few apartment buildings and condominiums in the neighborhoods, mostly near I-5 and Ravenna Boulevard.

The **Ravenna** neighborhood is named for the ravine that runs through the area, at one time connecting Green Lake with Union Bay and Lake Washington. Water still flows in the ravine, fed by underground streams and Seattle's ubiquitous rain. Ravenna Park follows the ravine, winding northwest toward the Green Lake area. It is a beautiful and lush city park with trails, tennis courts, and picnic areas. There are a variety of architectural styles in Ravenna, including modest Tudors, roomy Arts-and-Crafts homes, and 1960s bungalows. There are occasional opportunities for renting houses here, and a few apartments and townhouses line 25th Avenue East. Recent changes to Ravenna include the move of the familiar Honey Bear Bakery from its North 55th Street location to Northeast 65th Street and 20th Avenue.

The **University Park** neighborhood ranges from 16th Avenue NE in the west to 21st Avenue NE in the east. Its northern border is Ravenna Park, and NE 50th Street marks it southern edge. The tiny neighborhood, which is currently working to obtain official identification signs from the city to let visitors know where the community begins and ends, consists primarily of well preserved Arts-and-Crafts homes.

The **Bryant** neighborhood, east of University Village, has much in common with Ravenna. Houses here are mainly modest bungalows and Tudors, with a few scattered brick ranch houses. Ravenna and Bryant attract families,

UW faculty and staff members, and professionals who work downtown or on the Eastside. Commuters to the Eastside have few choices on their route to the 520 bridge from here, so the drive at rush hour can be time-consuming. Beyond that, you can't beat its offer of quiet streets and friendly neighbors.

Web Site: www.cityofseattle.net
Area Code: 206
Zip Codes: 98105, 98115
Post Office: University Station, 4244 University Way NE, 800-275-8777, www.usps.com
Library: University Library, 5009 Roosevelt Way NE, 206-684-4063, www.spl.lib.wa.us
Public Schools: Seattle Public Schools, P.O. Box 19116, Seattle, WA 98109-1116, 206-298-7000, www.seattleschools.org
Police: North Precinct, 10049 College Way North, 206-684-0850, www.cityofseattle.net/police
Emergency Hospital: University of Washington Medical Center, 1959 NE Pacific Street, 206-548-4000, www.washington.edu/medical/uwmc
Community Resources: University District Neighborhood Service Center, 4534 University Way NE, 206-684-7542, www.cityofseattle.net; Ravenna-Bryant Community Association, 6535 Ravenna Avenue NE, 206-528-0329, www.scn.org/neighbors/rbca; Ravenna Eckstein Community Center, 6535 Ravenna Avenue NE, 206-684-7534; Roosevelt Neighbors' Alliance, 4534 University Way NE, 206-632-7760, www.scn.org/neighbors/rna; University Park Community Club, www.upcc.org
Public Transportation: Metro Transit, 206-553-3000, www.transit.metrokc.gov
7: University District/Capitol Hill/Downtown/International District/Rainier Valley/Columbia City/Rainier Beach
9: University District/Capitol Hill/Rainier Valley/Columbia City/Rainier Beach
31: Magnolia/Fremont/Wallingford/University District
43: Downtown/Capitol Hill/Montlake/University District
45: Queen Anne/Wallingford/University District
46: Shilshole/Ballard/Fremont/Wallingford/University District
65: University District/Ravenna/Wedgwood/Lake City
67: University District/Maple Leaf/Northgate
68: University District/Ravenna/Wedgwood/Northgate
70: Downtown/Eastlake/University District
75: University District/Sand Point/Lake City/Northgate/Crown Hill/Ballard

78: University District/Maple Leaf/Jackson Park
133: University District/Burien
167: University District/Bellevue/Newport Hills/Renton/Kent/Auburn
197: University District/Federal Way
205: University District/Montlake/First Hill/Mercer Island
271: Issaquah/Eastgate/Bellevue/University District
272: University District/Crossroads/Eastgate
277: Juanita/Kingsgate/University District
370: University District/Jackson Park/Richmond Highlands/Shoreline/
Aurora Village
372:UniversityDistrict/Ravenna/Wedgwood/LakeCity/LakeForest
Park/Kenmore/Bothell/Woodinville

LAKE CITY

Boundaries: **North**: NE 145th Street; **West**: 5th Avenue NE; **South**: NE 95th Street; **East**: Lake Washington

Lake City is located near the north end of Lake Washington, just inside the city limits. When Seattle annexed Lake City in 1957, it was a quiet lakefront suburb with a small retail core along Lake City Way, a branch of the state highway system also known as Highway 522. Much of that small town character remains in Lake City, which attracts a mix of low- and middle-income families and professionals. The residential streets of Lake City are sheltered from the busy traffic of the highway, resulting in a slice of seclusion and a friendly small-town atmosphere.

Those looking to live in Lake City will find affordable homes and ample rental apartments. Homes here are modest, predominantly bungalows or modern split-levels. Many are on unusually large lots. Those east of Lake City Way may have views of Lake Washington and the Cascades. The Lake Washington waterfront in Lake City used to be lined with small weekend cottages, but as property values have soared many of those have been replaced with large, contemporary homes. Because of the distance from downtown and the Eastside, real estate prices and rents are generally lower here than in other residential neighborhoods in Seattle. However, living in Lake City makes for an easy commute to the north end of Lake Washington, Bothell, and Kenmore. Most apartment buildings are located in the few blocks to either side of Lake City Way and along NE 125th Street. Nearly half of the residents of Lake City rent apartments or houses, and the number of apartments in the area increased by about 30% between 1980 and the late '90s.

Lake City Way has changed significantly since it became part of Seattle; now crowded with strip malls, gas stations, second-hand and antique stores, and a variety of small locally owned retail businesses. Adult bookstores and strip clubs have given Lake City Way a slightly seedy reputation, although the businesses have had little impact on the residential areas of the neighborhood. The community has experienced some problems with criminal activity near the highway, but community watch groups and patrols have substantially reduced crime along Lake City Way and throughout the neighborhood.

This is a culturally diverse community, and the meld of cultures and languages is reflected in the assortment of new businesses that have sprouted up along Lake City Way, including ethnic art shops and restaurants. Because of the affordable rents and homes, residents are primarily blue-collar workers and their families. More recently, the area has begun to attract artists and college-educated professionals, as well as retirees with modest incomes. The neighborhood particularly appeals to renters because of its wide variety of housing and affordability.

Web Site: www.cityofseattle.net

Area Code: 206

Zip Code: 98125

Post Office: Lake City Station, 3019 NE 127th Street, 800-275-8777, www.usps.com

Library: Lake City Library, 12501 28th Avenue NE, 206-684-7518, www.spl.lib.wa.us

Public Schools: Seattle Public Schools, P.O. Box 19116, Seattle, WA 98109-1116, 206-298-7000, www.seattleschools.org

Police: North Precinct, 10049 College Way North, 206-684-0850, www.cityofseattle.net/police

Emergency Hospital: Northwest Hospital, 1550 N 115th St., 206-364-0500, www.nwhospital.org

Community Resources: Lake City Community Center, 12531 28th Avenue NE, 206-362-4378; Lake City Neighborhood Service Center, 12707 30th Avenue NE, 206-684-7526, www.cityofseattle.net

Public Transportation: Metro Transit, 206-553-3000, www.transit. metrokc.gov

   64: Downtown/Greenlake/Ravenna/Wedgwood/Lake City

   65: University District/Ravenna/Wedgwood/Lake City

   72: Downtown/Eastlake/University District/Maple Leaf/Lake City

   79: Downtown/University District/Maple Leaf/Lake City

NORTHGATE

JACKSON PARK
OAK TREE
AURORA

Boundaries: North: North 145th Street; **West:** Aurora Avenue North (Highway 99); **South:** NE 92nd Street; **East:** 5th Avenue NE

Northgate is a large neighborhood centered around the Northgate Mall, which opened in 1950 and claims to be the oldest shopping mall in North America. The mall itself is rather small by current standards, and the businesses located there tend to be scaled-down versions of their downtown or Bellevue Square counterparts. Nevertheless, ample parking around the mall, as well as its close proximity to I-5, make it a popular shopping destination. The mall was recently remodeled and expanded, which did not please some locals who believe the project failed to adequately address the effects of increased traffic.

While the immediate area around the Northgate Mall is filled with small retail businesses that benefit from the mall traffic—restaurants, drug stores, banks, and sporting goods stores—the heart of Northgate's residential community is north of the mall, stretching as far as the **Jackson Park** neighborhood at the city boundary. Houses in this area are 1950s brick ranch houses or modest split-levels on large lots, popular with first-time homebuyers. There are also a number of duplexes, townhouses, apartment buildings, and condominiums, as well as an increasing number of senior citizen residences. While real estate and rental prices are lower here than in other parts of the city, this is a close-knit community, complete with freshly painted houses, well-kept lawns, and friendly neighbors. Many contemporary apartments and condominiums are just off the main streets in the area surrounding Northgate Mall.

West of I-5, the **Oak Tree** area runs along Aurora Avenue, north of Green Lake. The Oak Tree Shopping Center, which gave this area its name, has a Starbucks, several good restaurants, a large multiplex theater, and Larry's Market, a gourmet supermarket. Nearby North Seattle Community College, an imposing concrete structure that resembles a small penitentiary, has a solid reputation, attracting students of all ages. The area around the college includes several small government agencies as well as the North Precinct for the Seattle Police Department. Also located in Oak Tree is a cultural center, formerly a public school, and a collection of modest homes and brightly painted townhouses.

North of Oak Tree is **Aurora**, which includes the area north of Northgate Way (105th Street) between Aurora Avenue North and I-5. Aurora Avenue North is a major business district, with a seemingly endless series of strip malls, car dealerships, small hotels, taverns, and appliance stores. While Aurora Avenue North has a reputation for petty crime and prostitution, residents who live even a few blocks off this main street rarely encounter any problems. A block or two east of Aurora Avenue North is a selection of modest split-level and contemporary brick homes. Real estate and rental prices in this area tend to be slightly lower than in those neighborhoods closer to downtown.

Web Site: www.cityofseattle.net
Area Code: 206
Zip Codes: 98133, 98125
Post Office: Northgate Station, 11036 Eighth Avenue NE, 800-275-8777, www.usps.com
Library: Lake City Library, 12501 28th Avenue NE, 206-684-7518, www.spl.lib.wa.us
Public Schools: Seattle Public Schools, P.O. Box 19116, Seattle, WA 98109-1116, 206-298-7000, www.seattleschools.org
Police: North Precinct, 10049 College Way North, 206-684-0850, www.cityofseattle.net/police
Emergency Hospital: Northwest Hospital, 1550 North 115th Street, 206-364-0500, www.nwhospital.org
Community Resources: Bitter Lake Community Center, 13035 Linden Avenue North, 206-684-7524, www.cityofseattle.net/parks
Public Transportation: Metro Transit, 206-553-3000, www.transit.metrokc.gov
　16: Downtown/Queen Anne/Wallingford/Green Lake/Northgate
　41: Downtown/Northgate
　66: Downtown/Eastlake/University District/Maple Leaf/Northgate
　67: University District/Maple Leaf/Northgate
　68: University District/Ravenna/Maple Leaf/Northgate
　302: Northgate/Shoreline/Aurora Village
　315: Northgate/Jackson Park/North City/Richmond Highlands/Shoreline/Richmond Beach
　318: Northgate

BROADVIEW

THE HIGHLANDS

Boundaries: North: NW 145th Street; **West:** Puget Sound; **South:** NW 110th Street; **East:** Aurora Avenue North (Highway 99)

Located in the northwest corner of Seattle, Broadview, with its quiet residential streets and unremarkable commercial district, is really more of a suburban community than an urban neighborhood. Most of the area bears a close similarity to the suburban Shoreline community located just north of the city.

Greenwood Avenue North is the commercial street in this neighborhood and is lined with a variety of retail businesses, restaurants, and several small strip malls. This avenue also serves as a dividing line down the center of the neighborhood, with more affluent residents to the west and working-class families to the east. Bitter Lake, just northeast of the intersection of 130th and Greenwood, is surrounded by single-family homes that attract middle-income professionals. There are some apartments and condominium complexes between Greenwood Avenue and Aurora Avenue North, particularly south of 130th Street. Because this area is not so close to downtown or I-5, these generally rent for less than comparable in-city units.

Houses in the Broadview neighborhood are mainly modern bungalows, ramblers, and split-levels, although the homes grow grander as you progress north along 3rd Avenue NW, especially on the west side of the street. Many of these homes have splendid views of the Puget Sound and the Olympic Mountains, similar to the more expensive homes just south in the North Beach area.

At the far north end of 3rd Avenue NW, the Seattle Golf Club and the entrance to **The Highlands** present a glimpse of one of the most exclusive developments in Seattle. The Highlands, designed in 1909 by the Olmsteds (who also designed Seattle's park system), remains an exclusive and private enclave for the very wealthy. Although the lots are smaller now than the original minimum of five acres, the winding wooded roads and gated entrance have preserved the quiet seclusion of this community.

Houses and apartments close to Aurora Avenue North offer the least expensive prices and rents, while still providing the comforts of a close-knit residential community. A variety of modest and affordable houses for young families and middle-income professionals can be found north of 130th Street between 3rd Avenue NW and Greenwood Avenue NW, and in the vicinity of Carkeek Park. While Broadview does not attract tourists, nor promise adventurous living, it will satisfy those looking for a stable suburban-style community within the city.

Web Site: www.cityofseattle.net
Area Code: 206
Zip Code: 98177
Post Office: Greenwood Station, 8306 Greenwood Avenue North, 800-275-8777, www.usps.com
Library: Broadview Library, 12755 Greenwood Avenue North, 206-684-7519, www.spl.lib.wa.us
Public Schools: Seattle Public Schools, P.O. Box 19116, Seattle, WA 98109-1116, 206-298-7000, www.seattleschools.org
Police: North Precinct, 10049 College Way North, 206-684-0850, www.cityofseattle.net/police
Emergency Hospital: Northwest Hospital, 1550 North 115th Street, 206-364-0500, www.nwhospital.org
Community Resources: Bitter Lake Community Center, 13035 Linden Avenue North, 206-684-7524, www.cityofseattle.net/parks
Public Transportation: Metro Transit, 206-553-3000, www.transit.metrokc.gov
28: Downtown/Fremont/Ballard/Whittier Heights/Broadview

SAND POINT

LAURELHURST
VIEW RIDGE
WEDGWOOD

Boundaries: North: NE 95th Street; **West**: 35th Avenue NE, Lake City Way; **South**: Union Bay; **East**: Lake Washington

On the shore of Lake Washington, the Sand Point neighborhood is best known as the location of the National Oceanic and Atmospheric Administration (NOAA) and Children's Hospital & Regional Medical Center. NOAA, a federal research facility that studies the weather and its impact upon the ocean and coastlines, shares a base with the Sand Point Naval Station on Lake Washington. Children's Hospital and Regional Medical Center, located on Sand Point Way, is a regional pediatric referral center that serves the special health care needs of children and their families.

Sand Point also features two public parks, both with access to the Lake Washington waterfront. Matthews Beach, located north of NOAA, is a summer favorite of sunbathers, picnickers, and swimmers. The Burke-Gilman trail stops off at Matthews Beach as it follows the edge of Lake Washington, giving bicy-clists and in-line skaters easy access to the park. South of NOAA, Magnuson Park offers visitors the use of several softball fields and a boat launch. Magnuson Park is also the home of the Soundgarden, a wind chime sculpture that inspired the name of the once-famous, now-defunct local band.

Laurelhurst, on the southern hill of the Sand Point neighborhood, is a quiet and determinedly private neighborhood. Residents here tend to be affluent professionals and retirees living in homes with incredible views of Lake Washington and Union Bay, with Mount Rainier and the snow-capped Cascades providing a stunning backdrop. Laurelhurst is a neighborhood of expensive homes with appropriately manicured lawns and private water-front access. Most houses are single-family residences, ranging in style from modest brick Tudors to palatial Georgians and colonials. The border of Laurelhurst, along Sand Point Way, includes a thriving upscale retail district, as well as Children's Hospital and other clinics. At the top of the hill, the Laurelhurst park and community center serves as a hub for neighborhood activities, including softball games, summer picnics, aerobics, and pottery classes. The few rental opportunities to be found in this neighborhood are in the handful of apartment buildings located along Sand Point Way.

View Ridge, north of Laurelhurst, tends to attract wealthy profession-als, affluent retirees, and UW professors. Homes in this area are modest brick Tudors and 1950s ranch houses with well kept lawns; many have panoramic views of the sun rising over Lake Washington and the Cascades. Near Matthews Beach are renovated beach cottages, a reminder of an ear-lier time when this area was an out-of-town destination for Seattle resi-dents. There are several newer "view" condominiums in this area as well. As with Laurelhurst, most rentals are limited to apartment buildings on busy Sand Point Way.

Located between Sand Point Way and a small retail district at the inter-section of NE 75th Street and 35th Avenue NE, **Wedgwood** offers a mix of affordable single-family homes, duplexes, townhouses, and apartment buildings with occasional views of the Cascade Mountains. Homes are less expensive here than elsewhere in the Sand Point area. Scan a *Seattle Times/Seattle P.I.* Sunday classifieds and you'll find the average home in Wedgwood will run you close to the quarter million dollar mark. Most homes are Cape Cod and Saltbox-style cottages, or Craftsman bungalows. Residents tend to be middle-income professionals and young families, as well as UW faculty and staff. Wedgwood has a strong and active Jewish community, with three synagogues located in the neighborhood.

Web Sites: www.cityofseattle.net, www.northeastseattle.com
Area Code: 206
Zip Codes: 98105, 98115

Post Office: Wedgwood Station, 7724 35th Avenue NE, 800-275-8777, www.usps.com

Library: North East Library, 6801 35th Avenue NE, 206-684-7539, www.spl.lib.wa.us

Public Schools: Seattle Public Schools, P.O. Box 19116, Seattle, WA 98109-1116, 206-298-7000, www.seattleschools.org

Police: North Precinct, 10049 College Way North, 206-684-0850, www.cityofseattle.net/police

Emergency Hospital: University of Washington Medical Center, 1959 NE Pacific Street, 206-548-4000, www.washington.edu/medical/uwmc

Community Resources: Laurelhurst Community Center, 4554 NE 41st Street, 206-684-7531; Sand Point Community Housing Association, 6940 62nd Avenue NE, 206-517-5499; View Ridge Community Council, P.O. Box 15218, Seattle, WA 98115, www.scn.org/neighbors/viewridge

Public Transportation: Metro Transit, 206-553-3000, www.transit.metrokc.gov

74: Downtown/University District/Ravenna/Sand Point

MADISON PARK

WASHINGTON PARK
DENNY BLAINE
BROADMOOR

Boundaries: North: Union Bay; **West**: Lake Washington Boulevard; **South**: Lake Washington Boulevard; **East**: Lake Washington

On the shore of Lake Washington, the community of Madison Park lies just south of Union Bay and the 520 floating bridge. During the late 1800s, Madison Park was a beachfront resort town frequented by Seattle residents. Many took the cable car from downtown Seattle to the shore to spend the day or rented a nearby cottage for the week. Festivities in the summer included a carnival with food and games, and a Ferris wheel.

Today, Madison Park is an affluent community with a small-town feel. Shop owners know the names of their local customers, traffic is slow and leisurely, people stroll the sidewalks and smile at one another. It's one of the few Seattle neighborhoods that is not on a shortcut route to other parts of the city, so it is spared the traffic problems of other less fortunate neighborhoods.

One-of-a-kind restaurants and cafes, fashionable boutiques, and fragrant bakeries offering scrumptious goodies line East Madison Street, Madison Park's main thoroughfare. Nowhere will you find sprawling supermarkets, warehouse stores, chain restaurants or fast food joints. Although First Hill and

Capitol Hill, with their mainstream business districts, are only ten minutes away, many Madison Park residents do most of their shopping locally.

Near the east end of East Madison Street, Colonial and Northwest Modern homes intermingle with more modest Cape Cods, reminiscent of the beach cottages that lined the shore in early Madison Park. Two traditionally expensive and fashionable Madison Park neighborhoods, **Washington Park** and **Denny Blaine**, lie further south along the shore of Lake Washington and on the hill facing the lake. Homes in these areas are an interesting mix, primarily Colonials and Northwest Moderns, as well as a few Elizabethan or Tudor homes. Many of the stately homes here were built when Seattle's wealthiest migrated to this area and other posh neighborhoods, such as Queen Anne and Capitol Hill, away from downtown and First Hill. Finally, the section called **Broadmoor** offers a variety of elegant homes in an ultra-exclusive golf and country club setting, tucked between Lake Washington and the Arboretum.

Just south of East Madison Street, high-rise condominiums face Lake Washington. Since these were completed, local zoning restrictions have changed, preventing other similar buildings from crowding out the homes that are the core of Madison Park. These condos offer the neighborly appeal of Madison Park and spectacular views of Lake Washington, the Cascades, and imposing Mount Rainier. On the north shore of the Madison Park peninsula, other contemporary and Colonial style condominiums offer views of Lake Washington and the 520 Bridge.

Madison Park continues to be a neighborhood of wealthy and influential Seattle citizens. The community has a median income more than twice that of the rest of the city, and the homes here are some of the more expensive in Seattle; even modest Cape Cod cottages run in the several hundred thousand dollar range. According to Northwest Multiple Listing Service, the median sale price in February 2002 was $330,000. That was nine percent higher than the median price of a home in Queen Anne or Magnolia at the time, and the highest median price of any other Seattle neighborhood for which data was collected. Though they rarely appear on the market, the grand residences in Broadmoor and Denny Blaine can break the million-dollar mark.

Web Site: www.cityofseattle.net
Area Code: 206
Zip Codes: 98112, 98122
Post Office: East Union Station, 1110 23rd Avenue, 800-275-8777, www.usps.com
Library: Montlake Library, 2300 24th Avenue East, 206-684-4720, www.spl.lib.wa.us

Public Schools: Seattle Public Schools, P.O. Box 19116, Seattle, WA 98109-1116, 206-298-7000, www.seattleschools.org

Police: East Precinct, 1519 12th Avenue, 206-684-4300, www.cityofseattle. net/police

Emergency Hospital: Swedish Medical Center, 747 Broadway, 206-386-2573, www.swedish.org

Community Resources: Denny-Blaine Park, 200 Lake Washington Boulevard East, www.cityofseattle.net/parks; Madison Park, 2300 43rd Avenue East, www.cityofseattle.net/parks

Public Transportation: Metro Transit, 206-553-3000, www.transit. metrokc.gov

  11: Madison Park/First Hill/Downtown

  84: (Night Owl) Downtown/First Hill/Madrona/Madison Park

MONTLAKE

PORTAGE BAY

Boundaries: **North**: Lake Washington Ship Canal; **West**: Fuhrman Avenue East; **South**: Boyer Avenue East; **East**: Lake Washington Boulevard

The Montlake Cut is a small, man-made waterway that connects Lake Union and Lake Washington. Each year on the first Saturday in May, the annual Opening Day celebration of boating season is celebrated here. Spectators, boating enthusiasts, and crew teams fill the cut for a day of races and boats on parade. The event's highlight is the Windermere Cup, the final race of the day that features the men's and women's Husky crew teams. Just south of the UW Husky Stadium, the Montlake Bridge crosses the cut, connecting Montlake Avenue to 24th Avenue East. The Montlake neighborhood includes all of the homes to the south side of this bridge and to either side of 24th Avenue East, which divides the community into east and west. Highway 520 further divides the area into north and south halves. Because it is located at the crossroads of two major thoroughfares, Montlake suffers from heavy traffic, particularly at rush hour. Despite this, the neighborhood feels tucked away from the cares of the city.

Homes in Montlake are a mix of imposing mansions, exquisite cottages, brick Tudors and elaborate colonials. Winding streets and cul-de-sacs add to the feeling of privacy in the neighborhood, though navigating the streets can be confusing. With the Montlake Cut to the north and the Arboretum to the east, Montlake's only close neighbor is **Portage Bay**, itself a tiny residential offshoot of the Eastlake and Capitol Hill neighborhoods. There are no shopping centers or malls, only a couple of small corner grocers and a freeway on-ramp gas station. University Village, a shopping center located just north of Montlake on 25th Avenue NE, offers everything from a Banana Republic and Eddie Bauer to a huge QFC Grocery. The neighborhood is home to two of Seattle's premier yacht clubs, the Seattle Yacht Club and Queen City Yacht Club, giving members easy access to both Lake Union and Lake Washington. Also, the Museum of History and Industry is here, as well as beautiful Foster Island Park, a popular place to rent canoes, rowboats or sailboats and paddle or sail through the Arboretum.

On the south side of Highway 520 and west of 24th Avenue East, the Montlake Playfield is a center of activity for the neighborhood, with quiet tennis courts and a popular activity center. Just across 24th Avenue East, Montlake homes brush up against the Washington Park Arboretum, a 200-acre public park with 5,500 different trees and shrubs and the University of Washington's Japanese Gardens. A quick drive through the Arboretum brings you to the edge of the Madison Park neighborhood, and provides access to the heavenly bakeries, elegant salons, and excellent restaurants that line Madison Street.

Most Montlake residents are middle- or high-income professionals who work downtown or on the Eastside. When lucrative high-tech jobs on the Eastside, including those at Microsoft, increased in the late 1990s, Montlake became a popular neighborhood for successful software engineers and other technical workers. Other residents include current and retired UW professors and UW Medical Center doctors. Convenient access to I-5 and the Highway 520 Bridge, and the secluded and quiet nature of the residential areas, make Montlake an attractive and sought-after location.

Web Sites: www.cityofseattle.net, www.montlake.net
Area Code: 206
Zip Code: 98112
Post Office: East Union Station, 1110 23rd Avenue, 800-275-8777, www.usps.com
Library: Montlake Library, 2300 24th Avenue East, 206-684-4720, www.spl.lib.wa.us
Public Schools: Seattle Public Schools, P.O. Box 19116, Seattle, WA 98109-1116, 206-298-7000, www.seattleschools.org
Police: East Precinct, 1519 12th Avenue, 206-684-4300, www.cityofseattle.net/police
Emergency Hospital: University of Washington Medical Center, 1959 NE Pacific Street, 206-548-4000, www.washington.edu/medical/uwmc
Community Resources: Montlake Community Center, 1618 East Calhoun Street, 206-684-4736, www.cityofseattle.net/parks; Northeast Neighborhood Service Center, 4534 University Way NE, 206-684-7542, www.cityofseattle.net

Public Transportation: Metro Transit, 206-553-3000, www.transit. metrokc.gov

44: Shilshole/Ballard/Wallingford/University District/Montlake

CENTRAL DISTRICT

JUDKINS PARK

Boundaries: North: East Madison Street, **West**: 12th Avenue East; **South**: I-90; **East**: Martin Luther King Jr. Way

The Central District or Central Area, referred to as "the CD" by most Seattle residents, cuts a long narrow swath through the center of Seattle. Most retail enterprises in the CD are located along 12th Avenue East and on 23rd Avenue East; many are family-owned restaurants and shops, and small African- or Asian-American groceries.

Sandwiched between Capitol Hill, First Hill, and the International District to the west, and Madison Park, Madrona, and Leschi to the east, the CD has long had an uneasy relationship with the rest of Seattle. Homes here are not all that different from those at this end of Capitol Hill—most are charming turn-of-the-century Victorians, 1920s Colonials, and Craftsman bungalows. Nevertheless, housing prices in the Central District, especially the eastern portion, have historically lagged behind prices in the rest of Seattle, in part because of geography. Steep slopes in the area slowed development and served as dividers from the rest of the city; the CD was further cut off by the expansion of I-90. Between 1970 and 1990, many homes in the area were neglected or even abandoned as residents moved out to the suburbs.

In the past decade, however, housing prices in the CD have risen as more affluent residents have moved to the area, particularly in the north end of the neighborhood. Although many houses in the CD are still run-down from years of neglect, some are being refurbished by newcomers and long-time residents. In fact, home prices in the central section of Seattle, which includes the Central Area, rose more than in any other neighborhood between February 2001 and February 2002, increasing nearly 18%, and surpassing the median price in the Ballard/Greenlake region.

Bordered by I-90 to the south, 20th Avenue South to the west, Yesler Way to the north, and Martin Luther King Jr. Way to the east, **Judkins Park** is a one-mile rectangle in the southeast corner of the Central Area. Once a neglected neighborhood decimated by the expansion of I-90 in the 1960s, Judkins Park, like much of the rest of the Central District, is now flourishing. Residents can buy freshly baked bread from Gai's Northwest Bakery on

South Weller Street. At the corner of South Jackson Street and 23rd Avenue South, there is a new Walgreen drugstore, Starbucks, Hollywood Video, and a Red Apple market.

At the center of the Central District is Garfield High School, which consistently produces National Merit Scholars, and boasts a number of famous former students, including Jimi Hendrix, Bruce Lee, Quincy Jones, and Ernestine Anderson. Other notable Central Area institutions include Providence Medical Center and Seattle University.

In 1997, in a series of articles about the Central District, the *Seattle Post-Intelligencer* examined the neighborhood's changing demographics. An analysis of census data showed that in 1980, the area was more than 80% black and about 11% white. By 1990 that had changed to about 70% black and 24% white, and by 2000, *The Seattle Times* reported that the CD was predominantly white, home to fewer African-Americans than at any other time in the previous 30 years. According to 2000 census figures, 43% of residents are white, 32% are black, 10% are Asian or Pacific Islanders, and eight percent are Hispanic. The Central District is also changing economically. Millions of dollars of new construction is under way or planned, including a four- to six-story building at 2211 East Madison Street. The project will include a supermarket, upper-level residential units, and an underground parking garage.

Prospective residents should be aware that racial tensions do exist in the Central District. Two incidents in particular include the shooting death of an African American man by white police officers in May 2001, and in July of that same year, the assault of Seattle's mayor by an African-American man. Ironically, the attack on then mayor Paul Schell occurred at a community festival organized to promote unity in the Central Area. The target of the neighborhood's anger, however, is the city and its law enforcement, not the CD's non-African-American residents, and steps are being taken to improve relations, including the formation of a civilian-led Office of Professional Accountability.

Web Sites: www.cityofseattle.net, www.centralarea.org
Area Code: 206
Zip Codes: 98122, 98144
Post Office: East Union Station, 1110 23rd Avenue, 800-275-8777, www.usps.com
Library: Douglass-Truth Library, 2300 East Yesler Way, 206-684-4704, www.spl.lib.wa.us
Public Schools: Seattle Public Schools, P.O. Box 19116, Seattle, WA 98109-1116, 206-298-7000, www.seattleschools.org
Police: East Precinct, 1519 12th Avenue, 206-684-4300, www.cityofseattle.net/police

Emergency Hospital: Swedish Medical Center, 747 Broadway, 206-386-2573, www.swedish.org

Community Resources: Central Area Development Association, 2515 South Jackson Street, 206-328-2240, www.cityofseattle.net; Central Area Motivation Program, 722 18th Avenue, 206-329-4111, www.cityofseattle.net; Central Area Youth Association, 119 23rd Avenue, 206-322-6640; Central Neighborhood Association, www.centralarea.org; Central Neighborhood Service Center, 1825 South Jackson Street, Suite 208, 206-684-4767, www.cityofseattle.net; Garfield Community Center, 2323 East Cherry Street, 206-684-4788, www.cityofseattle.net/parks; Langston Hughes Cultural Arts Center, 104 17th Avenue South, 206-684-4757; Meadowbrook Community Center, 10517 35th Avenue NE, 206-684-7522, www.cityofseattle.net/parks; Yesler Community Center, 835 East Yesler Way, 206-386-1245, www.cityofseattle.net/parks

MADRONA/LESCHI

Boundaries: **North**: Denny Way; **West**: Martin Luther King Jr. Way; **South**: I-90; **East**: Lake Washington

The Madrona and Leschi neighborhoods lie along Lake Washington, east of the Central District and the International District. While Madrona sits atop the hill facing west, Leschi, named for a Nisqually Indian executed for resisting the whites, faces east toward Lake Washington. Some consider Madrona and Leschi part of the Central District, but both neighborhoods are quite different from the CD. While the struggling CD, cut off from the rest of the city by steep hillsides, and further isolated with the construction of I-90, historically has been a neighborhood for those with moderate means, both Madrona and Leschi started out as affluent neighborhoods. It wasn't until after the 1960s when many of its wealthy residents moved to other areas of Seattle and outside Seattle that Madrona/Leschi declined. Fortunately for many, this shift made the area more affordable, and allowed for an influx of people from varied backgrounds. The result is that today these neighborhoods are a welcoming blend of various ethnic groups and income levels with both longtime residents and newcomers.

Madrona's center is the lively intersection of 34th Avenue East and East Union Street. Clustered here are the popular cafes and trendy shops. The few blocks surrounding this intersection create an idyllic urban village, with people sitting on storefront steps and at restaurant tables along the sidewalks. There are several small eateries here that cater to a Sunday brunch crowd. In Leschi, most businesses are located on the lake, and are primarily view restaurants and boat related ventures, including the Corinthian Yacht Club. The newly constructed condominium and retail complex, Lakeside at Leschi, is located on the shore of Lake Washington. To the south, Leschi Park features Victorian-style grounds, towering sequoias, and colorful tulip trees. Atop the hill, Frink Park offers lovely walking trails under grand maples.

Residents of Madrona and Leschi range from artists and artisans to young professionals, from retirees to families with young children. Homes also run the gamut in size and style, from opulent turn-of-the-century Victorians and Colonials to narrow abodes that were once corner groceries. Many of the splendid homes in Leschi have spectacular views of Lake Washington, the Cascade Mountains, and Mount Rainier. Other homes in both Madrona and Leschi share a view of downtown and the Olympics to the west.

Security concerns are evidenced by the bars on the windows on some businesses and houses in these neighborhoods. While there is a strong sense of community here, proximity to higher crime neighborhoods such as Rainier Valley and the Central District make both Madrona and Leschi more vulnerable than other Seattle neighborhoods. However, the crime rates are trending down in these areas and local neighborhood watch groups are organized and effective.

Web Site: www.cityofseattle.net

Area Code: 206

Zip Codes: 98122, 98144

Post Office: East Union Station, 1110 23rd Avenue, 800-275-8777, www.usps.com

Libraries: Douglass-Truth Library, 2300 East Yesler Way, 206-684-4704, www.spl.lib.wa.us; Madrona-Sally Goldmark Library, 1134 33rd Avenue, 206-684-4705, www.spl.lib.wa.us

Public Schools: Seattle Public Schools, P.O. Box 19116, Seattle, WA 98109-1116, 206-298-7000, www.seattleschools.org

Police: East Precinct, 1519 12th Ave., 206-684-4300, www.cityofseattle.net/police

Emergency Hospital: Harborview Medical Center, 325 9th Avenue, 206-731-3074, www.washington.edu/medical/hmc

Community Resources: Central Area Motivation Program, 722 18th Avenue, 206-329-4111, www.cityofseattle.net; Garfield Community Center, 2323 East Cherry Street, 206-684-4788, www.cityofseattle.net/parks; Madrona Community Council, 206-287-4837, www.madrona.org

Public Transportation: Metro Transit, 206-553-3000, www.transit.metrokc.gov

2: Madrona/Central District/First Hill/Downtown/Belltown/Queen Anne

3: Madrona/Central District/First Hill/Downtown/Belltown/Queen Anne

27: Downtown/Central District/Leschi

BEACON HILL

SOUTH BEACON HILL
HOLLY PARK
MOUNT BAKER

Boundaries: North: I-90 **West:** I-5; **South:** South Ryan Street (to Martin Luther King Jr. Way South), South Genesee Street; **East:** Lake Washington

At night, the Pacific Medical Center on Beacon Hill looms over the city like a huge gothic castle. Designed by architects Bebb & Gould, the building is the most recognized structure in the Beacon Hill neighborhood. Like many south Seattle communities, Beacon Hill tends to be overlooked by prospective homeowners or tenants, who prefer instead to set up house north of downtown. But, Beacon Hill is a flourishing, ethnically diverse neighborhood with a strong sense of community and comfortable, affordable homes.

North of South Spokane Street, quiet streets are lined with 1940s tract houses and modest bungalows on small but well-kept lots. Residents include middle-income families and young or retired couples. On the busier streets, brick Federal style apartment buildings offer studios and one-bedrooms for rents slightly below the city average. Some houses on the hill have pleasant views of downtown, the Cascades, or the Olympics.

South of South Spokane Street, small bungalows and contemporary split-levels sell for slightly less than comparable homes at the north end of the hill. Small family businesses such as Asian delis and groceries dot the neighborhood, and the Jefferson Public Golf Course is located here. Further south, the **South Beacon Hill** and **Holly Park** areas also offer modest yet affordable bungalows and simple tract houses.

The **Mount Baker** neighborhood, which clings to the east slope of Beacon Hill, is the most affluent section of Beacon Hill. Most homes here have spectacular views of the south end of Lake Washington and the Cascades; some may have views of majestic Mount Rainier to the southeast. Many wealthy professionals live in this area, and it is certainly one of the most racially diverse of Seattle's affluent neighborhoods.

Crime may be a concern in some parts of the Beacon Hill area, as gang-related activities occasionally spill into the neighborhoods, particularly in the southwest sections from nearby Rainier Valley (see next profile). Local crime prevention groups have been increasingly successful in holding the community together, but newcomers should be aware of the neighborhood dynamics before choosing a home here.

Web Site: www.cityofseattle.net

Area Code: 206

Zip Codes: 98118, 98144

Post Offices: Columbia Station, 3727 South Alaska Street, 800-275-8777, www.usps.com; International Station, 414 6th Avenue South, 800-275-8777, www.usps.com

Library: Beacon Hill Library, 2519 15th Avenue South, 206-684-4711, www.spl.lib.wa.us

Public Schools: Seattle Public Schools, P.O. Box 19116, Seattle, WA 98109-1116, 206-298-7000, www.seattleschools.org

Police: South Precinct, 3001 South Myrtle Street, 206-386-1850, www.cityofseattle.net/police

Emergency Hospital: Harborview Medical Center, 325 9th Avenue, 206-731-3074, www.washington.edu/medical/hmc

Community Resources: Greater Duwamish Neighborhood Service Center, 3801 Beacon Avenue South, 206-233-2044, www.cityofseattle.net; Jefferson Community Center, 3801 Beacon Avenue South, 206-684-7481, www.cityofseattle.net/parks

Public Transportation: Metro Transit, 206-553-3000, www.transit.metrokc.gov

38: Beacon Hill/Rainier Valley

RAINIER VALLEY

COLUMBIA CITY
RAINIER BEACH
DUNLAP

Boundaries: North: South Genesee Street; **West**: Martin Luther King Jr. Way South; **South**: South Juniper Street, South 116th Street; **East**: 48th Avenue South, Lake Washington

Until the construction of I-90 through the Central District, what is now Rainier Valley was a southerly extension of the CD. Today, Rainier Valley is one of Seattle's most ethnically diverse neighborhoods, with a large minority and immigrant population. Unfortunately, it has a high percentage of residents living in poverty and more problems with crime than many other areas of the city. Perhaps because of its physical isolation from the rest of Seattle, Rainier Valley has not received the attention that might have prevented or lessened many of its current socioeconomic problems.

Residents believe the neighborhood is a better place to live in now than it was a decade ago. Their optimism is well founded. According to the Seattle Police Department, the crime index for the South Precinct, which includes Rainier Valley, dropped 1.5% from 2000 to 2001. Specifically, robberies were down eight percent, from 492 to 452; assaults decreased by almost three percent from 2,910 to 2,831; and burglaries fell by two percent, from 1,997 to 1,959. While thefts of more than $200 increased by eight percent, and gang activity is still occasionally reported in Rainier Valley, there are hopeful signs that this is a community on the mend.

In spring 2001, Bill and Melinda Gates gave $1 million to the Boys and Girls Club of King County capital campaign. Part of the money will most likely help fund construction of a new state-of-the-art youth center in Rainier Valley. The project is tied to the city's redevelopment of the Rainier Vista public housing community, so a construction date has not yet been set. Home Sight, a community-based non-profit corporation, has built more than 100 affordable homes and townhouses near the I-90 Lid—the land above the I-90 tunnel—which start at just over $100,000. The city estimates that the valley's industrial north end will employ about 5,000 people by 2014.

The retail district is located along Rainier Avenue South, and is Rainier Valley's main thoroughfare. It is home to small, locally owned shops, delis, bakeries, and take-out restaurants. The renowned Borracchini's Bakery has been in the neighborhood for more than 70 years, and attracts people from all over Seattle for its delicious decorated-while-you-wait sheet cakes. It's one of the few reminders of Rainier Valley's Italian heritage when, almost a century ago, the area was settled by Italian immigrants and was referred to as "Garlic Gulch." Once the exclusive province of ethnic shops and eateries, the area has gained national chain retailers as well, permitting residents to shop for nearly everything in the neighborhood. For the alternative-minded, the neighborhood offers a PCC Natural Market (bordering the Seward Park neighborhood), specializing in organic produce, natural foods, and freshly baked treats. Overall, Rainier Valley seems to be benefiting from both the hard work of committed community groups and the increased prosperity of the greater Seattle area.

Columbia City, in the heart of Rainier Valley, is also experiencing revitalization. Beginning in 1995, residents joined together to fight increasing crime through an innovative crime-stopping dog walk. Several nights a week, residents and their pets would stroll through the community. The idea was to get people out of their homes, allow them to meet their neighbors, and send a message to criminals that they were not welcome. This, combined with other efforts, including those by the Columbia City Revitalization Committee, worked. As crime decreased, the commercial district, centered at Rainier Avenue South and South Ferdinand Street, began to expand to include new restaurants, coffee shops, an art gallery, and offices. A farmers' market at the corner of Rainier Avenue South and South Edmunds, and live-music walks are other popular attractions. Homes in Columbia City range from turn-of-the-century Victorians to modest bungalows. While homes here are slightly more expensive than those in the rest of Rainier Valley, the prices are still well below the city average.

Rainier Beach and **Dunlap**, located on the Lake Washington waterfront, offer lovely old homes, ranging from modest 1920s bungalows to stately turn-of-the-century mansions, most with spectacular views of Lake Washington and the Cascades. Crime rates in this part of the Rainier Valley are at or below the Seattle average. Just a couple of years ago, Seward Park Estates, the most run-down apartment complex in Seattle was renovated to provide quality low-income housing just steps from Lake Washington. In general, real estate prices in this neighborhood remain slightly lower than they are for comparable view homes in other parts of the city. According to the Northwest Multiple Listing Service, the median home sale price in Rainier Valley/Beacon had finally broke the $200,000 mark by spring of 2001, but remained 14% lower than the median price in West Seattle, the next most affordable neighborhood in the city. Dupre + Scott Apartment Advisors recently estimated that average rent here was about 50% less than downtown.

Rainier Beach reflects the racial diversity of the entire Rainier Valley, with a mixture of whites, blacks, Asian/Pacific Islanders, and Hispanics creating many of the ethnic background. Such diversity is reflected in the tiny business district (anchored by King Donut, at 9710 Rainier Avenue South), where you'll find a Filipino-owned coin-operated laundry, a Vietnamese jewelry store, a Mexican restaurant, and a Japanese teriyaki shop.

Newcomers to Seattle looking into Rainier Valley should keep in mind that gang-related activities and violent crimes are more common here than elsewhere in the city. Although most residents are respectable hard-working folks, and there are many wonderful streets in Rainier Valley, pockets of criminal activity may be only a block or two away.

Web Site: www.cityofseattle.net
Area Code: 206
Zip Codes: 98118, 98178
Post Office: Columbia Station, 3727 South Alaska Street, 800-275-8777, www.usps.com

Libraries: Columbia Library, 4751 Rainier Avenue South, 206-386-1908, www.spl.lib.wa.us; New Holly Library, 6805 32nd Avenue South, 206-386-1905, www.spl.lib.wa.us; Rainier Beach Library, 9125 Rainier Avenue South, 206-386-1906, www.spl.lib.wa.us

Public Schools: Seattle Public Schools, P.O. Box 19116, Seattle, WA 98109-1116, 206-298-7000, www.seattleschools.org

Police: South Precinct, 3001 South Myrtle Street, 206-386-1850, www.cityofseattle.net/police

Emergency Hospital: Harborview Medical Center, 325 9th Avenue, 206-731-3074, www.washington.edu/medical/hmc

Community Resources: Central Area Motivation Program, 77919 Rainier Avenue South, 206-722-2417, www.cityofseattle.net; Southeast Neighborhood Service Center, 4859 Rainier Avenue South, 206-386-1931, www.cityofseattle.net; Rainier Community Center, 4600 38th Avenue South, 206-386-1919, www.cityofseattle.net/parks; Rainier Beach Community Center, 8825 Rainier Avenue South, 206-386-1925, www.cityofseattle.net/parks; VanAsselt Community Center 2820 S Myrtle Street, 206-386-1921, www.cityofseattle.net/parks

Public Transportation: Metro Transit, 206-553-3000, www.transit. metrokc.gov

7: University District/Capitol Hill/Downtown/International District/ Rainier Valley/Columbia City/Rainier Beach

8: Rainier Valley/Capitol Hill/Queen Anne

9: University District/Capitol Hill/First Hill/Rainier Valley/Columbia City/Rainier Beach

36: Downtown/Beacon Hill/Jefferson Park/Rainier Beach

38: Rainier Valley/Beacon Hill

42: Downtown/Rainier Beach

48: Loyal Heights/Crown Hill/Greenwood/Ravenna/University District/Montlake/Central District/Columbia City/Rainier Beach

107: Rainier Beach/Lake Ridge/Bryn Mawr/Renton

SEWARD PARK

Boundaries: North: South Genesee Street; **West**: 48th Avenue South; **South**: South Holly Street; **East**: Lake Washington

The Seward Park neighborhood is located just south of Mount Baker, on Lake Washington. The park from which this community takes its name is a 277-acre peninsula filled with lush vegetation, including cherry trees, lofty Douglas firs, and silvery madrona trees. Whether or not you choose to live here, Seward Park is always worth a visit: during the summer, the park hosts jazz concerts and the annual Seafair celebration; and, in addition to nature trails and the lake, it is one of the best places in the city to savor breathtaking views of Mount Rainier. Residents take advantage of the Seward Park Art Studio, located in the original 1927 bathhouse, which offers pottery classes for all levels of students and serves as a workshop for several professional artists. And, residents and visitors alike line the streets for the annual Danskin Triathlon for women, held at either Seward Park or nearby Stan Sayres Park.

Residents of Seward Park are mostly affluent professionals, including local politicians and judges, and plenty of seniors, some of whom reside in the Kline Galland nursing home. While nearly half of Seward Park residents are Asian-American or African-American, the neighborhood is best known for its strong Jewish community. In fact, most of Seattle's Orthodox Jews live in or near Seward Park, attending one of the many synagogues located here. Bikur Cholim-Machzikay, the oldest synagogue in Washington, is located at 5145 South Morgan Street.

Homes in Seward Park range from 1950s brick ranch houses to stately modern mansions. Most have views of Lake Washington and Mount Rainier; many have waterfront access. While homes here are expensive due to the panoramic views, the neighborhood's proximity to Rainier Valley has kept real estate prices slightly lower than other Seattle neighborhoods.

Web Site: www.cityofseattle.net

Area Code: 206

Zip Code: 98178

Post Office: Columbia Station, 3727 South Alaska Street, 800-275-8777, www.usps.com

Library: Rainier Beach Library, 9125 Rainier Avenue South, 206-386-1906, www.spl.lib.wa.us

Public Schools: Seattle Public Schools, P.O. Box 19116, Seattle, WA 98109-1116, 206-298-7000, www.seattleschools.org

Police: South Precinct, 3001 South Myrtle Street, 206-386-1850, www.cityofseattle.net/police

Emergency Hospital: Harborview Medical Center, 325 9th Avenue, 206-731-3074, www.washington.edu/medical/hmc

Community Resources: Southeast Neighborhood Service Center, 4859 Rainier Avenue South, 206-386-1931, www.cityofseattle.net; Rainier Beach Community Center, 8825 Rainier Avenue South, 206-386-1925, www.cityofseattle.net/parks

DUWAMISH DISTRICT

SOUTH PARK
GEORGETOWN
SODO

Boundaries: North: South Royal Brougham Way, South Dearborn Street; **West:** Duwamish Waterway, Highway 509; **South:** South Barton Street; **East:** I-5

The Duwamish District is a primarily industrial area that starts just south of Safeco Field and follows the Duwamish River south to the city limits. Originally the land on either side of the river was fertile farmland, but eventually the farms were displaced by industries that used the river for shipping and, unfortunately, dumping. Today, most of the district remains strictly industrial, although there are pockets of residential and retail activity in the South Park and Georgetown areas. Boeing Field is located in the vicinity, but most employees commute to the area rather than live here. People from other parts of the city visit the Gai's Bakery outlet store and the nearby Museum of Flight at Boeing Field, or use the through streets in this neighborhood as shortcuts to the SeaTac Airport, Burien, and West Seattle.

South Park is a small community at the south end of this district, near the Duwamish River. This is a neighborhood of extremely modest bungalows, many of which are rentals. Quickly becoming known as "Little Tijuana," South Park is the only neighborhood in Seattle where Hispanic residents are heavily concentrated, 37% according to the 2000 census. Anchoring the neighborhood's four-block retail core on 14th Avenue South is the Mexi-Mart, a Mexican grocery, bakery, take-out restaurant, clothing and music store.

The **Georgetown** neighborhood, in the area around South Michigan Street, is an odd assortment of simple frame houses, breakfast cafes, warehouses, and other industrial buildings. Residents of Georgetown tend to be blue-collar workers who appreciate the lower housing prices. A growing number of artists have discovered Georgetown's affordable studio space, including several who collaborate and share resources in the former Rainier Cold Storage Plant on Airport Way South. The Seattle Design Center, a 360,000-square-foot complex of 60 designer showrooms on Sixth Avenue South, provides many of the city's contractors and homeowners with furnishings, fabrics, and accessories.

The **SODO** (**S**outh of the **Do**me) area borders downtown at Royal Brougham Street, south of the former Kingdome area. It's an industrial area, filled with warehouses and small manufacturing plants. The historic Sears building, now headquarters to Starbucks Coffee, is located here, as well as a sprawling new Home Depot. Few people actually live in SODO, but many of those who do are artists, residing in spacious lofts tucked inside converted warehouses. Though there are no grocery stores here, and the noise from passing cargo and passenger trains can be unbearable at times, creative types appreciate the lofts' high ceilings and plentiful elbow-room. In addition to the influx of artist residents, Art Wolfe Photography Gallery and Herban Pottery on First Avenue South provide additional clues to the emerging artistic community here.

Web Sites: www.cityofseattle.net, www.ci.seattle.wa.us/business/dc
Area Code: 206
Zip Codes: 98108, 98168, 98106
Post Office: Georgetown Station, 620 South Orcas Street, 800-275-8777, www.usps.com
Library: Delridge Library, 4555 Delridge Way SW, 206-937-7680, www.spl.lib.wa.us
Public Schools: Seattle Public Schools, P.O. Box 19116, Seattle, WA 98109-1116, 206-298-7000, www.seattleschools.org
Police: West Precinct, 610 3rd Avenue, 206-684-8917, www.cityofseattle.net/police
Emergency Hospital: Harborview Medical Center, 325 9th Avenue, 206-731-3074, www.washington.edu/medical/hmc
Community Resources: Duwamish Coalition, 516 3rd Avenue, www.ci.seattle.wa.us/business/dc; Georgetown Crime Prevention and Community Council, P.O. Box 80021, Seattle, WA 98108, www.ci.seattle.wa.us/commnty/georgetown; Greater Duwamish Neighborhood Service Center, 3801 Beacon Avenue South, 206-233-2044, www.cityofseattle.net; SODO Business Association, 2728 3rd Avenue South, 206-292-7449, www.cityofseattle.net

WEST SEATTLE

ADMIRAL
ALKI
FAUNTLEROY
DELRIDGE

Boundaries: North: Puget Sound, Elliott Bay; **West**: Puget Sound; **South**: Seola Beach Drive SW, SW Roxbury Street; **East**: Duwamish Waterway, Highway 509

In 1851, the schooner Exact landed on Alki Beach in what is now West Seattle, bringing the Denny party to the Puget Sound. Charles Terry, a member of the original party, remained behind while the rest of the group moved on to what is now the Seattle waterfront. By 1897, the peninsula had a large enough population to merit a ferry between downtown and West Seattle. Today, West Seattle is a comfortable residential hill connected to the rest of the city by the West Seattle Freeway, which bridges the Duwamish Waterway and the man-made Harbor Island.

Atop the hill, the West Seattle Junction at SW Alaska Street and California Avenue SW is a commercial center for West Seattle. Clothing boutiques, bookstores, small diners, and drug stores fill the ground floor retail space around "the Junction." Young couples and singles rent the quaint apartments above the storefronts. East of the junction, auto dealerships and ethnic take-out restaurants cluster around the intersection of SW Alaska Street and Fauntleroy Way SW.

With housing prices lower than in similar neighborhoods closer to the city, West Seattle continues to gain in popularity. Recent figures from the Northwest Multiple Listing Service put the average home sale price close to $270,000. Magnolia, which has similar views but from the opposite side of Elliott Bay, saw an average closer to $500,000. Apartment average between West Seattle and Magnolia are less remarkably different.

The intersection of SW Admiral Way and California Avenue SW is the second retail core on the hill. Here, the historic Admiral Theater presides over the intersection, which is lined with small shops, espresso joints, and funky restaurants. The **Admiral** district, which surrounds this intersection, is one of the more affluent areas in West Seattle. Homes at the top of the hill, mainly Craftsman bungalows and Northwest Moderns, have views of downtown to the northeast or of the Olympics to the west. Residents of the Admiral area tend to be middle- to upper-income professionals and their families.

The Admiral business district enjoys a magnificent Thriftway grocery store, filled with gourmet cheeses, fresh flowers, and fine wines, but suffers from a shortage of parking. Residents here lobbied for a parking garage near the Admiral Theatre, but the city council refused to approve funding. Instead, a local developer agreed to add an extra floor of parking to a condominium project. Nonetheless, parking on a Saturday night, when the district is filled with diners and moviegoers, continues to present a challenge.

Alki is a long, narrow beach neighborhood that stretches along the north and west sides of the peninsula and offers the atmosphere of an ocean resort town. In the summer, the beach is crowded with sunbathers, in-line skaters, bicyclists, and volleyball players. In the spring and fall, residents meet for coffee and dessert at the Alki Bakery, or stop for dinner at Spuds Fish & Chips or Pegasus Pizza. Although development has begun to change the face of this area, many 1960s condominiums and beach cottages are still located just a short walk or bicycle ride from the beach. Residents are generally middle-income service professionals, many of whom are longtime West Seattle residents. Alki has extraordinary views of both downtown Seattle and the Olympic peninsula. The most spectacular views of the Olympics come during early spring or late fall, when the sun is bright and the snow has not yet melted in the mountains. The Alki beachhead is a popular destination for couples watching the sunset during the summer, and many intrepid Seattle residents brave inclement winter weather to watch the waves crash against the shore. Salty's on Alki, at 1936 Harbor Avenue SW, is one of the city's favorite view restaurants, and a popular spot for wedding receptions and Sunday brunch. If there is a downside to Alki, it is the waves of tourists, short-term renters, and sun-worshippers who crowd the neighborhood during the summer. The city's anti-cruising ordinance stopped most of the circling of cars and motorcycles, but traffic on sunny days still slows to a crawl on Harbor Avenue SW.

Comparing Alki's views to those of Manhattan from Hoboken, NJ, the *Seattle Post-Intelligencer* calls this one of Seattle's hottest condo markets, with units selling for $275,000 to $1 million.

The **Fauntleroy** neighborhood lies along the southwest slope of the hill in West Seattle, facing the Puget Sound. Though Fauntleroy is best known throughout the rest of Seattle for its ferry dock, with services to Vashon Island and the Olympic Peninsula, it is also a comfortable, secluded neighborhood. Beautiful brick Tudors, classic Northwest Modern homes, and modest bungalows line winding streets and quiet cul-de-sacs. Fauntleroy was home to some of Seattle's original families, like the Colmans, who built the city's first brick building and its downtown ferry terminal. Another famous resident, Jim Whittaker, who was the first American to stand atop Mount Everest, grew up playing in the woods in Fauntleroy. Homes here have unparalleled views of the Puget Sound, Vashon Island, and the Olympics. Lincoln Park, at 8011 Fauntleroy Way SW, has grills for summer barbecuing, and a heated salt-water pool (Olympic size) right on the edge of the sound for spectacular summer swimming. Fauntleroy's tiny commercial district is easy to miss, and that suits residents just fine. A Greek restaurant, neighborhood bakery, gift shop, and beauty salon are concentrated in a single building at SW Wildwood Place and 45th Avenue SW.

As Fauntleroy's popularity grows, modest homes belonging to low- and middle-income families are being sold to wealthy retirees and professionals, though turn-over is occurring less quickly here than in other West Seattle neighborhoods. Interestingly, the transfer of property within families is not unusual, according to one local real estate agent.

In the southeast quarter of West Seattle, **Delridge** is a neighborhood of simple 1950s ramblers, contemporary split-levels, and tract houses. On its eastern edge near West Marginal Way, Delridge is primarily industrial. To the west, residential areas offer modest homes and modern apartment complexes. The median income in this neighborhood is lower than most of West Seattle; rents and real estate prices tend to be much lower as well. Community groups in Delridge work to improve the quality of life here. One such effort was the Delridge Neighborhoods Development Association's proposal to include affordable apartments on the top two floors of the new library. The impressive result is the full service Delridge Public Library, 5423 Delridge Way SW, which opened June 2002 and features 19 low-income housing units on the upper two floors. Home and car security is an issue in some areas of Delridge. Newcomers should explore this neighborhood carefully when considering housing here.

Though West Seattle is only a 20-minute drive from downtown, the neighborhood is not convenient for those working on the Eastside. The commute covers the West Seattle Freeway, I-5, and I-90, all of which have heavy traffic during rush hour. However, for people working downtown who would like to live in a neighborhood that feels utterly removed from the city, West Seattle may be the perfect spot.

Web Sites: www.cityofseattle.net, www.wschamber.com

Area Code: 206

Zip Codes: 98106, 98116, 98126, 98136

Post Office: West Seattle Station, 4412 California Avenue SW, 800-275-8777, www.usps.com

Libraries: Delridge Library, 4555 Delridge Way SW, 206-937-7680, www.spl.lib.wa.us; High Point Library, 6338 32nd Avenue SW, 206-684-7454, www.spl.lib.wa.us; Southwest Library, 9010 35th Avenue SW, 206-684-7455, www.spl.lib.wa.us; West Seattle Library, 2306 42nd Avenue SW, 206-684-7444, www.spl.lib.wa.us

Public Schools: Seattle Public Schools, P.O. Box 19116, Seattle, WA 98109-1116, 206-298-7000, www.seattleschools.org

Police: South Precinct, 3001 South Myrtle Street, 206-386-1850, www.cityofseattle.net/police

Emergency Hospital: Harborview Medical Center, 325 9th Avenue, 206-731-3074, www.washington.edu/medical/hmc

Community Resources: Alki Community Center, 5817 SW Stevens Street, 206-684-7430, www.cityofseattle.net/parks; Coalition of West Seattle Human Service Providers, www.wslyncs.org; Delridge Community Center, 4501 Delridge Way SW, 206-684-7423, www.cityofseattle.net/parks; Delridge Neighborhood Service Center, 5405 Delridge Way SW, 206-684-7416, www.cityofseattle.net; Hiawatha Community Center, 2700 California Avenue SW, 206-684-7441, www.cityofseattle.net/parks; High Point Community Center, 6920 34th Avenue SW, 206-684-7422, www.cityofseattle.net/parks; Southwest Community Center, 2801 SW Thistle Street, 206-684-7438, www.cityofseattle.net/parks; West Seattle Junction Association, 4750 California Avenue SW, 206-935-0904, www.wsjunction.com; West Seattle Neighborhood Service Center, 4750 California Avenue SW, 206-684-7495, www.cityofseattle.net

Public Transportation: Metro Transit, 206-553-3000, www.transit.metrokc.gov

37: Downtown/Harbor Island/Alki/West Seattle Junction

51: West Seattle Junction/Admiral District

55: Downtown/West Seattle Junction/Admiral District

56: Downtown/SODO/Admiral District/Alki

57: West Seattle Junction/Admiral District/SODO/Downtown

85: (Night Owl) Downtown/SODO/West Seattle Junction/White Center/Delridge

116: Downtown/West Seattle/Fauntleroy

128: Admiral District/West Seattle Junction/White Center/Southcenter

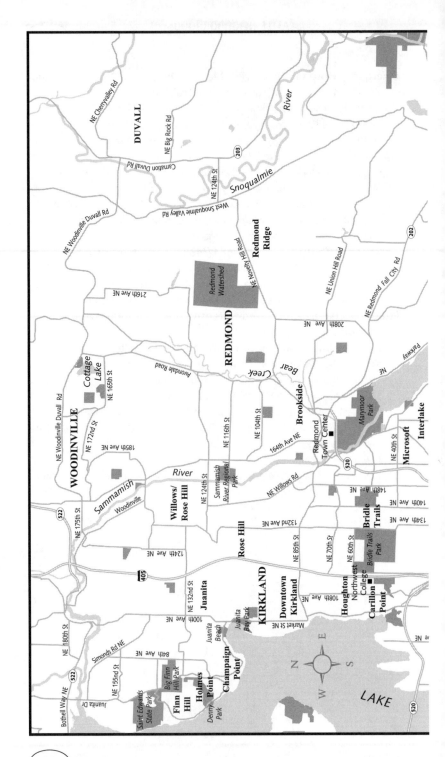

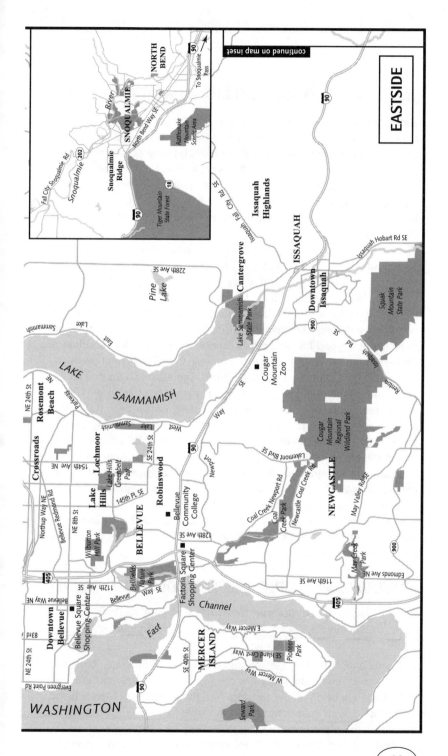

EASTSIDE

continued on map inset

WASHINGTON

Downtown Bellevue

MERCER ISLAND

NEWCASTLE

BELLEVUE

Lake Hills

Crossroads

Rosemont Beach

Lochmoor

Robinswood

Cantergrove

ISSAQUAH

Downtown Issaquah

Issaquah Highlands

SNOQUALMIE

NORTH BEND

Snoqualmie Ridge

LAKE SAMMAMISH

Pine Lake

Lake Sammamish State Park

Cougar Mountain Zoo

Cougar Mountain Regional Wildland Park

Squak Mountain State Park

Tiger Mountain State Forest

Rattlesnake Mountain Scenic Area

Seward Park

Pioneer Park

May Creek Park

Bellfields Nature Park

Wilburton Hill Park

Greenbelt Park

Bellevue Square Shopping Center

Factoria Square Shopping Center

Bellevue Community College

Coal Creek Park

To Snoqualmie Pass

83

SURROUNDING COMMUNITIES

Today, Seattle is composed of much more than simply the city itself. Beyond the city limits, many communities benefit from and contribute to Seattle's economy. A good number of Seattle residents go to work each day on the Eastside, to communities such as Bellevue, Kirkland or Redmond (where Microsoft is based). Both Seattle and Eastside residents commute to jobs in Tacoma to the south or Everett to the north. Many catch a ferry from Bainbridge Island west of downtown, or from towns and cities on the Olympic Peninsula.

According to local real estate agents, many newcomers arrive in Seattle with hopes of living in the city or very close to the city, only to find that housing prices are higher than they expected, or lot sizes smaller than they had hoped. Many choose to expand their search to include the Eastside, the north or south sides of greater Seattle, or along the I-5 corridor. When choosing a community outside Seattle, there are a few things to think about beyond housing prices. Consider if you want a suburban or rural environment—some make their homes in traditionally rural communities beyond the suburbs, including Duvall, Snoqualmie, and Bothell. Do you want new construction in a planned community, or an older home in a more established neighborhood? Do you prefer proximity to water or to mountains? Exclusive planned neighborhoods in some Eastside suburbs, particularly those with views of Lake Washington or Lake Sammamish, attract affluent residents looking for a suburban lifestyle. Communities like Issaquah and Redmond are filled with new developments, while mature communities like Burien or Shoreline offer established neighborhoods with spectacular views. And, perhaps most important, how much time do you want to spend in your car every day, commuting to work? Long commutes can negatively affect one's personal and professional life, not to mention harm done to the environment.

EASTERN COMMUNITIES (THE "EASTSIDE")—KING COUNTY

Mercer Island, Bellevue, Newcastle, Redmond, Kirkland,
Woodinville, Duvall, Issaquah, North Bend/Snoqualmie

A decade ago, "The Eastside" consisted primarily of Bellevue, Redmond, and Kirkland. Today, just about any city east of Seattle to Snoqualmie Pass is referred to as being on the Eastside. With the exception of Mercer Island, which has a limited amount of land available for new construction, the Eastside is the place to turn if you're looking for a large new home in a planned or gated community. Many eastern cities also feature wooded or semi-rural areas—a rarity in Seattle. The Eastside has always been known as an upscale region, so it's not surprising that Bill Gates—the world's richest man—lives here, in the affluent suburb of Medina.

MERCER ISLAND

ROANOKE

Located at the south end of Lake Washington, Mercer Island is an established, upscale community. While only minutes away from downtown Seattle, it feels miles away from the urban hubbub. This insular city with beautiful view homes, plentiful opportunities for recreation, and a compact but comprehensive commercial district, attracts affluent professionals and entrepreneurs. Though small, the city boasts numerous parks, including Luther Burbank Park at the north end of the island. A popular summer recreation area, Luther Burbank offers swimming, boating, a playground, and an off-leash dog area. During the summer months, performances are held at its small outdoor amphitheater. Not surprisingly, Mercer Island's school district is well-known for its academic accomplishments, and each year sends 95% of its seniors on to college. And, the cherry on the top, because Mercer Island is situated between Seattle and the Eastside, it's an easy commute for professionals in both regions—perfect for two career couples. The island measures 5 miles long and 2 $^1/_2$ miles wide, and in 2001 reported a population of just over 22,000 residents.

As you would expect, housing prices and rents on the island are high. Many of the homes here are sprawling estates and modern mansions, but there are a few modest houses around, mostly built between the 1950s and the 1980s. Houses in the half million-dollar range are the norm, and rents are expensive, just a bit higher than those in downtown Seattle.

Mercer Island's primary artery is Mercer Way—East Mercer Way on the eastern half of the island and West Mercer Way on the western side. The winding road hugs the lakeshore, and seemingly is used as much by runners and bicyclists as by cars. (In fact, Mercer Island is a fantastic place to train for triathlons or races, because of its opportunities for swimming, running and biking.) Island Crest Way bisects the island, running north/south. The community's commercial district is located adjacent to the freeway at the north end of the island, and is bounded by 27th and 32nd streets, Island Crest Way and 77th Avenue SE.

At the northern tip of Mercer Island is the **Roanoke** neighborhood. This is where you'll find two of Mercer Island's historic landmarks, the Roanoke Inn and the VFW Hall. The Roanoke Inn, at 72nd Avenue SE and North Mercer

Way, is a homey little tavern and eatery smack-dab in the middle of a residential community. Established in 1914, "the Roanoke" served as a speakeasy during Prohibition. Today, the restaurant is popular with both islanders and city folk for its weeknight dinner specials, cozy atmosphere, and patio dining during the summer. The VFW Hall, which began its history as the Keewaydin ("the north wind") Club and later the Mercer Island Community Club, was built by Mercer Island residents in 1922 to host social events.

Web Site: www.ci.mercer-island.wa.us
Area Code: 206
Zip Codes: 98040
Post Office: 3040 78th Avenue SE, 800-275-8777, www.usps.com
Libraries: 4400 88th Avenue SE, 206-236-3537, www.kcls.org
Public Schools: Mercer Island School District, 4160 86th Avenue SE, 206-236-3330, www.misd.wednet.edu
Police: City Hall, 9611 SE 36th Street, 206-236-3500, www.ci.mercer-island.wa.us
Emergency Hospital: Harborview Medical Center, 325 9th Avenue, 206-731-3074, www.washington.edu/medical/hmc; Overlake Hospital Medical Center, 1035 116th Avenue NE, 425-688-5000, www.overlakehospital.org
Community Resources: Community Center at Mercer View, 8236 SE 24th Street, 206-236-3545, www.ci.mercer-island.wa.us; Mercer Island Beach Club, 8326 Avalon Drive, 206-232-3125; Mercer Island Boys' & Girls' Club, 2825 West Mercer Way, 206-232-4548, www.positiveplace.org; Mercer Island Chamber of Commerce, 7613 SE 27th Street, 206-232-3404, www.mercerislandchamber.org; Mercer Island Country Club, 8700 SE 71st Street, 206-232-5600, www.mercerisland-cc.com; Mercer Island Historical Society, 206-232-1263, www.mihistory.org; Mercerwood Shore Club, 4150 East Mercer Way, 206-232-1622, www.mercerwood.com; Stroum Jewish Community Center of Greater Seattle, 3801 East Mercer Way, 206-232-7115, www.sjcc.org
Public Transportation: Metro Transit, 206-553-3000, www.transit.metrokc.gov
201: Mercer Island Park & Ride/West Mercer Way/South Mercer Island
202: Downtown Seattle/Mercer Island Park & Ride/South Mercer Island
203: Mercer Island Park & Ride/Downtown Mercer Island/East Mercer Way/Shorewood/North Mercer Island/City Hall
204: Mercer Island Park & Ride/Island Crest Way/South Mercer Island
205: University District/Montlake/First Hill/Mercer Island Park & Ride/South Mercer Island
213: Mercer Island Park & Ride/Downtown Mercer Island/East Mercer Way/Covenant Shores/North Mercer Island/City Hall

BELLEVUE

DOWNTOWN BELLEVUE
BRIDLE TRAILS
BROOKSIDE
MICROSOFT *(Unofficial moniker, mostly used by real estate agents for housing near Microsoft)*
CROSSROADS
ROSEMONT BEACH
INTERLAKE
LOCHMOOR
ROBINSWOOD
LAKE HILLS

A decade ago, Bellevue was a small city best known to Seattle residents as home to Bellevue Square, an upscale mall. Today, Bellevue is the state's fifth-largest city, and enjoys a thriving downtown, excellent schools and abundant parks. While the area has a reputation of being home to wealthy residents (the cost of living here tops the national average by more than 50%, according to Bestplaces.net), you'll find people of various incomes living in Bellevue. Suburban housing developments filled with modest split-level and contemporary homes dot the area, and homes close to Lake Washington to the west or Lake Sammamish to the east are more elegant and expensive. Most houses to the east are on the newer side, and range in style from traditional brick ranch houses to angular art deco homes to lavish new brick Tudors. Home prices in Bellevue range from $200,000 to the millions.

According to the City of Bellevue, the region's largest employers are Bellevue Community College, Boeing, Microsoft, PACCAR, Nordstrom, Safeway, Puget Sound Energy, and Overlake Hospital. Along with Microsoft, many high-tech companies are located in the Eastside. In fact, high-tech jobs account for about 20% of all Eastside jobs. Bellevue is also a popular choice for professionals who work in Seattle, as evidenced by the heavy morning and evening traffic across both bridges.

Though Bellevue is primarily a city of unassuming neighborhoods, recently **Downtown Bellevue** has become a hip place to live, with more than 4,000 residents now calling it home. Several condominiums have been erected here, and a host of new shops and restaurants have been added to the area near Bellevue Square. Completion of Lincoln Square, a soaring skyscraper with condos, retail and office space, restaurants, and the four-star Westin Bellevue Hotel is expected in late 2003. Also new, the Bellevue Art Museum, located at 510 Bellevue Way NE, site of the city's annual art fair, as well as the 3,500-square-foot Museum School.

Most of Bellevue's neighborhoods offer a range of housing styles and prices, though properties near the water will generally cost more than those inland. If you're looking for seclusion and large lots, consider the **Bridle Trails** community in northern Bellevue. Most homes in the neighborhood rely on septic tanks instead of sewers, but property is at a premium, and there are some incredible new estates peeking through the pines. Prices here range from $380,000 to nearly $3 million. To the southeast are the **Brookside** and **Microsoft** neighborhoods, popular choices for many Microsoft employees. Homes here are large and comfortable, and sell for a more modest but still hefty $400,000 to $800,000.

Crossroads is one of Bellevue's most culturally diverse neighborhoods. About 8,000 people live here and you are just as likely to hear residents speaking Russian, Spanish, or Chinese as English. Crossroads Shopping Center, at NE 8th Street and 156th Avenue NE, is a popular meeting place for members of the East European, Hispanic, and Asian communities. The mall frequently hosts live music and community celebrations. Also at the mall is the newly opened Library Connection; a public library with multi-language programs and materials, and internet access. In northeast Bellevue, near Lake Sammamish, are the **Rosemont Beach**, **Interlake** and **Lochmoor** neighborhoods. Homes in these communities sell for $200,000 to $350,000, though those with views are considerably more expensive. Most houses are large ramblers built in the mid to late 1970s.

The **Robinswood** and **Lake Hills** communities are located in southeast Bellevue, near Bellevue Community College. There are a variety of rentals in this area, which are popular with students and employees of nearby Factoria Mall. Most homes here are affordable, ranging in price from $230,000 to $450,000. The exception is the area overlooking the Glendale Golf & Country Club, where newly constructed homes can cost up to $800,000. Robinswood Community Park, at 148th Avenue SE and SE 22nd Street, is a favorite local attraction. It features soccer and baseball fields, and a quaint cottage for party and banquet rentals.

Web Site: www.ci.bellevue.wa.us
Area Code: 425
Zip Codes: 98004, 98005, 98006, 98007, 98008, 98009, 98015
Post Office: 1171 Bellevue Way NE; 11405 NE 2nd Place; 15731 NE 8th Street, 800-275-8777, www.usps.com
Libraries: 1111 110th Avenue NE, 425-450-1765; 15228 Lake Hills Boulevard, 425-747-3350; 14250 SE Newport Way, 425-747-2390, www.kcls.org
Public Schools: 12111 NE 1st Street, 425-456-4000, www.belnet.bellevue.k12.wa.us
Police: City Hall, 11511 Main Street, 425-452-6917, 877-881-2731; Factoria

Substation, 4098 Factoria Square Mall SE, 425-452-2891; Crossroads Substation, 15600 NE 8th Street, 425-452-2891; Spiritwood Substation, 1424 148th Avenue SE D-9, 425-452-6971, www.ci.bellevue.wa.us

Emergency Hospital: Overlake Hospital Medical Center, 1035 116th Avenue NE, 425-688-5000, www.overlakehospital.org

Community Resources: Bellevue Chamber of Commerce, 10500 NE 8th Street, Suite 212, 425-454-2464, www.bellevuechamber.org; Bellevue Community College, 3000 Landerholm Circle SE, 425-564-1000, www.bcc.ctc.edu; Bellevue Downtown Association, 500 108th Avenue NE, Suite 210, 425-453-1223, www.bellevuedowntown.org; Bellevue Historical Society, 425-450-1046, www.scn.org/arts/bellehist/frameset; Crossroads Community Center, 16000 NE 10th Street, 425-452-4874; Highland Park Community Center, 14224 NE Bel-Red Road, 425-452-7686; North Bellevue Community Senior Center, 4063 148th Avenue NE, 425-452-7681; Northwest Community Center, 9825 NE 24th Street, 425-452-4106

Public Transportation: Metro Transit, 206-553-3000, www.transit.metrokc.gov

220: Redmond/Rose Hill/Kirkland/Bellevue

222: Bellevue/Beaux Arts/South Bellevue/Factoria/Eastgate/Bellevue Community College/Overlake

232: Duvall/Cottage Lake/English Hill/Redmond/Bellevue

233: Redmond/Microsoft/Overlake/Bellevue

234: Kenmore/Juanita/Kirkland/Bellevue

237: Bellevue/Kingsgate/Woodinville

240: Clyde Hill/Bellevue/South Bellevue/Factoria/Newcastle/Renton

243: Jackson Park/Lake City/Ravenna/University District/Montlake/Bellevue

249: Redmond/Sammamish/Overlake//Bellevue

253: Bear Creek/Redmond/Overlake/Crossroads/Bellevue

261: Overlake/Crossroads/Bellevue/Clyde Hill/Medina/Montlake/Downtown Seattle

272: University District/Crossroads/Lake Hills/Eastgate

280: (Night Owl) Renton/Tukwila/Downtown Seattle/Bellevue

NEWCASTLE

CHINA CREEK

Situated between the cities of Bellevue, Renton, and Issaquah, Newcastle is a new community (incorporated as a city in 1994), with a population of about 8,000. Depending on whom you ask, Newcastle is either an Eastside neighborhood or a South End neighborhood. In fact, it is located southeast of Seattle, so both descriptions are accurate. But, Newcastle's numerous planned housing communities, like **China Creek**, and the public—but nonetheless swanky—Golf Club at Newcastle, give the city a distinctly Eastside feel. In general, homes in Newcastle are more expensive than in Renton to the south, ranging from $400,000 to $800,000. Many have views of the mountains, Lake Washington or the golf course. Condos and townhouses can be found for under $300,000.

Despite its proximity to the much larger city of Bellevue, Newcastle's leaders and residents take pride in the city's small-town feel and strong sense of community. Each year in September, the city hosts Newcastle Days. This two-day celebration is at Lake Boren Park, a 20-acre park located on SE 84th Avenue just off Coal Creek Parkway, one of Newcastle's major thoroughfares. Another impressive local treasure is Cougar Mountain Regional Wildland Park, the biggest park in King County, with more than 3,000 acres of trails and wildlife habitat.

Web Site: www.ci.newcastle.wa.us

Area Code: 425

Zip Codes: 98056, 98059

Post Office: 4301 NE 4th Street, Renton, 800-275-8777, www.usps.com

Libraries: 14250 SE Newport Way, Bellevue, 425-747-2390, www.kcls.org; 2902 NE 12th Street, Renton, 425-430-6790, www.ci.renton.wa.us

Public Schools: Issaquah School District, 565 NW Holly Street, 425-837-7000, www.issaquah.wednet.edu; Renton School District, 300 SW 7th Street, 425-204-2300, www.renton.wednet.edu

Police: 13020 SE 72nd Place, 425-649-4444, www.ci.newcastle.wa.us

Emergency Hospital: Overlake Hospital Medical Center, 1035 116th Avenue NE, 425-688-5000, www.overlakehospital.org

Community Resources: China Creek Homeowner's Association, 6947 Coal Creek Parkway SE #146, www.chinacreek.org; Cougar Mountain Regional Wildland Park, 18201 SE Cougar Mountain Drive, 206-296-4145; www.metrokc.gov/parks; The Golf Club at Newcastle, 15500 Six Penny Lane, 425-793-5566, www.newcastlegolf.com; Greater Newcastle Chamber of Commerce, 425-641-7590; Newcastle Historical Society, 425-226-4328

REDMOND

REDMOND RIDGE
WILLOWS/ROSE HILL

Though it is known as the bicycle capital of the Pacific Northwest, Redmond certainly is best known as the home of technology powerhouse Microsoft and renowned game maker Nintendo. Once a sleepy farming community, Redmond today is a thriving city of more than 43,000 residents. Most are in the middle- to upper-income bracket; many are affiliated with Microsoft or Nintendo. According to Bestplaces.net, Redmond's cost of living is a whopping 56% higher than the national average. Redmond increasingly attracts professionals and their families who seek larger homes and acreage that can't be found in the city.

Even before Redmond became a popular place to live, a variety of local attractions drew thousands of visitors to the city each year. Marymoor Park, along West Lake Sammamish Parkway, is one of the region's best parks. Along with the most popular off-leash dog area in Western Washington, the 640-acre park features a velodrome (hence the city's cycling moniker), numerous sports fields, tennis courts, and a venue designated specifically for remote-controlled airplanes. Sadly, the King County Heritage Festival, which was held in the park for 27 consecutive years, was cancelled due to budget cuts in the spring of 2001. The multicultural World of Music Arts and Dance (WOMAD) festival still takes place there each summer.

At the southern tip of Marymoor Park is Lake Sammamish, which covers almost 4,900 acres to touch the cities of Sammamish, Bellevue, and Issaquah. Idylwood Park, south of Marymoor on West Lake Sammamish Parkway NE, is a popular summertime recreation area on the western shore of the lake, and features picnic tables, outdoor grills, and a dock. The homes along the lakefront are a mix of summer cottages and large contemporary houses. Most have beach access and moorage. During the summer, the lake is busy with water skiers and boaters.

State Route 520 is the primary route in and out of Redmond, and ends at the city's southeastern border. Unfortunately, traffic jams on the highway are notorious, and Redmond residents can do little to avoid them. However, Redmond's explosive population growth over the past decade has delivered lots of new amenities and commercial endeavors to its confines, and unless you work in Seattle, you may never feel the need to leave. A modern new downtown has grown up around its original core, and stylish brick mixed-use buildings now surround the quaint city center. Residents no longer need trek to Bellevue Square now that the massive, open-air Redmond Town Center, comprised of 120 acres of stores, restaurants and offices, is right in their own backyards.

Though much of it looks new, Redmond is one of the Eastside's oldest communities, and despite traffic and parking issues here, there is a lovely small-town feel. Perhaps that stems from its deep agricultural roots, or from efforts to preserve open spaces. In **Redmond Ridge**, a popular planned community in the northeast part of the city, developers preserved 600 acres of forest, wetlands, and parks. The insular neighborhood has its own community center and parks, and will eventually have its own elementary school. In tune with the technology needs of Redmond's residents, the Ridge offers residents three internet and two cable television options. Single-family homes in this development cost between $200,000 and $500,000; condominiums range from $200,000 to $300,000. As of spring 2002, homes were still being built in Redmond Ridge, and construction had not yet begun on the planned school. To view progress in the community, visit www.redmondridge.com.

To the west of Redmond Ridge is the **Willows/Rose Hill** neighborhood, which borders Kirkland to the west and the Willows Run Golf Course to the east. Numerous high-tech offices are located along the community's eastern edge, including 3-Com, Nextel, and Metawave. Like many Eastside neighborhoods, old meets new here, with small ramblers on large lots perched next to contemporary planned communities. Along the neighborhood's outer edges are townhomes and apartment and condominium complexes, which are popular with students attending nearby Lake Washington Technical College.

Web Site: www.ci.redmond.wa.us
Area Code: 425
Zip Codes: 98052, 98053, 98073, 98074
Post Office: 16135 NE 85th Street, 800-275-8777, www.usps.com
Libraries: 15990 NE 85th, 425-885-1861, 425-895-7951 (TTY); 15990 NE 85th, 425-885-1861, 425-895-7951 (TTY), www.kcls.org
Public Schools: Lake Washington School District, 16250 NE 74th Street, 425-702-3200, www.lkwash.wednet.edu
Police: 8701 160th Avenue NE, 425-556-2500, www.ci.redmond.wa.us
Emergency Hospital: The Eastside Hospital (Group Health Cooperative), 2700 152nd Avenue NE, 425-888-5151, www.ghc.org
Community Resources: Friends of Marymoor Park, 206-205-8751, www.scn.org/fomp; Old Redmond Schoolhouse Community Center, 16600 NE 80th Street, 425-556-2300, www.ci.redmond.wa.us; Redmond Ridge, 10735 Cedar Park Crescent NE, 888-820-8188, www.redmondridge.com; Senior Center, 15670 NE 85th Street, 425-

556-2314, 425-556-2906 (TTD), www.ci.redmond.wa.us; Serve Our Dog Areas, 425-881-0148, www.soda.org

Public Transportation: Metro Transit, 206-553-3000, www.transit. metrokc.gov

220: Redmond/Rose Hill/Kirkland/Bellevue

230: Kingsgate/Totem Lake/Rose Hill/Kirkland/Bellevue/Cross-roads/Overlake/Microsoft/Redmond

233: Redmond/Microsoft/Overlake/Bellevue

247: Redmond/Overlake/Eastgate/Factoria/Newport Hills/Kennydale/ Renton/Kent

249: Redmond/Sammamish/Overlake/Bellevue

250: Redmond/Overlake/Montlake/Downtown Seattle

254: Kirkland/Redmond

265: Downtown Seattle/Redmond

268: Redmond/Bear Creek/Downtown Seattle

291: Kingsgate/Redmond

KIRKLAND

DOWNTOWN
HOUGHTON
CARILLON POINT
JUANITA
CHAMPAGNE POINT
HOMES POINT
FINN HILL
ROSE HILL

Kirkland is a small town on the shore of Lake Washington, just north of Highway 520. Real estate prices here are expensive, as many homes have views of the lake. In fact, some of the most spectacular views on the Eastside are found in Kirkland, with Lake Washington, the Seattle skyline, and Mount Rainier all visible from a few fortunate neighborhoods. The influx of nearby technology companies helped to fuel Kirkland's housing boom. Many choose to live here because of the short drive to Redmond, and because Kirkland is close to Highway 520 and Interstate 405, some residents commute west to Seattle or north to Everett.

Housing styles in Kirkland are a mixed bag, from turn-of-the-century homes like those on Seattle's Queen Anne Hill, to ultra-modern condominiums to 1960s ramblers. Because land is scarce in Kirkland, short-platting—the practice of building multiple homes on a piece of property that used to contain just one house—is increasingly common. Many neighborhoods offer an odd combination of homes; it's not uncommon to find quaint Craftsman bungalows rubbing elbows with massive newly built houses.

The **downtown** area is a sophisticated shopping district with a colorful marina, cozy cafes, trendy boutiques, and unique gift shops. This neighborhood also supports several bars that are popular with the early 20s crowd. Condos are the norm in downtown Kirkland, and can cost as little as $150,000 or as much as $2.5 million. Young professionals and empty-nesters alike live along the city's waterfront and in the **Houghton** area, just south of downtown. A handful of small beachfront parks cozy up to the lakeshore, and the upscale Woodmark Hotel perches on **Carillon Point**. If you're not ready to buy, or if you plan to rent until you find the perfect house, this area offers lots of rental properties, from apartments to condominiums to small houses. The eastern section of Houghton, near Northwest College, offers more affordable homes that start around $300,000, but homes with views can still garner up to $3 million.

The **Juanita** neighborhood, north of downtown Kirkland, is an up-and-coming community anchored by the new Juanita Village mixed-use property. Modeled after the village centers in northern Europe, the pedestrian-friendly project combines shops, banks, and restaurants with apartments, condominiums and townhomes. West of Juanita, the **Champagne Point** and **Homes Point** neighborhoods are private, funky communities with incredible views of Lake Washington. Homes are anywhere from 60 years old to brand new, and prices are high. Residents here can just as easily go for a sheltered walk in the woods or take a leisurely stroll along the beach.

For affordable homes, newcomers should look to the Finn Hill and Rose Hill neighborhoods. **Finn Hill** is located northwest of downtown and **Rose Hill** is situated to the northeast. Newcomers should be aware, however, that while most of Kirkland is free from traffic congestion except during rush hour, the area surrounding Rose Hill is frequently backed up along NE 85th Street.

Web Site: www.ci.kirkland.wa.us
Area Code: 425
Zip Codes: 98033, 98034, 98083
Post Office: 721 4th Avenue, 800-275-8777, www.usps.com
Libraries: 308 Kirkland Avenue, 425-822-2459; 12315 NE 143rd, 425-821-7686, www.kcls.org
Public Schools: Lake Washington School District, 16250 NE 74th Street, 425-702-3200, www.lkwash.wednet.edu
Police: 123 5th Avenue, 425-828-1183, www.ci.kirkland.wa.us

Emergency Hospital: Evergreen Hospital Medical Center, 12040 NE 128th Street, Kirkland, 425-899-1000, www.evergreenhealthcare.org

Community Resources: Greater Kirkland Chamber of Commerce, 401 Parkplace, Suite 102, 425-822-7066, www.kirklandchamber.org; Kirkland Arts Center, 620 Market Street, 425-822-7161, www.kirklandartscenter.org; Kirkland Heritage Society, 1032 4th Street, 425-828-4095, www.historylink.org/khs; North Kirkland Community Center, 12421 103rd Avenue NE, 425-828-1105, www.ci.kirkland.wa.us; Senior Center, 352 Kirkland Avenue, 425-828-1223, www.ci.kirkland.wa.us; Teen Center, 348 Kirkland Avenue, 425-822-3088, www.ci.kirkland.wa.us

Public Transportation: Metro Transit, 206-553-3000, www.transit.metrokc.gov

236: Kirkland/Juanita/Totem Lake/Kingsgate/Bothell/Woodinville
238: Kirkland/Rose Hill/Totem Lake/Kingsgate/Finn Hill/Bothell
245: Kirkland/Redmond/Overlake/Bellevue/Eastgate/Factoria
251: Kirkland/Redmond/Bear Creek/Cottage Lake/Woodinville/Bothell
254: Kirkland/Redmond
257: Downtown Seattle/Kirkland
277: Kirkland/University of Washington

WOODINVILLE

Woodinville is a close neighbor of Redmond, attracting many Microsoft employees and their families. The city is located in the north central region of King County, just east of the intersection of State Route 522 and Interstate 405. Most homes in Woodinville are large contemporary structures in suburban developments or modest farmhouses on acreage. The city epitomizes the goal of many formerly rural Eastside communities, which is to blend city living with a country attitude.

Formerly a heavily forested region of King County, Woodinville became an incorporated city in 1993. The community is comprised primarily of single-family homes, with about 40% of dwellings designated for multi-family use. Generally, older, modest homes dating from before Woodinville's housing boom of the late 1990s have a median price of $300,000. Most new properties sell for more than a half-million dollars, and larger palatial estates are priced in the millions.

Residents have access to the usual suburban shopping centers, grocery stores, fast food restaurants, and chain stores, plus the country's largest single-outlet garden center, Molbak's. This local gem serves as Woodinville's commercial hub, taking up 15 acres on NE 175th Street. A few yeas ago, the company added a high-tech 42-acre greenhouse complex near NE

124th Street and State Route 202. The city is also home to two wineries, Chateau St. Michelle and Columbia, and the Redhook Brewery's restaurant and bottling facility.

Web Site: www.ci.woodinville.wa.us
Area Code: 425
Zip Codes: 98072
Post Office: 17610 Woodinville Snohomish Road, 800-275-8777, www.usps.com
Libraries: Woodinville Library, 17105 Avondale Road NE, 425-788-0733; Kingsgate Library, 12315 NE 143rd, 425-821-7686, www.kcls.org
Public Schools: Northshore School District, 18315 Bothell Way NE, 425-489-6000, www.nsd.org
Police: 13203 NE 175th Street, 425-489-2700, www.metrokc.gov/sheriff
Emergency Hospital: Evergreen Hospital Medical Center, 12040 NE 128th Street, Kirkland, 425-899-1000, www.evergreenhealthcare.org
Community Resources: Woodinville Chamber of Commerce, 13205 NE 175th Street, 425-481-8300, www.woodinvillechamber.org; Woodinville Community Center, 13203 NE 175th Street, 425-398-9327, www.ci.woodinville.wa.us
Public Transportation: Metro Transit, 206-553-3000, www.transit.metrokc.gov
  236: Kirkland/Juanita/Totem Lake/Kingsgate/Bothell/Woodinville
  237: Bellevue/Kirkland/Woodinville
  307: Downtown Seattle/Northgate/Lake City/Kenmore/Bothell/Woodinville
  312: Downtown Seattle/Lake City/Kenmore/Bothell/Woodinville
  372: University District/Ravenna/Wedgewood/Lake City/Kenmore/Bothell/Woodinville

DUVALL

Duvall is a farming community in the valley east of Redmond and Bothell. The city offers country homes and a half-hour commute to Redmond or Bellevue. Many of the houses are hidden in wooded hills; some have views of the Snoqualmie River, lush farmland or the Cascades.

Despite its proximity to the larger cities of the Eastside, Duvall is a rural community. At the height of the 1990's high-tech boom, families flocked to Duvall for its short commute to Microsoft, but that influx has now tapered off. Today Duvall has fewer than 5,000 residents, and the city's commercial district consists of about three blocks on Main Street, home to city hall, the public library, restaurants, grocery stores, and gas stations.

Duvall's demographics are diverse and reflect the area's home prices, which range from $30,000 mobile homes to $700,000 for new construction. The average home price in 2001 was just shy of $400,000, but that figure was a bit inflated due to high-end new construction. Newcomers should have no problem finding a home for $200,000 to $300,000.

Short-platting—building multiple homes on a piece of property that used to contain just one house—is common in Duvall. As demand for housing in Duvall grew, property owners, many of them farmers, realized they could make more money by dividing and selling off pieces of land than by farming it. In some cases, this has resulted in a patchwork effect in the community, with small clusters of homes popping up next to large farms.

Web Site: www.cityofduvall.com
Area Code: 425
Zip Codes: 98014, 98019
Post Office: 26400 NE Valley Street, 800-275-8777, www.usps.com
Libraries: 15619 NE Main Street, Duvall, 425-788-1173, www.kcls.org
Public Schools: Riverview School District, 32240 NE 50th Street, 425-844-4500, www.riverview.wednet.edu
Police: 15535 Main Street NE, Duvall, 425-788-1519, www.cityofduvall.com
Emergency Hospital: Overlake Hospital Medical Center, 1035 116th Avenue NE, 425-688-5000, www.overlakehospital.org
Community Resources: Duvall Arts Commission, 425-788-2983, www.cityofduvall.com/DAC; Sno-Valley North Little League, 425-844-1991, www.svnll.org
Public Transportation: Metro Transit, 206-553-3000, www.transit.metrokc.gov
232: Duvall/Cottage Lake/English Hill/Redmond/Bellevue
311: Downtown Seattle/Woodinville/Duvall

ISSAQUAH

CANTERGROVE
ISSAQUAH HIGHLANDS
DOWNTOWN

If location is the most important tenet in real estate, then it is no wonder Issaquah's housing market is booming. Nestled midway between Seattle and Snoqualmie Pass, the once sleepy town is ideally located to take advantage of the best the city and the mountains have to offer. Unfortunately, the city's rapid growth has had a less-than-ideal side effect: some of the worst traffic on the Eastside.

In the last few years, Issaquah saw more than a million square feet of commercial space added, including a Krispy Kremes outlet. There is also a Costco, Lowe's Home Improvement Center, a movie theater, and numerous restaurants. The concentration of retail businesses just off the freeway results in frequent congestion in the downtown core. But, once you leave downtown, it is still possible to find the quieter rural atmosphere that attracted residents to Issaquah decades ago.

Issaquah is the community of choice for many of Seattle's highly paid athletes. Former Mariners Ken Griffey Jr. and Jay Buhner lived here, and at least one Seahawk is in residence, though real estate agents are mum about which player it is. Planned communities like **Cantergrove** in eastern Issaquah, offer million-dollar homes with huge, wooded lots and mountain views. Nearby, the **Issaquah Highlands** neighborhood resembles a movie set, rising above the city and surrounded by spectacular views that reach all the way to Bellevue. The Highlands community is a mix of new condos and homes situated around a village green complete with its own cash machine and nearby shopping center. Homes start at about a half-million dollars, with condos selling for around $350,000 and up.

In **Downtown** Issaquah is a small collection of historic homes and buildings, and most of the city's apartments. On Front Street, quaint brick buildings house shops and theatres; also in downtown are the recently constructed police department and library.

Web Site: www.ci.issaquah.wa.us
Area Code: 425
Zip Codes: 98027, 98029, 98075
Post Office: 400 NW Gilman Boulevard, 800-275-8777, www.usps.com
Libraries: 10 West Sunset Way, 425-392-5430; 960 Newport Way NW, 425-369-3200, www.kcls.org
Public Schools: Issaquah School District, 565 NW Holly Street, 425-837-7000, www.issaquah.wednet.edu
Police: 130 East Sunset Way, 425-837-3200, www.ci.issaquah.wa.us
Emergency Hospital: Valley Medical Center, 400 South 43rd Street, Renton, 425-228-3450, www.valleymed.org
Community Resources: Issaquah Community Center, 301 Rainier Boulevard South, 425-837-3300, www.ci.issaquah.wa.us; Issaquah Historical Society, 425-392-3500, www.issaquahhistory.org; Issaquah Little League, 425-391-9747, www.issaquahlittleleague.org; Issaquah Valley Senior Center, 105 2nd Avenue NE, 425-392-2381
Public Transportation: Metro Transit, 206-553-3000, www.transit. metrokc.gov
200: Issaquah Park & Ride/The Commons at Issaquah/Community Center/Senior Center

209: Issaquah/Preston/Fall City/Snoqualmie/North Bend
210: Downtown Seattle/Factoria/Eastgate/Issaquah
217: Downtown Seattle/Factoria/Eastgate/Issaquah
269: Issaquah/Redmond/Overlake
271: Issaquah/Eastgate/Bellevue/University District

NORTH BEND/SNOQUALMIE

SNOQUALMIE RIDGE

Located approximately 30 miles east of Seattle, the communities of North Bend and Snoqualmie are in the Snoqualmie Valley, surrounded by mountains and lush pasture. Before the area's high-tech boom in the 1990s, which brought tremendous growth here, the two towns were primarily a stop on the way to the mountain passes and to Eastern Washington.

It was in the early 1990s when the North Bend/Snoqualmie area was thrust into the limelight as the backdrop for David Lynch's groundbreaking television show, "Twin Peaks." (The region still hosts an annual Twin Peaks Festival each August). At the time, the area was rural, and the pace of life here was slower than in established suburbs like Bellevue. For that reason, although these two towns certainly lie to Seattle's east, North Bend and Snoqualmie were not generally included in the blanket description of "Eastside." That changed in the late 1990s, when high-tech employees and first-time homebuyers began moving to the region in droves. Today, North Bend and Snoqualmie are known as much for their housing developments as they once were for winter recreation.

In theory, North Bend and Snoqualmie are about a half-hour drive from Seattle and 20 minutes from Bellevue, but heavy traffic on Interstate 90 usually makes for a much longer commute. A trip to downtown Seattle during rush hour will take at least 45 minutes.

Despite the drive, both North Bend and Snoqualmie are well on their way to becoming suburban bedroom communities, as developments like **Snoqualmie Ridge** continue to attract families looking to buy bigger houses and pay lower prices. Snoqualmie Ridge is a sprawling, 1,300-acre community that boasts its own golf course and more than 500 acres of preserved open space. Homes in the mixed-use development sell for between $250,000 and $1 million.

Web Site: www.ci.north-bend.wa.us; www.ci.snoqualmie.wa.us
Area Code: 425
Zip Codes: 98045, 98065, 98068

Post Office: 451 East North Bend Way, North Bend; 8264 Olmstead Lane SE, Snoqualmie, 800-275-8777, www.usps.com

Libraries: North Bend Library, 115 East 4th, 425-888-0554; Snoqualmie Library, 38580 SE River Street, 425-888-1223, www.kcls.org

Public Schools: Snoqualmie Valley Public Schools, P.O. Box 400, 425-831-8000, www.snoqualmie.wednet.edu

Police: 1550 Boalch Avenue NW, North Bend, 206-296-0612, www.metrokc.gov/sheriff; 34825 SE Douglas Street, Snoqualmie, 425-888-3333, www.ci.snoqualmie.wa.us

Emergency Hospital: Snoqualmie Valley Hospital, 9575 Ethan Wade Way SE, 425-831-2300,

Community Resources: Northwest Railway Museum, 38625 SE King Street, Snoqualmie, 425-888-3030, www.trainmuseum.org; Upper Snoqualmie Valley Chamber of Commerce, 425-888-4440, www.snovalley.org

Public Transportation: Metro Transit, 206-553-3000, www.transit.metrokc.gov

209: Issaquah/Preston/Fall City/Snoqualmie/North Bend

214: Downtown Seattle/Issaquah/Preston/Fall City/Snoqualmie/North Bend

929: North Bend/Snoqualmie/Fall City/Carnation/Duvall/Redmond

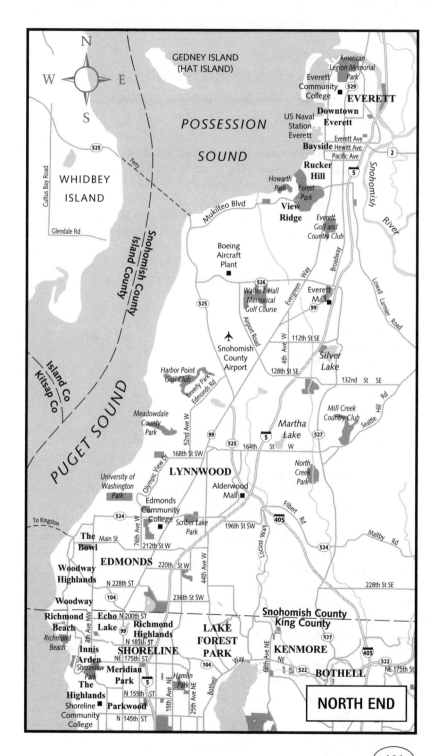

N

W · E

S

GEDNEY ISLAND
(HAT ISLAND)

POSSESSION

SOUND

WHIDBEY
ISLAND

525

Ferry

Cultus Bay Road

Glendale Rd

Snohomish County
Island County

Island Co
Kitsap Co

PUGET SOUND

American
Legion Memorial
Park

Everett
Community
College

529

EVERETT

Downtown
Everett

US Naval
Station
Everett

Everett Ave

Bayside Hewitt Ave

Pacific Ave

2

Rucker
Hill

5

Howarth
Park

Forest
Park

View
Ridge

Everett
Golf and
Country Club

Snohomish
River

Lowell Larimer Road

Mukilteo Blvd

Boeing
Aircraft
Plant

Evergreen Way

Broadway

526

Walter E Hall
Memorial
Golf Course

525

Everett
Mall

99

Airport Road

4th Ave W

112th St SE

Snohomish
County
Airport

128th St SE

Silver
Lake

132nd St SE

Harbor Point
Golf Club

Beverly Park
Edmonds Rd

Mill Creek
Country Club

Seattle Hill Rd

Meadowdale
County
Park

52nd Ave W

99

525

164th St W

Martha
Lake

527

168th St SW

Olympic View Dr

LYNNWOOD

Alderwood
Mall

North
Creek
Park

University of
Washington
Park

Edmonds
Community
College

Scriber Lake
Park

196th St SW

Filbert Rd

405

Maltby Rd

To Kingston

524

76th Ave W

Main St

212th St W

The
Bowl

EDMONDS

220th St W

44th Ave W

Locust Way

524

228th SE

Woodway
Highlands

N 228th ST

236th St SW

Woodway

104

Richmond
Beach

8th Ave NW

Echo
Lake

99

Richmond
Highlands

N 200th ST

Snohomish County
King County

228th St SE

Richmond
Beach

N 185th ST

LAKE
FOREST
PARK

KENMORE
NE

527

Innis
Arden

Shoreview
Park

NE 175th ST

SHORELINE

104

68th Ave NE

522

405

522

The
Highlands

Meridian
Park

5

Hamlin
Park

Bothell Way

BOTHELL

NE 175th St

Shoreline
Community
College

Parkwood

N 155th ST

N 145th ST

15th Ave NE

25th Ave NE

NORTH END

NORTHERN COMMUNITIES—KING COUNTY

Shoreline, Lake Forest Park, Bothell, Kenmore

The communities north of Seattle are often collectively referred to as the "North End." For the most part, homes in these cities are more affordable than in Seattle or the Eastside. The North End is popular with Boeing employees who commute to Everett, and with first-time homebuyers looking for less expensive housing than what can be found in Seattle. The North End is varied; with charming seaside communities like Edmonds just a few miles away from high-tech suburbs like Lake Forest Park.

SHORELINE

RICHMOND BEACH
INNIS ARDEN
THE HIGHLANDS
RICHMOND HIGHLANDS
ECHO LAKE
MERIDIAN PARK
PARKWOOD

Shoreline, home to over 53,000, is a growing community just north of Seattle. Known for its excellent schools and affordable contemporary homes, Shoreline is popular with young families increasingly priced out of Seattle and the Eastside. Before becoming a city in 1995, Shoreline was an unincorporated region of King County. It is surrounded by Edmonds and Woodway to the north, Lake Forest Park to the east, and Seattle to the south.

As its name implies, the city hugs the Puget Sound shoreline, offering spectacular sound and mountain views from expensive waterfront homes. Further inland, local architecture is best described as a mix of older split-levels, colonials, mid-century ramblers, and modern new construction. As you travel east toward I-5, homes in Shoreline become even more affordable. Neighborhoods east of Aurora Avenue offer smaller fixer-uppers and rental homes. Generally, home prices in Shoreline range from just under $200,000 to close to $400,000, depending on the neighborhood. Exceptions include **Richmond Beach**, in the northwest corner of the city, where most homes cost between $450,000 and $550,000, with view properties costing even more. Lots here are larger than those in Seattle, and charm and privacy are abundant. Not surprisingly, there is little turnover. The same is true for upscale **Innis Arden**, just south of Richmond Beach. Residents here are working and retired professionals who value the protections of covenant communities and the generous greenbelt. Lots are spacious and housing prices begin around the half-million-dollar mark. South of Innis Arden is **The Highlands**, where some of Seattle's wealthiest families have lived since the turn of the century. The gated waterfront/golf-course community is filled with multi-million-dollar mansions and sprawling estates. Some of the region's most incredible sound and mountain views are from the homes in this exclusive community.

A good bet for newcomers seeking moderately priced housing is the central Shoreline area, which includes the **Richmond Highlands, Echo Lake, Meridian Park,** and **Parkwood** neighborhoods. Situated between Aurora Avenue and I-5, these communities offer affordable homes typically built during the 1920s to 1930s, or during the post-World War II expansion of the 1950s and '60s. Many have been painstakingly restored or remodeled, but others could use a little tlc.

Shoreline boasts one of the region's most popular two-year colleges: Shoreline Community College, at Greenwood Avenue North and Arden Way, just east of The Highlands. About 14,000 students attend the college, with 10,000 pursuing degrees and 4,000 continuing their education in non-credit courses.

Shoreline doesn't really have a city center, but Aurora Avenue North's sprawling commercial district cuts through the city and offers ample opportunities for commerce, including Sears at North 155th Street, Fred Meyer and QFC at North 185th Street, and Home Depot and Costco at North 205th Street.

Just 15 miles north of downtown Seattle, Shoreline offers a relatively easy commute to the city. Both I-5 and Highway 99 connect Shoreline and Seattle, so drivers have two options when traveling between the two cities. An average commute takes about 20 minutes.

Web Site: www.cityofshoreline.com
Area Code: 206
Zip Codes: 98133, 98155, 98177
Post Office: Bitter Lake Station, 929 North 145th Street, Seattle; Gateway QFC Contract Station, 18300 Midvale Avenue North, Shoreline; North City Branch, 17233 15th Avenue NE, Shoreline; Richmond Beach Foods Contract Station, 2002 NW 196th Street, Shoreline; 800-275-8777, www.usps.com
Libraries: Richmond Beach Library, 19601 21st Avenue NW, Shoreline, 206-546-3522; Shoreline Library, 345 NE 175th, 206-362-7550, Shoreline, www.kcls.org
Public Schools: Shoreline School District, 18560 1st Avenue NE, Shoreline, 206-361-4412, 206-418-3386, www.shorelineschools.org

Police: Shoreline Police Station, 1206 North 185th Street, 206-546-6730; Eastside Police Center, 521 NE 165th Street, 206-363-8424; Westside Police Center, 630 NW Richmond Beach Road, 206-546-3636, www.cityofshoreline.com

Emergency Hospital: Northwest Hospital, 1550 North 115th Street, Seattle, 206-364-0500, www.nwhospital.org

Community Resources: Center for Human Services, 17018 15th Avenue NE, 206-362-7282 (Voice/TDD), www.chs-nw.org; Richmond Highlands Recreation Center, 16554 Fremont Avenue North, 206-542-6511; Shoreline Community College, 16101 Greenwood Avenue North, 206-546-4101, www.shoreline.ctc.edu; Shoreline-Lake Forest Park Arts Council, P.O. Box 55304, 206-542-6511, www.slfparts.org; YMCA, 1220 NE 175th Street, 206-364-1700, www.seattleymca.org

Public Transportation: Metro Transit, 206-553-3000, www.transit.metrokc.gov

5: Downtown/Fremont/Greenwood/Northgate/Shoreline

342: Shoreline/Aurora Village/Lake Forest Park/Kenmore/Bothell/Kingsgate/Bellevue/Newport Hills/Kennydale/Renton

355: Downtown/University District/Greenwood/Shoreline

LAKE FOREST PARK

Lake Forest Park, located north of Seattle and east of Shoreline, is a small community of approximately 13,000 residents. It has a mix of contemporary single-family homes on large lots, with a median home price of about $225,000. People choose Lake Forest Park as much for its lack of excitement as for its tree-covered hillsides. This is a quiet place, where kids play in the street and residents are surprised when they don't run into a friend or acquaintance at the grocery store.

The city's social and commercial center is the Lake Forest Park Towne Center, near the intersection of Bothell Way NE and Ballinger Way NE. The strip mall's newest addition is Third Place Books, a huge retail space that combines books, food, and entertainment. The bookstore is also home to the Northshore branch of Shoreline Community College.

Web Site: www.cityoflfp.com

Area Code: 206

Zip Codes: 98155

Post Office: 17233 15th Avenue NE, Seattle, 800-275-8777, www.usps.com

Libraries: 17171 Bothell Way NE, 206-362-8860

Public Schools: Shoreline School District, 18560 1st Avenue NE, Shoreline, 206-361-4412, 206-418-3386, www.shorelineschools.org

Police: 20150 45th Avenue NE, 206-364-8216, www.cityoflfp.com

Emergency Hospital: Northwest Hospital, 1550 North 115th Street, 206-364-0500, www.nwhospital.org

Community Resources: Lake Forest Park Stewardship Foundation, 17171 Bothell Way NE, 206-361-7076, www.lfpsf.org; Shoreline Community College/Northshore Center, 17171 Bothell Way NE, 206-306-1112, www.elmo.shore.ctc.edu/northshore; Shoreline-Lake Forest Park Senior Center, 18560 1st Avenue NE, Shoreline, 206-365-1536; Third Place Commons, 17171 Bothell Way NE, 206-366-3302, www.thirdplacecommons.org; YMCA, 1220 NE 175th Street, Shoreline, 206-364-1700, www.seattleymca.org

Public Transportation: Metro Transit, 206-553-3000, www.transit.metrokc.gov

308: Downtown Seattle/Jackson Park/Lake City/Lake Forest Park

314: Lake Forest Park/North City/Richmond Highlands/Shoreline

BOTHELL, KENMORE

Bothell is no longer just a bedroom community for Seattle and Eastside employees. More than 20,000 people now work in Bothell, instead of commuting to jobs in other areas. Major employers include high-tech, communications, medical equipment companies, and a regional University of Washington campus. Located just 12 miles north of Seattle, the city is home to about 30,000 residents. It straddles both King and Snohomish counties.

With median home prices of about $225,000, the city is a popular choice for young families and early career professionals. Though the city has grown considerably in the past decade, it retains a friendly downtown core that revolves around sleepy Main Street. Here you'll find cozy cafes and restaurants, plus furniture, retail, and antique stores. Another popular spot with residents is Bothell Landing, at 9919 NE 180th Street, just south of the city center. The site features playground equipment, a pedestrian bridge to the Sammamish River Trail, fishing, and small-boat mooring. It is also the site of the city's first schoolhouse and a log cabin.

West of Bothell is **Kenmore**. Incorporated in 1998, Kenmore is a fledgling city, about half the size and population of Bothell. Housing options include spacious homes overlooking Lake Washington, as well as more modest dwellings, some along partially forested hills. Housing prices are comparable to those in Bothell, making it a good bet for first time homebuyers. Key to the city's future is a proposed development called Lakepointe, a 45-acre site at the northeast end of Lake Washington, which would include 1,200 condos, a marina, a lakefront park, pedestrian walkways, an amphitheater and 600,000 square feet of commercial space. In January 2002, the project's development partnership dissolved because of concerns about the economy. According to the City of Kenmore, the property owner is still committed to completing the project, but for now, plans are on hold.

Web Sites: www.ci.bothell.wa.us; www.cityofkenmore.com
Area Code: 425
Zip Codes: 98011, 98012, 98021, 98028, 98041, 98082
Post Office: Bothell Main Office, 10500 Beardslee Boulevard, Bothell; Kenmore Branch, 6513 NE 181st, Kenmore, 800-275-8777, www.usps.com
Libraries: Bothell Library, 18215 98th Avenue NE, Bothell, 425-486-7811, 425-402-7071 (TTY); Kenmore Library, 18138 73rd NE, Kenmore, 425-486-8747, www.kcls.org
Public Schools: Northshore School District, 18315 Bothell Way NE, Bothell, 425-489-6000, www.nsd.org
Police: 18410 101st Avenue NE, Bothell, 425-486-1254, www.ci.bothell.wa.us; 18118 73rd Avenue NE, Kenmore, 206-296-4480, www.metrokc.gov/sheriff
Emergency Hospital: Northwest Hospital, 1550 North 115th Street, Seattle, 206-364-0500, www.nwhospital.org
Community Resources: Bothell Historical Museum, 9919 NE 180th Street, Bothell, 425-486-1889; Cascadia Community College, 18345 Campus Way NE, Bothell, 425-352-8000, www.cascadia.ctc.edu; Kenmore Heritage Society, 8124 NE 166th Street, Kenmore, 425-488-2818, www.scn.org/civic/kenmoreheritage; Northshore Chamber of Commerce, 18414 103rd Avenue NE, Suite A, Bothell, 425-486-1245, www.solveris.com/nshore; South Snohomish County Chamber of Commerce, 3500 188th Street SW, Suite 490, Lynnwood, 425-774-0507, www.sscchamber.org
Public Transportation: Metro Transit, 206-553-3000, www.transit.metrokc.gov
  234: Kenmore/Finn Hill/Juanita/Kirkland/Bellevue
  238: Kirkland/Rose Hill/Totem Lake/Kingsgate/Finn Hill/Bothell
  251: Kirkland/Redmond/Bear Creek/Cottage Lake/Woodinville/Bothell
  306: Downtown Seattle/Lake City/Kenmore
  341: Aurora Village/Lake Forest Park/Kenmore/Bothell

NORTHERN COMMUNITIES—SNOHOMISH COUNTY

Edmonds, Mountlake Terrace, Lynnwood, Everett

EDMONDS

THE BOWL
WOODWAY
WOODWAY HIGHLANDS

Edmonds, overlooking the Puget Sound just north of Seattle, is a peaceful village with a quaint shopping district. The Edmonds-Kingston Ferry Terminal, once the central attraction of the city, is now overshadowed by the popular downtown waterfront amenities, including restaurants, chic clothing boutiques, and funky gift shops. While there is tremendous wealth in Edmonds, you have to look hard to find it. This is a decidedly low-key community where residents are friendly and unpretentious, and consider Edmonds the gem of the Puget Sound.

The neighborhood that encompasses downtown and the surrounding hillside is **The Bowl**. The architecture here is varied, with a mix of Victorian homes, small bungalows, new condominiums, and older apartment buildings. Houses are staggered along the hillside for optimal views, and housing prices often depend on how much of the mountains and water you can glimpse—median price in 2001 was close to $370,000. Most city services are located right in downtown Edmonds, including the police and fire stations, civic center, city hall and museum. Condos are abundant in downtown Edmonds. Many are occupied by snowbirds who spend the spring and summer in the Northwest, and fly to warmer climes for fall and winter.

South of downtown is the community of **Woodway**, a secluded, woodsy neighborhood of expensive homes on large lots—one to five acres, due to the restrictions on short-platting here. Home prices range from $800,000 to two million. Also in Woodway is one of Edmonds' only planned communities, **Woodway Highlands**, which is similar to new developments on the Eastside: large homes nestled close together.

Web Site: www.ci.edmonds.wa.us
Area Code: 425
Zip Codes: 98020, 98026
Post Office: 201 Main Street, 800-275-8777, www.usps.com
Libraries: 650 Main Street, 425-771-1933, www.sno-isle.org
Public Schools: Edmonds School District, 20420 68th Avenue West, Lynnwood, 425-670-7000, www.edmonds.wednet.edu

Police: 250 5th Avenue North, 425-771-0200, www.ci.edmonds.wa.us

Emergency Hospital: Stevens Memorial Hospital, 21601 76th Avenue West, Edmonds, 425-640-4000, www.stevenshealthcare.org

Community Resources: Edmonds Art Commission, 700 Main Street, 425-771-0228, www.ci.edmonds.wa.us/artscomm; Edmonds Chamber of Commerce, 121 5th Avenue North, 425-670-1496, www.edmondswa.com/Chamber; Edmonds Community College, 20000 68th Avenue West, 425-640-1459, www.edcc.edu; Frances Anderson Cultural and Leisure Center, 700 Main Street, 425-771-0230, www.ci.edmonds.wa.us; South County Senior Center, 220 Railroad Avenue, 425-774-5555, www.ci.edmonds.wa.us/senior

Public Transportation: Community Transit, 425-353-RIDE, 800-562-1375, www.commtrans.org

110: Lynnwood/Edmonds

140: Edmonds/Mountlake Terrace/Lynnwood

180: Edmonds/Lynnwood

630: Lynnwood/Mountlake Terrace/Aurora Village/Edmonds

MOUNTLAKE TERRACE

Like Lake Forest Park in King County, Mountlake Terrace (pronounced Mont-lake) has a mix of contemporary single-family homes on large lots. This is a family-oriented community, with some of the city's most popular attractions revolving around children and recreation: Lake Ballinger is flanked by golf courses, and features a boat ramp and fishing pier; the city's public pavilion includes a swimming pool, racquetball courts, a weight room and a preschool facility; next to the pavilion are outdoor playing fields, tennis courts and a park.

When you consider the city's kid-friendly attitude and its median home price, which lingers well below $200,000, it's easy to understand why Mountlake Terrace is a good choice for young families. Major employers include Blue Cross of Washington and Alaska, and the Edmonds School District.

Web Site: www.ci.mountlake-terrace.wa.us

Area Code: 425

Zip Codes: 98043

Post Office: 6817 208th Street SW, Lynnwood, 800-275-8777, www.usps.com

Libraries: 23300 58th Avenue West, 425-776-8722, www.sno-isle.org

Public Schools: Edmonds School District, 20420 68th Avenue West, Lynnwood, 425-670-7000, www.edmonds.wednet.edu

Police: 5906 232nd Street SW, 425-670-8260, www.ci.mountlake-ter-race.wa.us

Emergency Hospital: Stevens Memorial Hospital, 21601 76th Avenue West, Edmonds, 425-640-4000, www.stevenshealthcare.org

Community Resources: Edmonds Community College, 20000 68th Avenue West, Lynnwood, 425-640-1459, www.edcc.edu; Mountlake Terrace Historical Committee, www.snonet.org/loscho/mlthc; South Snohomish County Chamber of Commerce, 3500 188th Street SW, 425-774-0507, www.sscchamber.org

Public Transportation: Community Transit, 425-353-RIDE, 800-562-1375, www.commtrans.org
167: Mountlake Terrace/Lynnwood

LYNNWOOD

For those who live outside it, Lynnwood is best known as the home of Alderwood Mall. But, if you can get beyond the sprawling shopping center and surrounding strip malls, you may find a gem of a home in the residential areas of Lynnwood. Tranquil suburban streets with modest affordable homes make Lynnwood the choice of many middle-income families and first-time homebuyers. Most residents either work in one of the community's numerous retail outlets, or commute south to Seattle or north to Everett. Lynwood's proximity to major thoroughfares, including I-5 and Highway 99, is advantageous for commuters.

Though about mid-way between Seattle and Everett, Lynnwood's residents generally turn to Seattle for attractions not found in their community. A few years ago, the city tried to pass a regional arts center bond request, but the initiative failed. City leaders plan to try again in a future election.

In Lynnwood, you can still find homes for less than $250,000, though they don't linger on the market. There is a pleasant mix of older construction and new developments, plus numerous condominiums and apartments, particularly near Edmonds Community College, which is located in Lynnwood. The city has done a good job of preserving open space, in the form of small neighborhood parks.

Web Site: www.ci.lynnwood.wa.us
Area Code: 425
Zip Codes: 98036, 98037, 98046
Post Office: 6817 208th Street SW; 3715 196th Street SW, Suite A; 800-275-8777, www.usps.com
Libraries: 19200 44th Avenue West, 425-778-2148, www.sno-isle.org

Public Schools: Edmonds School District, 20420 68th Avenue West, Lynnwood, 425-670-7000, www.edmonds.wednet.edu

Police: 19321 44th Avenue West, 425-744-6900, www.ci.lynnwood.wa.us

Emergency Hospital: Stevens Memorial Hospital, 21601 76th Avenue West, Edmonds, 425-640-4000, www.stevenshealthcare.org

Community Resources: Recreation Center, 18900 44th Avenue West, 425-771-4030, www.ci.lynnwood.wa.us; Senior Center, 5800 198th Street SW, 425-744-6464, www.ci.lynnwood.wa.us; South Snohomish County Chamber of Commerce, 3500 188th Street SW, Suite 490, Lynnwood, 425-774-0507, www.sscchamber.org

Public Transportation: Community Transit, 425-353-RIDE, 800-562-1375, www.commtrans.org

110: Lynnwood/Edmonds
120: Lynnwood/Bothell
140: Edmonds/Mountlake Terrace/Lynnwood
160: Lynnwood/Mill Creek
167: Mountlake Terrace/Lynnwood
170: Lynnwood/Mukilteo Ferry Terminal
180: Edmonds/Lynnwood
630: Lynnwood/Mountlake Terrace/Aurora Village/Edmonds

EVERETT

BAYSIDE
DOWNTOWN
RUCKER HILL
VIEW RIDGE
THE PRESERVE

Everett, a large city about forty minutes north of Seattle, was established in the late 1800s to support the infamous Monte Cristo gold mines. Although the mines never produced the expected amount of gold, the city continued as an industrial center. Today, Boeing and Naval Station Everett are the primary employers in Everett, although many other companies, including a sawmill, are also located here. As with Seattle, many distinct neighborhoods exist in Everett, each worth exploring if you are considering making your home here.

Broadway divides Everett into western and eastern halves, and is the city's major north-south thoroughfare. In the northern end of the city, west of Broadway, you'll find **Bayside**, a classic Everett neighborhood of turn-of-the-century homes, some with fantastic views of Possession Sound, the naval station, and the marina. Many of the houses here are handed down from generation to generation but when they do come on the market, they are usually more affordable than the Craftsman and Victorian homes for sale in Seattle's view neighborhoods. As you travel south along Marine View Drive toward downtown Everett, you'll find that many of these historic homes have been turned into multi-family rental units.

To fill Everett's growing need for affordable housing, a number of developers are constructing new condominiums in **Downtown** Everett. These new dwellings offer proximity to law firms, banks, and government buildings, some shops and restaurants, historic theatres, and the city's performing arts center. With its nine to five hours and a less-than-exciting reputation, city planners are working to overhaul Everett's sleepy downtown. Projects include building an 8,200 seat arena and adding pedestrian-friendly sidewalks to Hewitt Avenue. While the city's waterfront district lacks housing options, it does feature a small shopping center, a hotel, a marina, and the Everett Yacht Club.

Though Everett certainly claims its share of view properties and esteemed neighborhoods, newcomers will find a good selection of quiet, comfortable areas with affordable houses. **Rucker Hill** and **View Ridge** are attractive neighborhoods with many view homes and nearby parks. Houses are priced from about $350,000. **The Preserve** is a new community, complete with sidewalks and underground power lines; prices start at just under $300,000.

It is unlikely that you will choose to commute from Everett to Seattle each day, but if your job takes you north of Seattle or if you plan to work from home and want a little more bang for your buck, Everett is worth considering. The city offers many of the same attractions as Seattle, including performing arts, sporting events, a shopping mall, and popular city parks.

Web Site: www.everettwa.org
Area Code: 425
Zip Codes: 98201, 98203, 98204, 98205, 98206, 98207, 98208
Post Office: 3102 Hoyt Avenue, 800-275-8777, www.usps.com
Libraries: 2702 Hoyt Avenue, 425-257-8000, 9512 Evergreen Way, 425-257-8250, www.epls.org
Public Schools: Everett Public Schools, 4730 Colby Avenue, 425-745-1993, www.everett.k12.wa.us
Police: 3002 Wetmore Avenue, 425-257-8400, www.everettwa.org
Emergency Hospital: Providence Everett Medical Center, 1321 Colby Avenue, 425-261-2000; www.providence.org/everett
Community Resources: Boeing Everett Tour Center, 800-464-1476, www.boeing.com; The Children's Museum in Snohomish County, 3013 Colby Avenue, 425-258-1006, www.childs-museum.org; Downtown Everett Association, P.O. Box 5267, Everett, 98206,

info@downtowneverett.org, www.downtowneverett.com; Everett Area Chamber of Commerce, 11400 Airport Road, 425-438-1487, www.sno-biz.org; Everett Center for the Arts at Monte Cristo, 1507 Wall Street, 425-257-8380, www.everettwa.org; Everett Community College, 2000 Tower Street, 425-388-9100, www.evcc.ctc.edu; Everett Performing Arts Center, 2710 Wetmore Avenue, 425-257-8600, www.everettwa.org; Port of Everett, P.O. Box 538, Everett, 98206, 800-729-7678, www.portofeverett.com

Public Transportation: Community Transit, 425-353-RIDE, 800-562-1375, www.commtrans.org

210: Everett/Marysville/Arlington
280: Everett/Lake Stevens/Granite Falls
610: Aurora Village/Mountlake Terrace/Edmonds/Lynnwood/Everett
620: Aurora Village/Mountlake Terrace/Edmonds/Lynnwood/Everett
621: Aurora Village/Mountlake Terrace/Edmonds/Lynnwood/Everett
720: Everett/Snohomish/Monroe/Sultan/Gold Bar

WESTERN COMMUNITIES—KITSAP COUNTY

BAINBRIDGE ISLAND

WINSLOW

As Seattle residents search out alternatives to the bustle of living in the city, Bainbridge Island becomes more popular. A 30-minute ferry ride from the Seattle waterfront, Bainbridge Island is a community of lawyers, doctors, successful artisans, and architects, and others, many of them ex-Seattleites.

At just under 28 square miles, the island is comparable in size to Manhattan, but residents and real estate agents say it more closely resembles the idyllic California seaside communities of Sausalito or La Jolla. Many homes on the island have stunning views of the Puget Sound or the distant Seattle skyline, and as in any community with a good location and spectacular views, housing prices can be steep. Most homes on Bainbridge fall into the $325,000 to $450,000 range, and the housing market remains strong. Rentals are scarce, except for seasonal accommodations during the summer months.

The **Winslow** neighborhood, adjacent to the ferry terminal, is the current hot spot, offering shops, restaurants and the island's few condominiums. The community resembles Seattle's Madison Park neighborhood, with its spectacular water views and upscale boutiques. The neighborhood is popular with young professionals, who commute to the city and appreciate the short walk to the ferry terminal. Winslow is also where you'll find the island's only movie theater.

Despite its explosive growth, Bainbridge Island has managed to hang on to its rural feel, with abundant trees, parks, ponds, and beaches. Equestrian trails wind through the community, and many of the island's kids take riding lessons in addition to golf and swimming instruction. Like Mercer Island to the east of Seattle, Bainbridge is known for its excellent schools. The island also offers golf and country clubs, quaint restaurants and homey bed and breakfast inns.

So what are the drawbacks? Cell phone reception can be iffy on Bainbridge, island kids may suffer from a bit of pre-adolescent claustrophobia, and residents are dependent on the state ferry system. But, with Seattle's heavy traffic, Bainbridge Islanders are happy to forgo the messy daily grind of the Seattle's expressways. In emergency situations, island patients are airlifted to Seattle's Harborview Medical Center in minutes.

Web Site: www.ci.bainbridge-isl.wa.us

Area Code: 206

Zip Codes: 98110

Post Office: 10355 NE Valley Road, 800-275-8777, www.usps.com

Libraries: 1270 Madison Avenue North, 206-842-4162, www.krl.org

Public Schools: Bainbridge Island School District, 8489 Madison Avenue NE, 206-842-4714, www.bainbridge.wednet.edu

Police: 625 Winslow Way East, 206-842-5211, www.ci.bainbridge-isl.wa.us

Emergency Hospital: Harborview Medical Center, 325 9th Avenue, 206-731-3074, www.washington.edu/medical/hmc

Community Resources: Bainbridge Island Chamber of Commerce, 590 Winslow Way East, 206-842-3700, www.bainbridgechamber.com; Bainbridge Island Racquet Club, 8520 Renny Lane NE, 206-842-5661; Bainbridge Island Senior Center, 370 Brien Drive, 206-842-1616, www.bainbridgeseniors.org; Wing Point Golf & Country Club, 811 Cherry Avenue, 206-842-2688, www.wingpointgolf.com

Public Transportation: Washington State Ferries, 206-464-6400, 888-808-7977, www.wsdot.wa.gov/ferries

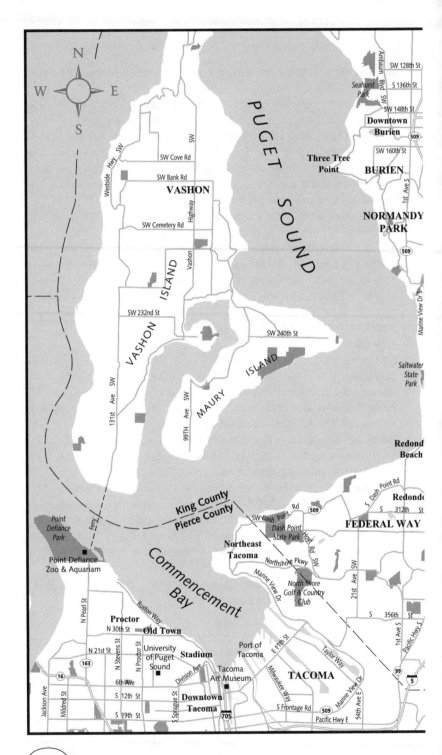

N
W E
S

SW 128th St
S 136th St
Seahurst Park
SW 148th St

Downtown Burien 509

Three Tree Point
SW 160th St
BURIEN

1st Ave S

NORMANDY PARK
509

Ambaum Blvd SW

Marine View Dr SW

PUGET SOUND

Westside Hwy SW

SW Cove Rd

SW Bank Rd

VASHON

Vashon Highway

SW Cemetery Rd

SW

VASHON ISLAND

SW 232nd St

SW 240th St

131st Ave SW

99TH Ave SW

MAURY ISLAND

Saltwater State Park

Redond Beach

Dash Point Rd

509

S Dash Point Rd
Redondo
S 312th St

King County
Pierce County

SW Dash Point Rd
Dash Point State Park

FEDERAL WAY

Hoyt Rd SW

21st Ave SW

Ferry

Point Defiance Park

Point Defiance Zoo & Aquarium

Commencement Bay

Northeast Tacoma

Northshore Pkwy

Marine View Dr

North Shore Golf & Country Club

S 356th St

1st Ave S

Pacific Hwy S

N Pearl St

Ruston Way

Proctor
N 30th St
Old Town

N 21st St

N Stevens St
N Proctor St

University of Puget Sound
Stadium

Division Ave

Port of Tacoma

E 11th St

Milwaukee Way

Taylor Way

TACOMA

Marine View Dr E

54th Ave E

99

5

16
163
6th Ave

S 12th St

S Sprague St

Tacoma Art Museum

Downtown Tacoma
705

Jackson Ave
Mildred St
S 19th St

S Frontage Rd

509 Marine View Dr E
Pacific Hwy E

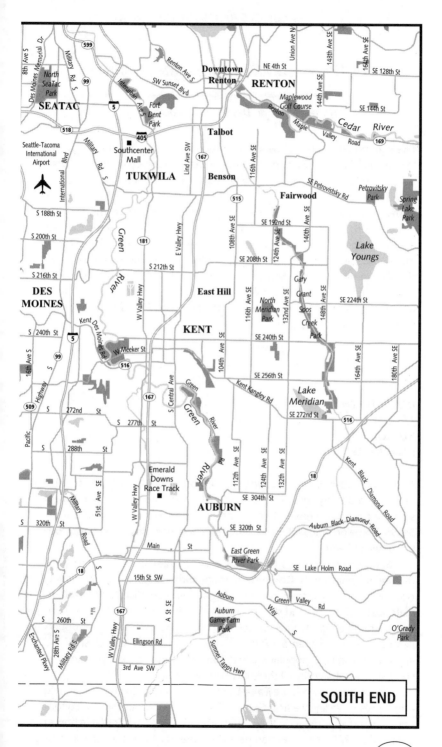

SEATAC

North
SeaTac
Park

Seattle-Tacoma
International
Airport

Downtown
Renton

RENTON

Maplewood
Golf Course

Cedar River

Talbot

Southcenter
Mall

TUKWILA

Benson

Fairwood

Petrovitsky
Park

Spring
Lake
Park

East Hill

Gary
Grant
Soos
Creek
Park

North
Meridian
Park

Lake
Youngs

DES
MOINES

KENT

Lake
Meridian

Emerald
Downs
Race Track

AUBURN

East Green
River Park

Auburn
Game Farm
Park

O'Grady
Park

Ellington Rd

SOUTH END

SOUTHERN COMMUNITIES—KING COUNTY

Renton, Kent, Burien, SeaTac, Tukwila,
Normandy Park, Des Moines, Federal Way

The communities south of Seattle are often collectively referred to as the "South End." For the most part, homes in these cities are more affordable than in Seattle or the Eastside. Many years ago, the common perception was that these areas were less desirable because they were further away from big city attractions like professional sports, theater, museums, and fine dining. Today, however, many of these communities have revitalized downtown cores, complete with nice restaurants and evening entertainment, and are increasingly attracting singles, couples, and young professionals and their families. Many neighborhoods to the west offer fantastic views of the sound and mountains, and most have thriving shopping centers. Today, the remaining drawback to the South End is airplane noise from nearby Sea-Tac Airport.

RENTON

DOWNTOWN
TALBOT
BENSON
FAIRWOOD

At the south end of Lake Washington, Renton, traditionally home to middle-income Boeing employees and a healthy working class population, is slowly attracting a crowd of young professionals. For the price of a small Seattle home on a tiny lot, prospective homeowners can buy a large, modern home in Renton.

Shopping centers or small business districts anchor most of Renton's mature neighborhoods. **Downtown**, mom-and-pop stores and restaurants occupy historic brick structures, while large chain stores like Wal-Mart dominate vast parking lots and strip malls. Housing here is limited to small bungalows, ramblers, and rental houses, and home prices are low. Fixer-uppers can be had for less than $200,000. Downtown residents are close to the city's main library, a popular walking trail along the Cedar River, and the sport stadium shared by all three city high schools.

Above downtown is the **Talbot** or **Benson** area, which is popular with employees of Valley Medical Center. There is a good selection of condominiums and apartments in this neighborhood, as well as affordable homes built in the 1980s. New developments here are small because they are limited by the hillside and I-405. Houses here start around $250,000, and some have views of downtown.

Fairwood is an established, up-scale community that revolves around the Fairwood Golf and Country Club. Built in the late 1960s and early 1970s, the neighborhood is a mix of colonials, brick ramblers, and contemporary homes. In most of the neighborhood, power lines are hidden underground, and many of the houses abut the golf course.

New housing developments began to spring up around Renton in the early 1990s. With names like Summerwind, The Orchards, Windwood, and Stonegate, they feature large homes in safe communities. There are houses in just about every price range, from $250,000 to half a million dollars, depending on construction, views, and lot size.

Web Site: www.ci.renton.wa.us

Area Code: 425

Zip Codes: 98055, 98056, 98057, 98058, 98059

Post Office: 17200 116th Avenue SE; 314 Williams Avenue South; 4301 NE 4th Street, 800-275-8777, www.usps.com

Libraries: 17009 140th SE, 425-226-0522, www.kcls.org;

Public Schools: Renton School District, 300 SW 7th Street, 425-204-2300, www.renton.wednet.edu

Police: 1055 South Grady Way, 425-430-7500, www.ci.renton.wa.us

Emergency Hospital: Valley Medical Center, 400 South 43rd Street, Renton, 425-228-3450, www.valleymed.org

Community Resources: Greater Renton Chamber of Commerce, 300 Rainier Avenue North, 425-226-4560, www.renton-chamber.com; Renton Community Center, 1715 Maple Valley Highway, 425-430-6700; Renton Community Foundation, 300 Rainier Avenue North, 425-235-2356, www.rentonfoundation.org; Renton Historical Museum, 235 Mill Avenue South, 425-255-2330; Renton Senior Activity Center, 211 Burnett Avenue North, 425-430-6633; Renton Technical College, 3000 NE 4th Street, 425-235-2352, www.renton-tc.ctc.edu

Public Transportation: Metro Transit, 206-553-3000, www.transit.metrokc.gov

101: Downtown Seattle/SODO/Renton

105: Renton Transit Center/Renton Technical College/Renton Highlands

106: Downtown Seattle/SODO/Rainier Beach/Skyway/Renton

107: Rainier Beach/Lake Ridge/Bryn Mawr/Renton

110: Southwest Renton/South Gate/FAA/Renton Transit Center/Renton Boeing/Paccar-Kenworth/North Renton

140: Burien/Sea-Tac Airport/Southcenter/Renton

148: Renton Transit Center/South Renton Park & Ride/Royal Hills/Fairwood
149: Renton/Maple Valley/Black Diamond
153: Kent/Renton
155: Fairwood/Cascade Vista/Valley Medical Center/Southcenter
169: Renton/Kent
240: Bellevue/Factoria/Newcastle/Renton
280: (Night Owl) Renton/Tukwila/Downtown Seattle/Bellevue
342: Shoreline/Aurora Village/Lake Forest Park/Kenmore/Bothell/Kingsgate/Kirkland/Bellevue/Newport Hills/Kennydale/Renton

KENT

EAST HILL

Formerly a rich agricultural valley, Kent today is one of the country's busiest distribution centers. It is the fourth-largest city in King County and the 10th largest in the state, and it's growing.

There is an abundance of designated parks and green space in Kent, ranging in size from the one-tenth of an acre, Gowe Street Mini Park (Kennebeck Avenue and Titus Street), to the 310-acre Green River Natural Resources Area, a wetland and wildlife refuge at 22000 Russell Road in the Kent Valley. The Green River Trail, a popular path for walking, running and biking, follows the east bank of the river from south Seattle through Kent and on into Auburn.

In Kent, renters outnumber homeowners, nearly two to one. There are dozens of multiple-family housing units, particularly on its **East Hill**, which is home to many strip malls and fast-food restaurants. Traffic in the teeming East Hill area is a constant challenge, as commuters headed toward Tacoma, Seattle, and Everett converge on the arterials and freeways.

This is a popular community for first-time homebuyers looking for new construction. The median home price in spring of 2002 barely brushed $200,000, making Kent one of the most affordable cities in the greater Seattle area. Likewise, apartments here are reasonably priced, averaging less than $800 per month.

Web Site: www.ci.kent.wa.us
Area Code: 253
Zip Codes: 98031, 98032, 98035, 98046, 98064
Post Office: 10612 SE 240th, 800-275-8777, www.usps.com
Libraries: 212 2nd Avenue North, 253-859-3330, 253-854-1050 (TTY), www.kcls.org

Public Schools: Kent School District, 12033 SE 256th Street, 253-373-7000, www.kent.wednet.edu

Police: 220 4th Avenue South, 253-856-5800, www.ci.kent.wa.us

Emergency Hospital: Valley Medical Center, 400 South 43rd Street, Renton, 425-228-3450, www.valleymed.org

Community Resources: Kent Chamber of Commerce, 524 West Meeker Street, Suite 1, 253-854-1770, www.kentchamber.com; Kent Commons, 525 4th Avenue North, 253-856-5000, www.ci.kent.wa.us; Resource Center, 315 East Meeker Street, 253-856-5030, www.ci.kent.wa.us; Senior Activity Center, 600 East Smith Street, 253-856-5150, www.ci.kent.wa.us

Public Transportation: Metro Transit, 206-553-3000, www.transit.metrokc.gov

153: Kent/Renton

158: Downtown Seattle/Kent

159: Downtown Seattle/Kent

160: Downtown Seattle/Tukwila/Kent

162: Downtown Seattle/Kent

163: Downtown Seattle/SODO/Tukwila/Kent

164: Kent/Green River Community College

166: Des Moines/Kent

168: Kent Transit Center/Lake Meridian Park & Ride/Timberlane

169: Renton/Kent

183: Federal Way/Kent

247: Redmond/Eastgate/Factoria/Newport Hills/Kennydale/Renton/Kent

BURIEN

DOWNTOWN
THREE TREE POINT

Like many south-end cities, Burien often hides its charms among strip malls and busy intersections. But, a closer look at this diverse community reveals sound and mountain views, saltwater beaches, affordable housing, and easy commutes to Seattle and Sea-Tac Airport. Burien is popular with medical professionals who work at Highline Community Hospital, pilots and flight attendants, and Weyerhaeuser employees.

The quickest route to Burien from downtown Seattle is Highway 509, a road much less traveled than the better-known I-5. Unfortunately, the route ends at the intersection of 1st Avenue South and Highway 518, a conglomeration of fast food restaurants and auto dealerships that doesn't give visitors a terribly good first impression of Burien. City planners are hoping to change that impression by renovating the downtown core with new sidewalks and a pedestrian-friendly town square.

Downtown Burien features a large park and community center, as well as a library and performing arts center. Rentals are plentiful in and around downtown, with a mix of old and new apartment buildings, condominiums and senior housing units. First-time homebuyers may be interested in areas east of downtown, like Chelsea Park, where post-World War II homes go for less than $200,000.

Three Tree Point is the jewel of Burien, an entirely residential neighborhood of artists, writers, doctors, and lawyers, among others, who seek privacy and spectacular Puget Sound views. The homes perched along the bluff and waterfront are varied, ranging from beach bungalows to turn-of-the-century farmhouses. The neighborhood is also popular with scuba divers who come to explore underwater shipwrecks, and hikers and history buffs, who climb the old Indian trail that winds up the hillside from the beach.

Web Site: www.ci.burien.wa.us

Area Code: 206

Zip Codes: 98146, 98148, 98166, 98168

Post Office: Burien Station, 609 SW 150th, Seattle; Seahurst Main Office, 2116 SW 52nd Street, Burien; 800-275-8777, www.usps.com

Libraries: 14700 6th Avenue SW, 206-243-3490, www.kcls.org

Public Schools: Highline School District, 15675 Ambaum Boulevard SW, 206-433-0111, www.hsd401.org

Police: 14905 6th Avenue SW, 206-296-3333, www.metrokc.gov/sheriff/city/burhome

Emergency Hospital: Highline Community Hospital, 16251 Sylvester Road SW, 206-244-9970, www.hchnet.org

Community Resources: Burien Community Center, 425 SW 144th Street, 206-988-3700; Burien Community Computer Center, 653 SW 152nd Street, 206-241-3551, www.burien.org; Burien Little Theatre, 206-242-5180, SW 146th and 4th Avenue South, www.burienlittletheatre.com; Southwest King County Chamber of Commerce, 16400 Southcenter Parkway #210, Tukwila, 206-575-1633, www.swkcc.org

Public Transportation: Metro Transit, 206-553-3000, www.transit.metrokc.gov

  133: University District/Burien

  135: Downtown Seattle/White Center/Burien

  136: Downtown Seattle/SODO/White Center/Burien

  137: Downtown Seattle/SODO/White Center/Burien

  139: Burien/Highline Community Hospital

  140: Burien/Sea-Tac Airport/Southcenter/Renton

SEATAC, TUKWILA

SeaTac (named for the Seattle Tacoma International Airport) is a modest middle-class suburb with pleasant and inexpensive contemporary homes. Airline and Boeing employees live in this area, but other local businesses employ many residents as well. SeaTac, and its neighbor, Tukwila, are subject to heavy airport noise. In fact, many homes have been vacated or torn down to make way for the airport's third runway. But, both communities enjoy a wealth of starter homes and apartments, and easy access to shopping and banking.

Tukwila is best known as the site of Southcenter Mall, (now officially known as the Westfield Shoppingtown Southcenter) a popular shopping center anchored by Nordstrom and The Bon Marché. There are numerous restaurant and strip malls surrounding Southcenter, and many industrial buildings. Because of the wealth of retail and industry, taxes in Tukwila are low, making the community attractive to young families and first-time homebuyers. Houses here range from $150,000 to $400,000.

The city of Tukwila provides a "welcome packet" on its web site at www.ci.tukwila.wa.us/infopack/welcome.

Web Site: www.seatac.wa.gov; www.ci.tukwila.wa.us
Area Code: 206
Zip Codes: 98108, 98138, 98148, 98158, 98168, 98178, 98188, 98198
Post Office: 15250 32nd Avenue South; 225 Andover Park West, 800-275-8777, www.usps.com
Libraries: 17850 Military Road South, 206-242-6044, 206-242-4335 (TTY); 4060 South 144th, 206-242-1640; 14475 59th South, 206-244-5140, www.kcls.org
Public Schools: Highline School District, 15675 Ambaum Boulevard SW, 206-433-0111, www.hsd401.org; Tukwila School District, 4640 South 144th Street, 206-901-8000, www.tukwila.wednet.edu
Police: 17900 International Boulevard, Suite 401, 206-241-9100, www.metrokc.gov/sheriff; 6200 Southcenter Boulevard, 206-433-1808, www.ci.tukwila.wa.us
Emergency Hospital: Highline Community Hospital, 12844 Military Road South, 206-248-4730, www.hchnet.org
Community Resources: North SeaTac Park Community Center, 13735 24th Avenue South, 206-439-9273; Southwest King County Chamber of Commerce, 16400 Southcenter Parkway #210, Tukwila, 206-575-1633, www.swkcc.org; Tukwila Community Center, 12424 42nd Avenue South, 206-768-2822, www.ci.tukwila.wa.us; Tukwila Golf Course, 13500 Interurban Avenue, 206-242-4221

Public Transportation: Metro Transit, 206-553-3000, www.transit. metrokc.gov

39: Downtown Seattle/SODO/Beacon Hill/Rainier Beach/Southcenter

124: Tukwila Park & Ride/Gateway Corporate Center/Allentown/ Tukwila/Southcenter

128: West Seattle/White Center/Southcenter

154: Tukwila/Kent/Auburn

155: Renton/Southcenter

NORMANDY PARK

About 20 miles south of Seattle is Normandy Park, a timeless seaside community between Burien and Des Moines. The city's location, small size, and reputable police force make it a popular choice with middle to upper income families and older residents. It lacks the suburban sprawl of other south end communities, and enjoys lots of green space and water views. There is little commerce here, however, so residents rely on nearby Burien or Des Moines.

As with any city situated on the water, Normandy Park offers a range of housing, from multi-million dollar estates with commanding views to large ramblers that sell for $300,000 to $500,000. Because lot and home sizes are larger here than in most Seattle suburbs, affording residents much treasured privacy, you won't find much for less than $300,000. Those lucky enough to land a beachfront home have access to The Cove, a parcel of jointly owned property that includes the beach, a playground, tennis and volleyball courts, and a community center. Beachfront property owners pay a small annual fee and split the property taxes for the privilege.

Normandy Park is known for its speeding restrictions, so if you come looking here, be sure to keep it to 25 miles per hour. The speed limit is in effect throughout the city, not just in the residential areas.

Web Site: www.ci.normandy-park.wa.us

Area Code: 206

Zip Codes: 98148, 98166, 98198

Post Office: 609 SW 150th Street, Seattle; 2003 South 216th Street, Des Moines, 800-275-8777, www.usps.com

Libraries: 21620 11th Avenue South, Des Moines, 206-824-6066, www.kcls.org

Public Schools: Highline School District, 15675 Ambaum Boulevard SW, Burien, 206-433-0111, www.hsd401.org

Police: 801 SW 174th Street, 206-248-7600, www.ci.normandy-park.wa.us

Emergency Hospital: Highline Community Hospital, 16251 Sylvester Road SW, Burien, 206-244-9970, www.hchnet.org
Community Resources: Des Moines Senior Center, 22030 Cliff Avenue South, Des Moines, 206-878-1642, www.ci.des-moines.wa.us; Normandy Park Community Club, 17655 12th Avenue SW, 206-242-3778

DES MOINES

Des Moines (pronounced De Moin) is a peaceful town located midway between Seattle and Tacoma. Marine View Drive, the primary artery through town, hugs the shoreline and meanders through the city's small commercial district.

Commerce revolves around the marina and waterfront, where a handful of seafood restaurants attract diners from all over the South End. The waterfront promenade is a safe and popular spot for walkers and runners. There is a dense concentration of condominiums near the Des Moines waterfront, many with gorgeous views. Like Edmonds to the north, Des Moines is popular with retirees who spend summers in the Northwest and escape to warmer climates during the winter.

Most homes in Des Moines are mature, comfortable ramblers and split levels built in the 1950s and later. There are small pockets of newer construction, but development is limited by geography. The South End's only co-op housing project is also located in Des Moines. The Seashore Club is a quaint cluster of 17 houses perched above the beach.

Web Site: www.ci.des-moines.wa.us
Area Code: 206
Zip Codes: 98148, 98198
Post Office: 2003 South 216th Street, 800-275-8777, www.usps.com
Libraries: 21620 11th Avenue South, 206-824-6066; 26809 Pacific Highway South, 253-839-0121, www.kcls.org
Public Schools: Highline School District, 15675 Ambaum Boulevard SW, Burien, 206-433-0111, www.hsd401.org
Police: www.ci.des-moines.wa.us
Emergency Hospital: Highline Community Hospital, 16251 Sylvester Road SW, Burien, 206-244-9970, www.hchnet.org
Community Resources: Des Moines Senior Center, 22030 Cliff Avenue South, 206-878-1642, www.ci.des-moines.wa.us; Greater Des Moines Chamber of Commerce, 206-878-7000; Mt. Rainier Pool, 22722 19th Avenue South, 206-296-4278, www.metrokc.gov/parks

Public Transportation: Metro Transit, 206-553-3000, www.transit.
metrokc.gov
130: Downtown Seattle/SODO/Georgetown/South Park/Burien/
Normandy Park/Des Moines
132: Downtown Seattle/SODO/South Park/Burien/Normandy Park/Des
Moines
166: Des Moines/Kent

FEDERAL WAY

REDONDO BEACH
REDONDO

Federal Way is a modest middle-class suburb with pleasant and inexpensive (compared to Seattle) contemporary homes. Airline, Boeing, and Weyerhaeuser employees live in this area, but other area businesses employ many residents as well. The median house price hovers just under $200,000, making it one of the area's most affordable communities. There are lots of nice starter homes here, many of them older ramblers that sell for $120,000 to $150,000. There are also pockets of new planned communities, with gorgeous homes on large lots. Adding to the city's diversity is a variety of apartments, condominiums and rental homes. The location, between Seattle and Tacoma makes sense for couples needing easy access to both communities.

As with many of the region's communities that hug Puget Sound, Federal Way also has a handful of waterfront communities that offer panoramic views. **Redondo Beach** is one such neighborhood. Formerly a vacation spot, the community is now a mix of beach bungalows, contemporary new homes, and condominiums. In **Redondo**, the community above the beach, you'll find large homes with partial views that sell for $350,000 to $550,000.

Like Lynnwood to the north of Seattle, Federal Way serves as a retail center for residents of many South End communities. SeaTac Mall is located here, along with numerous chain stores and restaurants. Other sources of local pride are the King County Aquatic Center, which was built for the 1990 Goodwill Games, and the rhododendron and bonsai garden, owned by the Weyerhaeuser Co.

Web Site: www.ci.federal-way.wa.us
Area Code: 253
Zip Codes: 98001, 98003, 98023, 98063, 98093
Post Office: 32829 Pacific Highway South, 800-275-8777, www.usps.com

Libraries: 34200 1st Way South, 253-838-3668; 848 South 320th Street, 253-839-0257, 206-296-5203 (TTY), www.kcls.org

Public Schools: Federal Way Public Schools, 31405 18th Avenue South, 253-945-2000, www.fwsd.wednet.edu

Police: 34008 9th Avenue South, 253-661-4600, www.ci.federal-way.wa.us

Emergency Hospital: St. Francis Hospital, 34515 9th Avenue South, 253-927-9700, www.fhshealth.org

Community Resources: Federal Way Chamber of Commerce, 34004 16th Avenue South, Suite 101, 253-838-2605, www.federalwaychamber.com; King County Aquatic Center, 650 SW Campus Drive, 206-296-4444, www.metrokc.gov/parks

Public Transportation: Metro Transit, 206-553-3000, www.transit.metrokc.gov

173: Duwamish Boeing/Federal Center South/Midway/Federal Way/Sea-Tac Mall/Federal Way Transit Center

174: Downtown Seattle/SODO/Sea-Tac Airport/ Federal Way

175: Downtown Seattle/Kent/Federal Way

176: Downtown Seattle/SODO/Federal Way

177: Downtown Seattle/SODO/Federal Way

178: Downtown Seattle/SODO/Federal Way

179: Downtown Seattle/Federal Way

181: Federal Way/Auburn

183: Federal Way/Kent

187: Federal Way Transit Center/South 320th Street/SW 320th Street/Twin Lakes

188: Federal Way Transit Center/South 320th Street/SW 320th Street/SW Federal Way

192: Downtown Seattle/Kent-Des Moines Park & Ride/Federal Way

194: Downtown Seattle/SODO/Sea-Tac Airport/Federal Way

196: Downtown Seattle/SODO/Federal Way

197: University District/Federal Way

SOUTHERN COMMUNITIES—PIERCE COUNTY

TACOMA

NORTHEAST TACOMA
DOWNTOWN
STADIUM DISTRICT
OLD TOWN
PROCTOR

As the second largest city in Western Washington (population 193,600), Tacoma doesn't quite count as a suburb, although some residents do commute to Seattle for work. An industrial and port city, Tacoma remains a less expensive alternative to Seattle. To truly appreciate Tacoma, you must get off I-5. Otherwise, it's easy to assume that the city's only attraction is the famous Tacoma Dome, the only dome remaining in Western Washington.

A decade ago, parts of Tacoma were troubled by gang activity, but efforts by the city and local community action groups have done much to contain and improve the situation. Today, home and personal security concerns for Tacoma residents are comparable to those in Seattle.

Tacoma has its own $100-million fiber optics network under the city, making it the most wired city in the country—according to its economic development director. So, it's not surprising that the city has been able to lure high-tech companies from other parts of the US, including Seattle. Other major employers in Tacoma include the Tacoma School District, the Frank Russell Company, University of Washington at Tacoma, Regence Blue Shield, DaVita Inc. (formerly Total Renal Care), and local hospitals. Recent cultural happenings include the opening of the Museum of Glass in July of 2002, and construction of the Tacoma Art Museum next to Union station. In addition, the city recently zoned warehouse district space for artists, and now has a fine arts high school (grades 10-12), the Tacoma School of the Arts, located at 1950 Pacific Avenue.

There are many distinct neighborhoods in Tacoma. If you're looking for new construction and a neighborhood of young, professional families, check out **Northeast Tacoma**, a conglomeration of planned developments staggered along the hillside. Homes started going up in the early 1980s, and construction continues; prices range from $250,000 to $400,000. There is no real commercial center here, but the conveniences of Federal Way and downtown Tacoma are just a short drive away.

Downtown Tacoma is experiencing something of a revival, though there is still little shopping available here. What you will find are refurbished apartments, condominiums and artists' lofts, quaint pubs, historic theaters, a gorgeous new art museum, and Washington State History Museum. Similar to Seattle's Belltown neighborhood, downtown Tacoma has become a hip spot to live, particularly for employees of the city's growing banking and finance community. One local developer, who moved his family here from Seattle, refers to Tacoma as the "promised land" because of the revitalization that is in progress here.

Some of Tacoma's most attractive neighborhoods are located in the city's northern sector. The **Stadium District** is home to Stadium High School and a nearly century-old French Renaissance castle, originally intended as a luxury hotel. The Stadium neighborhood is an eclectic mix of condominiums, turn-of-the-century Victorians, Craftsman bungalows, and mansions. Lively and diverse, the Stadium District is home to Tacoma's gay community, young professionals, and long-time residents. The neighborhood boasts spectacular views, good schools and wide, tree-lined streets. Except for the occasional mansion, homes here cost less than $700,000, and many go for under $400,000.

Old Town, above the city's bustling waterfront, is a former fishing village that offers modest homes at affordable prices. Tacoma's waterfront is a popular recreation area, with numerous docks and walkways, restaurants, and a new hotel. In the works is a planned community at the site of the former ASARCO smelter at the end of Ruston Way. The plan includes a mix of housing, parks and retail space, and is sure to raise property values in the area. **Proctor**, again in North Tacoma, is also popular with young professionals. With a quaint commercial district, Proctor offers the convenience of a small downtown with the charm of a residential neighborhood. Well-kept Craftsman homes line the quiet streets. Prices begin at around $200,000.

Tacoma has an expansive parks system, including a series of green spaces and trails along the Commencement Bay waterfront. On sunny days, the area resembles Seattle's Alki shorefront, with walkers, runners, and roller bladers jostling for position on the sidewalks—there's no place better for people-watching during the summer. Also in Tacoma are Point Defiance Park and Point Defiance Zoo & Aquarium, two of the South End's premier weekend destinations. At 698 acres, Point Defiance Park is among the 20 largest urban parks in the United States. It includes a replica of Fort Nisqually, a logging museum, rose and Japanese gardens, and 14 miles of hiking trails.

Web Site: www.cityoftacoma.org
Area Code: 253
Zip Codes: 98401, 98402, 98403, 98404, 98405, 98406, 98407, 98408, 98409, 98411, 98412, 98413, 98415, 98416, 98418, 98421, 98422, 98424, 98430, 98431, 98433, 98438, 98439, 98442, 98443, 98444, 98445, 98446, 98447, 98450, 98455, 98460, 98464, 98465, 98466, 98467, 98471, 98477, 98481, 98492, 98493, 98497, 98498, 98499

Post Office: 1220 Martin Luther King Jr. Way; 1102 A Street; 3801 North 27th Street, 3705 South G Street, 800-275-8777, www.usps.com

Libraries: 1102 Tacoma Avenue South, 253-591-5666; 765 South 84th Street, 253-591-5620; 1902 South Cedar Street, 253-591-5166; 212 Brown's Point Boulevard NE, 253-591-5630; 215 South 56th Street, 253-591-5650; 3523 East "G" Street, 253-591-5660; 3411 South 56th Street, 253-591-5670; 3828 Portland Avenue, 253-594-7805; 7001 6th Avenue, 253-591-5680; 3722 North 26th Street, 253-591-5640, www.tpl.lib.wa.us; 13718 Pacific Avenue South, 253-531-4656; 5107 112th Street East, 253-536-6186; 14916 Washington Avenue SW, 253-588-1014; 3605 Bridgeport Way West, 253-565-9447, www.pcl.lib.wa.us

Public Schools: Tacoma School District, 601 South 8th Street, 253-571-1000, www.tacoma.k12.wa.us

Police: 930 Tacoma Avenue South, 253-591-5905, www.tacomapolice.org

Emergency Hospital: Tacoma General Hospital, 315 Martin Luther King Jr. Way, 253-403-1000, www.multicare.com/TacomaGeneral1

Community Resources: Beacon Senior Center, 415 South 13th Street, 253-591-5083; Lighthouse Senior Center, 5016 A Street, 253-591-5080; Point Defiance Zoo & Aquarium, 5400 North Pearl Street, 253-591-5337, www.pdza.org; Port of Tacoma, One Sitcum Plaza, 253-383-5841, www.portoftacoma.com; Tacoma Art Museum, 1123 Pacific Avenue, 253-272-4258, www.tacomaartmuseum.org; University of Washington at Tacoma, 1900 Commerce Street, 253-692-4000, www.tacoma.washington.edu; YMCA of Tacoma-Pierce County, 1002 South Pearl Street, 253-564-9622; 9715 Lakewood Drive SW, 253-584-9622; 1144 Market Street, 253-597-6444, www.tacomaymca.org

Public Transportation: Pierce Transit, 3701 96th Street SW, 253-581-8000, 800-562-8109, www.ptbus.pierce.wa.us

    10: Tacoma Community College to Boathouse

    11: Downtown Tacoma to Boathouse

    13: Downtown Tacoma to Ruston

    16: Tacoma Community College to Downtown Tacoma

    25: Downtown Tacoma to Tacoma Community College

    26: Downtown Tacoma to Stadium High School

    27: Downtown Tacoma to Tacoma Community College

    28: Downtown Tacoma to Tacoma Community College

    41: Downtown Tacoma to 72nd & Portland Transit Center

    42: Downtown Tacoma to 72nd & Portland Transit Center

    45: Downtown Tacoma to Parkland Transit Center

    46: Downtown Tacoma to Graham

    48: Downtown Tacoma to Lakewood Mall Transit Center

51: Tacoma Mall Transit Center to Proctor Shopping District
52: Tacoma Mall Transit Center to Tacoma Community College
53: Downtown Tacoma to Tacoma Community College
54: Tacoma Mall Transit Center to McIlvaigh Middle School
55: Tacoma Mall Transit Center to Parkland Transit Center
56: Tacoma Mall Transit Center to 72nd & Portland Transit Center
57: Tacoma Mall Transit Center to Downtown Tacoma
59: Tacoma Mall Transit Center to Fred Meyer
60: Downtown Tacoma to Port Industrial Yard
61: Downtown Tacoma to North Shore Golf Club
65: Downtown Tacoma to Fife
100: Tacoma Community College to Purdy Park & Ride
102: Downtown Tacoma to Purdy Park & Ride
200: Tacoma Community College to Lakewood Mall Transit Center
202: Lakewood Mall Transit Center to Sumner
204: Lakewood Mall to Parkland Transit Center
206: Lakewood Mall Transit Center to Fort Lewis
210: Lakewood Mall Transit Center to Downtown Tacoma
212: Lakewood Mall Transit Center to McNeil Island Boat
214: Lakewood Mall Transit Center to Pierce College
220: Lakewood Mall Transit Center to North Tacoma
300: Tacoma Mall Transit Center to Ponders Corner
400: Downtown Tacoma to Puyallup
405: Downtown Tacoma to Bonney Lake
410: Parkland Transit Center to Puyallup
500: Downtown Tacoma to Federal Way
574: Lakewood Mall Transit Center to Sea-Tac Airport
582: Bonney Lake to Downtown Tacoma
585: Lakewood Mall Transit Center to Auburn

A DECADE AGO, FINDING A PLACE TO LIVE IN SEATTLE WAS EASY. Today, it will take persistence and some luck to find what you want. Situated between two bodies of water, with only narrow bridges and ferries to connect it to surrounding communities, Seattle faces the challenges of a growing population and substantial geographical constraints. Couple these factors with increasing anti-development sentiment and a tri-county population that grew by more than half a million people in the 1990s, and it's easy to understand the high price of area real estate.

Leveling off in the early 1990s, housing prices rose again in the mid 1990s, accounting for Seattle's listing by the National Association of Realtors and the Washington Center for Real Estate Research as being among the country's most expensive places to buy residential real estate. Though the national and regional economies slowed after 2000, home prices in King County continued to rise. By spring 2002, the median price for a single-family home in King County had risen to well over a quarter of a million dollars; region wide, the Multiple Listing Service listed the median home price at just over $209,000. (More about Seattle's cost of living can be found at www.BestPlaces.net, a non-ad driven site with information and statistics for 3,000 US cities and towns.)

Rental units, on the other hand, especially in downtown Seattle, experienced a downward pricing trend in 2001/2002. This renter's market is a simple supply and demand issue. Where just a few years ago there were not enough units on the market, the economic downturn that began in 2000, combined with the development of many rental units in Seattle's trendiest neighborhoods, particularly Belltown, has been a boon for apartment seekers. While this trend is not expected to be long term, it does offer some short term relief to renters.

Once a city primarily of single-family homes, the creation of duplexes and triplexes from older homes is now common. Condominiums and apartment buildings account for a large portion of current building projects, as do townhouses and multi-family houses. Rental rates in Seattle are high, although vacancies are now more common than they were in the late 1990s. Recent figures from Dupre + Scott Apartment Advisors, www.dsaa.com, listed $750 to $800 for a basic, one-bedroom apartment in King County; those areas that listed under $600 were Auburn, Rainier Valley and SeaTac. At the same time, 10% of the neighborhoods surveyed had rents that topped $1,100. Keep in mind that, despite the rise in vacancies, competition for rental properties—particularly for houses—is stiff. A landlord-hosted open house often attracts numerous applicants, and the event takes on the air of a job interview, with well-dressed renters vying for the landlord's attention. To get an edge over the competition, bring a prepared rental application with you, along with a list of references, and be ready to write a check for first and last month's rent and a damage deposit. If you are moving from out of state, you may be required to get a cashier's check or money order.

APARTMENT HUNTING

DIRECT ACTION

To find an apartment in Seattle on your own, consider a strategy using several methods. Searching the local classifieds, either online or in print, is the best way to begin. An early edition of the Sunday *Seattle Times/Seattle P.I.* arrives in stores on Friday night, allowing you to call landlords first thing Saturday morning. The listings should give you a good sense of prices in various neighborhoods. Since many local landlords don't run advertisements in the paper it's also a good idea to drive through the neighborhoods you're interested in, looking for posted rental notices.

If you'd like to be near a local university or college, late spring is the best time to look for vacancies. These neighborhoods include Fremont, Wallingford, or North Queen Anne near Seattle Pacific University; the University District, Green Lake and Ravenna near the University of Washington; or Capitol Hill and the Central Area, which border the Seattle University campus.

If you have narrowed your search to downtown Seattle, check out www.rentdowntownseattle.com, which lists vacancies in Belltown, Capitol Hill, First Hill, the International District and Queen Anne. The site also includes some helpful hints for living downtown and links to downtown interests. You should note, however, that only selected apartment complexes are included on the site; you should not expect a complete listing of all available rentals in that neighborhood.

Also, don't forget **word of mouth**. Some of the best apartments are found through the grapevine. Even if you are new to the area and haven't yet established such connections, you can still put the word out. Check college/university, coffee shop, and grocery bulletin boards (see below). When you call about vacancies, ask about any others that may be opening up in the neighborhood. Chances are, even if the apartment you are calling about has been taken, someone knows someone up the street who is moving on. In addition, the neighborhood profiles include a list of neighborhood organizations, which may be a good resource for finding out about available apartments, as well as area safety and neighborhood events.

CLASSIFIED ADVERTISEMENTS

In **Seattle**, check out these news sources for the best selection of classified ads:
- *Seattle Post-Intelligencer/The Seattle Times*; get the joint Sunday edition, which has the most comprehensive rental and real estate listings for Seattle and surrounding communities. Rentals are divided into apartments and houses in the "NWclassifieds" section, and further subdivided by location. Houses for sale are listed in the "Home/Real Estate" section, also organized by location. The newspapers share an online classifieds section at http://classifieds.nwsource.com/classified. New listings appear daily in both the print and online versions.
- *Seattle Weekly*; a free newspaper, the *Weekly* is distributed on Thursdays and is available in newspaper vending boxes, cafés, bars, and convenience and grocery stores. The paper often lists rental opportunities not found in the larger publications. To view ads online, visit www.seattleweekly.com. New ads are posted to the web site every day.
- *The Stranger*; a free weekly newspaper that can be found in restaurants and bars throughout Seattle. *The Stranger* is distributed on Thursdays, and contains rental and real estate classifieds. Online ads, which are updated daily, can be found at www.thestranger.com.

Community newspapers are excellent avenues for finding an apartment; many run local classifieds that will give you first crack at vacancies that may not appear in the citywide papers. These papers are usually available free of charge at neighborhood businesses and cafes.
- *Ballard News Tribune,* www.robinsonnews.com
- *Magnolia News,* www.zwire.com/site/news
- *Queen Anne News*, www.zwire.com/site/news
- *West Seattle Herald,* www.robinsonnews.com
- *White Center News,* www.robinsonnews.com

To find housing in Seattle's **surrounding communities**, check out the classified ads in these major newspapers:

- *Eastside Journal*, www.eastsidejournal.com
- *Everett Herald*, www.heraldnet.com
- *Issaquah Press*, www.isspress.com
- *Mercer Island Reporter*, www.mi-reporter.com
- *South County Journal*, www.southcountyjournal.com
- *Tacoma News Tribune*, www.tribnet.com

All of the newspapers listed above have "roommate wanted" or "room available" sections, worth a look if you're on a limited budget. Shared houses are common in some areas of Seattle, particularly in the University District and the southeast side of Capitol Hill. These can be a good option if you plan to move again in several months, as many do not require a long-term lease.

OTHER RENTAL PUBLICATIONS
Several companies publish free rental guides. Most list newer apartment complexes or apartments that are maintained by large property management companies. You can pick up rental guides at most grocery or convenience stores.

- *For Rent*, www.forrent.com
- *Apartment Guide*, www.apartmentguide.com

BULLETIN BOARDS

Check out bulletin boards on college campuses, or in laundromats, coffee shops, and convenience stores in the neighborhoods that interest you.

- **Seattle University**: a classifieds ads bulletin board is located on the first floor of the Student Union Building.
- **University of Washington**: off-campus housing information is available in Room G20 of the Husky Union Building.
- **Seattle Central Community College**: two community bulletin boards are available in the Broadway Edison Building.
- **North Seattle Community College**: housing information can be found on campus at Baxter Center.
- **South Seattle Community College**: a student bulletin board is located in the Jerry Brockey Building.
- **Seattle Pacific University**: bulletin boards can be found on campus at Weter Hall and in the Student Union Building.
- **Bellevue Community College**: housing opportunities are posted in the college cafeteria.

ONLINE RESOURCES

These local and national apartment-listing and roommate referral sites may be worth a look. Each lists vacancies in the Seattle area.
- **Apartment Rental Guide.com**, www.apartmentrentalguide.com
- **MetroRent Roommates**, www.metrorent.com
- **Roomie.com**, www.roomie.com
- **Roommate Express**, www.e-roommate.com
- **Rent Tech**, 206-322-5544, www.renttech.com
- **Rent Downtown Seattle.com**, www.rentdowntownseattle.com
- **Rentals.com**, www.rentals.com
- **SeattleRenter.com**, www.seattlerenter.com

APARTMENT SEARCH FIRMS

One way to find an apartment, particularly if your time is limited, is to use an apartment search firm. These can be especially helpful if you want to set up your rental before arriving in town, as most agents will do a lot of the legwork for you. When speaking to an apartment search firm agent, be specific about your needs and budget. Also, find out if there is a fee. Some services charge to view their listings, while others get their revenue from the property owners. Of the firms listed below, the first three offer free searches to renters. Rent Tech charges a fee that allows you access to its listings for 90 days.
- **Apartment Finders of Seattle**, 206-213-0127, 800-473-3733, www.seattleapartmentfinder.com
- **Apartment Hunters**, 206-658-8015, www.apthunters.com
- **RentDowntownSeattle.com**, www.rentdowntownseattle.com
- **Rent Tech**, 206-322-5544, www.renttech.com

CHECKING IT OUT

You're on your way to the day's first rental appointment, you haven't had breakfast, the old college friends you're staying with are getting restless, your back is aching from a bad night's sleep on their sofa-bed, and twenty other people are waiting outside the prospective apartment when you drive up. You panic, take a quick glance around, like what you see, and grab an application. Three months later you're wondering how you landed in such a dump.

To avoid this scenario, tour each apartment with a clear idea of what you want. Beyond personal likes and dislikes, there are some specific things to check for as you look:

- Is the apartment on the first floor? If so, does it have burglar bars? First-floor apartments are easy targets for burglary.
- Are the appliances clean and in good working order? Test all of the stove's burners. Does the kitchen sink have one or two basins? Is there sufficient counter space? Is the freezer compartment of the refrigerator a frost-free variety?
- Check the windows to make sure they open, close and lock. Do the windows, especially the bedroom windows, open onto a busy street or alley? Alleys are especially notorious for late-night car horns and loud early morning trash removal.
- Are there enough closets? Are the closets big enough to accommodate your belongings?
- Is there private storage space in a secure area?
- Is there adequate water pressure for the shower, the sink and the toilet? Turn them on and check.
- Flush all toilets and check for leaks or unusual noises.
- Check the number of electrical outlets. In older buildings it is common to have one or two outlets per room. Are there enough outlets for all your plug-in appliances?
- Are there laundry facilities in the building? Is there a laundromat within walking distance?
- How close is the building to public transportation and grocery stores?
- If you are looking at a basement apartment, check to see if there are any water stains along the walls. They're a sure sign of flooding.
- Does it smell funny? They may have sprayed the apartment for bugs. You should think twice before taking it.
- Is there a smoke and/or carbon monoxide detector in the apartment?

Ed Sacks' *Savvy Renter's Kit* contains a thorough renter's checklist for those interested in augmenting theirs.

If it all passes muster, be prepared to stake your claim without delay!

STAKING A CLAIM

When you view a unit, come prepared. Bring your checkbook. If you are moving from out of state, you may be required to provide a cashier's check or money order instead of a check. Have cash on hand in case you cannot get to the bank and need to purchase a money order from a convenience store or check-cashing outlet. Also bring a copy of your credit report for the building manager. Prepare a renter's resume with addresses of your last three residences, including the names, phone numbers, fax numbers, and e-mail addresses of your previous landlords, building managers, and room-mates. Better yet, before you come to the Seattle area, bring letters of recommendation from the aforementioned that vouch for your sterling qualities. Employment information may also be helpful. If you have secured a job, ask your employer to write a letter on company stationary that verifies your start date and salary.

It won't hurt to mention casually that you don't have a dog, cat or monkey, and that you don't smoke or play the drums. Feel free to rave about the unit and how great it feels (after all, a landlord is human, too). If there is a garden, mention that you love gardening and have a very green thumb. If you do have a pet, ask former landlords to write letters praising its good behavior. If your dog is well behaved, you may want to bring him with you to show how well trained he is (if, of course, he actually is well trained).

When applying for a place, consider that landlords will want your monthly earnings to be equal to at least three times the monthly rent. They can request only non-smokers, they can prohibit pets other than a working dog, and they can bar you from having overnight guests for more than a certain number of nights per year. (If you think you'll have lots of visitors, watch out for a lease containing such a clause, as this may not bode well for your tenant/landlord relationship.)

In Seattle's competitive job market, it isn't just the early bird that gets the worm, it can also be the polite worm, the well-dressed worm and the worm with the highest bid. Treat the open house or appointment like a job interview. If competition is particularly stiff, you may want to offer to sign a lease for longer than the required time period.

According to The Tenants Union (see below), the renter's most powerful moment is right before the rental agreement is signed. Once you sign an agreement, you will be bound by its terms, except for provisions that are illegal under the Landlord-Tenant Act. The union says these issues should be discussed before you agree to move in:

- How much is the rent, and when is it to be paid?
- Are there any rate charges for delinquent payments?
- Who will pay for the utilities?
- Is the tenancy for a fixed period, like one year, or is it for an indefinite period?
- What are the rules on guests, pets, parking, etc.?
- What repairs or cleaning has your landlord agreed to complete before you move in? (Get all promises in writing.)
- Is there a deposit? If so, how much, and when will it be refunded? (A non-refundable fee may not be called a deposit.)

TENANT/LANDLORD RELATIONS

LEASES/RENTAL AGREEMENTS AND SECURITY DEPOSITS

Most landlords in Seattle require your first month's rent, a security or "damage" deposit, and a signed lease agreement prior to moving in. Many also require the last month's rent to be paid either prior to renting or within the first three months of tenancy. Make sure that you read your lease agreement before signing, and before paying anything. Check to see how and when the rent can be increased and by how much; don't assume that it can't be increased during the initial term of your lease. Such details should be negotiated before you sign the lease.

In Washington, the type of your tenancy (month-to-month or fixed period) will determine your rights and duties under the Landlord-Tenant Act, according to The Tenants Union. If you have an agreement with your landlord to stay for a fixed period at the same rent, you have a lease. To be valid, it must be in writing. If it is to be in effect for more than one year, it must not only be in writing, but it must also be signed by the landlord before a notary public. Rent cannot be increased during the fixed period, and the tenancy rules cannot be changed, unless both you and your landlord agree about it. At that time, says The Tenants Union, you must initial any changes that are made.

In the city of Seattle, month-to-month rental agreements are legal but a minimum stay requirement or penalties for not fulfilling a minimum stay on a month to month agreement are illegal. (These agreements usually state that if the tenant does not stay for a minimum number of months, usually six, he/she forfeits the deposit.) If a tenant loses a deposit because of such illegal provisions, the tenant is entitled to collect from the landlord double the deposit, plus actual damages incurred and attorney's fees and costs. Before a tenant sues in small claims court, he/she must request that the landlord return the deposit. For more information, contact The Tenants Union at 206-723-0500 or visit www.tenantsunion.org.

If a landlord charges a deposit, the lease or rental agreement must be in writing, and must include the terms under which any of the deposit will be returned. A deposit cannot be withheld for normal wear and tear, according to the Washington State Bar Association. If a tenant pays a deposit, the landlord must provide a written document describing the condition of the rental unit, and keep the deposit in a trust account. The landlord has 14 days after a tenant moves out to return a deposit, or give a written explanation why it was not refunded.

RENT AND EVICTION CONTROL

There is no rent control in Washington State. In fact, a state law prohibits cities and counties from passing any kind of rent control measure. According to The Tenants Union, a tenant's only protection against a rent increase is a lease. In a month-to-month agreement, a landlord can raise the rent as often as he/she pleases, but must give 30 days written notice. Landlords are prohibited from raising rent as a means of either discrimination or retaliation.

In Seattle, landlords are required to give tenants a minimum of 60 days written notice when rent is to be increased by 10% or more during a 12-month period. The same rule applies to other housing costs like water or sewage. The notice must coincide with the beginning of the rental period, usually the first day of the month.

The landlord-tenant rules in Washington tend to favor landlords. A landlord has the right to ask a tenant who is only three days late with the rent to vacate. Even if the tenant pays rent within five days of the date it is due, the landlord is not obliged to accept payment. Many landlords will accept rent within five days of the date it is due, but may charge a late fee. Emergencies that prevent a tenant from paying rent on time should be discussed with the landlord, who may agree to accept partial payment or to set up a payment plan. If alternate terms are agreed upon, tenants should be sure to get them in writing, and ask the landlord to sign and date them. If additional assistance is necessary, contact The Tenants Union.

In 1996, Seattle passed a Just Cause Eviction Ordinance that prohibits landlords from evicting tenants without a court order. For the full text of the law, visit The Tenants Union web site at www.tenantsunion.org.

LANDLORD/TENANT RIGHTS AND RESPONSIBILITIES

Washington landlords have a list of obligations that they must fulfill, including being accessible to their tenants and obeying the rules of the rental agreement. In addition, they must keep the rental property up to code, maintain the roof, walls, and structural components of the building, keep common areas safe and clean, provide a pest-control program, and provide the facilities necessary to supply heat, electricity, and hot and cold water. They must also provide adequate locks and maintain the appliances that come with the rental unit.

Contrary to what some believe, a landlord may not enter your apartment whenever he/she wishes. A landlord must have tenant consent to inspect the premises, make repairs, supply necessary services, or show the unit to a prospective renter. The time of entry must be reasonable, and he/she must notify you two days in advance. Of course, in an emergency, your landlord can enter your apartment without notice or permission.

A tenant must also meet a series of legal responsibilities. He/she must pay rent, keep his/her dwelling clean and sanitary, dispose of garbage, and properly use fixtures and appliances. He/she must not damage or permit damage to the property, and property must be restored it to its original condition, except for normal wear and tear, before moving out. He/she must also comply with the rental agreement.

The Federal Fair Housing Act of 1968 makes it illegal for a landlord to discriminate based on a person's race, sex, national origin or religion. In addition, various local laws forbid discrimination against unmarried persons, children, gays, and disabled persons.

If you have any problems with your landlord while you're renting, or if you feel that you were discriminated against while you were hunting for an apartment or house, the resources listed below may help:

- **City of Seattle Office for Civil Rights**, 206-684-4500, 206-684-4503 (TTY), www.cityofseattle.net/civilrights
- **City of Seattle Office of Housing**, 206-684-0721, www.cityofseattle.net/housing
- **The Tenants Union**, 206-723-0500, 206-723-0523 (TDD), www.tenantsunion.org
- **Washington State Attorney General's Office**, 206-464-6684, 800-551-4636, www.wa.gov/ago/consumer/lt
- **Washington State Bar Association**, 206-448-WSBA, 800-945-WSBA, www.wsba.org

RENTER'S/HOMEOWNER'S INSURANCE

You've moved into your new apartment, and the last boxes have been cleared away. Take a look around and ask yourself, "How much would it cost to start over if everything I own was destroyed by fire?" Probably more than you might think. Imagine having to replace your clothing, television, stereo, furniture, computer and other accumulations of a lifetime. No small bill.

Typically, with renter's insurance you are protected against fire, hail, lightning, explosion, aircraft, smoke, vandalism, theft, building collapse, frozen plumbing, defective appliances, and sudden electrical damage. Renter's insurance also may cover personal liability as well as damage done (by you) to the property of others.

By now you should be convinced that renter's insurance is a good idea, especially because your belongings would not be insured under your landlord's policy. The good news about renter's insurance is that it is not a huge expense. For $20,000 in coverage your annual rate may run between $150 to $200 if you live in an apartment, and $200 to $250 if you live in a house.

When shopping for renter's insurance, be sure to ask whether the insurance company pays as soon as the claim is filed and whether it pays cash-value or replacement value. If you have a cash-value policy, you will only be paid what your five-year-old television is worth, not what it costs to replace it. Some big-ticket items, such as computers or jewelry, are insured only to a certain amount. Find out what these limits are. A higher deductible usually gives you a lower premium. You can purchase renter's insurance through almost any insurance agency.

Web sites worth investigating as you search for renter's insurance are Quotesmith, www.quotesmith.com, which offers instant quotes from more than 300 insurance companies; QuickenInsurance, www.insuremarket.com, which is good for finding inexpensive insurance rates online. For answers about general insurance questions, check www.insure.com; this site is geared toward professionals in the insurance business as well as consumers, and offers details about what a policy should cover, provides tips on making a claim, and has a listing of complaints filed against insurance companies.

Whether you get renter's insurance or not, it's a good idea to keep an inventory of all items of value and record their serial numbers. You may also want to take photographs of your belongings, or walk through your apartment with a video camera and record them on tape. Make a copy of these records and keep one at a friend's house or in a safe deposit box.

Below is a list of some of the major insurers in the Seattle area:

- **Allstate**, www.allstate.com
- **Farmers Insurance Group**, www.farmersinsurance.com
- **Pemco**, www.pemco-ins.com
- **Safeco**, www.safeco.com
- **Unigard**, www.unigard.com

BUYING

Many people come to Seattle intending to buy a house in the city, but find that the cost of a home is just too high. Newcomers can avoid sticker shock by thoroughly researching home prices and neighborhoods before they arrive, and by keeping an open mind about the types of housing and the locations they are willing to consider. For instance, you will get more bang for your buck in Renton or Snoqualmie, but your commute to the city will be longer. Or, maybe you had your heart set on living in Queen Anne or Magnolia, but you find a really wonderful Craftsman home in the Central Area that's in your price range. It's important to determine your priorities ahead of time, but to be flexible when possible.

Most streets in Seattle are lined with single-family homes on roomy lots. Over the last decade, home values grew steadily with the economy, and in the late 1990s the Seattle housing market exploded. Homes were on the market for just days before selling, and bidding wars were common. Today, while home prices continue to climb, the pace is slower. That, combined with low interest rates, has created more of a buyer's market. Home prices are slightly less expensive in those neighborhoods without direct freeway access, and in nearby suburbs, such as Renton, Bothell, and Edmonds.

Property taxes are another expense to consider. The **King County Department of Assessments** is responsible for collecting property taxes in Seattle and most surrounding communities. You can estimate your annual property taxes if you know the assessed value of your property and your tax levy rate. Divide the value of your home by 1,000 and multiply by the tax levy rate. In Seattle in 2001, the tax levy rate was $11.85. Thus, for a home valued at $300,000, property taxes would be about $3,555. The tax levy rate varies by city; to find the rate in the city of your choice, visit the Department of Assessments web site at www.metrokc.gov/Assessor.

Before buying a house, it's a good idea to hire an independent building inspector or engineer to examine the foundation and overall structure, heating and plumbing systems, and the roof. Also request that the inspector check for mold, particularly if the roof has been replaced recently or if there are signs of water damage in the basement. Your lender will appraise the house, but only to determine if its value will safely secure the loan. If possible, you should include language in your purchase offer that allows you to take back the offer if your inspection uncovers a serious problem. At the very least, your real estate agent should be willing to negotiate with the seller on any major flaws turned up during the inspection. For more see below under **Purchase Agreements**.

How should you go about finding a home to buy in Seattle? Any good real estate agent will tell you there are three things to consider when purchasing a house: location, location, location. The **Neighborhoods** chapter of this book will give you a good overview of the neighborhoods in Seattle, as well as profiles of many of the city's suburbs. From there, visit the neighborhood(s) you're considering. Get a general feel for the area; visit the schools and parks; drive to or from the neighborhood during rush hour to evaluate traffic flow and freeway noise. Attend a few open houses to find a realtor that knows the area. The *Seattle Times/Seattle Post-Intelligencer* Sunday edition has a Home/Real Estate section that lists many of the open houses in Seattle and surrounding communities. The paper is available on Friday evenings, so you can get a drive-by preview. Or, visit the classifieds' web site at http://classifieds.nwsource.com; new open house announcements are added daily. Additional newspaper sites are listed previously in this chapter under **Classified Advertisements**.

The **Washington State Housing Finance Commission** offers free home ownership programs and homebuyer education seminars (see below under **Additional Resources**). For more information, visit the agency's web site at www.wshfc.org or call 206-464-7139 (in Seattle) or 800-767-4663. You can also find information on buying or selling a home at the **National Association of Realtors** web site, www.realtor.com.

CONDOMINIUMS, CO-OPS, AND CO-HOUSING

Buying a home in Seattle doesn't necessarily mean buying a traditional single-family house. Condominiums, co-ops, and co-housing projects are all options, depending on your needs. All three are usually less expensive than traditional houses, and may be a good first step for first-time homeowners.

A **condominium** is a type of joint ownership. Each housing unit is individually owned and residents collectively own the common areas—grounds, lobbies, elevators, hallways, surrounding property, and recreational facilities. You own the apartment outright, so you can usually make improvements to it, rent it out, or resell it as you see fit. However, some restrictions apply to condo ownership. Generally, a condo association oversees the rules of the complex, making decisions about building repairs, external improvements and landscaping. Some condo associations impose rules on subletting. Be sure to review, with your real estate lawyer, the association rules and regulations and the current operating budget. Consider any major improvements or repairs that will be required in the next few years, and see if the budget will be able to cover most of the cost.

If your building has jointly owned amenities, such as a hot tub, rooftop deck or pool, the association coordinates maintenance on those facilities as well. All of these services come at a cost; expect to pay between $100 and $300 in monthly association dues, as well as a one-time fee for capital improvements or emergency repairs, such as a new roof. While these dues may add up over time to little more than the maintenance on your own house, you'll need to factor them in when evaluating your monthly house payments.

A **co-op** (cooperative apartment) is another option for home ownership in Seattle. When you buy a co-op, you are buying shares in the ownership of a building. Co-ops tend to be much less expensive than comparable condominiums, but there are some important trade-offs. Co-ops are tightly controlled by the shareholders in the building—in other words by all of the co-op owners. This can make it difficult to buy a cooperative apartment, since the co-op board will interview you, consider both your financial status and neighborly qualities, and may require several letters of reference. You may not have the option to remodel your unit, rent it out, or even sell it quickly, should you need to (as the co-op board must approve prospective buyers). If you're short on cash, buying into a co-op can be challenging because many lenders will not approve mortgages for them. Unfortunately, many co-ops do not accept anything but a full cash payment at the time of purchase. Co-ops are most common in the Capitol Hill, Eastlake, and First Hill neighborhoods.

Those thinking about buying a condominium or co-op should seriously consider that owning a condo or co-op obligates you socially a bit more than does a freestanding house. While your co-op or condo neighbors could turn out to be great friends and neighbors, the opposite could also be true.

Co-housing projects are catching on in Seattle as residents seek to recapture the aura of a close-knit neighborhood in a rapidly growing city. Also called "intentional communities," co-housing projects offer communal living with affordable condo-style ownership opportunities. Each household owns its own unit, but shares communal space such as a "common house." Co-housing residents often prepare and eat meals together, share gardening responsibilities, and environmental initiatives like recycling and composting are common. Currently, co-housing communities exist in Seattle's Jackson Place and West Seattle neighborhoods, in the Rose Hill community of Redmond, and near Bothell. For more information on co-housing, visit The Co-housing Network at www.cohousing.org, or contact one of the co-housing communities listed here:

- **Duwamish Co-housing**, Seattle, http://boutell.com/~ciel
- **Rose Hill Co-housing**, Redmond, 425-827-0659, www.rosehillcohousing.org
- **Seattle Co-housing**, Seattle, 206-522-3099, http://seattlecohousing.org
- **Songaia Co-housing**, Snohomish County, 425-486-2035, www.songaia.com

WORKING WITH REALTORS

If you are unfamiliar with the city, it may be helpful to find a real estate agent or broker to help you with your search. Friends or co-workers may be able to recommend someone, or consider the agents who host open houses in your neighborhood of choice. The agent should be someone you trust, who listens to you, knows the city and the neighborhoods you like, and understands the market. A good realtor will not expect you to pay more than you can afford, although you may find that the house you can afford and the house you want are very different things.

Generally, home buyers in Seattle do not use a real estate lawyer. Often the only lawyer involved is an employee of the escrow company. Nevertheless, it is a good idea to have the name of a real estate attorney available just in case. Ask friends or co-workers for recommendations, or ask your agent to suggest a reputable attorney.

The major national and regional real estate companies offer online lists of agents. To begin your search you may want to visit one of the realtor web sites listed below, or go to **HomeGain**, www.homegain.com—a company that states as its threefold mission: "finding out what your current or future home is worth; preparing your home for sale; and finding the right real estate agent."

- **Coldwell Banker**, www.coldwellbanker.com
- **John L. Scott**, www.johnlscott.com
- **Prudential**, www.prudential.com/realestate
- **RE/MAX**, Northwest Seattle, http://northwestrealtors.com/ remax_northwest, 206-522-5500
- **Windermere**, www.windermere.com

If you already have a chosen area, consider contacting one of the agents listed here.

SEATTLE

- **Cynthia Creasey and Mack McCoy**, Lake & Company Real Estate, 7801 Green Lake Drive North, 206-276-8292, www.seattlehomes.net
- **Val Ellis**, Coldwell Banker Bain Associates, 1200 Westlake Avenue North #406, 206-216-3461, www.valellis.com
- **Peter Greeley**, ReMax Metro Real Estate, 2312 Eastlake Avenue East, 206-322-5700
- **Maury King**, Windermere Real Estate, 4919 South Genesee Street, 206-954-9010, www.realestateseattle.com
- **Karen Lavallee**, Windermere Real Estate, 4526 California Avenue SW, 206-937-6574, www.windermere.com
- **Virginia Mason**, Coldwell Banker Bain Associates, 1200 Westlake Avenue North #406, 206-216-3418, www.soldinseattle.com
- **Michael Smith Realtors**, Prudential, 1008 140th Avenue NE, Bellevue, 425-453-9100, http://prumsr.com

EASTSIDE

- **Laura Bernard**, Windermere Real Estate, 11656 98th Avenue NE, Kirkland, 425-823-4600, www.laurabernard.com
- **Linda Gray**, Coldwell Banker Bain Associates, 15410 Main Street NE, Suite E, Duvall, 800-768-7875, www.cbba.com
- **Carole Tinker**, Coldwell Banker Bain Associates, 1151 NW Sammamish Road, Suite 103, Issaquah, 425-391-5600, www.cbba.com
- **Oscar Diaz**, Windermere Real Estate, 13000 NE 20th Street, Bellevue, 425-883-1800, http://oscardiaz.mywindermere.com
- **Michael Smith Realtors**, Prudential, 1008 140th Avenue NE, Bellevue, 425-453-9100, http://prumsr.com

WEST
- **Ty Evans**, Windermere Real Estate, 220 Madison Avenue South, Bainbridge Island, 206-842-5626, www.bainbridge-realestate.com

NORTH
- **North Central Washington Association of Realtors**, http://ncwarfp. internetcrusade.com/new
- **Lee Lageschulte**, Windermere Real Estate, 900 North 185th Street, Seattle, 206-546-5731, www.windermere.com
- **Gary Biddle**, Huber Development and Real Estate, 7304 10th Street East, Everett, 425-252-5805, www.garybiddle.com
- **Tonya Robison Tye**, Windermere Real Estate, 4211 200th Street SW, Suite 110, Lynnwood, 206-793-7996, www.seattleabodes.com
- **Emoke Rock**, Windermere Real Estate, 210 5th Avenue South, Suite 102, Edmonds, 425-672-1118, www.windermere.com

SOUTH
- **Sharon Benson**, Coldwell Banker Hawkins-Poe, 5929 North Westgate Boulevard, Tacoma, 800-455-4102, www.sharonbenson.com
- **Marge Hering**, Windermere Real Estate, 33438 1st Way South, Federal Way, 253-838-8900, www.southseattle.com/fedway
- **Jim Poh**, Coldwell Banker Bain Associates, 17650 140th Avenue SE, Suite B8, Renton, 425-981-3022, www.cbba.com
- **Kay Storhoff**, Windermere Real Estate, 401 SW 152nd, Burien, 206-244-5900, www.windermere.com

PURCHASE AGREEMENTS, CREDIT, MORTGAGES, INSURANCE

The purchase agreement is a legally binding document signed by the buyer and seller that states the price and all the terms of the sale. It is the most negotiable, variable, and important document produced in the home-buying process. The purchase agreement is the document to which a buyer may attach contingencies. Such contingencies can protect you, the buyer, from being legally bound by the purchase agreement if, for example, you cannot sell the house you live in now, the house you are buying does not pass mechanical and structural inspection, the seller is not able to give you possession by a certain date, or you cannot qualify for a loan.

Washington does not regulate purchase agreements, but it does require Form 22J, the disclosure of lead-based paint. If a seller does not give a buyer this form, the buyer can rescind the sale up until the closing date. The state also requires the seller to deliver to the buyer a property disclosure statement (Form 17). The statement provides the buyer with information about the condition of the property, and may outline known or potential problems, like a leaky roof or drainage problems.

It's a good idea to get pre-approved for a loan before looking for houses in earnest. Most sellers will not seriously consider an offer from a buyer who is not pre-approved. The pre-approval process should not commit you to a particular lender or interest rate. It is simply a document that indicates to the seller that when you formally apply for a loan, you will most likely qualify to purchase the home. Most banks or mortgage brokers will process a pre-approval application without a fee. In addition to making your offer more attractive to the seller, the pre-approval process gives you, the buyer, an accurate idea of how much you can spend on a house.

A key factor when seeking a loan is your credit history. Check your credit report to make sure it is accurate *before* meeting with a loan officer. You can check your credit report with all three national credit bureaus listed here. You will need to provide your name, address, previous address, and Social Security number with your request. Check with each company for specific instructions, or contact all three online at www.icreditreport.com. Reports are free if you have been denied credit based on your credit report within the last 30 days, otherwise, expect to pay $8 per report. The national credit bureaus are:

- **Equifax**, P.O. Box 105873, Atlanta, GA 30348, 800-685-1111
- **Experian**, P.O. Box 2104, Allen, TX 75002-2104, 888-397-3742
- **TransUnion Corporation**, P.O. Box 390, Springfield, PA 19064-0390, 800-916-8800

When contemplating buying a house, you'll want to evaluate your personal finances. How much can you afford to pay up front, and how much will you then be able to pay per month? Generally, you will be able to qualify for a loan of about three or four times your yearly income, depending on your credit record and other debts. The loan won't cover your down payment and closing costs, however. In most cases closing costs, which are in addition to the down payment, run three to seven percent of the purchase price. These can include loan origination fees, attorney's fees, title search, title insurance, inspections, and tax and insurance premiums held in escrow. As a buyer you will probably not be expected to pay the broker's fees, which are commonly paid by the seller. Expect your down payment to be 10% to 20% of the price of the home. Additional fees, such as mortgage insurance or higher loan origination fees, are often required if the down payment is less than 20%.

Finally, a few words about getting a loan: it may be most convenient to get your pre-approval from a local bank, but shop around before you sign for your loan. While many banks offer competitive interest rates, mortgage brokers can often match or beat their best offers. Make sure you ask about loan origination fees (points) when requesting interest rate quotes. Usually the lowest interest rate includes a hefty one-time fee, one that may not be mentioned until you're ready to sign the papers. The Bank Rate Monitor web site, www.bankrate.com, provides mortgage and interest rate data on over 2,000 lending institutions.

Major banks and mortgage-lending institutions usually have web sites, and most now allow you to get pre-approved online. See **Mortgages** below for a list.

Once your loan is approved, your lender will require you to buy **homeowner's insurance** to protect their investment (your home). Be sure the policy you choose covers the house, its contents and outbuildings, and includes earthquake coverage. You'll also want to protect yourself in case of liability. Policies vary, so check restrictions and exclusions carefully to make sure you have the coverage you need. A basic homeowner's policy includes liability insurance to protect you if someone is injured on your property; property protection, which insures your house and personal belongings against damage or loss; and living expense coverage that will pay for you to live elsewhere while repairs are being made.

You may also need mortgage insurance, which is required by many lenders as well as the FHA to cover them if you default on your loan, and title insurance, which protects the lender in case the legal title to the property isn't clear. It doesn't protect you though, so, in addition, you may want to buy an owner's title insurance policy, or get an attorney's opinion on your title. If the seller has purchased title insurance in recent years, you may be able to get the same title company to issue you a new policy at a lower cost, so be sure to ask for a re-issue credit. See **Renter's Insurance** above for a list of insurance companies.

ONLINE RESOURCES—HOUSE HUNTING

You can start your search on the internet before you arrive in Seattle. While searching the web probably won't get you a house—many are sold shortly after they are listed—it will give you a good idea about what's on the market, where you should look once you get here, and about how much you can expect to pay. Not every site lists every home in the Seattle area, but most homes will be listed on at least one site. Also, don't forget the newspaper classifieds (see above under **Apartment Hunting**).

- **Cyberhomes**, www.cyberhomes.com
- **HomeSeekers.com**, www.homeseekers.com
- **Homestore.com**, www.homestore.com
- **MSN HomeAdvisor**, www.homeadvisor.com
- **National Association of Realtors**, www.realtor.com
- **Realty Locator**, www.realtylocator.com
- **Yahoo! Real Estate**, http://realestate.yahoo.com
- **ZipRealty**, www.ziprealty.com

FOR SALE BY OWNER

If you prefer to buy or sell a home without an agent, check out the sites below; they specialize in home listings by owners:
- **4SaleByOwner.com**, www.4salebyowner.com
- **FiSBO Registry Inc.**, www.fisbos.com
- **HomesByOwner.com**, www.homesbyowner.com
- **Owners.com**, www.owners.com

MORTGAGES

The following sites might be useful:
- **Freddie Mac**, www.freddiemac.com; offers information on current mortgage averages.
- **Interest.com**, www.interest.com; includes a section for first-time home-buyers, details on how to find a lender close to home, and mortgage rate comparisons.
- **E-Loan**, www.eloan.com; rated first in the *Smart Money 2000 Internet Guide* for ease of use, finding low rates for customers, and low origination fees.
- **MSN HomeAdvisor**, www.homeadvisor.com; the Microsoft Network's directory allows users to apply for loans, compare rates and estimate payments.
- **iOwn**, www.iown.com; CitiMortgage's site lets visitors prequalify for loans, shop and compare rates and apply for loans online.
- **Quicken Loans**, www.quickenmortgage.com; easy-to-use calculators help expedite and clarify the finance process.
- **Countrywide**, www.countrywide.com; includes a section for buyers with less-than-perfect credit.
- **Home Finance of America**, www.bestrateloans.com; offers competitive home financing rates.

ADDITIONAL RESOURCES

If you want to buy a house, especially if you are a first time homebuyer, consider taking a real-estate class, often available at area colleges. The **Washington State Housing Finance Commission** offers free home ownership programs and homebuyer education seminars. For more information, visit the agency's web site at www.wshfc.org or call 206-464-7139 (in Seattle) or 800-767-HOME. If you don't have the time or inclination for a class, but are willing to conduct your own research, look for a book on home buying how-tos. One such publication specifically about the Seattle area is *Seattle Homes: Real Estate Around the Sound* by Jim Stacey. Another invaluable resource is the **Washington Center for Real Estate Research (WCRER)**, 800-835-9683 or www.cbe.wsu.edu/~wcrer. The WCRER, a division of the Washington State University College of Business and Economics, provides research and education materials to consumers.

The following resources that may be of interest for those in the market for a new home:

- *100 Questions Every First Time Homebuyer Should Ask* by Ilyce R. Glink.
- *Opening the Door to a Home of Your Own*, a pamphlet published by the Fannie Mae Foundation for first-time homebuyers, can be obtained by calling 800-834-3377.
- *Your New House: the Alert Consumer's Guide to Buying and Building a Quality New Home*, now in its third edition and picked by the *San Francisco Chronicle* as one of its top ten "Best Real Estate Books," can be ordered by calling 800-888-0385.
- Check www.scorecard.org if you are concerned about toxic waste issues in or near your prospective neighborhood. This site is sponsored by the Environmental Defense Fund.

B EFORE YOU CAN START YOUR NEW LIFE IN SEATTLE, YOU AND YOUR worldly possessions have to get here. How difficult that will be depends on how much stuff you've accumulated, how much money you're willing or able to spend on the move, and where you're coming from.

TRUCK RENTALS

The first question you need to answer: am I going to move myself or will I have someone else do it for me? If you're used to doing everything your-self, you can rent a vehicle and head for the open road. Look in the Yellow Pages under "Truck Rental," and call around and compare; also ask about any specials. Below we list four national truck rental firms and their toll-free numbers and web sites. For the best information, you should call a local office. Note: most truck rental companies now offer "one-way" rentals (don't forget to ask whether they have a drop-off/return location in or near your destination), as well as packing accessories and storage facilities. Of course, these extras are not free. If you're cost-conscious you may want to scavenge boxes in advance of your move and, if you haven't yet found your new residence, make sure you have a place to store your belongings upon arrival. Also, if you're planning to move during the peak moving months of May through September, call well in advance of when you'll need the vehi-cle—a month at least.

Once you're on the road, keep in mind that your rental truck may be a tempting target for thieves. If you must park it overnight or for an extend-ed period (more than a couple of hours), try to find a safe spot, preferably a well-lit place you can easily observe.

- **Budget**, 800-428-7825, www.budget.com
- **Penske**, 800-222-0277, www.penske.com
- **Ryder**, 800-467-9337, www.ryder.com
- **Uhaul**, 800-468-4285, www.uhaul.com

Not sure if you want to drive the truck yourself? Commercial freight carriers, such as **Consolidated Freightways** and **ABF** offer an in-between service: they deliver a 28-foot trailer to your home, you pack and load as much of it as you need, and they drive the vehicle to your destination (usually with some commercial freight filling up the empty space). Available through their web sites at www.cfmovesu.com and www.upack.com.

MOVERS

Surveys show that most people find movers through the Yellow Pages. If that's too random for you, probably the best way to find a mover is through a personal recommendation. Absent a friend or relative who can point you to a trusted moving company, try the internet; just type in "movers" on a search engine and you'll be directed to dozens of moving-related sites. For long distance or interstate moves, the **American Moving and Storage Association**'s site, www.moving.org, identifies member movers both in Washington and across the country. In the past, *Consumer Reports* (www.consumerreports.org) has published useful information on moving. Members of **AAA** can call their local office and receive discounted rates and service through AAA's Consumer Relocation Service.

Disagreeable moving experiences, while common, aren't obligatory. To aid you in your search for a hassle-free mover, we offer a few general recommendations. First and foremost, make sure any moving company you consider hiring is **licensed by the appropriate authority**:

- **The Washington Utilities and Transportation Commission (WUTC) regulates intrastate moves**. All movers operating within the state of Washington are required to have a valid state UTC permit. The permit number must appear on the mover's vehicles, advertisements, correspondence, business cards, and web site. A licensed mover must comply with UTC safety, insurance and service standards, and must perform its services at reasonable rates and within a reasonable time. WUTC offers a free "Moving Survival Kit" on its web site at www.wutc.wa.gov, where you also will find a list of registered movers. To check on your mover by phone, call WUTC consumer information at 800-562-6150 (toll-free in Washington), or 360-664-1160. When you call, you will be informed if the moving company is registered, and whether there have been complaints lodged against it.
- **Interstate moves** are regulated by the US Department of Transportation's **Federal Motor Carrier Safety Administration (FMCSA)**. When reviewing prospective carriers, make sure the carrier has a Department of Transportation MC ("Motor Carrier") or ICC MC number that should be displayed on all advertising and promotional material as well as on the truck. With the MC number in hand, you can

contact the Washington office of FMCSA at 360-753-9875 or check www.fmcsa.dot.gov to see if the carrier is licensed and insured. Before a move takes place, federal regulations require interstate movers to furnish customers with a copy of "Your Rights and Responsibilities When You Move." If they don't give you a copy, ask for one. FMCSA's role in the regulation of interstate carriers concerns safety issues, not consumer issues. To find out if any complaints have been filed against a prospective mover check with the Better Business Bureau (www.bbb.org) in the state where the moving company is licensed, as well as with that state's Consumer Protection Office.

ADDITIONAL RECOMMENDATIONS:

- If someone recommends a mover to you, get names (the salesperson or estimator, the drivers, the loaders). To paraphrase the NRA, moving companies don't move people, people do.
- Once you've narrowed your search down to two or three companies, ask a mover for references, particularly from customers who recently did moves similar to yours. If a mover is unable or unwilling to provide such information or tells you that it can't give out names because their customers are all in the federal Witness Protection Program . . . perhaps you should consider another company.
- Even though movers will put numbered labels on your possessions, you should make a numbered list of every box and item that is going in the truck. Detail box contents and photograph anything of particular value. Once the truck arrives on the other end, you can check off every piece and know for sure what did (or did not) make it. In case of claims, this list can be invaluable. Even after the move, keep the list; it can be surprisingly useful.
- Be aware that during the busy season (May through September), demand can exceed supply and moving may be more difficult and more expensive than during the rest of the year. If you must relocate during the peak moving months, call and book service well in advance, a month at least of your moving date. If you can reserve service way in advance, say four to six months early, you may be able to lock in a lower winter rate for your summer move.
- Whatever you do, *do not* mislead a salesperson about how much and what you are moving. And make sure you tell a prospective mover how far they'll have to transport your stuff to and from the truck as well as any stairs, driveways, obstacles or difficult vegetation, long paths or sidewalks, etc. The clearer you are with your mover, the better he or she will be able to serve you.

- You should ask for and receive a written estimate of the probable cost of your move. The estimate should clearly and accurately describe all charges. In Washington, there are two types of estimates: A **non-binding estimate** is an educated guess of what your move would cost based on the mover's survey of your belongings. In this scenario your final cost can exceed the non-binding estimate—though there is a limit on how much over the estimate the company can charge. A **binding estimate** is a written agreement that guarantees the price you pay based on the items to be moved and the services listed on the estimate, inventory or tally sheet.

- Remember that price, while important, isn't everything, especially when you're entrusting all of your worldly possessions to strangers. Choose a mover you feel comfortable with.

- Think about packing. Depending on the size of your move and whether or not you do the packing yourself, you may need a lot of boxes, tape and packing material. Boxes provided by the mover, while not cheap, are usually sturdy and the right size. Sometimes a mover will give a customer free used boxes. It doesn't hurt to ask. Also, *don't* wait to pack until the last minute. If you're doing the packing, give yourself at least a week to do the job, two is better.

- Listen to what the movers say; they are professionals and can give you expert advice about packing and preparing. Also, be ready for the truck on both ends—don't make them wait. Not only will it irritate your movers, but it may cost you. Understand, too, that things can happen on the road that are beyond a carrier's control (weather, accidents, etc.) and your belongings may not get to you at the time or on the day promised. (See note about insurance below.)

- Treat your movers well, especially the ones loading your stuff on and off the truck. Offer to buy them lunch, and tip them if they do a good job.

- Ask about insurance, the "basic" 60 cents per pound industry standard coverage is not enough. If you have homeowner or renter's insurance, check to see if it will cover your belongings during transit. If not, consider purchasing "full replacement" or "full value" coverage from the carrier for the estimated value of your shipment. Though it's the most expensive type of coverage offered, it's probably worth it. Trucks get into accidents, they catch fire, they get stolen—if such insurance seems pricey to you, ask about a $250 or $500 deductible. This can reduce your cost substantially but still give you much better protection in the event of a catastrophic loss. Transport irreplaceable items, such as jewelry, photographs or key work documents, yourself.

- Be prepared to pay the full moving bill upon delivery. Cash or bank/cashier's check may be required. Some carriers will take VISA and MasterCard but it is a good idea to get it in writing that you will be permitted to pay with a credit card since the delivering driver may not be aware of this and may demand cash. Unless you routinely keep thousands of dollars of greenbacks on you, you could have a problem getting your stuff off the truck.

- Above all, ask questions and if you're concerned about something, ask for an explanation in writing.
- Finally, before moving pets, attach a tag to your pet's collar with your new address and phone number in case your pet accidentally wanders off in the confusion of moving.

Those **moving within the Seattle area** with minimal belongings probably won't need a huge truck to complete the task. If you (and your friends) are not interested in loading and unloading a rented truck, you may consider hiring one of the following local movers. All were registered with the WUTC and held current permits at the time of publication:

- **Aviv Moving & Storage**, 13846 NE 12th Avenue #204, Bellevue, 206-381-8488, www.avivmovers.com
- **Bekins Northwest**, 425-775-8950, www.bekinsnorthwest.com
- **Cascade Moving & Storage**, 430 South Cloverdale Street, Seattle, 206-762-9100
- **Hansen Bros. Moving & Storage**, 910 North 137th Street, Seattle, 206-365-4454, www.hansenbros.com
- **Joe the Mover**, 206-441-5418, www.joethemover.com

According to the WUTC, moving costs in Washington are calculated in one of two ways, depending on the distance. For moves of 35 miles or more, rates are based on the weight of your goods and the distance hauled. For moves of less than 35 miles, rates are based on the number of workers used, the amount of time necessary to load, move and unload your goods, and the mover's hourly rate.

CONSUMER COMPLAINTS—MOVERS

If you have a problem with your mover that you haven't been able to resolve directly, you can file a complaint about an intrastate move with the **Washington Utilities and Transportation Commission**. Call the Consumer Affairs Section at 800-562-6150, or use the online complaint form at www.wutc.wa.gov. If yours was an interstate move, your options for government intervention or assistance are limited. Years ago the now-defunct Interstate Commerce Commission (ICC) would log complaints against interstate movers. Today, you're pretty much on your own. The Federal Motor Carrier Safety Administration recommends that you contact the Better Business Bureau in the licensing state, as well as that state's consumer protection office to register a complaint. If satisfaction still eludes you, begin a letter writing campaign: to the state Attorney General, to your congressional representative, to the newspaper, the sky's the limit. Of course, if the dispute is worth it, you can hire a lawyer and seek redress the all-American way.

STORAGE

If your new pad is too small for all of your belongings or if you need a temporary place to store your stuff while you find a new home, self-storage is the answer. Most units are clean, secure, insured, and inexpensive, and you can rent anything from a locker to your own mini-warehouse. You'll need to bring your own padlock and be prepared to pay first and last month's rent up front. Many will offer special deals to entice you, such as second month free. Probably the easiest way to find storage is to look in the Yellow Pages under "Storage—Self Service" or "Movers & Full Service Storage." To conduct your search online, visit the site of local yellow pages provider QwestDex at www.qwestdex.com and check under "Storage—Household and Commercial." To narrow the search to the ten units closest to your home click on "narrow search." Another online site is www.storagelocator.com.

Keep in mind that demand for storage surges in the prime moving months (May through September), so try not to wait until the last minute to rent storage. If you don't care about convenience, your cheapest storage options may be out in the boonies. You just have to figure out how to get your stuff there and back.

A word of warning: Unless you no longer want your stored belongings, pay your storage bill and pay it on time. Storage companies may auction the contents of delinquent customers' lockers.

- **12th & Madison Self Storage**, 1111 East Madison Street, 206-322-8408, www.u-storage.com
- **A-1 Self Storage**, 2648 15th Avenue West, 206-282-0200
- **Aaron's Mini-Storage Center**, 2030 Dexter Avenue North, 206-286-9155
- **Door-to-Door Storage**, 888-366-7222, www.doortodoor.com
- **Downtown Self Storage**, 1915 3rd Avenue, 206-441-2999
- **Magnolia Bridge Self Storage**, 1900 15th Avenue West, 206-286-1900
- **Nickerson Street Self Storage**, 1300 West Nickerson Street, 206-285-5800, www.nickersonstreetstorage.com
- **Public Storage**, 800-447-8673
- **Roosevelt Self Storage**, 6910 Roosevelt Way NE, 206-526-0900
- **Seattle Self Storage**, 1100 Poplar Place South, 206-323-3000
- **Shurgard Storage**, 800-SHURGARD, www.shurgard.com

CHILDREN

Studies show that moving can be hard on children. According to an American Medical Association study, children who move often are more likely to suffer from such problems as depression, worthlessness, and aggression. Often their academic performance suffers as well. If you must move there are a few things you can do to help your children through this stressful time:

- Talk about the move with your kids. Be honest but positive. Listen to their concerns. To the extent possible, involve them in the process.
- Make sure the child has his/her favorite possessions on the trip; *don't* pack "blankey" in the moving van.
- Make sure you have some social life planned on the other end. Your child may feel lonely in your new home and such activities can ease the transition.
- Keep in touch with family and loved ones as much as possible. Photos and phone calls are important ways of maintaining links to the important people you have left behind.
- If your child is of school age, take the time to involve yourself in his/her new school.

For younger children, there are dozens of good books on the topic. Just a few include, *Alexander, Who's Not (Do You Hear Me? I Mean It!) Going to Move* by Judith Viorst; *The Moving Book: A Kid's Survival Guide* by Gabriel Davis; *Goodbye/Hello* by Barbara Hazen; *The Leaving Morning* by Angela Johnson; and the *Little Monster's Moving Day* by Mercer Mayer.

For older children, try: *Amber Brown is Not a Crayon* by Paula Danziger; *Kid in the Red Jacket* by Barbara Park; *Hold Fast to Dreams* by Andrea Davis Pinkney; *Flip Flop Girl* by Katherine Paterson and *My Fabulous New Life* by Sheila Greenwald.

For general guidance, read *Smart Moves: Your Guide through the Emotional Maze of Relocation* by Nadia Jensen, Audrey McCollum and Stuart Copans (Smith & Krauss)

Visit www.firstbooks.com to order any of the above resources.

TAXES

If your move is work-related, some or all of your moving expenses may be tax-deductible—so you will want to keep those receipts. Though eligibility varies, depending, for example, on whether you have a job or are self-employed, the cost of moving yourself, your family and your belongings is generally tax deductible, even if you don't itemize. The criteria: In order to take the deduction your move must be employment-related, your new job must be more than 50 miles away from your current residence, and you must be at your new location for at least 39 weeks during the first 12 months after your arrival. If you take the deduction and then fail to meet the requirements, you will have to pay the IRS back, unless you were laid off through no fault of your own, or transferred again by your employer. It's probably a good idea to consult a tax expert regarding IRS rules related to moving. If you're a confident soul, get a copy of IRS Form 3903 (www.irs.gov) and do it yourself!

ONLINE RESOURCES—RELOCATION

- **www.erc.org**, Employee Relocation Council; if your employer is a member of this professional organization, you may have access to specialized reports and services. Non-members can use the online database of real estate agents and related services.
- **www.firstbooks.com**, relocation resources and information on moving to Atlanta, Boston, Chicago, Los Angeles, Minneapolis-St. Paul, New York City, San Francisco and the Bay Area, Washington, D.C., as well as London, England
- **www.homefair.com**, realty listings, moving tips, and more
- **www.jobrelocation.com**, consulting firm that works with employers and employees to design custom relocation aid packages
- **www.monstermoving.com**, comprehensive web portal featuring a tool that lets you compare movers' rate quotes online.
- **www.moverquotes.com**, comparison shop for mover quotes
- **www.moving.com**, a moving services site: packing tips, mover estimates, etc.
- **www.moving.guide.com**, movers and moving services
- **www.moving.org**, American Moving and Storage Association site; referrals to interstate movers, local movers, storage companies, and packing and moving consultants
- **http://realestate.yahoo.com**, national real estate and rentals listings; relocation advice
- **www.rent.net**, apartment rentals, movers, relocation advice and more
- **www.springstreet.com**, apartment rentals, moving tips, movers, and more
- **www.movedoc.com**, visit this site to order a copy of *Steiners Complete How to Move Handbook* by Clyde and Shari Steiner for $14.95, or to browse sample tips.
- **www.unitedrentals.com**, referrals to van lines
- **www.usps.com**, relocation information from the United States Postal Service

BANKING

A S SOON AS YOU FIND A PLACE TO HANG YOUR HAT, YOU WILL want to find a home for your money. For major deposits, shop around for interest rates, but for routine checking and savings, you'll be more interested in ATM fees, online banking options, and direct deposit services—an increasingly common alternative to getting a paycheck in the mail or on your desk. Although opening an account is fairly simple, it's a good idea to keep your old checking account current until you've completed the task of setting up a new one here. This can be particularly important if you're going to try to rent a home or apartment before opening a local account; many landlords won't accept a tenant who doesn't have a bank account.

The largest Seattle banks offer the convenience of branches through-out the Puget Sound area. There are also many smaller community banks offering competitive rates and services. Your employer or alma mater may offer membership in a credit union, which may give you better interest rates, lower loan fees, and low-fee checking.

Most of the following area banks have several branch offices in the city:

- **Bank of America**, 800-900-9000, www.bankofamerica.com
- **EvergreenBank**, 800-331-7922, www.evbank.com
- **First Mutual Bank**, 800-735-7303, www.firstmutual.com
- **HomeStreet Bank**, 800-719-8080, www.homestreetbank.com
- **KeyBank**, 800-KEY-2YOU, www.keybank.com
- **Northstar Bank**, 206-632-0200, www.northstarbankwa.com
- **Pacific Northwest Bank**, 206-624-0600, www.pnwbank.com
- **Seattle Savings Bank**, 888-262-8324, www.seattlesavingsbank.com
- **Sterling Savings Bank**, 888-678-7800, www.sterlingsavingsbank.net
- **US Bank**, 800-US-BANKS, www.usbank.com
- **United Savings & Loan Bank**, 206-624-7581
- **Viking Community Bank**, 206-784-2200, www.vikingbank.com

- **Washington Federal Savings Bank**, 206-624-7930, www.washington-federal.com
- **Washington First International Bank**, 206-292-8880, www.wfib.com
- **Washington Mutual**, 800-756-8000, www.wamu.com
- **Wells Fargo**, 800-TO-WELLS, www.wellsfargo.com

BANK ACCOUNTS AND SERVICES

You'll probably want to call around to find out about special promotions; many banks offer special deals or extra perks for opening a **checking account**. Be sure to ask if a **debit card** is available to use with your account. Debit cards, often displaying a VISA or MasterCard symbol, take the place of a written check, deducting the amount of your purchase directly from your checking account, usually at no charge. They can be used as an ATM card for cash withdrawals and deposits.

To open a checking account, you'll need to apply at the bank's web site, or visit a local branch office and bring the minimum deposit required (this amount varies from bank to bank, so call ahead). You will also need photo ID and proof of address (a letter or utility bill mailed to your new address, or your rental contract).

You may also want to open a **savings account** in addition to your checking account. With some banks, you will save on fees by having two accounts at the same location. Other services offered by banks include credit cards, loans, mortgages, and lines of credit.

Most banks in the Seattle area charge non-members a fee to use their ATM machines. This charge can range from 75 cents to $2.50. One notable exception is **Washington Mutual**. For a list of ATM locations, visit www.wamu.com.

CREDIT UNIONS

A low-cost alternative to a bank checking account is a similar type of account at a credit union.Normally, you must belong to a union or an employee organization to have access to these consumer-friendly nonprofits. Two large local credit unions are the Washington State Employee Credit Union and the Group Health Credit Union. Contact information for these and other local credit unions is listed here:

- **Boeing Credit Union**, 800-233-2328, www.becu.org
- **Group Health Credit Union**, 800-562-5515, www.ghcu.org
- **King County Credit Union**, 800-248-6928, www.kccu.com
- **Qualstar Credit Union**, 800-848-0018, www.qualstarcu.com
- **Seattle Metropolitan Credit Union**, 800-334-2489, www.smcu.com

- **US First Federal Credit Union**, 800-488-3300, www.usfirstfcu.org
- **Washington School Employees Credit Union**, 888-628-4010, www.wsecu.org
- **Washington State Employees Credit Union**, 800-562-0999, www.wastatecu.org

INTERNET BANKING

While online banking has been provided by traditional brick and mortar banks for years, there is a new breed of institutions, the so-called "stand-alone online banks" like **E*TRADE Bank**, www.etradebank.com, and **NetBank**, www.netbank.com. Although word is still out whether online banks really can stand alone (several have partnered up with other banks or businesses to diversify offerings), some believe that stand-alone online banks are the future of banking. Only time will tell whether consumers will give up the comfort and personal service provided by traditional banks. Even if you choose to do most of your banking at a traditional bank, it might be worth your while to investigate an online bank for high interest rate products like CDs.

According to a search of Bankrate.com (an industry-tracking site where you'll find information about auto loan rates, credit cards, CDs, home-equity loans, etc.), online banks that offer free checking and no minimum balance (though some may require a minimum amount to open the account) include:

- **Bank CaroLine**, 877-692-2765, www.bankcaroline.com
- **Bank of Internet USA**, 877-541-2634, www.bankofinternet.com
- **Directbanking**, 888-666-5500, www.directbanking.com
- **First Internet Bank of Indiana**, 888-873-3424, www.firstib.com
- **Giantbank.com**, 877-446-4200, www.giantbank.com
- **National InterBank**, 877-468-7265, www.nationalinterbank.com
- **NetBank**, 888-256-6932, www.netbank.com
- **Nexity Bank**, 877-738-6391, www.nexitybank.com
- **RBCCentura**, 800-236-8872, www.rbccentura.com
- **Stonebridge Bank**, 800-807-1666, www.stonebridgebank.com
- **USAccess Bank**, 877-363-2265, www.usaccessbank.com
- **Umbrella Bank**, 888-250-1585, www.umbrellabank.com

CONSUMER PROTECTION

If you have a problem with your financial institution, first try to resolve the issue through their customer service department or with a bank officer. If the matter concerns a discrepancy on your statement, time is usually important. Find out how long you have to resolve the situation, and file a written complaint with the bank as soon as possible. If attempts to resolve the issue are unsuccessful, call the **Washington State Attorney General's Office**, Consumer Protection Division complaints hotline at 206-464-6684, or visit www.wa.gov/ago/consumer.

CREDIT CARDS

As soon as you've established a new address in Seattle, chances are you'll start receiving plenty of credit card offers in the mail. In the unlikely event they don't find you, here are credit card companies you can contact:

- **American Express**, 800-THE-CARD, www.americanexpress.com
- **Department store credit cards**; check at the customer service counter or at the checkout counter. Many stores offer a discount on your first purchase, with some restrictions. Department store cards are sometimes easier to qualify for than traditional credit cards, and can be used to establish a credit history if you have none. Seattle-area department stores that offer credit cards include The Bon Marché (www.federated-fds.com/retail/bon_1_3.asp), Nordstrom (www.nordstrom.com), Mervyn's (www.mervyns.com), JC Penney (www1.jcpenney.com), Sears (www.sears.com) and Target (www.target.com).
- **Diner's Club**, 800-2DINERS, www.dinersclub.com
- **Discover Card**, 800-347-2683, www.discovercard.com
- **MasterCard and VISA**, www.mastercard.com, www.visa.com; most banks offer one of these two major credit cards, and you can sign up for the card when opening your bank account. However, you may be able to find a more competitive interest rate by shopping around. See **Additional Credit Card Resources** below.

A word of warning to credit card users: the biggest revenue sources for credit card issuers are penalty charges for late credit card payments. If you want to avoid high finance charges, determine your grace period—the period between the end of a billing cycle and the payment due date—and pay off your balance within this period. For some cards, grace periods have been eliminated (often the case for cards issued with rewards programs, such as university cards or frequent-flyer cards). Another method to calculate finance charges compounds interest daily instead of monthly. Called "daily periodic rate" billing, this may only squeeze a few extra pennies out of you, but they're still your pennies. Since credit card issuers are always coming up with new ways to improve their profits be sure to read the fine print in your contract. For additional consumer information access **CardWeb**, 800-344-7714, www.cardweb.com, or the **Consumer Action Organization**, www.consumer-action.org.

ADDITIONAL CREDIT CARD RESOURCES

A list of low-rate card issuers can be found on the internet at CardWeb, the Consumer Action Organization site, **BankRate.com**, www.bankrate.com, and **iMoneynet.com**, www.imoneynet.com.

To see your personal credit report, go to www.icreditreport.com. At this site, you can receive a copy (for $8) of your credit report from the three main credit bureaus. Just don't do it more than once a year or it could adversely affect your credit rating. You can also visit each credit bureau individually:

- **Equifax**, 800-685-1111, www.equifax.com
- **Experian**, 888-397-3742, www.experian.com
- **Trans Union Corporation**, 800-916-8800, www.transunion.com

TAXES

SALES TAX

Washington state residents do not pay a state income tax. Instead, there is a high sales tax (7% to 8.8%) that is charged on all purchases other than food and most prescription drugs. The sales tax is a combination of state and local taxes, so the rate varies by region. In Seattle, the sales tax rate is 8.8% (6.5% for the state, 1.9% for the city and .4% for the Regional Transit Authority.) After you've lived here for a while, you'll get used to paying more than the listed price for most items.

FEDERAL INCOME TAX

The IRS's Tax Help Line, 800-829-1040 is available for consumers with questions and/or in need of forms. For free publications about IRS tax services, call 800-829-3676. During tax season, IRS forms are available at local libraries and post offices. You can also find forms online at www.irs.gov. When filing federal tax forms, the following numbers may be useful:

- **Federal Teletax Information System**, 800-829-4477
- **Internal Revenue Service, Local Taxpayer Advocate**, 915 2nd Avenue, Room 456, 206-220-6037, outside Seattle, 877-777-4778
- **Washington State Department of Revenue**, 800-647-7706

ELECTRONIC INCOME TAX FILING

According to estimates by the IRS, in 2001, about 40 million taxpayers filed their taxes electronically. That figure is expected to grow. Filing electronically can be done with the proper software and an online service, or through an accredited agency for a much quicker return. Web sites for those considering filing online are: www.securetax.com, www.turbotax.com and www.onetax.com.

The IRS web site, www.irs.gov, includes such features as convenient payment options or direct deposit for those expecting a refund. This site also will direct you to IRS-accepted software brands. For some qualified individuals (single or married couples below a certain income level), the IRS accepts electronic filing over the telephone. Call 800-829-5166 for more details.

STARTING OR MOVING A BUSINESS

When Boeing decided to move its corporate headquarters from Seattle to Chicago in 2001, the company cited traffic, education, and taxes as its top complaints. However, according to an article published in the *Seattle Post-Intelligencer*, most believe the Puget Sound region remains a healthy place to do business. In fact, the *P.I.* reported that Washington was the third-most entrepreneur-friendly state in the nation, according to an index released by the Small Business Survival Committee in July of 2001, and the Corporation for Enterprise Development included Washington on its year 2000 honor role, scoring the state high on the competitiveness of existing industries and the vitality of new companies.

Business owners in Washington are subject to a business and occupation tax and/or a public utility tax. These are based on the gross receipts of the business. The rates vary depending on the type of business, from .0138% to 5.019%. The tax can be easy on established companies, but hard on start-up companies that have yet to show a profit, according to the *P.I.* article. In a report from the Washington Alliance for a Competitive Economy, "Washington's tax structure is a mixed bag for business," pointing out the state's drawbacks, but highlighting the fact that the state lacks a corporate and a personal income tax.

If you do choose to start a business in Washington, the state has created a simple, one-stop system called the Master License Service that will walk you through the process. For details, visit the **Department of Licensing** at www.wa.gov/dol, or call 360-664-1400.

ONCE YOU'VE FOUND A PLACE TO CALL HOME, YOU'LL NEED TO arrange phone service, electric and/or gas accounts, trash pick-up and so on. Most of your utilities can be hooked up with a phone call, although in some cases you may be required to mail or fax documents. Other services in this chapter, such as auto registration or photo ID, will require a visit to an office but you can probably live without these for a few days or even weeks. Also included in this chapter: a list of broadcast media; passport, voter, and library registration details; assistance with finding a doctor and/or vet; and consumer protection and safety information.

UTILITIES

ELECTRICITY

Seattle City Light, 206-684-3000, 206-684-3225 (TTY), www.ci.seattle.wa.us/light, supplies electricity for all residences within the city limits. You may use the City's automated voice response line to open a new account with Seattle City Light and Seattle Public Utilities: 206-684-4969. You should be prepared with your name, telephone number, place of employment, billing information and service address. You will also need to get a meter reading at your new address.

Outside the Seattle city limits, **Puget Sound Energy**, 888-225-5773, 800-962-9498 (TTY), www.pse.com, provides electrical service for the remainder of King County and much of Pierce County. Customer service is accessible at the above number 24 hours a day, 365 days a year. Multi-lingual representatives are available. In sections of Pierce County not reached by Puget Sound Energy, a dozen local municipal districts and small vendors serve residents. For instance, the City of Lakewood delivers electricity to residents there. If your community is not covered by any of the power companies listed here, contact your local city or county government for information about electric service (see **Useful Telephone Numbers and Web Sites**).

In Tacoma, electric service is provided by **Tacoma Power**, 253-502-8600, 253-502-8343 (TTY), www.tacomapower.com. In Snohomish County, including Everett, contact the **Snohomish County Public Utility District**, www.snopud.com, 425-783-1000; 425-783-8660 (TTY), or toll free in Western Washington at 877-783-1000, Monday-Friday, 8 a.m. to 5:30 p.m.

NATURAL GAS OR OIL HEAT

In Seattle, heating options are electric, natural gas or oil. Most likely you will go with whatever is already at your new house, apartment, or condominium. Unless the cost is included in your rent or condominium dues, you will be responsible for setting up a new account and for filling the existing tank (if using oil). If you decide to install a new furnace, water heater, or stove, you must be home for the line hook-up. If you choose the same fuel as the previous resident, just call for service; the gas or oil company will handle the rest. Natural gas is supplied to Seattle and Seattle suburbs by **Puget Sound Energy**, 888-225-5773, www.pse.com.

Heating oil may be purchased from any of several local companies; a few are listed here. Check the Yellow Pages for additional companies.

- **Ballard Oil Co.**, 206-783-0241, www.ballardoil.com
- **Bowman Oil, King County**, 800-660-4733, www.bowmanoil.com
- **Cascade Oil Company**, 800-823-6050, www.cascadeoil.com
- **Olson Energy Service**, 206-782-5522, www.olsonenergy.com
- **Pacific Heating Oil Company**, 206-632-1966
- **Rainier Petroleum Inc.**, 206-623-3480
- **Rossoe Energy Systems**, 206-725-7555, www.rossoe.com

TELEPHONE

You'll need a home phone number for most applications so you'll want to get your residential telephone service established before anything else. **Qwest** provides local telephone service in Seattle. Call 800-244-1111 (TTY), 800-223-3131, 7 a.m. to 7 p.m., weekdays to set up your account, or go to www.qwest.com, to order service online. Be prepared with the following information: home address, preferred long distance company, information on your previous phone account (including your former address and telephone number), and employment and credit information. A deposit may be required when you set up service depending on your credit status and previous telephone service history.

AREA CODES

The area code in Seattle, and just north and south of the city limits, is 206. A large block of cities located to the north, east, and south of Seattle use the 425 area code. In cities farther south, like Kent and Tacoma, the area code is 253. Other areas in Western Washington use 360 (both north and south of Seattle). East of the Cascades the area code is 509. Long distance calls require 11 digits (1 + area code + number).

The following area codes represent the Seattle local calling area and surrounding communities:

- 206: Bainbridge Island, Des Moines, Richmond Beach, Seattle, Vashon
- 253: Auburn, Des Moines, Kent, Tacoma
- 425: Ames Lake, Bellevue, Bothell, Duvall, Everett, Halls Lake, Issaquah, Kirkland, Maple Valley, North Bend, Redmond, Renton, Snoqualmie

LONG DISTANCE

Long distance service providers frequently advertise very low per-minute rates, but be sure to read the fine print. If you have to pay $5.95 a month to get the five-cents per minute deal, and you don't make many long distance calls, it may make more sense for you to use a pre-paid calling card— or even your cell phone for long distance. For help comparing long distance and wireless calling plans, visit the **Telecommunications and Research and Action Center** (**TRAC**) (not affiliated with the telecommunications industry), www.trac.org, or call them at 202-263-2950. Major long distance service providers include:

- **AT&T**, 800-222-0300, www.att.com
- **MCI**, 800-955-0925, www.mci.com/service
- **Sprint**, 800-877-4000, www.sprint.com

CELLULAR PHONES

There are many choices for cellular service in Seattle. Shop around, as rates and telephone prices can vary widely, and always ask about current promotions or discounts before committing yourself to a contract. If you will be working for a large company or government agency, ask your employer whether there is a company service plan. Often these offer much lower rates than you could get on your own. Listed here are some cellular companies that serve the Seattle area:

- **AT&T Wireless Services**, 800-888-7600, www.attws.com
- **Cingular Wireless**, 866-246-4852, www.cingular.com
- **Qwest Wireless**, 800-222-3772, www.qwest.com/wireless
- **Sprint PCS**, 800-480-4727, www.sprintpcs.com
- **Verizon Wireless**, 866-256-4646, www.verizonwireless.com
- **VoiceStream Wireless**, 888-787-3267, www.voicestream.com

PREPAID CELLULAR PHONE SERVICE

With only slightly higher rates and no 12-month contract or monthly fees, prepaid cellular phone service is catching on with those who need mobile phone service. Simply purchase a phone that comes with a prepaid card. Activate the card. When the money runs out, the card is easily replenished with a payment.

Bartell Drugs sells prepaid cellular phone service at all 50 of its Seattle-area stores. For a location near you check the Yellow Pages or visit www.bartelldrugs.com.

DIRECTORY ASSISTANCE

In today's web-oriented world, directory assistance need no longer be fee-laden. An online Yellow Pages directory is available from Qwest, www.qwestdex.com, and numerous sites are dedicated to providing telephone listings and web sites, including the following:

- www.555-1212.com
- www.altavista.com
- www.anywho.com
- www.superpages.com
- www.switchboard.com
- www.trac.org
- www.whowhere.lycos.com
- www.worldpages.com

Of course, you can still pay to access a local or national number by dialing 411. In Washington, a directory assistance call will cost you $1.25, for both local and national numbers.

ONLINE SERVICE PROVIDERS

There are many online service providers that offer basic internet access and e-mail service via existing phone lines. Some of these provide free service but often bombard you with advertisements. For a complete list of internet service providers located near you check the Yellow Pages under "Internet Access Providers."

For high-speed internet access, consider signing up for service on a digital subscriber line (known as DSL), or via cable modem access. DSL runs over copper wires like those used for telephone calls, but on a separate line. Unlike a dial-up option, a DSL connection is always on, so logging onto the internet is nearly instantaneous. Cable Internet access is available from cable TV providers. Like DSL, the cable modem is always on. One possible disadvantage with cable modem is that your access speed may decrease if your neighbors also use cable. Before you sign up for cable modem, ask the provider what speed they guarantee.

Whatever type of connection you select, here are a few questions you may want to ask:

- What must the provider do to your home when installing the system?
- Does the provider offer technical support?
- What are the tech support hours?
- What is the average wait on the telephone for technical support? How long is it before tech support e-mail is answered?
- Does the provider offer e-mail accounts?
- Will the provider host your web site?
- What is the monthly fee?

Here are a few companies that offer dial-up access, DSL and/or cable modem:

- **America Online**, 888-265-8003, www.aol.com
- **AT&T Worldnet Service**, 800-967-5363, www.att.com
- **Compuserve**, 800-848-8199, www.compuserve.com
- **Earthlink**, 800-511-2041, www.earthlink.com
- **Qwest Internet Services**, 877-660-6342, www.qwest.com/internet
- **Seanet**, 800-973-2638, www.seanet.com
- **Verizon**, 877-863-0151, www.verizon.net

WATER

Seattle Public Utilities supplies drinking water to more than 1.3 million people in the Seattle/King County area. If you are renting, the property owner must notify the utility of changes in occupancy, but it's likely you will be responsible for the monthly bill. If you have purchased a home, you must change the current service to your name. Call 206-684-3000, Monday-Friday, 7:30 a.m. to 6 p.m., Saturday 8 a.m. to 5 p.m., or visit www.cityofseattle.net/util.

According to Seattle Public Utilities, the water it provides, which is supplied by the Cedar River and Tolt River watersheds, meets or exceeds all federal drinking water quality standards. The Cedar River Watershed, 141 square miles in size, at an elevation ranging from 538 feet to 5,447 feet, collects between 57 and 140 inches of precipitation each year and supplies over 65% of the area's drinking water. The South Fork Tolt River in the foothills of the Cascades east of Carnation at an elevation ranging between 760 and 5,535 feet, collects between 90 and 160 inches of precipitation each year and supplies about 30% of Seattle's drinking water.

Like electricity, water service outside Seattle is provided by local public utility districts or private companies. If you live outside the Seattle Public

Utilities district, the Department of Ecology recommends that you call the city nearest you to determine your supplier. See the **Useful Phone Numbers and Web Sites** chapter to contact your local government office.

If you have questions or concerns about water quality, call the King County Department of Health, 206-296-4932, or the state Department of Ecology, 360-407-6000. For current reports on water quality and legislative activity related to the state's water supply, visit www.wa.gov.

GARBAGE AND RECYCLING

Seattle Public Utilities provides trash and recycling services. The Seattle Municipal Code requires that all residents have garbage containers and pay for garbage collection. Charges appear every other month on a combined utility bill, along with water and sewer fees. Garbage is collected once a week on an assigned day. The cost of the service depends on the number and size of garbage containers. Call 206-684-3000 for customer service or recorded information on rates and services. To view a rate table, visit www.cityofseattle.net/util/services/rates.

For most apartments and condominiums, sanitation and recycling fees are included in your monthly rent or dues. For single-family residences, your must buy a garbage can from the city or from a hardware store, and you must set up service with the city. The most common usage level is one 32-gallon can per week at a monthly cost of $16.10, but other options are available. There are also charges for additional garbage collected beyond your usual level of service. Yard waste is collected every other week, on the same day of the week as your garbage. The city requires that yard waste be contained in rigid cans, placed in Kraft paper or reusable polyethylene bags, or bundled with twine. A monthly charge of $4.25 covers up to four units of yard waste per collection.

The city also offers recycling pick-ups every other week at both houses and apartments in the city; scheduled on the same day as your garbage collection day. (Yard waste and recycling alternate weeks.) One recycling container is provided for newspapers, mixed papers, aluminum, plastic and tin. Glass must be collected in a separate container. Again, call 206-684-3000 for customer service or recorded information on rates and services. If you live in an apartment or condominium, these services should be provided for all tenants. If you are renting or have purchased a house, the recycling containers should be with the house.

The City of Seattle runs two recycling and disposal stations. Both transfer stations are open seven days a week, except for Thanksgiving, Christmas, and New Year's Day. Go to www.ci.seattle.wa.us/util for hours or directions.

- **North Recycling and Disposal Station**, 1350 North 34th Street
- **South Recycling and Disposal Station**, 8100 Second Avenue South

Residents outside Seattle should check with their local municipality regarding trash pick-up and recycling.

CONSUMER PROTECTION—UTILITY COMPLAINTS

It's always a good idea to try to resolve billing or other disputes directly with the utility company. If that fails you can file a formal complaint with the appropriate consumer complaint office. A division of the Department of Neighborhoods, the **Citizens Service Bureau** fields all complaints about city departments. According to the City of Seattle, the office responds to more than 54,000 citizen questions and complaints annually. Call the Citizens Service Bureau at 206-684-8811, or send an e-mail to city.action@ci.seattle.wa.us.

To file a complaint about a state department or independent company, contact the state **Consumer Protection Division** at 800-551-4636. You may also file a complaint online, or download a complaint form, at www.wa.gov/ago/consumer.

AUTOMOBILES

Details about licensing, operating and parking a car in Seattle, auto insurance, and seatbelt laws are covered here. For information about auto repair and consumer protection related to automobiles, check the **Helpful Services** chapter. Additional auto related listings, such as auto impound numbers, parking tickets and traffic violations line, and who to call about illegally parked and/or abandoned vehicles are in the **Useful Phone Numbers and Web Sites** chapter.

DRIVER'S LICENSE, STATE IDENTIFICATION

You must apply for a Washington State driver's license within 30 days of becoming a resident. You are considered a resident when you establish a permanent home in the state, register to vote, receive state benefits, apply for any state license, or seek in-state tuition fees. To obtain a license, you must pass a written exam, and a driving skills test may be required. If you have a valid driver's license from another state, the driving test may be waived. If you currently live out of state, you can order a Washington State Driver's Guide by phone, or find it on the Department of Licensing web site: www.wa.gov/dol/drivers/guide. The cost of your first five-year license is $32; $7 for your written exam and $25 for your license. The cost of a state photo ID is $4.

You must visit a department of licensing to obtain your license, temporary permit, or photo ID card. Recent customer service improvements have greatly increased the efficiency of these offices, but you're still better off going on a weekday rather than a Saturday when the lines are longer. Bring your current (valid or expired) license, other proof of identification, and proof of state residence, such as a utility bill or rental agreement. If you've recently been married and need your name changed on your driver's license, bring your marriage certificate. Finally, don't forget to bring cash or a personal check. The Department of Licensing does not accept credit cards. Most offices are open Tuesday, Wednesday, Friday, and Saturday from 8:30 a.m. to 4:30 p.m. and Thursday from 9:30 a.m. to 4:30 p.m., but office hours vary by location. Call to confirm hours of operation before you visit, or check their web site, www.wa.gov/dol.

- **Bellevue**, 525 156th SE, 425-649-4281
- **Downtown Seattle** (renewals only), 380 Union Street, 206-464-6845
- **East Seattle**, 5811 Rainier Avenue South, 206-721-4560
- **Everett**, 5313 Evergreen Way, 425-356-2967
- **Federal Way**, 1617 324th Street, 253-661-5001
- **Greenwood**, 320 North 85th Street, 206-706-4268
- **Kent**, 25410 74th Avenue South, 253-872-2782
- **Kirkland**, 10639 NE 68th Street, 425-827-0317
- **Lynnwood**, 18023 Highway 99, Suite E, 425-672-3409
- **North Bend**, 1535 North Bend Avenue, 425-888-4040
- **North Seattle**, 907 North 135th Street, 206-368-7261
- **Renton**, 1314 Union Avenue NE, 425-277-7230
- **Tacoma West**, 8313 27th Street West, 253-534-3218
- **Tacoma South**, 6402 South Yakima Avenue, Suite C, 253-593-2990
- **West Seattle**, 8830 25th Avenue SW, 206-764-4144

Low-income seniors and disabled persons may apply for a City of Seattle identification card, entitling them to discounts in the Seattle area. Call the Mayor's Office for Senior Citizens, 206-684-0500 for more information.

AUTO REGISTRATION

You must license your automobile or motorcycle within 30 days of becoming a Washington resident, even if your tabs from your previous state of residence are still valid. The fine for driving an unregistered vehicle is a minimum of $330.

To license your automobile in Washington you will pay a basic license fee of $30. In addition, you will pay various county and state fees totaling approximately $30. You may pay an $8.50 surcharge if you get your registration from a sub-agent (often worth the additional charge for the added efficiency; see below), a $15 emissions test charge (for vehicles manufactured after 1967; see below), and a $15 out-of-state fee if your vehicle was previously registered or titled in another state. The **State of Washington Department of Licensing** web page at www.wa.gov/dol offers tips on vehicle, vessel, and driver's licensing, or contact them at 1125 Washington Street SE, Olympia, 360-902-3600, 360-664-8885 (TDD). For more information on vehicle licensing in Washington, contact the **King County License and Regulatory Service Division**, 500 4th Avenue Room 401, 206-296-4000, www.metrokc.gov/lars/autoboat.

VEHICLE/VESSEL LICENSE SUB-AGENTS

- **Bellevue**: Alpine Management Services, 3927 Factoria Boulevard SE, Suite D-5, 424-747-2816; Bel-Red Auto License, 15600 NE 8th Suite O-14, 425-747-0444
- **Bothell**: Canyon Park Vehicle Licensing Agency, 20631-D Bothell-Everett Highway, 425-481-7113; Worthington Brokerage, 10035 NE 183rd Street, 425-481-1644
- **Edmonds**: Edmonds Auto License Agency, 550 5th Avenue South, 425-774-6657
- **Everett**: Bev's Auto Licensing Inc., 9111 Evergreen Way, 425-353-5333; Claremont Vehicle Licensing, 5319 Evergreen Way, 425-353-5557; Julie's Licensing Service, 1001 North Broadway, Suite A-7, 425-252-3518; Snohomish County Auditor Auto License, 3000 Rockefeller Avenue, 425-388-3371; Village Licensing, 9327 4th Street NE, Suite 7, 425-334-7311
- **Federal Way**: Federal Way Auto License Agency, 32610 17th Avenue South, Suite C4, 253-874-8375
- **Kent**: Kent Licensing Agency, 331 Washington Avenue South, 253-852-3110
- **Kirkland**: Lee Johnson Auto License, 12006 NE 85th Street, 425-828-4661
- **Lakewood**: Active Military/Civilian Agency, 12500 Bridgeport Way SW, 253-588-7786; Military Retired Bureau, 10644 Bridgeport Way SW, 253-588-9049
- **Lynnwood**: Lynnwood Auto License Agency, Fred Meyer, 4615 196th Street SW, Suite 150, 425-774-7662
- **Mountlake Terrace**: McMahan License Agency, 22911 56th Avenue West, 425-670-3874
- **Renton**: Fairwood/Maple Valley License Agency, 14276 SE 176th Street, 425-228-7234; Renton License Agency, 329 Williams Avenue South, 425-228-5640
- **Seattle**: Ballard Licensing Agency, 2232 NW Market Street, 206-781-0199; Bill Pierre License Agency, 12531 30th Avenue NE, 206-361-5505; Georgetown License Agency, 5963 Corson Avenue South,

206-767-7782; Puget Sound License Agency, 3820 Rainier Avenue South, Suite C, 206-723-9370; Siler Licensing, 628 SW 151st Street, 206-243-8222; University License Agency, 5615 Roosevelt Way NE, 206-522-4090; Wendels License and Service, 13201 Aurora Avenue North, Suite 2, 206-362-6161; West Seattle Licenses, 5048 California Avenue SW, 206-938-3111; White Center License Agency, 10250 16th Avenue SW, 206-763-7979

- **Snoqualmie**: Sno Falls Credit Union, 9025 Meadow Brook Way SE, 425-888-8705
- **Tacoma**: North Pacific Financial Service Inc., 5442 South Tacoma Way, 253-475-4112; Western Auto Licensing Inc., 215 South Garfield Street (Parkland), 253-537-3112; Pierce County Auditor Auto License, 2401 South 35th Street, Suite 200, 253-798-3649; Quik Stop Licensing II, 6722 West 19th Street (University Place), 253-564-6555
- **Woodinville**: Woodinville License Agency, 17403 139th Avenue NE, 425-486-0289

EMISSIONS TEST INFORMATION

In Clark, King, Pierce, Snohomish and Spokane counties, most vehicles must pass an emissions test every two years, even if the vehicle is certified in another state. The fee for testing is $15, and must be paid in cash. Testing station hours are Tuesday-Saturday, 9 a.m. to 5 p.m. For more information, call the state **Department of Ecology** at 800-272-3780, or visit the agency's web site at www.ecy.wa.gov.

- **Bellevue**: 15313 SE 37th Street, 425-644-1803
- **Des Moines**: 22406 Pacific Highway South, 206-824-2904
- **Kirkland**: 12415 132nd Avenue NE, 425-821-1002
- **Redmond**: 18610 NE 67th Court, 425-882-3317
- **Renton**: 805 SW 10th Street, 425-228-6453
- **Seattle**: 12040 Aurora Avenue North, 206-362-5173; 3820 6th Avenue South, 206-624-1254

AUTOMOBILE INSURANCE

The State of Washington requires drivers to have automobile insurance for all owned or leased vehicles, providing liability coverage for damage to the other driver's vehicle, as well as bodily damage to the driver and passengers of the other car. Minimum requirements are $25,000 for bodily injury to the other driver; $50,000 for total bodily injury to driver and all passengers; and $10,000 for property damage to the other driver's car. The fines for not carrying automobile insurance are steep, close to $400. You are required to show proof of insurance if stopped for a moving violation or if involved in an automobile accident. Coverage is available from area and national insurance companies. Contact your homeowners' insurance agent first, and ask about a possible discount for carrying multiple policies with the same company. Check the Yellow Pages under "Insurance" for listings of area companies. The **Washington State Insurance Commissioner** provides a free online consumer guide to auto insurance at www.insurance.wa.gov.

AUTOMOBILE SAFETY

Washington is a pretty safe place for drivers. According to the state Traffic Safety Commission, that's largely due to the region's reliance on freeways, which are roughly three times safer than other roads and city streets. When highway accidents do occur, they are often caused by the combination of drinking and driving.

In 1996, alcohol-related deaths accounted for nearly half of the state's traffic fatalities. This was much higher than the corresponding National Highway Transportation Safety Administration's nationwide statistic. To halt this alarming trend, in 1999, Washington became the 16th state to drop its legal blood-alcohol level for drivers to 0.08 %.

According to the Washington State Patrol, the new laws give police more power when arresting people charged with DUI (driving under the influence), allowing them to suspend driver's licenses, impound vehicles, and pursue drivers across state lines. The rules also require breath-triggered ignition locks for at least a year, for those drivers convicted of DUI with alcohol levels above 0.15 %, and limit to once in a lifetime the opportunity to avoid DUI prosecution by entering an alcohol-treatment program.

Washington also regulates the use of seat belts and child restraints. Every person riding in a motor vehicle must wear a seat belt. Child guidelines are: kids under one year or less than 20 pounds must ride in a rear-facing infant seat; kids between one and four years, or up to 40 pounds, must be in a forward-facing safety seat; and kids between four and six, or up to 60 pounds, must ride in a booster seat. Driving without a seatbelt is considered a primary offense, meaning officers can pull you over for that reason alone. The fine for driving without a seatbelt is $86. For tips on properly installing car seats check with your local fire department or go to www.safekids.org.

PARKING

Parking in Seattle can be challenging at times, but if you're moving here from another large city you'll probably be pleasantly surprised. While parking for a few hours in the business district can be very expensive, there are affordable lots in some parts of downtown. Street parking is also available throughout downtown, at a cost of $1 per hour, but be sure to read the signs carefully. Some streets restrict parking during the busiest traffic hours;

other parking meters have special time restrictions or fees. Parking fines are not insignificant: $25 for a street parking infraction. (See below for more about parking tickets.) The good news on street parking downtown is that you only need to pay between 8 a.m. and 6 p.m. Monday-Saturday. Meters are also free on holidays.

If you'll be commuting to downtown Seattle, your least expensive, and possibly most convenient, option may be to take the bus. If that's not practical, consider setting up or joining a carpool, and take advantage of reduced parking fees. Call **City of Seattle Commuter Services** at 206-684-0816 to arrange for a carpool-parking permit. The cost for downtown carpool parking is $250 per quarter (three months) for a two-person carpool or $125 per quarter for a three-person carpool. (See **Transportation** for more information.) Your employer may offer discounts at nearby parking lots or offer incentives to carpool or ride mass transit.

If you prefer to drive to work by yourself, arrange to rent a space in a parking lot or garage. Street parking is too expensive and inconvenient for all-day parking. Here is a partial list of downtown parking garages.

- **1111 3rd Avenue Garage**, 1111 3rd Avenue, 206-623-0226
- **4th & Columbia Parking**, 723 4th Avenue, 206-622-7373
- **520 Pike Building Garage**, 520 Pike Street, 206-340-8803
- **Harbor Steps Garage**, 1200 Western Avenue, 206-622-4846
- **IBM Building Garage**, 1200 5th Avenue, 206-623-2675
- **Key Tower Garage**, 700 5th Avenue, 206-628-9042
- **King Street Garage**, 83 South King Street, 206-340-0738
- **Norton Building Garage**, 800 1st Avenue, 206-622-2870
- **Parking at Pacific Place**, 600 Pine Street, 206-652-0416
- **Public Market Parking**, 1531 Western Street, 206-621-0469
- **Seattle Tower Garage**, 3rd Avenue at University Street, 206-624-2473
- **Securities Building Garage**, 1922 3rd Avenue, 206-623-9937; 1913 4th Avenue, 206-269-0762
- **Third Avenue Building Garage**, 1111 Third Avenue, 206-623-0226
- **U-Park**: Tower Lot, 1825 7th Avenue; 7th Avenue & Marion Street; 100 4th Avenue South, 206-284-9797
- **Union Square Garage**, 601 Union Street, 206-447-5664
- **United Airlines Building Garage**, 2020 5th Avenue, 206-448-9992
- **Union Station Parking Garage**, 550 4th Avenue South, 206-652-4602

RESIDENTIAL PARKING PERMITS

In Seattle proper, residential neighborhood parking has become a problem within the last ten years. Although there is still free street parking in residential neighborhoods, restrictions are common. Restricting parking on busy streets is done to keep traffic flowing, and parking time limits keep spaces available for shoppers. Other restrictions that limit parking on residential streets during certain hours of the day target habitual long-term parking by people who do not live in the area. For instance, neighborhoods with popular theaters and restaurants may have evening parking restrictions; areas with office buildings or hospitals nearby may have daytime parking restrictions. If your neighborhood has restricted parking, you'll want to get a residential parking permit. These permits cost $27 and are usually good for two years. Call **Seattle Transportation** at 206-684-7623 for more information, or visit www.cityofseattle.net.

PARKING TICKETS

If you get a parking ticket, you must pay it within 15 days, or you'll be charged a penalty. The city will also notify the state Department of Licensing and a collection agency. To pay in person, visit the **Municipal Court of Seattle** in the Public Safety Building, 600 3rd Avenue: 8 a.m. to 5 p.m. Monday-Friday. The court will accept cash, cashier's check, money order, VISA or MasterCard. If you can't get away during business hours, there is a green deposit box in front of the building, but only cashier's checks or money orders are accepted. Finally, you can mail payments to the Municipal Court of Seattle, 600 3rd Avenue, Room 100, Seattle, WA 98104. For more information about parking tickets, call 206-684-5600 or visit www.cityofseattle.net/courts.

TOWED OR STOLEN CARS

There are five impound lots in Seattle that are operated by the city. If you believe that your vehicle has been impounded by order of the police department, call 206-684-5444 (have your license number ready) and you will be directed to the appropriate lot. If your car was towed while on private property, call the owner or manager of that property or the posted towing company number. To report a stolen vehicle, call the **Seattle Police Department** non-emergency line at 206-625-5011.

SOCIAL SECURITY

It is the rare American citizen who does not have a Social Security number. Non-citizens who are working or studying here will also need a number. This can be done by mail, by first calling 800-772-1213 and answering five automated questions, then mailing a completed application form with the necessary documents (the form will be sent after the initial telephone interview); or go online to www.ssa.gov. You may also visit the nearest Social Security office (see the telephone book or get the address from the 800 number above or at www.ssa.gov), no appointment necessary.

Bring with you a certified birth certificate and two other pieces of iden-tification: passport, driver's license, school or government ID, health insur-ance card, military records, an insurance policy. A Social Security employee will complete the application, and you should receive a card with your number within several weeks.

Non-citizens need a birth certificate and/or a passport and a green card or student documentation, as well as whatever immigration docu-ments you have. It may take a month or more to receive a card.

If you already have a number but have lost your card, call the number above to apply for a new card.

VOTER REGISTRATION

To register to vote in Seattle, you must be at least 18 years old, a citizen of the United States, and a legal resident of the state of Washington. To vote in an upcoming election, you must register at least 30 days prior. You may register to vote at government offices, schools, and public libraries. You can also register through the mail or through the "Motor Voter" program. "Motor Voter" registration is completed when you apply for or renew your driver's license. It takes only an extra minute or two. You need not declare your political affiliation or party membership when you register. Absentee ballots are available up to 45 days before an election. The rules for receiving absentee ballots are not particularly rigid in Washington, and many voters use absentee ballots even when they expect to be in the area on election day. For more information or to register by mail, call the Secretary of State's **Voter Information and Elections Hotline** at 800-448-4881, 800-422-8683 (TTY), or go to www.secstate.wa.gov/elections/register.

LIBRARY CARDS

The Seattle metropolitan area has two overlapping library systems, the Seattle Public Library and the King County Library System. Both libraries offer an extensive selection of books and other materials, and upon request, will reserve books at other libraries in their system for your use.

The **Seattle Public Library** free service area includes the City of Seattle, the City of Bothell, and most of King County. The exceptions are the cities of Enumclaw, Renton, Yarrow Point, and Hunts. Anyone who lives, works, attends school, or owns property within the service area quali-fies for a free library card. Seattle Public Library cards are available at any neighborhood library. Check the **Neighborhoods** chapter for listings of Seattle libraries near you. You must show identification, such as a driver's license or passport. If you live outside the library's free service area, you can purchase a non-resident library card for an annual fee of $50. For more information, call Borrower Services at 206-386-4190.

To borrow books from the **King County Library System (KCLS)**, you must apply for a King County Library card, which is available to anyone who lives in the KCLS service area, or in the service area of another library system that has a reciprocal borrowing agreement. This includes residents of Seattle, Renton, and Enumclaw. The KCLS service area consists of unincorporated King County and just about every city in the county. For the complete list, visit www.kcls.org. You can apply for a card at any King County Library branch or online at www.kcls.org. You must provide ID and verification of your address. Call the following for more information:

- **Seattle Public Library**, **Central Library**, 800 Pike Street, 206-386-4636, www.spl.lib.wa.us
- **King County Library System**, Main Office, 960 NW Newport Way, 800-462-9600, www.kcls.org

Seattle residents also benefit from proximity to the University of Washington and its libraries. Free services to visitors include in-library use of most materials, limited access to library computers, reference assistance, tours, and classes. Call 206-543-0242 or visit www.lib.washington.edu for more information. See the **Literary Life** section of the **Cultural Life** chapter for a list of UW libraries.

PASSPORTS

In Seattle, passports are processed at the **Seattle Passport Agency**, located downtown at the US Department of State, 915 2nd Avenue Suite 992, 206-808-5700 (appointment line). This office serves only those customers who are traveling within two weeks or who need foreign visas for travel, and is by appointment only. Hours are Monday-Friday, 8 a.m. to 3 p.m. Those not meeting that criteria may pick up passport applications at the Lake City, University District, Ballard, Delridge, West Seattle, Southeast and Central neighborhood service centers. Check the **Neighborhoods** chapter for locations. Bring two standard passport photos, a picture ID, and proof of US citizenship, such as a previous US passport, certified birth certificate, naturalization certificate or certificate of citizenship. The cost is $85 for a new passport and $55 to renew a passport less than 12 years old. The standard turnaround time for a new passport is 25 days, but an expedited three-day passport can be requested for an additional $60 fee. For appointments and recorded information, call the Seattle Passport Agency office. To use the internet for your passport application go to the web site for the **Bureau of Consular Affairs**, www.travel.state.gov.

TELEVISION

CABLE

AT&T Broadband provides cable television service to all of Seattle except for some parts of the Central District, where residents are served by **Millennium Digital Media**, 800-829-2225. Millennium also serves Duvall, the Sammamish Plateau (east of Redmond and north of Issaquah), Redmond, Issaquah, and Bellevue. AT&T Broadband currently offers more than 200 channels in Seattle, with similar lineups in King, Pierce and Whatcom counties. The range of channels may vary slightly by city, depending on the number of city-required education and government channels. The company also offers digital cable, which allows for more channels, and better picture and sound. Installation fees and monthly rates vary depending on which package you choose, but the company frequently offers special packages to new customers. Prices can range from $12 per month for basic cable to a $80 for the full spectrum of channels. To order new service, call 877-824-2288, or visit www.attbroadband.com/services. AT&T Broadband office locations are listed here:

- Auburn, 4020 Auburn Way North
- North Seattle, 1140 North 94th Street
- Redmond, 14870 NE 95th Street
- South Seattle, 15241 Pacific Highway South

LOCAL STATIONS

If you signed up for cable or satellite service, the local broadcast stations listed here may differ:

- Channel 4, KOMO-TV, ABC
- Channel 5, KING-TV, NBC
- Channel 6, KONG-TV, NBC
- Channel 7, KIRO-TV, CBS
- Channel 9, KCTS-TV, PBS
- Channel 11, KSTW-TV, UPN
- Channel 13, KCPQ-TV, FOX
- Channel 10/22, KTZZ-TV, WB

RADIO STATIONS

Seattle area residents love their music! Here's a guide to local radio stations:

ADULT CONTEMPORARY
- KBKS, 106.1 FM
- KLSY, 92.5 FM
- KMIH, 104.5 FM
- KMTT, 103.7 FM
- KPLZ, 101.5 FM
- KYPT, 96.5 FM

ALTERNATIVE/MODERN ROCK
- KCMU, 90.3 FM
- KGRG, 89.9 FM
- KKBY, 104.9 FM
- KNDD, 107.7 FM

CHRISTIAN
- KCIS, 630 AM
- KCMS, 105.3 FM
- KGNW, 820 AM
- KLFE, 1590 AM

CLASSIC SOUL
- KSRB, 1150 AM

CLASSICAL
- KING, 98.1 FM

COUNTRY
- KMPS, 94.1 FM
- KRPM, 1090 AM

JAZZ
- KBCS, 91.3 FM
- KPLU, 88.5 FM
- KWJZ, 98.9 FM

KIDS
- KKDZ, 1250 AM

KOREAN
- KSUH, 1450 AM
- KWYZ, 1230 AM

NEWS, NPR
- KIRO, 710 AM
- KNWX, 770 AM
- KOMO, 1000 AM
- KPLU, 88.5 FM
- KRKO, 1380 AM
- KUOW, 94.9 FM

OLDIES
- KBSG, 97.3 FM
- KBSG, 1210 AM

PUBLIC AFFAIRS
- KSER, 90.7 FM

ROCK
- KISW, 99.9 FM
- KIXI, 880 AM
- KRWM, 106.9 FM
- KZOK, 102.5 FM

SPORTS
- KIRO, 710 AM
- KJR, 950 AM

TALK RADIO
- KJR, 950 AM
- KKOL, 1300 AM
- KOMO, 1000 AM
- KQBZ, 100.7 FM
- KRKO, 1380 AM
- KVI, 570 AM

TOP 40/DANCE
- KNHC, 89.5 FM

URBAN CONTEMPORARY
- KRIZ, 1420 AM
- KUBE, 93.3 FM
- KYIZ, 1620 AM

WORLD MUSIC AND FOLK
- KBCS, 91.3 FM
- KCMU, 90.3 FM

LOCAL NEWSPAPERS AND MAGAZINES

In March 2000, the *Seattle Post-Intelligencer* and *The Seattle Times*, the city's two metropolitan daily newspapers, squared off in head-to-head competition as *The Times* moved from afternoon publishing to morning. Six months after the switch, the Audit Bureau of Circulations calculated the *P-I*'s circulation at 175,794, and *The Times*' at 225,687. *The Seattle Times*, locally owned by the Blethen family since 1896, and the *Post-Intelligencer*, founded in 1863 and now part of the Hearst Corporation, though separately owned and managed, share a joint operating agreement that allows *The Times* to handle advertising, circulation, production and promotion for both. News and editorial functions remain separate.

The following newspapers and magazines serve Seattle and surrounding communities:

- *Eastside Journal*, 1705 132nd Avenue NE, Bellevue, 425-455-2222, www.eastsidejournal.com
- *The Herald*, 1213 California Avenue, Everett, 425-339-3000, www.heraldnet.com
- *Issaquah Press*, 425-392-6434, www.isspress.com
- *Mercer Island Reporter*, 7845 SE 30th Street, 206-232-1215, www.mi-reporter.com
- *Puget Sound Business Journal*, 720 Third Avenue, Suite 800, 206-583-0701, http://seattle.bcentral.com/seattle
- *Seattle Daily Journal of Commerce*, 83 Columbia Street, 206-622-8272, www.djc.com
- *Seattle Homes and Lifestyles*, 1221 East Pike Street, 206-322-6699, www.seattlehomesmag.com
- *Seattle Magazine*, 423 3rd Avenue West, 206-284-1750, www.seattlemag.com
- *Seattle Post-Intelligencer*, 101 Elliott Avenue West, 206-464-2121, www.seattle-pi.com
- *The Seattle Times*, 1120 John Street, 206-464-2111, www.seattletimes.com
- *Seattle Weekly*, 1008 Western Avenue, Suite 300, 206-623-0500, www.seattleweekly.com
- *South County Journal*, 600 South Washington Avenue, Kent, 253-872-6600, www.southcountyjournal.com
- *The Stranger*, 1535 11th Avenue, 3rd Floor, Seattle, 206-323-7101, www.thestranger.com
- *Tacoma News Tribune*, 1950 South State Street, 253-597-8742, www.tribnet.com
- *Valley Record*, 8124 Falls Avenue, Snoqualmie, 425-888-2311
- *Washington CEO*, 200 West Thomas Street, Seattle, 206-441-8415, www.waceo.com

FINDING A PHYSICIAN

When searching for a doctor in Seattle you will find plenty of options. Begin by determining your needs: are you looking for a general family practitioner or a specialist? An MD or a naturopath? Do you prefer the comforts of a small clinic or the more extensive services of a large hospital? And perhaps most importantly, does your health plan limit who you can see? Many new residents rely on recommendations from friends or co-workers when looking for a doctor. Another option is to contact the **King County Medical Society** at 206-621-9393 or www.kcmsociety.org. Their web site allows you to search by physician's last name, zip code, specialty or language. Or, call a physician referral line or local hospital. Here is a list of local referral lines, many of which are affiliated with major area hospitals.

- **Children's Hospital and Regional Medical Center**, 877-526-2500, www.seattlechildrens.org
- **King County Medical Society**, 206-621-9393, www.kcmsociety.org
- **Northwest Hospital Physician Referral**, 206-633-4636, www.nwhospital.org
- **Overlake Hospital Medical Center**, 425-688-5211, www.overlakehospital.org
- **PacMed Clinics**, 888-472-2633, www.pacmed.org
- **Swedish Medical Center**, 800-793-3474, www.swedish.org
- **UW Physicians**, 800-489-3627, www.uwphysicians.org
- **Valley Medical Center**, 425-656-4636, www.valleymed.org
- **Virginia Mason**, 888-862-2737, www.virginiamason.org
- **Washington Association of Naturopathic Physicians**, 206-547-2130
- **Washington Osteopathic Medical Association**, 206-937-5358

Should you have a **serious complaint** about a medical provider, which you cannot resolve directly with your provider, contact the **Washington Medical Quality Assurance Commission**, P.O. Box 47866, Olympia, WA 98504, 360-236-4700, or the Washington State Board of Osteopathic Medicine and Surgery (same address and phone number).

The Office of the Washington State Insurance Commissioner assists consumers with questions about health insurance concerns, from Medicare to HMOs to long-term care, through their **Statewide Health Insurance Benefits Advisors (SHIBA)**. Call their consumer hotline, 800-562-6900 (7 a.m. to 7 p.m.) or their referral line, 800-397-4422 (24 hours).

PET LAWS & SERVICES

Pets in Seattle must be licensed annually, even those that generally are kept inside. A dog license costs $33.00 ($15.00 if the dog is spayed or neutered); cats are $20.00 ($10.00 if the cat is spayed or neutered). To qualify your pet for a license, you must provide proof that your pet has received a current rabies vaccination. The reduced license fee for a spayed or neutered pet requires a copy of a veterinarian's spay or neuter certificate. Low-income senior citizens and disabled persons with a City of Seattle ID card qualify for a 50% discount on all fees. (See the **Driver's License, State Identification** section of this chapter for more information about ID cards.)

All four-legged pets (except cats) must be on a leash or held by the owner when in public places in Seattle, including sidewalks. In addition, Seattle has strict "scoop laws" that require the person in charge of the animal to clean up after the pet.

Six city parks have "off-leash" areas where pets are allowed to roam freely, but there are a few rules. Owners must have voice control over their pets, dogs must be licensed, and poop must be scooped.

- **"Blue Dog Pond,"** Martin Luther King Jr. Way South and South Massachusetts
- **Genesee Park**, 46th Avenue South and South Genesee Street
- **Golden Gardens Park**, 8498 Seaview Place NW
- **Sand Point Magnuson Park**, 6500 Sandpoint Way NE
- **Westcrest Park**, 8806 8th Avenue SW
- **Woodland Park**, West Greenlake Way

Pilot dog-park sites are also open at **Northacres Park,** west of I-5 at North 130th Street, and at **Jose Rizal Park**, 1008 12th Avenue South on North Beacon Hill. One of the area's most popular dog parks is located outside the city limits in Redmond. This off-leash area at **Marymoor Park** covers over 40 acres and provides dogs with swimming and fetching opportunities. A non-profit group, **Serve Our Dog Areas**, is dedicated to its maintenance and preservation. To volunteer, call 425-881-0148.

If you're interested in adopting an animal, you can visit the **Seattle Animal Control Center** at 2061 15th Avenue West (in the Interbay area), 206-386-4254. Fees range from $20 to $90 depending on the size and breed of the animal. You must provide current photo ID, and your landlord's name and phone number if you live in a rental property. For more information about Seattle Animal Control and pets available for adoption, visit the SAC web site at www.ci.seattle.wa.us/rca/animal.

Organizations that may prove useful for those who have lost a pet or have found a stray are:

- **Humane Society for Seattle/King County**, 13212 SE Eastgate Way, Bellevue, 425-641-0080, www.seattlehumane.org
- **King County Animal Control Shelter**, 821 164th Avenue NE, Bellevue, 206-296-3940; 21615 64th Avenue South, Kent, 206-296-7387, www.metrokc.gov/lars/animal
- **King County Animal Control Enforcement**, 206-296-7387

- **Progressive Animal Welfare Society (PAWS)**, 15305 44th Avenue West, Lynnwood, 425-787-2500, www.paws.org
- **Seattle Animal Control Shelter**, 2061 15th Avenue West, 206-386-4254, www.cityofseattle.net/rca/animal
- **Seattle Animal Control Hotline** (Lost Pets), 206-386-4254, www.city-ofseattle.net/rca/animal

PET CARE SERVICES

If the of off-leash areas in the city's parks aren't enough to convince you that Seattle has gone to the dogs in recent years, consider the rise in the canine comfort industry, and the increase in pet-sitting and dog-walking providers. If you must leave your dog or cat home alone for the day—or for weeks—consider hiring a surrogate or sending your pet to daycare.

- **Atwood Pet Resorts**, 206-241-0880, www.petresort.com
- **Bone-A-Fide Dog Ranch**, 206-501-9247, www.bone-a-fide.com
- **Cat Calls**, 206-286-1366
- **Central Bark Productions**, 206-322-8874
- **Dogvana**, 206-223-1131, www.dogvana.com
- **Happy Camper Pet Service**, 206-784-5291, www.happycamperpets.com
- **Lap of Luxury**, 206-217-0317
- **The Pet Au Pair**, 206-200-5357, www.mypetaupair.com
- **Kitty Love Cat Sitting Service**, 206-781-0208, www.kittyluv.com
- **Pet Sitters of Puget Sound Referral Line**, 206-622-7387
- **Whisker Watchers**, 206-322-1210, www.whiskerwatchers.com

SAFETY AND CRIME

According to statistics compiled by the FBI, in 2001, 21,451 crimes were reported in Seattle, a 5.5% drop from the previous year. (Nationally, the number of reported offenses decreased 0.3%.) The FBI Crime Index categories that experienced increases in Seattle were burglary, which grew from 2,960 reported incidents in 2000 to 3,044 in 2001, and arson, which grew from 68 incidents to 105.

If the state of Washington and the city of Seattle have an Achilles heel when it comes to crime, it is auto thefts, which have plagued the region for more than a decade. In 1999, according to *The Seattle Times*, 587 cars were stolen per 100,000 in the state, above even California's rate of 508. Areas that suffered most were Fremont, Green Lake, Northgate, Queen Anne, and Broadview. These neighborhoods all posted increases of 60% or more when comparing 1994-1996 with 1998-2000. The problem persists: in 2001, Seattle police reported 4,195 motor vehicle thefts.

Auto theft is a crime of opportunity, so your best defense is to deny a thief the opportunity to take your automobile. Also protect yourself from car prowls or smash and grabs by not leaving anything in the car. Valuable or not, items left in cars are tempting to thieves. The Seattle Police Department Car Prowl Task Force recommends the following preventive measures:

- Always lock your car, and remove valuables when parking.
- Park in well-lighted areas, even at home.
- Park in areas of busy pedestrian traffic.
- Call 911 to report suspicious activity.

Auto thefts and car prowls notwithstanding, most Seattle neighborhoods are safe. Take precautions, however, especially in unfamiliar areas. The following safety tips may be helpful: walk quickly and with a purpose, especially at night; don't dawdle or slow your pace, even when approached, and keep clear of alleyways, deserted areas and dead ends. If riding in a bus, stay close to the front, near the driver. Most of all, trust your instincts. If you feel uneasy about a person or situation, there may be a good reason for it. For more personal safety tips, visit the Seattle Police Department's crime page at www.cityofseattle.net/police.

Many neighborhoods participate in **Block Watch**, a free program sponsored by the Seattle Police Department. For more information, call 206-684-7555 or visit www.cityofseattle.net/police.

N OW THAT YOU HAVE A PLACE TO CALL HOME, AND HAVE TAKEN care of the basics like setting up electricity and gas accounts, you might have time to investigate and benefit from some of the area's helpful services. Services, such as **House Cleaning, Pest Control** or **Automobile Repair** can make your life a bit simpler. Other sections in this chapter include **Postal and Shipping Services, Consumer Protection, Services for People with Disabilities**, and **Gay and Lesbian Life**.

DOMESTIC SERVICES

For those who need a little extra help around the house, the following services might be of interest. Check the Yellow Pages for more listings.

DIAPER SERVICES

- **Baby Diaper Service**, 206-634-2229, www.diapers.com
- **Pure & Natural Diaper Service**, 206-767-1807, www.seattlediaper.com
- **Sunflower Diaper Service**, 206-782-4199

DRY CLEANING DELIVERY

- **AmeriCleaners.com**, www.americleaners.com
- **Fashion Care Cleaners**, 1822 Terry Avenue, 206-382-9265
- **Four Seasons Cleaners**, 2800 15th Avenue West, 206-286-9696, www.fourseasonscleaners.com
- **Hogan's Corner Drycleaners**, 5501 25th Avenue NE, 206-526-9754
- **Stadium Cleaners**, 3307 NE 65th Street, 206-522-9125
- **Village Cleaners**, 2672 NE University Village Mall, 206-522-1033

HOUSE CLEANING

You may decide to use a house-cleaning service before you move into your new home or for routine chores on an ongoing basis. A few house-cleaning businesses are listed below. As with all lists in this guide, inclusion does not indicate endorsement. If you are not satisfied with the service you receive from a company during the initial cleaning, request that they clean again at no charge.

- **Best Homemakers**, Seattle: 206-682-2556; Eastside: 425-455-5533
- **Dana's Housekeeping–Housekeeper Referral Service**, Seattle/South Snohomish County: 206-368-7999, Burien/Des Moines/West Seattle: 206-433-0070; Bellevue north to Woodinville: 425-827-2220; Kent/Renton/Newport Hills: 425-227-6777; Everett: 425-355-4999; www.housekeeping.com
- **Maid Brigade**, Lynnwood/North Seattle: 206-362-8439; Federal Way/South Seattle: 253-874-1044; Redmond: 425-702-2155; Kirkland/Woodinville: 425-487-2367; North Bellevue: 425-454-1731; Issaquah/Kent/Mercer Island/Renton/South Bellevue: 425-251-5013; Auburn/Black Diamond: 253-939-2397; www.maidbrigade.com
- **Maid in the Northwest**, Seattle: 206-622-7783; North Seattle: 206-365-5087; Federal Way/Kent: 253-859-9029; Bellevue/Eastside: 425-455-0655; Edmonds/Lynnwood: 425-775-3888; Des Moines/Tacoma: 425-927-4122; www.maidinthenw.com
- **The Maids**, North King County/South Snohomish County: 425-742-2779; www.maids.com
- **Merry Maids**, Seattle/University District: 206-527-2984; West Seattle: 206-937-7083; North Seattle/South Snohomish County: 425-778-3355; Eastside: 425-881-6243; South King County: 253-833-6171; www.merrymaids.com
- **Mighty Maids**, West Seattle: 206-938-9662; South King County: 253-630-2799
- **Rent-A-Yenta House Cleaning Service**, Seattle: 206-325-8902; Eastside: 425-454-1512; http://rent-a-yenta.qwest.com
- **Student Cleaning**, Seattle: 206-527-4290; Bellevue/Eastside: 425-649-8610

PEST CONTROL

Rats have long been a problem in Seattle, and the pesky rodents are an increasing nuisance in the suburbs as well. According to *The Seattle Times*, mild winters have encouraged breeding and increased construction has disrupted habitat, forcing rats to find new homes. If that includes your home or yard and setting traps yourself hasn't worked or is not an option, consider calling an exterminator, or visit www.pestweb.com to find tips for dealing with unwelcome house "guests." These local pest control experts can also help you with ants, spiders, termites and other pests that might be bugging you.

- **A Complete Pest Control**, Seattle: 206-362-2847; Eastside: 425-454-2847; 800-394-2847
- **AAA Pest Control**, Seattle: 206-781-9729; West Seattle: 253-932-8222
- **Agricultural Pest Control Services**, 425-702-9272; 866-500-3777
- **Bio Bug Pest Management**, Seattle/Mercer Island: 206-246-7632; Bothell/Kenmore: 425-488-1011; Redmond/Kirkland/Woodinville: 425-869-0811; Bellevue/Issaquah/North Bend: 425-688-0884; www.biobug.com
- **Cascade Pest Control**, Seattle: 206-525-0882; South Snohomish County: 425-353-8888; Eastside: 425-641-6264; South King County: 253-631-2030
- **Eden Advanced Pet Technologies**, Seattle: 206-282-8988; Bellevue: 425-882-3205; Everett: 425-357-8282; 800-401-9935; www.edenpest.com
- **Orkin**, Seattle: 206-632-5882; Bellevue: 425-462-6690; Edmonds: 425-742-4331; Federal Way: 253-529-0252; Issaquah: 425-391-0491; Kent: 253-395-7814; Kirkland: 425-803-0454; Lynnwood: 425-745-4706; Mercer Island: 206-232-7259; Tukwila: 206-575-0111; Woodinville: 425-481-8258; www.orkin.com
- **Terminix**, Seattle/Bothell/Kirkland: 425-487-6643; Renton: 425-251-5943; Kent/Auburn: 253-872-3462; Des Moines/Federal Way: 253-839-0808; Bellevue/Redmond: 425-451-7876; North Bend: 425-888-4474; www.terminix.com

POSTAL AND SHIPPING SERVICES

If you are between addresses and in need of a place to receive mail, you can rent a box at a local post office or choose a private receiving service. Many of the private services allow call-in mail checks and mail forwarding, but they are often more expensive than the post office.

MAIL RECEIVING SERVICES

- **The Mail Box**, Seattle: 300 Lenora Street, 206-728-1228; 300 Queen Anne Avenue North, 206-285-0919; 3213 West Wheeler Street, 206-285-4843; 6201 15th Avenue NW, 206-789-7564; Bellevue: 10020 Main Street, 425-453-9019

- **Mail Boxes Etc.**, Seattle: 10002 Aurora Avenue North, 206-527-5065; 4756 University Village Place NE, 206-524-2558; 800 5th Avenue, Suite 101, 206-382-9177; 9594 1st Avenue NE, 206-523-7353; Everett: 10121 Evergreen Way, 425-353-9144; Federal Way: 1911 SW Campus Drive, 253-874-6583; Issaquah: 700 NW Gilman Boulevard, 425-557-0777; Totem Lake: 11410 NE 124th Street, 425-823-3198; Lynnwood: 13619 Mukilteo Speedway, 425-745-0539; Mercer Island: 7683 SE 27th, 206-232-3053; Mill Creek: 914 164th Street, 425-787-5100; Puyallup: 4441 South Meridian, 253-840-0807

PACKAGE DELIVERY SERVICES

- **Airborne Express**, 800-247-2676, www.airborne.com
- **DHL Worldwide Express**, 800-225-5345, www.dhl.co.id
- **FedEx**, 800-463-3339, www.fedex.com/us
- **FedEx Ground** (formerly RPS), 800-463-3339, www.fedex.com/us
- **United Parcel Service (UPS)**, 800-742-5877, www.ups.com
- **US Postal Service Express Mail**, 800-222-1811, www.usps.com

JUNK MAIL

To curtail the deluge of mail you surely will receive after relocating, send a written note, including name and address, to the Direct Marketing Association, asking to be purged from their list: Direct Marketing Association's Mail Preference Service, P.O. Box 9008, Farmingdale, NY 11735. This should help, but you must contact some catalog companies directly with a purge request. (Keep in mind; you might actually appreciate some of the mass-market mail, as many retailers and household service providers welcome new residents with coupons and special offers.)

AUTOMOBILE REPAIR

Finding a mechanic you can trust is often difficult. The most popular way to find a shop is to ask around—co-workers, neighbors, friends. Though often pricey, auto dealers are generally reliable, and will have the right equipment and parts to work on your car. Check the Yellow Pages for listings.

Those considering an independent mechanic shop may want to check with the Better Business Bureau to determine if any complaints have been filed against it. The local chapter serves Oregon and Western Washington, and is located at 4800 South 188th Street, Suite 222, in SeaTac. Call 206-431-2222 or visit www.thebbb.org.

If it's just "advice" you need, consider tuning your radio to NPR's "Car Talk." Locally, the program can be heard on KPLU, 88.5 FM, on Saturday from 10 to 11 a.m., and Sunday from 2 to 3 p.m.

If the question isn't who will repair your car, but rather who to call to have it towed, your best resource may be an automobile club like the American Automobile Association. For information about membership benefits and services, visit www.aaawa.com, or call 800-562-2582. The Seattle office is at 330 6th Avenue North. Additional locations are Bellevue, Everett, Lynnwood, Renton, and Tacoma.

CONSUMER PROTECTION—AUTOMOBILES

If you are looking for a new car, Washington has a lemon law to protect owners who have "substantial or continuing problems with warranty repairs." A lemon is defined as a vehicle that has one or more substantial defects, which has been subject to a "reasonable number of attempts" to diagnose or repair the problem(s) under the manufacturer's warranty. The law does not cover problems caused by owner abuse or negligence, or any unauthorized modifications made to the vehicle. Nor does it cover some motorcycles and large commercial trucks, motor homes used as homes, office or commercial space, or vehicles purchased as part of a fleet of 10 or more. The law allows the owner to request an arbitration hearing through the office of the **Washington Attorney General** within 30 months of the vehicle's original retail delivery date. If you are not the original owner, you can still apply the lemon law if the vehicle was purchased within two years of delivery to the original retail consumer, and within the first 24,000 miles of operation. For more details, visit the Attorney General's Consumer Protection web site at www.wa.gov/ago/consumer, or call 800-551-4636.

Information about vehicle recalls and crash tests can be found at the **US Department of Transportation's Auto Safety Hotline**, 800-424-9393, or visit www.nhtsa.dot.gov.

CONSUMER PROTECTION—RIP-OFF RECOURSE

Got a beef with a merchant or company? There are a number of agencies that monitor consumer-related businesses and will take action when necessary. The best defense against fraud and consumer victimization is to avoid it—read the contracts down to the smallest print, save all receipts and canceled checks, get the name of telephone sales and service people with whom you deal, check a contractor's license number with the state's Consumer Protection Division for complaints. Despite such attention to details, sometimes you still get stung. A dry cleaner returns your blue suit, but now it's purple and he shrugs. A shop refuses to refund, as promised, on the expensive gift that didn't suit your mother. After $898 in repairs to your engine, your car now vibrates wildly, and the mechanic claims innocence. Negotiations, documents in hand, fail. You're angry, and embarrassed because you've been had. There *is* something you can do.

- **Attorney General's Office, Consumer Protection Division**, 900 4th Avenue, Suite 2000, 800-551-4636, www.wa.gov/ago/consumer; in 1999, problems with telecommunications and online services, credit/mortgages, retail business, travel tours, and motor vehicle repair topped the list of consumer complaints received by the Attorney General's Office. The Consumer Protection Division web site outlines how to resolve and file complaints. Seven neighborhood consumer resource centers are also available throughout the state.
- **Better Business Bureau**, 4800 South 188th Street, Suite 222, 206-431-2222, www.thebbb.org; the local chapter serves both Western Washington and Oregon. The BBB can supply you with a reliability report for a business. The agency also accepts complaints when a breakdown in communication occurs between you and a business.
- **City of Seattle Department of Neighborhoods, Citizens Service Bureau**, 600 Fourth Avenue, Room 105, 206-684-8811; www.cityof-seattle.net/don; the Citizens Service Bureau employs four full-time complaint resolution coordinators who collectively respond to more than 50,000 questions and complaints annually.
- **King County Office of Citizen Complaints**, 516 Third Avenue, Room 213, 206-296-3452, www.metrokc.gov/ombuds; if your dispute is with a county agency, contact the county Ombudsman's Office. Though the office cannot take legal action on your behalf, they can generally resolve the matter through a fact-finding effort with the agency involved.
- **King County Small Claims Court**, King County Courthouse, W-1034, 206-296-3594, www.metrokc.gov/KCDC; with some exceptions, an individual, business, partnership or organization can bring a small claims suit for the recovery of money only, up to $4,000. The filing fee is $21.
- **The Tenants Union**, 3902 South Ferdinand Street, 206-723-0500, www.tenantsunion.org; their web site provides a series of online brochures to answer renters' commonly asked questions. You may visit the office in person on Monday, Tuesday, Wednesday and Friday between 11 a.m. and 5 p.m., and Thursday from 11 a.m. to 7 p.m.

MEDIA SPONSORED CONSUMER ADVOCACY PROGRAMS

The following consumer advocacy and assistance programs are operated by Seattle area television stations.

- **KOMO 4 Buyer Beware and People Helper**, 206-404-4000, 140 4th Avenue North, www.komotv.com/buyerbeware, www.komotv.com/peoplehelper
- **KING 5 Legally Speaking**, 206-448-5555, 333 Dexter Avenue North, www.king5.com/localnews/legallyspeaking
- **KIRO 7 Consumer Alert Team**, 206-728-7777, 2807 3rd Avenue, www.seattleinsider.com/partners/kirotv/specialreports

LEGAL RESOURCES

- **Center for Consumer Law**, 1809 7th Avenue, 206-464-1011, www.consumerrights.net
- **Columbia Legal Services**, 101 Yesler Way, 206-464-5911, 800-542-0794
- **King County Lawyer Referral Service**, 206-623-2551
- **Northwest Justice Project**, 401 Second Avenue South, 206-464-1519, 888-201-1012, www.nwjustice.org
- **Senior Services Elder Law Legal Clinic**, 1601 2nd Avenue, 206-448-5720, www.seniorservices.org
- **Washington State Bar Association**, 206-443-9722, 800-945-9722, 2101 4th Avenue, www.wsba.org

SERVICES FOR PEOPLE WITH DISABILITIES

There are a number of organizations in the Seattle area that serve as resources for disabled persons. The **Washington Coalition of Citizens with Disabilities (WCCD)** offers legal services concerning civil rights violations; an employment program, which provides assistance in finding a job; a travel training program, to help disabled persons use the Metro bus system; a technical assistance program, providing job training; and a self-advocacy program, to teach disabled persons how to speak up for their rights. The **Northwest Disability and Business Technical Assistance Center (NWDB-TAC)** supports the integration of all persons with disabilities into the community and provides publications on workplace accessibility and other topics. The **Washington Assistive Technology Alliance (WATA)** increases access to and awareness of technologies that provide assistance and accessibility for people with disabilities. The **University of Washington's Assistive Technology Resource Center (ATRC)** provides information, referral services, training, and consultation regarding assistive technology devices, services, and funding. The **Easter Seal Society of Washington** provides housing assistance programs, vocational rehabilitation, including interview skills training, job search techniques, and on the job support. They also publish a pamphlet listing accessible sites in the Seattle area.

Metro Transit issues Regional Reduced Fare Permits to individuals with disabilities. The permit costs $3 and is valid for Metro transportation, Washington State Ferries, Community Transit, Pierce Transit and most other bus agencies in the region. Buses are equipped with wheelchair lifts and special seating. For those individuals who require assistance in riding the bus, a special Personal Care Attendant permit allows the disabled person's escort to ride free. Depending on the nature of the disability, a letter of certification from a physician, psychiatrist, psychologist or audiologist is required. Call Metro Transit at 206-263-3113, 206-263-3116 (TTY) for more information and to receive a copy of the certification form.

Here's a list of addresses and phone numbers for the above centers and some other national and local organizations:

- **Center for Technology and Disability Studies**, University of Washington, 206-685-4181 (Voice), 206-616-1396 (TTY), 800-841-8345 (Voice/TTY), http://uwctds.washington.edu
- **Community Service Center for the Deaf and Hard of Hearing**, 1609 19th Avenue, 206-322-4996 (Voice/TTY), 877-301-0006 (Voice/TTY), www.cscdhh.org
- **Community Services for the Blind and Partially Sighted**, 9709 3rd Avenue NE, Suite 100, 206-525-5556, 800-458-4888, www.csbps.com
- **Deaf-Blind Service Center**, 2366 Eastlake Avenue East, Suite 206, 206-323-9178 (Voice/TTY)
- **Easter Seal Society of Washington**, 521 2nd Avenue West, 800-678-5708, www.seals.org
- **Hearing, Speech and Deafness Center**, 1620 18th Avenue, 206-323-5770 (Voice/TTY), www.hsdc.org
- **Learning Disabilities Association of Washington**, 7819 159th Place NE, Redmond, 425-882-0792; Seattle Chapter: 206-527-7420
- **Metro Transit**, 206-263-3113, 206-263-3116 (TTY), http://transit.metrokc.gov
- **National Council on Disability (NCD)**, 1331 F Street NW Suite 1050, Washington, DC, 20004, 202-272-2004 (Voice), 202-272-2074 (TTY), www.ncd.gov
- **Northwest ADA/IT Center**, P.O. Box 574, Portland, Oregon 97207-0574, 800-949-4232, www.nwada.org
- **Self Help for Hard of Hearing People (SHHH)**, P.O. Box 4025, Kent, WA 98032, 360-659-9438 (Voice), www.wasa-shhh.org
- **Washington Assistive Technology Alliance (WATA)**, Eastern Assistive Technology Resource Center, West 606 Sharp, Spokane, WA, 509-328-9350 (Voice/TTY), 800-214-8731 (Voice/TTY), http://wata.org/wata
- **Washington Coalition of Citizens with Disabilities**, 4649 Sunnyside Avenue North, 206-545-7055, 206-632-3456 (TTY), www.wccd.org

- **Washington Protection and Advocacy System**, 180 West Dayton, Suite 102, Edmonds, 425-776-1199, 425-776-1648 (TTY), 800-562-2702, 800-905-0209 (TTY), www.wpas-rights.org
- **Washington State Department of Social and Health Services**, Deaf Services, 1009 College Street SE, Lacey, 800-422-7930, 800-422-7941 (TTY)
- **Washington Telecommunications Relay Services**, 800-833-6384, 800-833-6388 (TTY), 800-833-6385 (Telebraille)

GAY AND LESBIAN LIFE

When the census counted same-sex partners for the first time in 2000, figures indicated that Seattle has one of the nation's highest percentages of gay households. At the count, one out of every 21 couples living together in Seattle listed themselves as homosexual. Of 15,900 same-sex pairs in Washington, about half resided in King County, and nearly one-fifth lived within three miles of Lake Union in Seattle. While this may be news to some, it is not news to Seattle's thriving and well-established gay community. There are numerous organizations, businesses, and publications that address the concerns and interests of Seattle's lesbian, gay, bi-sexual, and transgender community—too many to detail here. We mention the following as starting points.

- **City of Seattle Commission for Sexual Minorities**, 700 3rd Avenue, Room 250, 206-684-4500, 206-684-4503 (TDD), www.ci.seattle.wa.us/scsm
- **Dignity Seattle**, 206-325-7314, www.dignityusa.org, is the country's largest and most progressive organization of gay, lesbian, bisexual and transgender Catholics.
- **Freedom Day Committee (FDC)**, 1122 East Pike Street, 206-324-0405, www.seattlepride.org, FDC organizes and promotes the annual Seattle Pride parade and march.
- **Greater Seattle Business Association**, 2150 North 107th Street, Suite 205, 206-363-9188, www.thegsba.org; GSBA's goal is to strengthen and expand business and career opportunities in the gay and lesbian community.
- **Lambert House Gay Youth Center**, 1818 15th Avenue, 206-322-2515, www.lamberthouse.org; an activities and resource center for lesbian, gay, bisexual, transgendered and questioning youth between the ages of 14 and 22.
- **Lesbian Resource Center**, 2214 South Jackson, 206-322-3953, www.lrc.net; established in Seattle in 1971, LRC promotes empowerment, visibility, and social change.

- **Parents, Families and Friends of Lesbians and Gays (PFLAG)**, Seattle Chapter, 1122 East Pike Street, 206-325-7724, www.seattle-pflag.org, promotes the health and well-being of sexual minorities through support, education and advocacy.
- **Seattle Gay Couples**, P.O. Box 567, Seattle, WA 98111, 206-762-7198, www.seattlegaycouples.com, provides a comfortable environment to meet other couples, strengthen relationships and explore gay-related issues.
- **Seattle LGBT Community Center**, 1122 East Pike Street, 206-323-2227

NEWSPAPERS

- *Seattle Gay News*, 1602 12th Avenue, 206-324-4297, www.sgn.org
- *Seattle Gay Standard*, 605 29th Avenue East, 206-322-9027, www. gaystandard.com
- *The Stranger*, 1535 11th Avenue, 206-323-7101, www.thestranger.com

ENTERTAINMENT

Most of Seattle's gay bars and restaurants are located in the Capitol Hill neighborhood.
- **C.C. Attle's**, 1501 East Madison, 206-726-0565
- **Changes**, 2103 North 45th, 206-545-8363
- **The Cuff**, 1533 13th Avenue, 206-323-1525
- **Elite**, 622 Broadway East, 206-324-4470
- **Madison Pub**, 1315 East Madison, 206-325-6537
- **Neighbours Disco**, 1509 Broadway, 206-324-5358
- **R Place**, 619 East Pine, 206-322-8828
- **Re-Bar**, 1114 Howell Street, 206-233-9873
- **Sea Wolf Saloon**, 1413 14th Avenue, 206-323-2158
- **Sonya's Bar & Grill**, 1919 1st Avenue, 206-441-7996
- **Thumper's**, 1500 East Madison, 206-328-3800
- **Timberline Tavern**, 2015 Boren Avenue, 206-622-6220
- **The Vogue**, 1516 11th Avenue, 206-324-5778
- **Wild Rose**, 1021 East Pike Street, 206-324-9210

WHEN MOVING TO A NEW AREA, ONE OF THE MOST CHALlenging and overwhelming tasks parents face is finding good childcare and/or schools for their kids. While the process is not an easy one, with time and effort it is possible to find what is best for your children, whether it be in-home or on-site daycare, an after-school program, or a good public or private school. The keys, of course, are research and persistence.

Note: mention in this book of a particular childcare organization or business is not an endorsement. We recommend that you scrutinize any persons or organizations before entrusting your youngster(s) to them.

CHILDCARE

DAYCARE

Often, the best advice when looking for childcare is to ask for referrals from friends or co-workers. As a newcomer who may be lacking such resources, a good place to start is the **Washington State Child Care Resource & Referral Network**, 800-446-1114, www.childcarenet.org. This private, non-profit agency will send you a packet of age-specific childcare, health, and parenting information, and tell you about a local referral program in your area. In the city of Seattle, that program is **Child Care Resources**, 206-329-1011, www.childcare.org. Based on your criteria, Child Care Resources will give you a list of providers from its database of more than 2,000 facilities in King County. While referrals are for state-licensed facilities, be sure to visit prospective sites and interview caregivers, regardless of any recommendations you may receive about an organization. Many local employers offer a benefits package that includes a similar service; check with your place of work for details.

Childcare in Washington is regulated by the state **Division of Child Care & Early Learning (DCCEL)** (formerly the Office of Child Care Policy), www.wa.gov/dshs/occp. The agency offers several helpful publications on its web site, including "Child Care Options for Parents" and "Choosing Child Care." The staff at the division of Child Care & Early Learning is responsible for licensing more than 2,000 childcare homes and centers, which provide care for approximately 50,000 children in King County. Licensors process background checks, inspect and monitor facilities, investigate complaints, and take corrective action when necessary. In June 2002, the *Seattle Post-Intelligencer* reported that each licensor is responsible for inspecting/monitoring either 152 in-home day cares or 85 large centers, the goal being at least one visit per center per year. While most agree this is not enough supervision, no changes to the system are expected anytime soon. Furthermore, a facility that is under investigation for licensing violations or allegations of abuse/neglect is not required to report the investigation to inquiring parents. Add to this the current shortage of trained teachers and aides in King County and it's easy to understand why diligent and thorough research is in order when looking for childcare.

In Washington, a license is required for anyone paid to care for children on a regular basis (unless the children are related to the caregiver). The state imposes minimum licensing requirements for three different types of childcare facilities: licensed childcare centers; licensed school age centers; and licensed family homes. A **childcare center** is a facility that provides regularly scheduled care for a group of children age one month through age 12. A **school age center** is a program operating in a facility other than a private residence, accountable for school age children when school is not in session. The program must provide adult-supervised care and a variety of developmentally appropriate activities. A **licensed family home** is a facility in the family residence of the licensee that provides regularly scheduled care for 12 or fewer children from birth to age 11. Before receiving a license from Child Care & Early Learning, a prospective day care provider must have a business license, undergo a criminal history background check, attend a first aid/CPR class that includes infant/child CPR and pediatric first aid, attend an HIV/AIDS awareness class, and pass a state licensing inspection at the place of business. Only licensed daycare providers qualify for liability insurance. However, because liability insurance is not required by the state, you must ask the daycare providers you interview if their business is covered. You can check the license status of your childcare provider through the DCCEL web site at www.wa.gov/dshs/occp, or call 866-48-CHECK.

The **Service Employees International (SEIU)** Local #925, the local union for childcare workers, may be able to offer some help in your search for good childcare. The SEIU district office is located at 2900 Eastlake Avenue East. Call 206-328-7275 or go to www.seiu925.org for more information.

- **Child Care Resources**, Seattle, 253-329-5544; Eastside, 425-865-9350
- **City of Seattle Child Care Information and Referral**, 206-461-3207, 206-461-4571 (TTY)
- **South King County Family Child Care Association**, Child Care Referral Line, 253-639-1417
- **Southwest King County Family Child Care Association**, 253-854-7869

WHAT TO LOOK FOR IN DAYCARE

When searching for the best place for your child, be sure to visit prospective daycare providers—preferably unannounced. In general, look for a safe environment and caring attitude. Check that the kitchen, toys, and furniture are clean and safe. Observe the other kids at the center. Do they seem happy? Are they well behaved? Are the teacher/child ratios acceptable? Ask for the telephone numbers of other parents who use the service and talk to them before committing. It's a good idea to request a daily schedule—look for both active and quiet time, and age appropriate activities. In the winter months, weather in Seattle doesn't allow for a lot of outdoor activities, but make sure that sports, games, and field trips are still included in the curriculum.

Keep in mind that a license does not guarantee the service of the quality you may want. If you think a provider might be acceptable, call the Licensed Child Care Information System at 866-48-CHECK to determine their licensing status, and call on parent referrals.

ONLINE RESOURCES—DAYCARE

The state Division of Child Care and Early Learning suggests the following child related online resources:
- **Consumer Product Safety**, www.cpsc.gov
- **Office of the Superintendent of Public Instruction**, www.k12.wa.us
- **Governor's Commission on Early Learning**, www.governor.wa.gov
- **Washington State Child Care Coordinating Committee**, www.ccccwa.org
- **Washington State's Early Childhood Education and Assistance Program**, www.ocd.wa.gov/info/csd/waeceap
- **Washington State's Infant Toddler Early Intervention Program**, www.wa.gov/dshs/iteip

NANNIES

A number of agencies match families with nannies. While these services tend to be pricey, some include background checks or psychological testing during the applicant screening process. Nannies are not licensed by the state, and screening processes vary among agencies, so you may want to ask for interview specifics at the various agencies. That said, a nanny can be a wonderful addition to your family. Whether you're employed outside your home or simply need some assistance while working at home, a considerate and hard-working nanny may be the best option for your childcare needs. Area nanny services include:

- **A Nanny for U**, 425-745-9882, www.anannyforu.com
- **Annie's Nannies**, 206-784-8462, www.anniesnannies.cc
- **CareWorks**, 206-325-7510, www.careworkseattle.com
- **Home Details**, 206-285-7656, www.homedetailsinc.com
- **Judi Julin, RN, Nannybroker Inc.**, Seattle, 206-624-1213, Eastside, 425-392-5681, www.nannybroker.com
- **Keepsake Nannies**, 253-875-1601, www.keepsakenannies.com
- **McDonald Employment/Nanny Services**, 206-284-5244
- **The Seattle Nanny Network Inc.**, Seattle, 206-374-8688, Eastside, 425-803-9511, www.theseattlenanny.com
- **Theresa Snow Homecare Inc.**, 206-623-7091

Be sure to check all references before hiring a nanny. These companies offer pre-employment screening services, and can provide criminal background checks, driving records, and credit reports:

- **Active Employment Screening**, 800-555-1420
- **Alliance Credit Services Inc.**, 206-622-1933
- **Background Investigations Inc.**, 888-338-1550, www.wedobackgroundchecks.com
- **Sound Screening Services Inc.**, 800-300-0138, www.soundscreening.com
- **Verifacts**, 800-568-5665, www.usascreening.com

For those hiring a nanny without an agency, there are certain taxes that must be paid, Social Security and Medicare, and possibly unemployment. For assistance with such issues, check the **Nanitax** web site, www.4nannytaxes.com, or call them at 800-NANITAX.

AU PAIRS

If you'd like the convenience of a nanny at a considerably lower cost, or if you're simply interested in a cultural exchange, consider the services of an au pair. Young women (and a few men), usually from Europe, provide a year of childcare and light housekeeping in exchange for airfare, room and board, and a small stipend. Au pairs work up to 45 hours a week, and often go to school or sightsee during their time off.

It is a good program for those families and au pairs who understand the trade-offs of the system. Nevertheless, you may want to confirm that you and the au pair have mutual expectations for your year together. The au pair will be in a foreign country and interested in traveling and meeting people her age. While most agencies outline specific responsibilities, make sure the au pair understands what is expected during her year of employment; your au pair may not have fully considered how restricted her free time will be. Additionally, some parents may have unrealistic expectations of an au pair, assuming that she will be a combination nanny, babysitter and full time housekeeper, with few social interests. That said, if you and your au pair come to an agreement early in the relationship, and follow the guidelines detailed by the agency, most likely you will be very pleased with the au pair experience.

The US Department of State **Bureau of Educational and Cultural Affairs** is responsible for authorizing the organizations that conduct au pair exchange programs. For answers to frequently asked questions, visit http://exchanges.state.gov/education. The following organizations administer the au pair program:

- **American Institute for Foreign Study**, Au Pair in America, 800-727-2437, www.aifs.org
- **AYUSA International**, AuPairCare, 800-428-7247, www.aupaircare.com
- **EF Au Pair**, 800-333-6056, www.efaupair.org
- **Euraupair Intercultural Child Care Programs**, 800-333-3804, www.euraupair.com
- **Go Au Pair**, 800-574-8889, www.goaupair.com
- **InterExchange Au Pair**, 800-287-2477, www.interexchange.org

BABYSITTERS

If you haven't found a reliable babysitter in your neighborhood, or the one you found just called and cancelled, the following companies offer babysitting services. Be prepared pay more for immediate response.

- **Annie's Nannies**, 206-784-8462, www.anniesnannies.cc
- **Judi Julin, RN, Nannybroker Inc.**, Seattle, 206-624-1213, Eastside, 425-392-5681, www.nannybroker.com
- **The Seattle Nanny Network Inc.**, Seattle, 206-374-8688, Eastside, 425-803-9511, www.seattlenanny.com

CHILD SAFETY

Numerous public agencies, private organizations, and hospitals offer resources to help keep your kids safe. The **Seattle Public Library** provides parents and teachers with a list of internet safety organizations on its web site, www.spl.org/children/safety. **Public Health of Seattle & King County** will deliver health and safety news alerts via e-mail; to subscribe, visit www.metrokc.gov/health. The **Seattle Fire Department** offers a program for children called Fire Stoppers—call 206-386-1338 for details. Several hospitals offer infant and child CPR programs, including **Children's Hospital & Regional Medical Center**, 206-789-2306, www.seattlechildrens.org, and **Swedish Medical Center**, 206-386-3606, www.swedish.org.

SCHOOLS

SEATTLE PUBLIC SCHOOLS (K-12)

In recent years, public schools in Seattle have experienced a shortage of teachers. This was mostly due to the statewide approval of Initiative 728, which mandated smaller classrooms, coupled with the city's high cost of living and the relatively low pay scale for new teachers. According to *The Times*, in 2000, new teachers in Seattle earned less than their counterparts in 92 of the nation's 100 largest cities. To attract more teachers, voters then passed initiative 732, which gives teachers automatic pay raises based on the rising cost of living. While administrators and principals had to scramble for a bit to cover classrooms, all in all, most are happy with the smaller class sizes, particularly students and parents.

Seattle schools have made enormous strides in quality of education. Several years ago, now deceased Superintendent John Stanford, with his controversial brand of military-style planning and organization, set out to improve the Seattle Public School system. As a result, test scores went up at most schools; graduation requirements were made more challenging; and standardized exit tests were required for students to pass up from grades five, eight, and eleven. The district also implemented safety measures in schools, including identification badges for high school students and anti-violence campaigns.

In February of 1999, Joseph Olchefske, the district's former chief operating officer, became superintendent, and won praise for bringing tens of millions of dollars into the schools, for improving the professional training of teachers, and for ousting marginal principals. However, reported *The Seattle Times* in June of 2001, he has also been taken to task for the reassignments of several popular principals, and the continued existence of racial disparities in discipline and academics. According to the *Times*, African-American middle- and high-school students are disciplined more than twice as often as students of other races, and whites pass the Washington Assessment of Student Learning test at a rate seven times that of African-Americans.

While the district continues to wrestle with issues of racial disparity, it is succeeding in improving test scores and raising standards. In the fall of 2000 students of the K-8 **African American Academy** moved into a new $24 million facility on Beacon Hill. The school's mission is to help African-American children meet and exceed Seattle public's academic standards. The three-story building houses a science lab, photo darkroom, art room, music room, gymnasium and 90-seat lecture hall. Another development in Seattle Public Schools is the addition of **The Center School**, the district's newest high school, and the only school located in downtown Seattle. In fact, the small high school, which opened on the second floor of a Queen Anne church in the fall of 2001, will enjoy a permanent home on the grounds of the Seattle Center. While the school's emphasis is on mathematics, English, social studies, and science, students will benefit from internships within the scientific, communications, and artistic communities in and around the facility, including the Pacific Science Center and Seattle Repertory Theatre.

Other notable public school programs include **TOPS**, a K-8 program known for its strong parent involvement and state-of-the-art school building, and **Summit**, Seattle's only K-12 school, which prides itself on utilizing the cross-age learning opportunities that arise from having kids of all ages in the same building.

For younger students, Seattle Public Schools offers both half-day and full-day kindergarten. There is a huge demand for full-day programs, and some are fee-based. Check with area schools for more information. The Seattle school district also offers Montessori programs at two schools—**Graham Hill Elementary** and **Daniel Bagley Elementary**. (See below for a list of private Montessori programs.)

The **Homeschool Resource Center** serves parents who choose to teach their students at home. The center offers academic support, encouragement and guidance to parents who are their kids' primary educators. Resources include six classrooms, a computer lab, an extensive resource library, family lounges, playground access and a gym.

For more information about these schools go to www.seattleschools.org:

- **African American Academy K-8**, 8311 Beacon Avenue South, 206-252-6650
- **The Center School**, 0160 John Street, 206-956-3235
- **Daniel Bagley Elementary**, 7821 Stone Avenue North, 206-729-3290
- **Graham Hill Elementary**, 5149 South Graham Street, 206-252-7140
- **Homeschool Resource Center**, 9250 14th Avenue NW, 206-706-4270
- **Summit**, 11051 34th Avenue NE, 206-366-7820
- **TOPS**, 2500 Franklin Avenue East, 206-252-3510

ENROLLMENT—SEATTLE PUBLIC SCHOOLS

The Seattle Public Schools enrollment process is a bit complicated—and not without controversy—but most parents consider it a vast improvement over the former school assignment program. The old system did not allow voluntary school selection and involved busing large numbers of students throughout the city to improve the racial balance at each school. While busing successfully integrated the schools, it also took its toll on the overall well-being of the public school community. With bus rides as much as 90 minutes each way, many students found it difficult to get to and from school, let alone participate in after-school sports and activities. With such inconveniences, those who could afford to chose private schools instead.

In 1993, the school district offered the community a voluntary school selection process, which is limited only by space and the racial integration standards set by the state. The goal is to give all students their first choice school. The district has consistently come close to the goal. According to *The Seattle Times*, most high school students in 2001 were assigned to the school of their choice, and 91% of families of kindergartners received one of their top two choices. Slight changes are made to the program each year, but generally the **enrollment guidelines** are as follows. Each elementary school has a "reference area." Your child's reference area school is determined by your address. Further, elementary schools are grouped into geographic clusters—nine groups of schools defined by location (North, Northeast, Northwest, Queen Anne/Magnolia, Central, South, Southeast, West Seattle North, and West Seattle South). Elementary school students may choose any school in the district, but your child will receive priority assignment only when you choose your reference area school and register on time (dates vary according to school year, generally it's some time in February for elementary, and in March for middle and high schools). When more children apply to a school than space allows, students are assigned based on a series of "tiebreakers." In this order, a child will get priority if he/she: has a sibling at the same school, lives in the school's reference area, positively impacts the school's racial integration, lives closer to the school than other students who have applied, or wins a random lottery.

In middle school and high school, students are also assigned reference areas, and schools are grouped into geographic regions. Middle and high-school students may also choose any school, and receive priority assignment if they register on time, as long as there are enough spots to accommodate all the students who want to go there. If too many students choose a particular school, the following tiebreakers are applied in this order: the student has a sibling at the same school, the student lives in the region (middle school only), the student positively impacts racial integration, the student lives closer to the school than another waiting student, or the student wins a random lottery.

To enroll your child in Seattle Public Schools, you must obtain a registration form by visiting one of the enrollment service centers or by calling 206-252-0760. You can also print the application from the district's web site at www.seattleschools.org. The centers can provide you with your child's reference area or cluster assignment. To complete the registration process, you must bring two proofs of address, such as a rent receipt, driver's license or pre-printed check, and your child's immunization records.

- **Bilingual Family Center, Aki Kurose Middle School**, 3928 South Graham Street, 206-252-7750
- **Central Enrollment Service Center**, Meany Middle School, 301 21st Avenue East, 206-252-2480
- **North Enrollment Service Center**, Wilson Pacific Building, 1330 North 90th Street, 206-252-0765
- **South Enrollment Service Center**, Columbia Annex Building, 3100 South Alaska Street, 206-252-7732
- **West Seattle Enrollment Service Center**, Sealth High School, 2600 SW Thistle Street, 206-252-8660

If you can register your child for school during the regular enrollment period (February for elementary, March for middle and high school), you have a much better chance to receive your first choice school assignment. All applications received before the period deadline are processed together and each carries equal weight. After the regular enrollment period ends, applications are processed on a "first-come, first-served" basis. Some schools fill up quickly based on special programs or popularity; others simply have smaller buildings and cannot accommodate as many students. Alternative schools and classes, such as honors, special education, multi-cultural or bilingual programs, often have additional requirements that restrict enrollment.

An important element of the registration program is the appeals process. If your child does not receive his/her first-choice school, you may appeal to the school district and, if necessary, request a hearing before the Student Assignment Appeals Board. It is always worth taking this step if you are truly dissatisfied with your child's school assignment. Grounds for appeal include medical or psychological concerns, extreme hardship, and district failure to follow district guidelines.

While the Enrollment Service Centers can provide information on any of the Seattle Public Schools, another excellent resource for statistics and information on schools and programs is *The Seattle Times School Guide*, which contains information on more than 600 private and public schools in the greater Seattle area. The guide is on the web at http://texis.seattle-times.nwsource.com/cgi-bin/texis/schoolguide/vortex. In addition, you may want to contact School Match, in Westerville, Ohio, to request its report on Seattle schools. The three-page report will include information on student-teacher ratios, test scores, and even property values in your chosen neighborhood. Call School Match at 800-992-5323 to order the report, which costs $19.

All of the above mentioned resources, as well as some other Seattle Public Schools resources, are listed here.

- **School Match**, 800-992-5323, 614-890-1573, www.schoolmatch.com
- **Seattle Public Schools**, P.O. Box 19116, Seattle, WA 98109-1116, 206-252-0010, www.seattleschools.org
- **Automated Enrollment Services Line**, 206-252-0410
- **Appeals**, 206-252-0586
- **Bilingual Services**, 206-252-7750
- **Special Education Services**, 206-252-0055
- **Highly Capable Services**, 206-252-0130
- **Transportation Services**, 206-252-0900
- **Wait List Automated Info Line**, 206-252-0212

SURROUNDING COMMUNITIES

For information on public schools outside the city of Seattle, contact your local school district, or visit its web site. A selection of districts is listed here:

- **Auburn School District**, 915 4th Street NE, Auburn, WA 98002, 253-931-4900, www.auburn.wednet.edu
- **Bellevue Public Schools**, P.O. Box 90010, Bellevue, WA 98009-9010, 425-456-4000
- **Edmonds School District**, 22901 106th Avenue West, Lynnwood, WA 98036, 425-670-7000, www.edmonds.wednet.edu
- **Everett Public Schools**, P.O. Box 2098, Everett, WA 98203, 425-745-1993, www.everett.k12.wa.us
- **Federal Way Public Schools**, 31405 18th Avenue South, Federal Way, WA 98003, 253-945-2000, www.fwsd.wednet.edu
- **Highline Public Schools**, 15675 Ambaum Boulevard SW, Burien, WA 98166, 206-433-0111, www.hsd401.org
- **Issaquah School District**, 565 NW Holly Street, Issaquah, WA 98027, 425-837-7000, www.issaquah.wednet.edu
- **Kent School District**, 12033 SE 256th Street, Kent, WA 98031, 253-373-7000, www.kent.wednet.edu
- **Lake Washington School District**, P.O. Box 97039, Redmond, WA 98073, 425-702-3200, www.lkwash.wednet.edu
- **Mercer Island School District**, 4160 86th Avenue SE, Mercer Island, WA 98040, 206-236-3330, www.misd.wednet.edu

- **Northshore School District**, 18315 Bothell Way NE, Bothell, WA 98011, 425-489-6000, www.nsd.org
- **Renton School District**, 700 SW 7th Street, Renton, WA 98055, 425-204-2300, www.renton.wednet.edu
- **Shoreline Public Schools**, 18560 1st Avenue NE, Shoreline, WA 98155, 206-361-4412, www.shorelineschools.org
- **Tacoma Public Schools**, P.O. Box 1357, Tacoma, WA 98401-1357, 253-571-1000, www.tacoma.k12.wa.us
- **Tahoma School District**, 25720 Maple Valley-Black Diamond Road SE, Maple Valley, WA 98038, 425-413-3400, www.tahoma.wednet.edu
- **Tukwila School District**, 4640 South 144th Street, Tukwila, WA 98168, 206-901-8000, www.tukwila.wednet.edu

PRIVATE SCHOOLS

If you are considering a private school there are many options in the greater Seattle area, most of which provide bus service. A few of the private schools in Seattle and its surrounding communities are listed here; check the Yellow Pages for more. Entrance requirements vary widely. Be sure to call or visit the school for more information.

- **Annie Wright School** (P-12), 827 North Tacoma Avenue, Tacoma, 253-272-2216, www.aw.org; situated on Commencement Bay, Annie Wright is a co-ed day school through grade 8 and an all-girls' boarding-day school grades 9 through 12.
- **Bellevue Christian School** (P-12), 1601 98th Avenue NE, Bellevue, 425-454-4402, www.bellevuechristian.org; with a comprehensive program that serves preschool through 12th-grade students, Bellevue Christian educates close to 1,350 children, and promotes socioeconomic and religious diversity.
- **Bishop Blanchet High School** (9-12), 8200 Wallingford Avenue North, 206-527-7711, www.blanchet.k12.wa.us; a Catholic, college preparatory school, sends approximately 98% of its graduates on to higher education. The north Seattle high school is a member of the Class AAA division of the Seattle Metro League.
- **Bush School** (K-12), 405 36th Avenue East, 206-326-7736, http://helen.bush.edu, commands nine acres in the Madison Valley neighborhood. Emphasis is placed on cooperative learning, with students working in groups to reach common goals.
- **Cascade Christian Schools** (P-12), 815 21st Street SE, Puyallup, 253-841-1776, www.cascadechristianschool.org, support early childhood centers and elementary schools in Puyallup, Spanaway and Tacoma, as well as Cascade Christian Junior/Senior High School in Puyallup.

- **Charles Wright Academy** (K-12), 7723 Chambers Creek Road West, Tacoma, 253-620-8300, www.charleswright.org, is located on 90 acres in suburban Tacoma. The school provides a challenging college-prep curriculum at all grade levels.
- **The Clearwater School** (ages 4-19), 11006 34th Avenue NE, 206-306-0060, www.clearwaterschool.com, is part of a national network of Sudbury Schools, modeled after the Sudbury Valley School in Massachusetts. Students direct their own activities and engage in a participatory democracy.
- **Concordia Lutheran School** (K-8), 7040 36th Avenue NE, 206-525-7407, http://concordia.seattle.wa.us; owned and operated by the Lutheran School Association of Greater Seattle, Concordia offers a strong Christian atmosphere where children develop academically, socially, and physically.
- **Holy Family School**, 505 17th Street SE, Auburn, 253-833-5130, www.hfsauburn.com; the philosophy of this Catholic school is that parents have the primary responsibility for their child's education, and that the church, school and community complement this role.
- **Holy Names Academy** (9-12), 728 21st Avenue East, 206-323-4272, www.holynames-sea.org; a Catholic, college preparatory school for girls, is a three-time winner of the US Department of Education's blue ribbon of excellence. Athletes compete in the Class AAA division of the Seattle Metro League.
- **Islamic School of Seattle** (P-6), 720 25th Avenue, 206-329-5735, http://islamicschool-seattle.org; founded in 1980, the Islamic School has since added an accredited Montessori pre-school and a full-immersion Arabic program.
- **The Jewish Day School of Metropolitan Seattle**, 15749 NE 4th Street, Bellevue, 425-460-0200, www.jds.org; the Jewish Day School provides a challenging curriculum of general and Jewish studies, along with enrichment opportunities.
- **King's School** (P-12), 19303 Fremont Avenue North, Seattle, 206-546-7218; **King's West** (P-12), 4012 Chico Way NW, Bremerton, 360-377-7700, www.kingsschools.org, serves Seattle and Kitsap families seeking a college preparatory program that emphasizes strong academics, positive discipline, and Christian faith.
- **Lakeside School** (5-12), 14050 1st Avenue NE, 206-368-3600, www.lakesideschool.org, is a co-ed school that enrolls about 700 students, with an average student to teacher ratio of 7.5 to 1, and an average class size of just 16 students. The school's most famous alumni are Microsoft co-founders and Seattle residents Bill Gates and Paul Allen.
- **Meridian School** (K-5), 4649 Sunnyside Avenue North, 206-632-7154, www.meridianschool.edu; located in the Wallingford neighborhood,

Meridian School combines its academic curriculum with thematic studies like raising salmon or recreating a pioneer encampment.

- **The Northwest School** (6-12), 1415 Summit Avenue, 206-682-7309, www.northwestschool.org, is a college preparatory day and boarding school that offers cross-disciplinary study in the humanities, sciences, and performing and fine arts.
- **St. Edward** (P-8), 4212 South Mead Street, 206-725-1774; instruction at St. Edward takes place in multi-age, non-graded classrooms. Catholic values and church teachings permeate all aspects of the school community.
- **St. Joseph School** (K-8), 700 18th Avenue East, 206-329-3260, www.stjosephsea.org; classrooms at this Catholic school are all equipped with e-mail and internet capabilities.
- **Seattle Jewish Community School** (K-5), 7330 35th Avenue NE, 206-522-5212, www.sjcs.net; at SJCS, girls and boys participate equally in all areas of academics and Jewish ritual. The school stresses parental involvement and a non-competitive environment.
- **Seattle Lutheran High School** (9-12), 4141 41st Avenue SW, 206-937-7722, www.seattlelutheran.org; the mission of this Lutheran high school in West Seattle is to prepare students for a lifetime of learning, service, and leadership.
- **Seattle Preparatory School** (9-12), 2400 11th Avenue East, 206-324-0400, www.seaprep.org, provides college preparatory instruction in the Jesuit tradition. Known for its athletic success, the school is a member of the Class AAA division of the Seattle Metro League.
- **Seattle Urban Academy** (9-12), 3800 South Othello Avenue, 206-723-0333, specializes in meeting the needs of at-risk students, helping them earn full or partial credit toward their high school diploma.
- **Shoreline Christian School** (P-12), 2400 NE 147th Street, Shoreline, 206-364-7777, www.shorelinechristian.org, is a multi-denominational Christian school.
- **Soundview School** (P-8), 6515 196th Street SW, Lynnwood, 425-778-8572, www.soundview.org; in 2001 Soundview added five acres to its campus, and built a separate middle school to accommodate the upper grades.
- **University Preparatory Academy** (6-12), 8000 25th Avenue NE, 206-525-2714, www.universityprep.org; with fewer than 500 students, University Prep stresses small classes, a commitment to diversity and a balanced curriculum.

MONTESSORI SCHOOLS

Dr. Maria Montessori developed the Montessori theory of education in the early 1900s. The Montessori Foundation estimates that there are more than

4,000 schools in the United States that follow her strategies. For informa-
tion about the Montessori philosophy, visit the Pacific Northwest
Montessori Association's web site at www.pnma.org, or call 800-550-
PNMA. The following is a list of Montessori schools in Seattle:

- **Blue Skies Montessori Preschool**, 2310 California Avenue SW, 206-938-9663, www.blueskiesmontessori.org
- **Catkins Montessori**, 4014 South 152nd Street, 206-241-6004
- **Chelsea House Montessori**, 13742 30th Avenue NE, 206-363-5212
- **Children's Niche Montessori**, 1412 NW 67th Street, 206-782-1886
- **Cinquegranelli Montessori**, 1405 NW 85th Street, 206-789-2942
- **Discovery Montessori School**, 2836 34th Avenue West, 206-282-3848
- **Learning Tree Montessori**, 1721 15th Avenue, 206-324-4788
- **Mary's Montessori Preschool**, 7925 10th Avenue SW, 206-767-4314
- **Montessori for Kids**, 14410 Greenwood Avenue North, 206-361-2264
- **Montessori Garden**, 8301 5th Avenue NE, 206-524-8307
- **Montessori School of Seattle**, 720 18th Avenue East, 206-325-0497
- **Mt. Baker Montessori**, 2714 34th Avenue South, 206-723-8265
- **Northwest Montessori Schools**, 7400 25th Avenue NE, 206-524-4244
- **Pacific First Montessori**, 1420 5th Avenue, #300, 206-682-6878
- **Paideia Academy Montessori**, 1211 Post Alley, 206-382-2625, www.paideiamontessori.com
- **Sunnyside Montessori**, 3939 South Americus Street, 206-725-5756
- **Tricycle Montessori School**, 904 16th Avenue East, 206-323-5561
- **Veranda Montessori School**, 526 North 105th Street, 206-782-5250
- **Wedgewood Montessori Preschool**, 6556 35th Avenue NE, 206-525-4432
- **West Seattle Montessori**, (K-8), 4536 38th Avenue SW, 206-935-0427

WALDORF SCHOOLS

Waldorf education is based on the philosophy of Austrian philosopher
Rudolf Steiner. For more information on the Waldorf method, visit the
Association of Waldorf Schools of North America at www.awsna.org. The
following is a list of Waldorf schools in Western Washington:

- **Seattle Waldorf School**, 2728 NE 100th Street, 206-524-5320, www.seattlewaldorf.org
- **Whidbey Island Waldorf School**, 6335 Old Pietila Road, Clinton, 360-341-5686, www.icelu.com/wiws
- **Waldorf Tacoma Kinderhaus**, 3315 South 19th Street, Tacoma, 253-383-8711
- **Olympia Waldorf School**, 8126 Normandy Street SE, Olympia, 360-493-0906, www.olympiawaldorf.org
- **Whatcom Hills Waldorf School**, 941 Austin Street, Bellingham, 360-733-3164, www.whws.org

S HOPPING IS GOOD IN SEATTLE AND MADE EVEN BETTER IN RECENT years with the addition of upscale stores to newly remodeled malls and shopping squares. Bellevue Square and University Village in particular have become destinations for the fashionable and affluent. Seattle's downtown shopping core also has been made more cosmopolitan with the arrival of stores like Kenneth Cole, Coach, Tommy Hilfiger, and Tiffany & Co. Heady espresso stands, swank cocktail lounges, and trendy eateries complete the day out.

Most of the shopping locations listed in this chapter are found in Seattle or in nearby suburbs such as Lynnwood, Tukwila or the Eastside, but some may be in surrounding communities just a bit farther away, like the bargain-filled outlet malls in North Bend and Mount Vernon. Unless otherwise noted, all of the following are Seattle addresses.

SHOPPING DISTRICTS

While nearly every neighborhood in Seattle has its own small retail core, the following **Seattle districts** are well known for their shopping opportunities.

- If you are in a spending mood, some of the best shopping **downtown** can be found in and around the soaring new Pacific Place mall at the intersection of 6th Avenue and Pine Street, and just west, is the equally impressive new Nordstrom flagship store in the former Frederick & Nelson building. Since 1993 this area of downtown has been undergoing a concerted and expensive retail makeover as many upscale, locally owned retailers, as well as big names in international fashion and entertainment, have located here.
- Originally a simple farmers' market, the popular and famous **Pike Place Market** is located downtown at 1st Avenue and Pike Street. In addition to the traditional fish, meats, fruits and vegetables, stalls are filled with

local arts, crafts, flowers, teas, and clothing. Surrounding the market-place, unique clothing shops, gardening and home decorating stores, antique malls and importers share space with tiny restaurants and fragrant bakeries.

- Located at the north end of Fremont Bridge, the **Fremont** shopping district is known for kitschy boutiques, vintage clothing stores, funky bakeries, and the local Red Hook Brewery. Fremont is a great location to visit for a strong cup of coffee and enjoyable window shopping. Every Sunday during summer the Fremont Fair attracts local artisans and their wares.
- Capitol Hill's busy **Broadway** shopping district runs along Broadway, from East Roy Street to Madison Street. Usually crowded until late at night, the district has almost as many restaurants, cafes and bakeries as retail stores. Shops cater to a young crowd, with several new and used music stores, bookstores such as the popular Bailey-Coy Books, costume jewelry and bead shops, tattoo and body-piercing parlors, movie theaters, and funky clothing stores.

MALLS

Most Seattle area malls offer a combination of shopping options, from reasonably priced, practical stops, to high-end department stores, to one-of-a-kind boutiques—though not much in the way of discount stores. In the last decade, specialty retailers and popular national chains replaced many of the malls' bargain-oriented shops and dollar stores, which are now often located outside the malls. Mall cross streets are listed for each location, followed by mailing addresses.

- **Alderwood Mall**, I-5 and Alderwood Mall Boulevard; 184th Street SW, Lynnwood, 425-771-1121
- **Bellevue Square**, NE 8th Street and Bellevue Way; 302 Bellevue Square, Bellevue, 425-454-2431, www.bellevuesquare.com
- **Crossroads Shopping Center**, NE 8th Street and 156th Avenue NE; 15600 NE 8th Street, Bellevue, 425-644-1111, www.crossroadsbellevue.com
- **Everett Mall**, I-5 and Everett Mall Way; 1402 SE Everett Mall Way, Everett, 425-355-1771, http://everettmall.org
- **Factoria Mall**, 128th Avenue SE and SE 41st Place; 4055 Factoria Mall SE, Bellevue, 425-747-7344
- **Lakewood Mall**, Gravelly Lake Drive SW and Wildaire Court SW; 10509 Gravelly Lake Drive SW, Tacoma, 253-584-6191
- **Northgate Shopping Center**, I-5 and Northgate Way; 401 NE Northgate Way, Seattle, 206-362-8768, www.northgateshoppingctr.com
- **Pacific Place**, 6th Avenue and Pine Street; 600 Pine Street, Seattle, 206-405-2655, www.pacificplaceseattle.com

- **Redmond Town Center**, NE 74th Street and 164th Avenue NE; 16945 NE 74th Street, Redmond, 425-869-2479, www.shopredmondtown-center.com
- **SeaTac Mall**, South 320th Street and Pacific Highway South; 1928 South SeaTac Mall, Federal Way, 253-839-6150, www.seatacmall.com
- **Totem Lake Shopping Center**, Totem Lake Boulevard and 120th Avenue NE; 12620 120th Avenue NE, Kirkland, 425-821-9420
- **University Village**, 25th Avenue NE and Montlake Avenue NE; 2673 University Village, Seattle, 206-523-0622, www.uvillage.com
- **Westfield Shoppingtown Southcenter** (formerly named and still referred to as the **Southcenter Mall**), I-5 and I-405; 633 Southcenter Mall, Tukwila, 206-246-7400
- **Westlake Center**, 4th Avenue and Pine Street; 400 Pine Street, Seattle, 206-467-1600

FACTORY DISCOUNT STORES AND OUTLET MALLS

Great bargains can be found in factory discount stores, which often stock overruns and imperfect goods. Pay attention to price and merchandise quality. Most of these malls are quite a drive from Seattle, so check the locations on a map or call ahead for directions before you leave the city.

- **Centralia Factory Outlet Center**, 1342 Lum Road, Centralia, 360-736-3327, www.centraliafactoryoutlet.com
- **Factory Stores at North Bend**, 461 South Fork Avenue SW, North Bend, 425-888-4505
- **Peace Arch Factory Outlets**, 3400 Birch Bay-Lynden Road, Custer, 360-366-3127, www.peacearchoutlets.com
- **Prime Outlets at Burlington**, 448 Fashion Way, Burlington, 360-757-3549, www.primeoutlets.com
- **SuperMall of the Great Northwest**, Highway 18 and Highway 167, Auburn, 253-833-9500, www.supermall.com

WAREHOUSE STORES

Warehouse stores now offer good deals on just about anything, from clothing and groceries to furniture and appliances. One caveat: you have to buy many items in bulk, so unless you have room for 100 rolls of toilet paper… Both of the warehouse chains listed here have membership requirements; call for more details.

- **Costco**, 4401 4th Avenue South, 206-622-3136; 1175 North 205th Street, 206-546-0480; 10200 19th Avenue SE, Everett, 425-379-7451; 35100 Enchanted Parkway South, Federal Way, 253-874-3652; 1801 10th Avenue NW, Issaquah, 425-313-0965; 8629 120th Avenue NE,

Kirkland, 425-827-1693; 19105 Highway 99, Lynwood, 425-640-7700; 1201 39th SW, Puyallup, 253-445-7543; 10000 Mickleberry Road NW, Silverdale, 360-692-1140; 2219 South 37th Street, Tacoma, 253-475-2093; 1160 Saxon Drive, Tukwila, 206-575-9191; 5500 Littlerock Road, Tumwater, 360-357-6580; www.costco.com

• **Sam's Club**, 13550 Aurora Avenue North, 206-362-6700; 1101 Super Mall Way, Auburn, 253-333-1026; www.samsclub.com

DEPARTMENT STORES

Nordstrom (*not* Nordstrom*s*) originated in Seattle, and still dominates the local market for high-end clothing and shoes. However, Seattle offers many alternatives for both home and personal shopping. A few of the largest stores are here:

• **The Bon Marché**, 3rd and Pine, 206-506-6000; Alderwood Mall, 425-712-6000; Bellevue Square, 425-688-6000; SeaTac Mall, 253-529-6000; Northgate Shopping Center, 206-440-6000; Southcenter Mall, 425-656-6000, www.federated-fds.com

• **Gottschalks**, Northgate Mall, 206-367-7690; Bellevue, 425-644-2921; Burien, 206-433-0676; Issaquah, 425-557-6550; Kent, 253-872-9895; Lake Forest Park, 206-367-7716, www.gottschalks.com

• **Nordstrom**, 5th and Pine, 206-628-2111; Alderwood Mall, 425-771-5755; Bellevue Square, 425-455-5800; Northgate Shopping Center, 206-634-8800; Southcenter Mall, 206-246-0400, www.nordstrom.com

• **JC Penney**, Alderwood Mall, 425-771-9555; Bellevue Square, 425-454-8599; Kent, 253-852-3260; Northgate Shopping Center, 206-361-2500; Puyallup, 253-845-6669; Southcenter Mall, 206-246-0850, www1.jcpenney.com

• **Sears Roebuck & Co.**, 76 South Lander, 206-344-4830; 15711 Aurora Avenue North, 206-364-9000; Everett, 425-355-7070; Federal Way, 253-529-8200; Lynnwood, 425-771-2212; Puyallup, 253-770-5700; Redmond, 425-644-6749; Tukwila, 206-241-3422, www.sears.com

DISCOUNT DEPARTMENT STORES

Discount chains, such as K-mart, Target, and Wal-Mart do business throughout the Seattle area. Check the Yellow Pages for the nearest location of your favorite. Below are a few of the discount department stores in the region.

• **Fred Meyer**, 18325 Aurora Avenue North, 206-546-0720; 417 Broadway East, 206-328-6920; 100 NW 85th Street, 206-784-9600; Auburn, 253-931-1299; Bellevue, 425-865-8560; Burien, 206-433-6411; Everett, 425-348-8400; Federal Way, 253-952-0100; Gig Harbor, 253-858-4100; Kent, 253-639-7400; Kirkland, 425-820-3200; Lake

City, 206-440-2400; Lynnwood, 425-670-0200; Renton, 425-235-5350; Spanaway, 253-875-4000; Shelton, 360-432-5340; Tacoma, 253-534-3000, www.fredmeyer.com

- **K-mart**, 13200 Aurora Avenue North, 206-363-6319; 7345 Delridge Way SW, 206-767-7004; Kent, 253-852-9071, www.bluelight.com
- **Marshalls**, 15801 Westminster Way North, 206-367-8520; Lynnwood, 425-771-6045; Redmond, 425-644-2429, www.marshallsonline.com
- **Mervyn's California**, Bellevue, 425-643-6554; Federal Way, 253-941-8800; Lynnwood, 425-672-7765; Redmond, 425-558-9500; Tukwila, 206-439-1919, www.mervyns.com
- **Ross Dress for Less**, 1418 3rd Avenue, 206-623-6781; 13201-B Aurora Avenue North, 206-367-6030; Bellevue, 425-644-2433; Federal Way, 253-941-2122; Kent, 253-852-6442; Issaquah, 425-313-9616; Tukwila, 206-575-0110, www.rossstores.com
- **Target**, 302 NE Northgate Way, 206-494-0897, 2800 SW Barton, 206-932-1153; Bellevue, 425-562-0830; Everett, 425-353-3167; Federal Way, 253-839-3399; Issaquah, 425-392-3357; Kent, 253-850-9710; Lynnwood, 425-670-1435; Redmond, 425-556-9533; Tukwila, 206-575-0682; Woodinville, 425-482-6410, www.target.com
- **Wal-Mart**, Auburn, 253-735-7855; Federal Way, 253-941-9974; Renton, 425-227-0407, www.walmartstores.com

HOUSEHOLD SHOPPING

APPLIANCES/ELECTRONICS/COMPUTERS & SOFTWARE

For your stereo, television, cellular phone, home theater and technology purchases, there is a wide variety of electronics and computer stores in Seattle. While JC Penney and The Bon Marché no longer have home electronics departments, large department and warehouse stores such as Sears and Costco are worth a visit when shopping for home audio or video options. One Seattle location well known for its concentration of electronics stores is just north of the University District on Roosevelt Way NE, between NE Ravenna Boulevard and NE 65th Street.

- **Adcom Systems**, 8917 Lake City Way NE, 206-524-6828
- **The Audio Connection**, 5621-A University Way NE, 206-524-7251
- **Bang & Olufsen**, 412 University Street, 206-467-4494; 239 Bellevue Square, Bellevue, 425-452-9292, www.bang-olufsen.com
- **Best Computers**, 3600 Stone Way North, 206-545-4216, http://bcicomputers.com
- **Classic Audio**, 7313 Greenwood Avenue North, 206-706-1561
- **Compro Computers**, 14320 NE 20th Street, Bellevue, 425-643-9880

- **CompUSA**, 12526 Totem Lake Boulevard, Kirkland, 425-825-5500; 17400 Southcenter Parkway, Tukwila, 206-575-2922, www.compusa.com
- **CompuStar Computers**, 2373 Eastlake Avenue East, 206-329-3840
- **Computer Renaissance**, 2827 2nd Avenue, 206-448-9566; 2120 South 320th, Federal Way, 253-941-0900; 17306 Southcenter Parkway, Tukwila, 206-575-2225
- **The Computer Store**, 815 NE 45th Street, 206-522-0220, www.thecomputerstore.com
- **Definitive Audio**, 6017 Roosevelt Way NE, 206-524-6633, www.definitive.com
- **The Good Guys**, 601 106th Avenue NE, Bellevue, 425-688-0029; 19800 44th Avenue West, Lynnwood, 425-640-5514; 300 Andover Park West, Tukwila, 206-575-8000, www.goodguys.com
- **Hawthorne Stereo**, 6303 Roosevelt Way NE, 206-522-9609, www.hawthornestereo.com
- **Madison Audio**, 909 Western Avenue, 206-292-9262
- **Magnolia Hi-Fi**, 6308 Roosevelt Way NE, 206-525-1961; 14404 NE 20th Street, Bellevue, 425-747-0850; 4201 196th SW, Lynnwood, 425-775-7288; 6053 Tacoma Mall Boulevard, Tacoma, 253-475-2321; 16600 Southcenter Parkway, Tukwila, 206-575-0851, www.magnoliahifi.com
- **Office Depot**, 13501 Aurora Avenue North, 206-364-2404; 4900 25th Avenue NE, 206-527-3220; 1751 Airport Way South, 206-587-2582; 100 108th Avenue NE, Bellevue, 425-453-2900; 34950 Enchanted Parkway South, Federal Way, 253-661-2900; 1810 12th NW, Issaquah, 425-837-9501; 6805 South 217th, Kent, 253-872-1700; 5710 196th Avenue SW, Lynnwood, 425-771-2582; 15301 NE 24th, Redmond, 425-747-9019; 300 Andover Park West, Tukwila, 206-575-0101, www.officedepot.com
- **Radio Shack**, 115 West Mercer, 206-283-4502; 1523 3rd Avenue, 206-682-7980; 2032 NW Market, 206-784-8986; 2600 SW Barton, 206-937-8040; 3048 NE 127th, 206-365-2179; 3820 Rainier Avenue South, 206-725-5000; 4223 University Way NE, 206-632-4720; 4505 California Avenue SW, 206-935-0900; 6310 Martin Luther King Jr. Way South, 206-723-9988, www.radioshack.com
- **SpeakerLab**, 6220 Roosevelt Way NE, 206-523-2269, www.speakerlab.com
- **Stereo Warehouse**, 13728 Aurora Avenue North, 206-365-5622
- **University Bookstore Computer & Electronics Center**, 4300 University Way NE, 206-545-4382, www.bookstore.washington.edu
- **Video Only**, 707 Westlake Avenue North, 206-623-3388; 14339 NE 20th Street, Bellevue, 425-644-9400; 290 Andover Park East, Tukwila, 206-444-1650
- **Westwind Computing**, 510 NE 65th Street, 206-522-3530, www.westwind.com

BEDS, BEDDING & BATH

Some area department stores sell bedding as well as beds. For their names, locations and phone numbers, see the previous entries under **Department Stores**.

- **All About Down**, 352 N 78th Street, 206-784-3444
- **Bed Bath & Beyond**, 1930 3rd Avenue, 206-448-7905; 1101 Super Mall Way, Suite 1260, Auburn, 253-931-8583; 15600 NE 8th Street, Bellevue, 425-564-0304; 3115 196th Street SW, Lynnwood, 425-672-7530; 7589 170th Avenue NE, Redmond, 425-558-7978; 400 Strander Boulevard, Tukwila, 206-241-2226, www.bedbathandbeyond.com
- **Bedrooms and More**, 300 NE 45th Street, 206-633-4494; 18910 28th West, Lynnwood, 425-672-2078; 16701 Cleveland Street, Redmond, 425-869-1183, www.bedroomsandmore.com
- **Comfort by Akiko**, 705 East Pike Street, 206-328-3173
- **Down Factory**, 3427 4th Avenue South, 206-467-7072, www.downfactory.com
- **Feathered Friends**, 409 Yale Avenue North, 206-292-9911, www.featheredfriends.com
- **Futon 123**, 3409 Stone Way North, 206-634-0630; 10416 Aurora Avenue North, 206-528-2440
- **Linens 'n' Things**, 1718 South 320th Street, Federal Way, 253-941-4300; 190 SE 58th Street, Issaquah, 425-837-9597; 19401 Alderwood Mall Parkway, Lynnwood, 425-775-7110; 1200 SW Cooper Point Road, Olympia, 360-705-1109; 17170 Redmond Way, Redmond, 425-558-9436; 10001 Mickelberry Road NW, Silverdale, 360-613-0422; 17501 Southcenter Parkway, Tukwila, 206-575-3068; 17849 Garden Way NE, Woodinville, 425-486-9921; www.lnt.com
- **McKinnon Furniture**, 1015 Western Avenue, 206-622-6474, www.mckinnonfurniture.com
- **Scandia Down**, 129 Bellevue Square, Bellevue, 425-455-5535
- **Sleep Country USA**, 1900 3rd Avenue, 206-464-1513, 551 NE Northgate Way, 206-364-1380; 2337 148th Avenue NE, Bellevue, 425-643-4277; 31610 Pacific Highway South, Federal Way, 253-839-6289; 730 NW Gilman Boulevard, Issaquah, 425-313-9415; 377 Strander Boulevard, Tukwila, 206-575-2115, www.sleepcountry.com
- **Sleep Train**, 809 NE Northgate Way, 206-364-8150; 833 Bellevue Way NE, Bellevue, 425-452-9703; 31423 Pacific Highway South, Federal Way, 253-941-8626; 1810 12th Avenue NW, Issaquah, 425-369-1712; 2172 148th Avenue NE, Redmond, 425-865-8615; 16830 Southcenter Parkway, Tukwila, 206-575-9323, www.sleeptrain.com

- **Soaring Heart Futons**, 101 Nickerson Street, Suite 400, 206-282-1717, www.soaringheart.com
- **Yves Delorme**, 2669 North University Village Mall, 206-523-8407, www.yvesdelorme.com

CARPETS & RUGS

If it's an Oriental rug you need, a fun place to begin your search is in the many galleries and shops in the Pioneer Square area of downtown.

- **ABC Carpet Company**, 1110 19th Avenue East, 206-323-8567
- **Birdem Turkish Rugs & Kilims**, 7321 Greenwood Avenue North, 206-782-9205
- **Caravan Carpets**, 3500 Fremont Avenue North, 206-547-6666
- **Carpet Exchange**, 1251 1st Avenue South, 206-624-7800
- **Carpet World**, 920 NW Leary Way, 206-782-4856
- **The Color Store**, 1122 E Madison Street, 206-328-3908
- **Consolidated Carpet**, 200 N 85th Street, 206-789-7737; 11724 Lake City Way NE, 206-440-8609
- **Decker Brothers Interiors**, 4435 California Avenue SW, 206-937-7707
- **Nielsen Brothers Carpets**, 2031 NW 56th Street, 206-783-3040; 13700 Bellevue Redmond Road, Bellevue, 425-746-1962; 453 SW 153rd, Burien, 206-242-6900; 121 SE Everett Mall Way, Everett, 425-347-4040; 6814 196th SW, Lynnwood, 425-776-9191
- **Pande Cameron**, 815 Pine Street, 206-624-6263
- **Pitcher Brothers Carpet One**, 5034 University Way NE, 206-522-4611, http://pitcherbrothers.com
- **Ravenna Interiors**, 2251 NE 65th Street, 206-525-5794
- **Yam Oriental Rugs**, 78 South Washington Street, 206-622-2439

FURNITURE

A home furnishings store may be one of the first places you visit as you try to fill your new home or apartment. For a huge selection of reasonably priced contemporary furnishings, check out the IKEA store in Renton, south of Seattle. Many department stores offer good selections of traditional home furnishings. Call ahead for details, or check the newspaper for sales and special promotions. Catalog favorites, such as Pottery Barn, Restoration Hardware, and Crate and Barrel, allow consumers to shop in-person, by mail, or online.

- **The Bon Marché**, 3rd and Pine, 206-506-6000; Alderwood Mall, 425-712-6000; Bellevue Square, 425-688-6000; SeaTac Mall, 253-529-6000; Northgate Shopping Center, 206-440-6000; Southcenter Mall, 425-656-6000, www.federated-fds.com

- **Crate and Barrel**, 555 Bellevue Square NE, Bellevue, 425-646-8900, www.crateandbarrel.com
- **Dania Home and Office Interiors**, 6416 Roosevelt Way NE, 206-524-9611; 12230 116th NE, Kirkland, 425-823-9160; 1251 Andover Park West, Tukwila, 206-575-1918
- **Ethan Allen Home Interiors**, 2209 NE Bellevue Redmond Road, Bellevue, 425-641-3133; 4029 Alderwood Mall Boulevard, Lynnwood, 425-775-1901; 17333 Southcenter Parkway, Tukwila, 206-575-4366, www.ethanallen.com
- **IKEA Home Furnishings**, 600 SW 43rd, Renton, 425-656-2980; 800-570-4532, www.ikea.com
- **Levitz Furniture**, 17601 Southcenter Parkway, Tukwila, 206-575-0510, www.levitz.com
- **McKinnon Furniture**, 1015 Western Avenue, 206-622-6474, www.mckinnonfurniture.com
- **Miller-Pollard Interiors**, 2575 NE University Village, 206-527-8478; 4218 East Madison Street, 206-325-3600
- **Norwalk-The Furniture Idea**, 1010 Western Avenue, 206-622-0282, www.norwalkfurnitureidea.com
- **Olsen Furniture**, 5354 Ballard Avenue NW, 206-782-6020, www.olsenfurniture.com
- **Pottery Barn**, 600 Pine Street, 206-621-0276; 4645 University Village Plaza NE, 206-522-6860; 212 Bellevue Square, Bellevue, 425-451-0097, www.potterybarn.com
- **Restoration Hardware**, 600 Pine Street, 206-652-4545; 4635 University Village Plaza NE, 206-522-2775, www.restorationhardware.com
- **Ryan's Fine Furniture**, 11306 Lake City Way NE, 206-364-4030
- **Sears Roebuck & Co.**, 76 South Lander, 206-344-4830; 15711 Aurora Avenue North, 206-364-9000; Everett, 425-355-7070; Federal Way, 253-529-8200; Lynnwood, 425-771-2212; Puyallup, 253-770-5700; Redmond, 425-644-6749; Tukwila, 206-241-3422, www.sears.com
- **Seva**, 3212 Harvard Avenue East, 206-323-9920

HOUSEWARES

- **The Bon Marché**, 3rd and Pine, 206-506-6000; Alderwood Mall, 425-712-6000; Bellevue Square, 425-688-6000; SeaTac Mall, 253-529-6000; Northgate Shopping Center, 206-440-6000; Southcenter Mall, 425-656-6000, www.federated-fds.com
- **City People's**, 500 15th Avenue East, 206-324-9510; 5440 Sand Point Way NE, 206-524-1200

- **Cost Plus Imports**, 2103 Western Avenue, 206-443-1055; 10300 NE 8th Street, Bellevue, 425-453-1310; 17680 Southcenter Parkway, Tukwila, 206-575-0646
- **Crate and Barrel**, 555 Bellevue Square NE, Bellevue, 425-646-8900, www.crateandbarrel.com
- **Eddie Bauer Home Store**, 1330 5th Avenue, 206-622-2766; 2720 NE University Village Mall, 206-526-8193; 2012 Bellevue Square, Bellevue, 425-637-0690, www.eddiebauer.com
- **The Mrs. Cooks**, 2810 NE University Village, 206-525-5008
- **Pier 1 Imports**, 4345 University Way NE, 206-545-7397; 905 Bellevue Way NE, Bellevue, 425-451-8002; 15725 Westminster Way North, Shoreline, 206-361-0984; 17197 Southcenter Parkway, Tukwila, 206-575-4113, www.pier1.com
- **Pottery Barn**, 600 Pine Street, 206-621-0276; 4645 University Village Plaza NE, 206-522-6860; 212 Bellevue Square, Bellevue, 425-451-0097, www.potterybarn.com
- **Restoration Hardware**, 600 Pine Street, 206-652-4545; 4635 University Village Plaza NE, 206-522-2775, www.restorationhardware.com
- **Sur La Table**, 84 Pine Street, 206-448-2244; Kirkland, 90 Central Way, 425-827-1311, www.surlatable.com
- **Williams Sonoma**, 600 Pine Street, 206-621-7405; 2530 NE University Village, 206-523-3733; 216 Bellevue Square, Bellevue, 425-454-7007, www.williamssonoma.com

LAMPS & LIGHTING

Many hardware and department stores stock a wide selection of lamps and lighting fixtures. The Bon Marché, Eagle Hardware, and Home Depot are worth a visit when looking for contemporary lighting options.

- **Antique Lighting Company**, 8214 Greenwood Avenue North, 206-622-8298, www.antiquelighting.com
- **Bogart, Bremmer & Bradley Antiques**, 8000 15th Avenue NW, 206-783-7333
- **Hansen Lamp and Shades**, 6510 Phinney Avenue North, 206-783-6859
- **Harold's Lamps & Shades**, 1912 North 45th Street, 206-633-2557
- **Highlights**, 999 Western Avenue, 206-382-9667
- **Lighting Supply Inc.**, 2729 2nd Avenue, 206-441-5075
- **Seattle Lighting**, 222 2nd Avenue South, 206-622-4736; 12828 Bellevue Redmond Road, Bellevue, 425-455-2110; 6710 Tacoma Mall Boulevard, Tacoma, 253-838-3365, www.seattlelighting.com

HARDWARE & GARDEN CENTERS

For paint and wallpaper, light fixtures, and anything else you might need for your Saturday projects, the following list might be useful.

- **City People's**, 500 15th Avenue East, 206-324-9510; 5440 Sand Point Way NE, 206-524-1200
- **Chubby & Tubby**, 7906 Aurora Avenue North, 206-524-1810; 3333 Rainier Avenue South, 206-723-8800; 4110 A NE 4th Street, Renton, 425-793-9600
- **Crawford-Waage Hardware**, 2217 3rd Avenue, 206-441-4393
- **Five Corners Hardware**, 305 West McGraw Street, 206-282-5000
- **The Home Depot**, 2759 Utah Avenue South, 206-467-9200; 11616 Aurora Avenue North, 206-361-9600; 1335 North 205th, 206-546-1900; 325 120th NE, Bellevue, 425-451-7351; 1715 South 352nd, Federal Way, 253-661-9200; 6200 East Lake Sammamish Parkway SE, Issaquah, 425-391-8467; 26120 104th SE, Kent, 253-852-1017; 6810 South 180th, Tukwila, 206-575-9200, www.homedepot.com
- **Junction True Value Hardware**, 4747 44th Avenue SW, 206-932-0450
- **Lowe's Home Improvement Warehouse**, 12525 Aurora Avenue North, 206-366-0365; 2700 Rainier Avenue South, 206-760-0832; 1232 "A" Street NE, Auburn, 253-804-2600, 3102 West Valley Highway, Auburn, 253-804-8770; 11959 Northup Way, Bellevue, 425-646-9031; 35205 16th South, Federal Way, 253-838-2233; 1625 11th Place NW, Issaquah, 425-391-3355; 101 Andover Park East, Tukwila, 206-243-5470, www.lowes.com
- **Madison Park Hardware**, 1837 42nd Avenue East, 206-322-5331
- **Magnolia Ace Hardware**, 2420 32nd Avenue West, 206-282-1916
- **Stephenson Ace Hardware**, 9000 Roosevelt Way NE, 206-522-3324
- **Stewart Lumber & Hardware**, 1761 Rainier Avenue South, 206-324-5000
- **Stoneway Hardware & Supply**, 4318 Stone Way North, 206-545-6910
- **Tweedy & Popp Ace Hardware**, 1916 North 45th Street, 206-632-2290
- **University Hardware**, 4731 University Way NE, 206-523-5353
- **Winkelman True Value Hardware**, 14401 Greenwood Avenue North, 206-363-7211

SECOND HAND SHOPPING

Second-hand shopping is a favorite pastime of many Seattle residents. What better way to spend a drizzly afternoon than digging for treasures that cost so little?

THRIFT STORES

- **Chicken Soup Brigade**, 1508 11th Avenue, 206-329-4563; 2501 South Jackson Street, 206-322-7550; 4542 University Way NE, 206-633-5083
- **Children's Hospital Thrift Stores**, 15835 Westminster Way North, 206-448-7609; 303 West Meeker, Kent, 253-850-8216; 15137 NE 24th, Redmond, 425-746-3092
- **Goodwill**, 1400 South Lane Street, 206-860-5711; 14506 NE 20th Street, Bellevue, 425-649-2080; 4209 Wheaton Way, Bremerton, 360-479-4013; 3002 Hoyt Avenue, Everett, 425-743-6470; 19505 52nd Avenue West, Lynnwood, 425-774-6157; 1174 Andover Park West, Tukwila, 206-575-4944
- **Shop & Save**, 102 Cross Street SE, Auburn, 253-939-4245; 21558 Highway 99, Edmonds, 425-771-8323; 4920 Evergreen Way, Everett, 425-258-9347; 24034 104th Avenue SE, Kent, 253-850-8760; 6613 132nd Avenue NE, Kirkland, 425-881-0803; 10014 15th Avenue SW, White Center, 206-762-8099
- **Value Village**, 8700 15th Avenue NW, 206-783-4648; 12548 Lake City Way NE, 206-235-8232; 1525 11th Avenue, 206-322-7789; 3449 Wheaton Way, Bremerton, 360-479-7998; 131 SW 157th Street, Burien, 206-246-6237; 6220 Evergreen Way, Everett, 425-355-8320; 32945 Pacific Highway South, Federal Way, 253-874-3966; 17216 Highway 99, Lynnwood, 425-745-6603; 16771 Redmond Way, Redmond, 425-883-2049; 1222 Bronson Way North, Renton, 425-255-5637

ANTIQUE SHOPS & DISTRICTS

There are many antique and vintage stores in Seattle, particularly near the Pike Place Market and in the Greenwood, Ballard and Fremont neighborhoods. Several towns beyond the city limits, most notably Duvall, Issaquah, and Snohomish, are known for their many antique stores. Also, check the Sunday newspapers for estate sales or auctions. Most are open to the public, some also hold previews so you can judge whether to arrive early.

Here are just a few antique stores and malls:

- **Antique Gallery Mall**, 117 Glen Avenue, Snohomish, 360-568-7644
- **Antique Mall of West Seattle**, 4516 California Avenue SW, 206-935-9774
- **Antique Station**, 1108 1st Street, Snohomish, 360-568-4913
- **Antiques & Heirlooms**, 6019 15th Avenue NW, 206-706-5650; 916 First Street, Snohomish, 360-568-4646
- **Antiques at Pike Place**, 92 Stewart Street, 206-441-9643
- **Aurora Antique Pavilion**, 24111 Highway 99, Edmonds, 425-744-0566

- **Bogart Bremmer, & Bradley Antiques**, 8000 15th Avenue NW, 206-783-7333
- **Country Collections**, 15525 Main Street NE, Duvall, 425-788-2939
- **Designers Warehouse at Heritage Square**, 1011 2nd Street, Snohomish, 360-568-5775 (new made to look old)
- **Fremont Antique Mall**, 3419 Fremont Place North, 206-548-9140
- **Gilman Antique Gallery**, 625 NW Gilman Boulevard, Issaquah, 425-391-6640
- **Greenwood Antique Mall**, 8414 Greenwood Avenue North, 206-297-1904
- **Kirkland Antique Gallery**, 151 3rd Street, Kirkland, 425-828-4993
- **McCoy's Mercantile**, 15515 Main Street NE, Duvall, 425-788-7920
- **Michael's First Street Antique**, 1202 1st Street, Snohomish, 360-568-9735
- **Pelayo Antiques**, 7601 Greenwood Avenue North, 206-789-1999
- **Seattle Antique Market**, 1400 Alaskan Way, 206-623-6115
- **The Trading Post**, 551-B 156th Avenue SE, Bellevue, 425-643-6693
- **Tuxedo's Junction**, 15918 Main Street NE, Duvall, 425-788-9678
- **Woodinville Antique Gallery**, 14450 Woodinville Redmond Road, Woodinville, 425-402-6459

FOOD

Now comes the fun part, eating! Seattle has a great selection of eateries, ranging from greasy spoons to elegant seafood restaurants. Almost every neighborhood in Seattle has at least one espresso stand, a cafe or bakery, and a local pub or micro-brewery. Ask your neighbors for recommendations or check the paper for restaurant reviews.

At-home chefs are in luck too. In addition to the well-stocked supermarkets common in any city, Seattle has a nice selection of specialty grocers, food co-ops, farmers' markets, and fresh seafood markets.

GROCERY STORES

Many of the large grocery stores in the city are open 24-hours, and most feature well-stocked delis and on-site bakeries. The current trend in the new and remodeled stores is to offer an in-house floral department, espresso stand, and a take-out food counter with sandwiches, salads and hot entrees. Many have adjoining businesses such as bakery, bagel or coffee shops, and small bank branches. **Larry's Market**, www.larrysmarkets.com, **Thriftway**, www.thriftway.com, and **Albertson's**, www.albertsons.com, each have several locations throughout the city, but the predominant chains—almost 70% according to a recent *Post Intelligencer* article—are **QFC**, www.qfconline.com, **Fred Meyer**, www.fredmeyer.com (both owned by food giant Kroger), and **Safeway**, www.safeway.com. Selection, good sales, and convenience are consumers' oft-sited reasons for shopping at large chains, some even have in-store pharmacies. But don't miss out on the unique offerings at the smaller grocers. Larry's is known for their well-stocked wine selections and knowledgeable wine stewards, and Thriftway for their organic produce, specialty foods, and customer service.

Two warehouse stores in the Seattle area offer good deals on bulk foods and other household items. These are **Costco**, www.costco.com, and **Sam's Club**, www.samsclub.com. See above under **Warehouse Stores** for locations. Both have membership requirements. Call ahead for details.

SPECIALTY/HEALTH FOOD GROCERS

- **Essential Baking Co.**, 1604 North 34th Street, 206-545-3804, www.essentialbaking.com
- **Whole Foods**, 6400 Roosevelt Way NE, 206-985-1500; www.wholefoods.com
- **Pioneer Organics**, 901 NW 49th Street, 206-632-3424, http://pioneerorganics.com
- **Madison Market**, 1600 East Madison Street, 206-329-1545
- **Fremont Fresh Market**, 3601 Fremont Avenue North #2112, 206-633-3663
- **Greenwood Market**, 8500 Third Avenue NW, 206-782-1610

Another grocery shopping option is the food cooperative. With seven neighborhood stores in the city, Seattle's largest is **PCC (Puget Consumers Co-Op)**, which offers a wide selection of natural and organic foods. Visit www.pccnaturalmarkets.com or call your nearest store for membership information.

- **PCC Fremont**, 716 North 34th Street, 206-632-6811
- **PCC Greenlake**, 7504 Aurora Avenue North, 206-525-3586
- **PCC Issaquah**, 1810 12th Avenue NW, 425-369-1222
- **PCC Kirkland**, 10718 NE 68th Street, 425-828-4622
- **PCC Seward Park**, 5041 Wilson Avenue South, 206-723-2720
- **PCC View Ridge**, 6514 40th Avenue NE, 206-526-7661
- **PCC West Seattle**, 2749 California Avenue SW, 206-937-8481

ETHNIC DISTRICTS AND MARKETS

Small grocery stores specializing in delicacies from other parts of the world are scattered throughout the Seattle area and surrounding communities. Immigrants and natives alike are attracted to these unique stores.

AFRICAN
- **Kilimanjaro Market**, 12515 Lake City Way NE, 206-440-1440

ASIAN
There are numerous Asian markets in Seattle's International District, also known as Chinatown. Start at the intersection of 4th Avenue South and Jackson Street and head east. You will also find a collection of Asian groceries along Aurora Avenue in North Seattle.
- **Asia Market**, 9615 15th Avenue SW, 206-762-8658
- **Cambodian Market**, 9419 16th Avenue SW, 206-767-0531
- **Center Oriental Grocery**, 9641 15th Avenue SW, 206-762-5620
- **Foulee Market**, 2050 South Columbian Way, 206-764-9607
- **Hop Thanh Supermarket**, 1043 South Jackson Street, 206-322-7473
- **Phnom Penh Market**, 7123 Martin Luther King Jr. Way South, 206-723-4341
- **Uwajimaya**, Seattle, 4601 6th Avenue South, 206-624-3215; Bellevue, 15555 NE 24th, 425-747-9012
- **Vientian Asian Grocery**, 6059 Martin Luther King Jr. Way South, 206-723-3160
- **Viet Hoa Seafood & Meat Company**, 700 South Jackson Street, 206-622-5297
- **Viet Wah Super Foods**, 6040 Martin Luther King Jr. Way South, 206-760-8895

GREEK-MIDDLE EASTERN
- **Aladdin Gyro-Cery**, 4139 University Way NE, 206-632-5253

INDIAN-PAKISTANI
- **Pakistani and Indian Grocery**, 12325 Roosevelt Way NE, 206-368-7323

ITALIAN
- **De Laurenti Specialty Food Market**, 1435 1st Avenue, 206-622-0141

SPANISH-MEXICAN-LATIN AMERICAN
Seattle's South Park neighborhood is known for its concentration of Hispanic businesses and residents. Readily available items include savory chorizo, fresh corn tortillas, hot peppers, and sweet mangoes.
- **La Bonita Grocery Store**, 9431 Rainier Avenue South, 206-725-2896
- **El Mercado Latino**, 1514 Pike Place, 206-623-3240
- **La Bodeguita Specialty Foods**, 2528A Beacon Avenue South, 206-329-9001
- **Mexican Grocery**, 1914 Pike Place, 206-441-1147

FARMERS' MARKETS

If you're searching for the highest quality in fruits and vegetables, your best bet is to buy right from the growers. During the summer, you can often find corn, cherries, raspberries, strawberries, apples, and peaches sold from truck beds on city street corners. For a bigger selection, try one of the farmers' markets in Seattle. The largest is **Pike Place Market**, in downtown Seattle at the west end of Pike Street. Don't be fooled by the fact that Pike Place is a popular tourist attraction; it is also a year-round destination for locals in search of fresh produce—succulent nectarines, perfect tomatoes or flavorful Walla Walla sweet onions. You can also find fresh fish and shellfish, homemade jams, jellies and honey, and brilliantly colored tulips, daffodils and dahlias. Neighborhood farmers' markets are open either on weekends or on an assigned weekday, and offerings include fresh produce from local farmers, and arts and crafts. Except for the year round Pike Place Market and the Fremont Sunday Market, all the markets here are open from late spring to early fall.

SEATTLE
- **Ballard Farmers' Market**, NW 56th Street and 22nd Avenue NW, Sundays, 10 a.m. to 4 p.m.
- **Columbia City Farmers' Market**, 4801 Rainier Avenue South, Wednesdays, 3 to 7 p.m.
- **Fremont Sunday Market**, 400 North 34th Street, Sundays, 10 a.m. to 4 p.m.
- **Pike Place Market**, 1st Avenue and Pike Street, Monday-Saturday, 9 a.m. to 6 p.m.; Sunday 10 a.m. to 5 p.m.
- **University District Farmers' Market**, NE 50th Street and University Way NE, Saturdays, 9 a.m. to 2 p.m.
- **West Seattle Farmers' Market**, SW Alaska Street and California Avenue SW, Sundays, 10 a.m. to 2 p.m.

SURROUNDING COMMUNITIES
- **Bothell Country Village Farmers' Market**, 23732 Bothell-Everett Highway, Fridays, 10 a.m. to 3 p.m.
- **Edmonds Museum Summer Market**, Bell Street between 5th and 6th avenues, Saturdays, 9 a.m. to 3 p.m.
- **Enumclaw Farmers Market**, Cole and Initial streets, Saturdays, 10 a.m. to 3 p.m.
- **Everett Farmers' Market**, Everett Marina at Port Gardner Landing, Sundays, 11 a.m. to 4 p.m.

- **Issaquah Public Market**, SE 56th and 10th Avenue NW, Saturdays, 9 a.m. to 2 p.m.
- **Kirkland Farmers' Market**, Park Lane East, between 3rd and Main, Wednesdays, 1 to 7 p.m.
- **North Bend Farmers' Market**, Main and Park, at State Route 202, Saturdays, 9 a.m. to 1 p.m.
- **Redmond Saturday Market**, 7730 Leary Way, Saturdays, 8 a.m. to noon
- **Vashon Island Growers Association Farmers' Market**, 1/2 block north of Bank Road on Vashon Highway SW, Saturdays, 9 a.m. to 1 p.m.
- **Woodinville Farmers' Market**, 17301 133rd Avenue NE, Saturdays, 9 a.m. to 4 p.m.

COMMUNITY GARDENS

For the ultimate in freshness you could grow your own herbs and veggies. It doesn't take much space; a window box will do for many herbs. If you prefer a little more growing room when you garden, but don't have the space in your own backyard, consider a community garden. In Seattle, residents of 44 neighborhoods share "P-Patches," community gardens that boast more than 1,900 plots on 12 acres of land. **P-Patch** gardeners supply seven to ten tons of fresh organic vegetables to Seattle food banks each year. Many gardens have waiting lists—some up to three years long. According to the Seattle Department of Neighborhoods, only 10% to 20% of plots turn over each year, so you might want to get on the list as soon as you are settled into your new neighborhood. To sign up, or for more information, call the P-Patch Program at 206-684-0264, or visit www.cityofseattle.net.

RESTAURANTS

Depending on your degree of interest in food, dining out here can be a convenience, a diversion, a hobby, a sport, a religion or a vocation. Offering every cuisine imaginable, Seattle is beginning to catch up to food meccas like San Francisco and New York City. To find popular eateries in your neighborhood, visit www.seattle.citysearch.com or www.zagat.com. For helpful printed guides, consider buying the *Zagat Survey, Seattle/Portland Restaurants* or *The Food Lover's Guide to Seattle* by Katy Calcott.

Thanks to a new cookbook from authors Cynthia Nims and Kathy Casey, Seattle's cooks can reproduce their favorite restaurant meals at home: *Best Places Seattle Cookbook: Recipes From the City's Outstanding Restaurants and Bars* features 125 recipes and 24 essays about local food and drink.

TAKEOUT MEALS

If you're tired after a long day of work and prefer to eat in without the hassle of cooking, consider picking up some food to go. Nearly all restaurants as well as some local grocery stores and specialty food shops offer take-out. Most of the chain grocery stores, particularly Larry's Market, QFC and Thriftway, have a wide selection of take-out meals. Here are some other places to consider:

- **Pagliacci Pizza**, 4529 University Way NE, 206-632-0421; 426 Broadway East, 206-324-0730; 550 Queen Anne Avenue North, 206-285-1232, www.pagliacci.com
- **Pasta & Co.**, 2109 Queen Anne Avenue North, 206-283-1182; 815 East Pike Street, 206-322-4577; 2640 NE University Village Mall, 206-523-8594; www.pastaco.com
- **Red Mill Burgers**, 312 North 67th Street, 206-783-6362; 1613 West Dravus, 206-284-6363
- **Taco del Mar**, 5431 Ballard Avenue NW, 206-706-9933; 800 Union, 206-628-8982; 823 3rd Avenue, 206-467-4878; 1336 1st Avenue, 206-623-8741; 2932 4th Avenue South, 206-521-8887; 3526 Fremont Place North, 206-545-8001; 5963 Corson Avenue South, 206-764-4956; 8004 Greenwood Avenue North, 206-706-4063; 615 Queen Anne Avenue North, 206-281-7420; 90 Yesler Way, 206-467-5940; 6501 Roosevelt Way NE, 206-729-0670; 1520 Broadway, 206-328-4868; 1165 Harrison, 206-624-2114; 1815 North 45th Street, 206-545-3720, www.tacodelmar.com
- **Toshi's Teriyaki**, 14705 Aurora Avenue North, 206-364-7057; 10716 5th Avenue NE, 206-361-9134; 111 15th Avenue East, 206-329-5838; 617 3rd Avenue, 206-467-6689; 2500 SW Barton, 206-937-9442; 3401 Stone Way North, 206-547-5330; 6421 15th Avenue NW, 206-789-7998; 20320 Ballinger Way NE, 206-361-9088

DRINKING WATER

Most Seattle residents drink plain tap water, though some use a simple home filtering system, such as a Brita water pitcher. For less trusting souls, some companies will deliver drinking water to your home or business:

- **Crystal Springs**, 888-686-9283
- **Culligan**, 888-575-0234, www.culligan.com
- **Mountain Mist**, 800-232-7332, www.mountainmist.com
- **PureWater**, 800-822-5889, www.purewaterinc.com
- **Sparkletts**, 800-453-0293, www.sparkletts.com

THOUGH SEATTLE LANDED ON THE WORLD MUSIC MAP AS THE birthplace of grunge, it is not just a music mecca for alternative rock and its fans. Seattle is home to big and small fine art venues that offer top-notch live performances in classical music, opera, comedy, and theater. Area residents flock to film openings, improvisational theater, traveling Broadway shows, and readings by visiting authors. The months of inclement winter weather guarantee large audiences for most performances. In the summer, entertainers simply move to the enticing outdoors. Music concerts are held in local parks, on the waterfront, and in concert halls. Another concert venue about two and half hours east of Seattle is "The Gorge," a huge amphitheater that attracts big names in contemporary and classic rock, blues, and jazz. Several summer festivals feature fabulous musical and theatrical performances; see **A Seattle Year** for more details.

Also covered in this chapter, **Museums, Literary Life,** and **Culture for Kids**. Unless otherwise noted, the following establishments are in Seattle.

TICKETS

Like nearly every major city in the US, tickets to most shows in Seattle can be bought through **Ticketmaster**: 206-628-0888 or online at www.ticketmaster.com. For especially popular events, such as rock concerts and professional sports playoffs, you may have no choice but to buy from Ticketmaster. However, for many events and performances you can avoid paying the extra Ticketmaster fees by purchasing tickets directly at the event venue's box office. Ticketmaster outlets are located in most area Rite Aid stores.

Several local live entertainment venues, including the Crocodile Café, Comedy Underground, Pacific Science Center, and Tractor Tavern, use the online ticket service **TicketWeb**, www.ticketweb.com. Still other attractions, like Argosy Cruises and the Showbox Theater, use **Fastixx**; go to www.fastixx.com or call 800-992-TIXX for a list of venues using this service. **TicketWindow**, 206-325-6500, www.ticketwindowonline.com, is a local online box office that also provides discount walk-up service at its three **Ticket/Ticket** outlets. The outlets, located in Capitol Hill's Broadway Market, at the Pike Place Market information booth, and at Bellevue's Meydenbauer Center, offer half-price, day-of-show tickets to a variety of arts events; sales are cash and walk-up only. Call 206-324-2744 to find out what events are available.

If you have your heart set on a sold-out performance, a broker can usually provide a ticket, but expect to pay dearly for the opportunity. Broker services can charge top dollar because they operate outside the city and avoid Seattle's anti-scalping ordinance. Look in the Yellow Pages under "Ticket Sales—Entertainment & Sports."

CLASSICAL MUSIC AND DANCE

PROFESSIONAL—SYMPHONIC, CHORAL, OPERA, CHAMBER MUSIC

- **Northwest Chamber Orchestra**, 1305 4th Avenue, Suite 522, 206-343-0445, www.nwco.org; the area's only professional chamber orchestra, the group presents performances of contemporary and classical works, September through May.
- **Seattle Choral Company**, 1518 NE 143rd Street, 206-363-1100, www.seattlechoralcompany.org; performances are held November through May at various venues.
- **Seattle Men's Chorus**, 319 12th Avenue, 206-323-2992, www.seattle-menschorus.org; a popular local choir representing Seattle's large gay community, the Seattle Men's Chorus is well known for its raffish and entertaining performances.
- **Seattle Opera**, 1020 John Street, 206-389-7676, www.seattleopera.org; world renowned, the Seattle Opera features five productions from August to May, as well as a bi-yearly summer presentation of "The Ring" cycle by Wagner. A typical season includes several traditional performances of popular operas, as well as contemporary works and fresh takes on old standards. The opera routinely attracts international stars for lead roles, and longtime patrons recognize the local performers filling out each performance. Renovation at the Seattle Center Opera House will force the company to perform in Mercer Arts Arena from January 2002 to spring 2003. The opera house will reopen as Marion Oliver McCall Hall.
- **Seattle Pro Musica**, 1756 NW 56th Street, 206-781-2766, www.seattlepromusica.org; this award-winning group performs a four-concert season that ranges from medieval chant to the works of living composers.

- **Seattle Symphony**, 200 University Street, 206-215-4700, www.seat-tlesymphony.org, presents weekly performances September through June in Benaroya Hall, an acoustic masterpiece with seating for 2,500.
- **Tacoma Opera**, P.O. Box 7648, Tacoma, WA 98407, 253-627-7789, www.tacomaopera.com; performances are held at the Pantages Theater in downtown Tacoma.

COMMUNITY—SYMPHONIC, CHORAL, OPERA, CHAMBER MUSIC

- **Choral Arts Northwest**, 1820 South 261st Place, Des Moines, 877-404-2269, www.choralartsnorthwest.org; a chamber ensemble of 26 musicians, the group presents concerts in Seattle and Tacoma.
- **Federal Way Symphony**, P.O. Box 4513, Federal Way, WA 98063, 253-529-9857, www.federalwaysymphony.org; performances take place at St. Luke's Church, 515 South 312th Street, in Federal Way.
- **Masterworks Choral Ensemble**, P.O. Box 1091, Olympia, WA 98507, 360-491-3305, www.mce.org, presents five concerts from October to June at the Washington Center for the Performing Arts in Olympia.
- **Northwest Symphony Orchestra**, 7520 30th Avenue SW, 206-242-6321, www.northwestsymphonyorchestra.org, performs works by Pacific Northwest composers, as well as classical pieces.
- **Thalia Symphony Orchestra**, 3307 3rd Avenue West, 206-281-2048, www.thaliasymphony.org; Seattle Pacific University's orchestra-in-residence performs October through June.

DANCE

- **On the Boards**, 100 West Roy, 206-217-9888, www.ontheboards.org; approximately 200 experimental and contemporary performances are presented October through December in two theaters at the Behnke Center for Contemporary Performance, and at theaters throughout Seattle.
- **Pacific Northwest Ballet (PNB)**, 301 Mercer Street, 206-441-9411, www.pnb.org, presents six programs September through June, including several performances of short contemporary works and one or two longer traditional pieces. The annual Christmas show is a beloved version of The Nutcracker, featuring sets designed by author and illustrator Maurice Sendak. Like the Seattle Symphony, renovation at the Seattle Center Opera House will force the company to perform in Mercer Arts Arena from January 2002 to spring 2003.
- **Spectrum Dance Theater**, 800 Lake Washington Boulevard, 206-325-4161, www.spectrumdance.org; Seattle's premier jazz dance company

draws on influences from swing to scat and tango to blues. Performances are held at a variety of venues throughout Seattle and the Eastside.

- **UW World Dance Series**, 4001 University Way NE, 206-543-4880; as part of the UW World Series, Meany Theater presents a selection of dance performances from around the globe. The series runs from October to May. Meany Theater is located on the UW campus, at 15th Avenue NE and Campus Parkway.

CONTEMPORARY MUSIC

Seattle burst onto the national music scene a decade ago as the home of "grunge" rock. While bands like Pearl Jam, Soundgarden, Alice In Chains, and Nirvana put the city on the map for alternative music, other musical genres thrive in Seattle. The following bars, clubs and concert halls are best known for the category under which they are listed, but many book a variety of acts. Check out the *Seattle Weekly*, www.seattleweekly.com, or *The Stranger*, www.thestranger.com—both free local newspapers found in bars, cafes and music stores—to find out each venue's schedule.

CONCERT VENUES

- **Benaroya Hall**, S. Mark Taper Auditorium, 200 University Street, 206-215-4747, www.benaroyahall.com
- **Chateau Ste. Michelle Winery**, 14111 NE 145th Street, Woodinville, 425-488-3300, www.ste-michelle.com
- **Gorge Amphitheatre**, 754 Silica Road NW, George, 509-785-2267, www.hob.com
- **Key Arena**, Seattle Center, 206-684-7200, www.seattlecenter.com
- **Memorial Stadium**, Seattle Center, 206-684-7200, www.seattlecenter.com
- **Mercer Arena**, Seattle Center, 206-684-7200, www.seattlecenter.com
- **Paramount Theatre**, 911 Pine Street, 206-682-1414, www.theparamount.com
- **Piers 62/63**, Summer Nights at the Pier, 200 Alaskan Way West, 206-281-8111, www.summernights.org
- **Stadium Exhibition Center**, 1000 Occidental South, 206-381-7500, www.stadiumexcenter.com
- **Tacoma Dome**, 2727 East "D" Street, Tacoma, 253-272-3663

BARS AND NIGHTCLUBS

ALL AGES

- **DV8**, 131 Taylor Avenue North, 206-448-0888
- **Paradox Theater**, 5510 University Way NE, 206-524-7677, www.theparadox.org

ALTERNATIVE, INDUSTRIAL, ROCK

- **Ballard Firehouse**, 5429 Russell Avenue NW, 206-784-3516, http://theballardfirehouse.com
- **The Breakroom**, 1325 East Madison Street, 206-860-5155
- **Catwalk**, 172 South Washington Street, 206-622-1863, www.catwalkclub.net
- **Central Saloon**, 207 1st Avenue South, 206-622-0209, www.centralsaloon.com
- **Club Broadway**, 1611 Everett Avenue, Everett, 425-259-3551
- **Crocodile Café**, 2200 2nd Avenue, 206-441-5611, www.thecrocodile.com
- **Doc Maynard's**, 610 1st Avenue, 206-682-3705, www.docmaynards.com
- **Experience Music Project**, Sky Church, 325 5th Avenue North, 206-770-2777, www.emplive.com
- **Graceland**, 109 Eastlake Avenue East, 206-381-3094
- **King Cat Theatre**, 2130 6th Avenue, 206-269-7444
- **Moore Theatre**, 1932 2nd Avenue, 206-682-1414, www.themoore.com
- **Rocksport**, 4209 SW Alaska Street, 206-935-5838, www.rocksport.net
- **Showbox**, 1426 1st Avenue, 206-628-3151
- **Sit & Spin**, 2219 4th Avenue, 206-628-3151
- **Sliders Pub**, 221 Main Street, Renton, 425-254-3800, www.sliderspub.com
- **Waldo's**, 12657 NE 85th Street, Kirkland, 425-827-9292

BLUES, JAZZ

- **Bad Albert's**, 5100 Ballard Avenue NW, 206-782-9623
- **Dimitriou's Jazz Alley**, 2033 6th Avenue, 206-441-9729, www.jazzalley.com
- **Larry's Greenfront Restaurant and Lounge**, 209 1st Avenue South, 206-624-7665
- **Latona by Green Lake**, 6423 Latona Avenue NE, 206-525-2238
- **New Orleans Restaurant**, 114 1st Avenue South, 206-622-2563
- **Old Timer's Café**, 620 1st Avenue South, 206-623-9800
- **Tula's Restaurant and Jazz Club**, 2214 2nd Avenue, 206-443-4221

COUNTRY

- **Little Red Hen**, 7115 Woodlawn Avenue NE, 206-522-1168, www.littleredhen.com

DANCE, DJs

- **The Backdoor (Ultra) Lounge**, 503 3rd Avenue, 206-622-7665, www.backdoorlounge.com
- **The Ballroom**, 456 North 36th Street, 206-634-2575
- **Baltic Room**, 1207 Pine Street, 206-625-4444
- **Belltown Billiards**, 90 Blanchard Street, 206-448-6779
- **Contour**, 807 1st Avenue, 206-748-9834
- **Down Under**, 2407 1st Avenue, 206-728-4053
- **I-Spy**, 1921 5th Avenue, 206-374-9492
- **Last Supper Club**, 124 South Washington Street, 206-748-9975
- **Neighbours**, 1509 Broadway, 206-324-5358
- **Paragon Bar and Grill**, 2125 Queen Anne Avenue North, 206-283-4548
- **Polly Esthers/Culture Club**, 332 5th Avenue North, 206-441-1970
- **Re-bar**, 1114 Howell Street, 206-233-9873
- **Vogue**, 1516 11th Avenue, 206-324-5778

FOLK, ROCKABILLY, SWING

- **Fiddler's Inn**, 9219 35th Avenue NE, 206-525-0752, www.fiddlersinn.org
- **Tractor Tavern**, 5213 Ballard Avenue NW, 206-789-3599, www.tractortavern.com

FUNK, HIP HOP, R&B, SOUL

- **Art Bar**, 1516 2nd Avenue, 206-622-4344, www.artbar.com

IRISH AND CELTIC

- **The Dubliner Pub**, 3405 Fremont Avenue North, 206-548-1508
- **Fado Irish Pub**, 801 1st Avenue, 206-264-2700, www.fadoirishpub.com
- **Kells**, 1916 Post Alley, 206-768-728-1916, www.kellsirish.com
- **Mulleady's Pub**, 2017 West Dravus Street, 206-283-8843
- **The Owl 'n' Thistle**, 808 Post Avenue, 206-621-7777, www.owlnthistle.com

THEATER AND FILM

While many residents become season ticket subscribers, you'll find this is a city of last-minute ticket buyers. Even the most popular shows may not sell out until the day of the performance, though it's always good to call ahead and check availability.

PROFESSIONAL THEATER

- **A Contemporary Theater (ACT)**, 700 Union Street, 206-292-7676, www.acttheatre.org; referred to as "ACT theater" or "the CT," presents contemporary works by both established and little-known playwrights.
- **Empty Space Theatre**, 3509 Fremont Avenue North, 206-547-7500, www.emptyspace.org; situated on the top floor of a building in the center of the Fremont neighborhood, the Empty Space Theatre has been producing contemporary shows in Seattle for more than 25 years. The Empty Space is a favorite of Seattle theatergoers, who enjoy the boisterous comedies and cutting edge dramas performed (and often written) by talented local players.
- **The 5th Avenue Musical Theatre Company**, 1326 5th Avenue, 206-625-1900, www.5thavenuetheatre.org; like the Paramount Theater, The 5th Avenue hosts traveling productions of major Broadway shows, as well as some concerts. The performance hall is exquisitely decorated with Oriental style carvings and opulent fabrics.
- **Intiman Theatre**, Playhouse, Seattle Center, 201 Mercer Street, 206-269-1900, www.intiman.org; once considered the poor cousin to the nearby Seattle Repertory Theater (also at the Seattle Center), the Intiman Theatre has come into its own in recent years. Presenting a variety of modern and classic works, the Intiman addresses contemporary issues with ambitious and dynamic interpretations of new and established plays.
- **Paramount Theater**, 911 Pine Street, 206-682-1414, www.theparamount.com; the recently refurbished Paramount Theater hosts traveling productions of Broadway shows, as well as some concerts and special charitable functions. The plush lobby and ornate performance hall make this an elegant venue for any play or musical.
- **Seattle Public Theater**, 7312 West Green Lake Drive North, 206-524-1300, www.seattlepublictheater.org; the company performs at the Greenlake Bathhouse, a cozy brick building which used to serve as the lake's bathhouse. The theater produces classic shows with a good dose of humor.

- **Seattle Repertory Theatre**, Bagley Wright Theater, Seattle Center, 155 Mercer Street, 206-443-2222, www.seattlerep.org; perhaps Seattle's best-known theater, "The Rep" presents a mix of classical and contemporary plays each season, from October to April. The theater often performs plays that have recently completed successful Broadway runs, but never hosts touring shows.
- **SecondStory Repertory**, Redmond Town Center, 16587 NE 74th Street, Redmond, 425-881-6777, www.secondstoryrep.org; a non-profit, professional ensemble, SecondStory presents comedies, revues, and dramas September through June. The company also performs a series of original musicals.
- **Tacoma Actors Guild (TAG)**, Theatre on the Square, 915 Broadway, Tacoma, 253-272-2145; productions range from classic to contemporary, serious drama to light-hearted comedy. The *San Francisco Chronicle* described TAG as "... an asset as rare as Tacoma's zoom lens view of Mount Rainier."

COMMUNITY THEATER

- **Annex Theatre**, 1017 East Pike Street, 206-728-0933, www.annextheatre.org
- **Valley Community Players**, Carco Theatre, 1717 Maple Valley Highway, Renton, 425-226-5190, www.valleycommunityplayers.com
- **Renton Civic Theatre**, 507 South Third Street, Renton, 425-226-5529, www.rentoncivictheatre.org
- **Bellevue Civic Theatre**, Meydenbauer Center, 11100 6th Street, Bellevue, 425-235-5087, http://bellevuecivic.org
- **Driftwood Players**, Wade James Theatre, 950 Main Street, Edmonds, 425-774-9600, www.driftwoodplayers.com
- **Theater Schmeater**, 1500 Summit Avenue, 206-324-5801, www.schmeater.org
- **Village Theatre**: Francis J. Gaudette Theatre, 303 Front Street North, Issaquah, 425-392-2202; Everett Performing Arts Center, 2710 Wetmore Avenue, Everett, 425-257-8600, www.villagetheatre.org

IMPROV

A combination of stand-up comedy and acting, improvisational theater uses audience suggestions to create a scene, which is then played for laughs. Most improv groups perform only on the weekends; make sure you call ahead as times and locations change.

- **Jet City Improv**, University Heights Center, 5031 University Way NE, and ArtsWest Playhouse, 4711 California Avenue SW, 206-781-3879, www.jetcityimprov.com
- **TheatreSports**, 1428 Post Alley, 206-781-9273, www.unexpectedproductions.org

COMEDY

- **Comedy Underground**, 222 South Main Street, 206-628-0303, www.comedyunderground.com
- **Giggles Comedy Nite Club**, 5220 Roosevelt Way NE, 206-526-JOKE

FILM

There are numerous movie theatres in Seattle, and multi-screen outlets continue to rise in developing areas outside of Seattle. For general multi-screen movie complexes, visit www.movies.com or check the Yellow Pages under "Theatres-Movies." The following is a list of **alternative and fine art movie houses.**

- **Aurora Cinema Grill**, 13000 Aurora Avenue, 206-364-8880, www.cinemagrill.com
- **Broadway Market Cinemas**, 425 Broadway East, 206-323-0231, www.landmarktheatres.com
- **Grand Illusion Cinema**, 1403 NE 50th Street, 206-523-3935, www.wigglyworld.org/grandillusion
- **Seven Gables Theater**, 911 NE 50th Street, 206-632-8820, www.landmarktheatres.com
- **Egyptian Theatre**, 805 East Pine Street, 206-323-4978, www.landmarktheatres.com
- **Harvard Exit**, 807 East Roy, 206-323-8986, www.landmarktheatres.com
- **Neptune Theatre**, 1303 NE 45th Street, 206-633-5545, www.landmarktheatres.com
- **Varsity Theatre**, 4329 University Way NE, 206-632-3131, www.landmarktheatres.com

FILM FESTIVALS

- **Fremont Outdoor Film Festival**, North 35th and Phinney Avenue, 206-781-4230, www.outdoorfilmfestival.com
- **Seattle International Film Festival**, 911 Pine Street, 206-324-9997, www.seattlefilm.com

- **Seattle Jewish Film Festival**, 1402 3rd Avenue, Suite 1415, 206-390-7791, www.ajcseattle.org
- **Seattle Underground Film Festival**, 206-382-0926, www.seattleundergroundfilm.com
- **Seattle Lesbian and Gay Film Festival**, 1122 East Pike Street, #1313, 206-323-4274, www.seattlequeerfilm.org

MUSEUMS

Rainy days are perfect for strolling through the quiet (and dry) halls of fine museums—and Seattle has plenty of both! From art to science to culture and history, area museums offer interesting and diverse exhibits, and many host traveling exhibits. Be sure to call ahead or go online to find out about the latest offerings and to check on days and hours of operation (several museums are closed on Monday).

ART

- **Bellevue Art Museum**, 510 Bellevue Way NE, 425-519-0770, www.bellevueart.org, is located across the street from Bellevue Square, the Eastside's most popular shopping mall. The museum combines traditional art exhibits and programs with a school, art studio, and community center, and hosts the annual Bellevue Art Museum Fair each summer. Hours are Tuesday, Wednesday, Friday, Saturday from 10 a.m. to 5 p.m., Thursday 10 a.m. to 8 p.m., and Sunday noon to 5. Admission is $6 for adults, $4 for seniors and students. Kids under 6 are free.
- **Frye Art Museum**, 704 Terry Avenue, 206-622-9250, www.fryeart.org; located on First Hill in an International Style building designed in 1952 by Paul Thiry, the Frye Art Museum houses a collection of 19th century paintings by European artists, as well as a large collection of works by 18th century German artists. Open Tuesday, Wednesday, Friday, Saturday 10 a.m. to 5 p.m., Thursday 10 a.m. to 9 p.m., and Sunday noon to 5. No admission charged.
- **Henry Art Gallery**, University of Washington, 15th Avenue NE and NE 41st Street, 206-543-2280, www.henryart.org; the 19th century and early 20th century American and European works originally donated by local businessman Horace C. Henry are still the backbone of this museum's collection. Housed in a recently renovated brick Tudor designed by Carl Gould, it provides a pleasant respite from the bustle of the city. Hours of operation are Tuesday, Wednesday, Friday, Saturday, Sunday 11 a.m. to 5 p.m., and Thursday 11 a.m. to 8 p.m. General admission is $6, $4.50 for seniors, and no charge for students, UW faculty and staff, and kids 13 and younger. Thursday evenings, 5 to 8, are free.

- **Museum of Glass**, 1801 Dock Street, Tacoma, 253-284-4750, 866-4-MUSEUM, www.museumofglass.org; opened in July of 2002, and devoted to the exhibition and interpretation of contemporary art with a focus on the medium of glass. A 500-foot pedestrian tunnel crafted by legendary glass artist Dale Chihuly links the museum to downtown Tacoma. Hours are Tuesday, Wednesday, Friday, Saturday 10 a.m. to 5 p.m., Thursday 10 a.m. to 8 p.m. Admission is $8 for adults, $6 for seniors, $3 for children, 6 to 12. Free every third Thursday of the month from 5 p.m. to 8 p.m.

- **Museum of Northwest Art (MoNA)**, 121 South 1st Street, 360-466-4446, www.museumofnwart.org; the Skagit Valley, north of Seattle, has long been a haven for Northwest artists. MoNA opened in 1981 to present the works of these artists, and to serve as a source of education. The museum's small permanent collection consists of paintings, sculpture, glass and works on paper. Open Tuesday-Saturday 10 a.m. to 5 p.m. Admission is $4 for adults, $2 for students and free for children 12 and under.

- **Seattle Art Museum (SAM)**, 100 University Street, 206-654-3255, www.seattleartmuseum.org; located near the Pike Place Market, the Seattle Art Museum houses an exceptional collection, which includes a variety of African, Chinese and Native American pieces, as well as European and American art. SAM is Seattle's preeminent art museum, showcasing international traveling exhibits of photography, painting and sculpture. Open Tuesday-Sunday, 10 a.m. to 5 p.m., Thursday until 9 p.m. Suggested admission for adults is $7, $5 for seniors and students, and those 12 and under are admitted free. The first Thursday of the month admission is free.

- **Seattle Asian Art Museum**, Volunteer Park, 1400 East Prospect Street, 206-654-3206, www.seattleartmuseum.org; housed in a 1933 Art Deco building designed by Carl Gould, and previously occupied by the Seattle Art Museum, this gallery presents art from Japan, China, Korea and India. The museum is a focal point of Volunteer Park, located at the northeast corner of Capitol Hill. Open Tuesday-Sunday, 10 a.m. to 5 p.m., Thursday until 9 p.m. Suggested admission for adults is $3; those 12 and under are admitted free. Admission on the first Saturday of the month is free.

- **Tacoma Art Museum (TAM)**, 1123 Pacific Avenue, Tacoma, 253-272-4258, www.tacomaartmuseum.org; TAM's exhibits emphasize art and artists from the Northwest. A collection Dale Chihuly's glass works is a permanent fixture. Every other summer, the museum hosts the Northwest Biennial, a juried competition for artists from Washington, Oregon, Idaho and Montana. Hours are Tuesday-Saturday 10 a.m. to 5 p.m., Thursday 10 a.m. to 8 p.m., and Sunday noon to 5 p.m. Admission is

$5 for adults, $4 for seniors and students, and free for kids 6 and under. Admission on the third Thursday of each month is free.

ART GALLERIES

Each month, various communities in the Puget Sound region host "art walks," where neighborhood galleries stay open late and often provide food and live music. This is a great way to see the exhibits without fighting daytime traffic and crowds. Pioneer Square holds its art walk on the first Thursday of the month; Everett on the second Thursday; Tacoma on the third Thursday; Bremerton, and Vashon Island on the first Friday; Capitol Hill, Fremont, Port Townsend, and Langley on the first Saturday; Ballard on the second Saturday; and Bainbridge Island on the first Sunday. Call ahead for hours and showings or look in the local newspapers for weekly reviews. Listed below are some of the galleries in downtown Seattle:

- **Benham Studio**, 1216 1st Avenue, 206-622-2480, www.benham-gallery.com
- **Linda Cannon Gallery**, 617 Western Avenue, 206-233-0404
- **Center of Contemporary Art**, 65 Cedar Street, 206-728-1980, www.cocaseattle.org
- **Davidson Galleries**, 313 Occidental Avenue South, 206-624-7684, www.davidsongalleries.com
- **Foster/White Gallery**, 3112 Occidental Avenue South, 206-622-2833, www.fosterwhite.com
- **G. Gibson Gallery**, 122 South Jackson Street, 206-587-4033, www.ggibsongallery.com
- **The Grover/Thurston Gallery**, 309 Occidental Avenue South, 206-223-0816
- **Lisa Harris Gallery**, 1922 Pike Place, 206-443-3315, www.lisaharrisgallery.com
- **Linda Hodges Gallery**, 316 1st South, 206-624-3034, www.lindahodgesgallery.com
- **Kimzey Miller Gallery**, 1225 2nd Avenue, 206-682-2339
- **Kurt Lidtke Gallery**, 318 2nd Avenue South, 206-622-5082
- **Meyerson & Nowinski**, 123 South Jackson Street, 206-223-1700
- **Jeffrey Moose Gallery**, 1333 5th Avenue, 206-467-6951, www.jeffreymoosegallery.com
- **Bryan Ohno Gallery**, 155 South Main Street, 206-667-9572, www.bryanohnogallery.com
- **Soil Gallery**, 1205 East Pike Street, 206-264-8061, www.soilart.org
- **William Traver Gallery**, 110 Union Street, 206-587-6501, www.travergallery.com

CULTURE, HISTORY

- **Burke Museum**, University of Washington, NE 45th Street and 17th Avenue NE, 206-543-5590, www.washington.edu/burkemuseum; the Thomas Burke museum houses fascinating exhibits on Pacific Rim geology, natural history and anthropology. Native American artifacts, including masks, beads and totem poles, and displays of dinosaur skeletons and fossils are especially popular with children. Open seven days a week, 10 a.m. to 5 p.m., Thursdays until 8 p.m. General admission for adults is $8, $6.50 for seniors, $5 for students, and free for children 5 and under.
- **Coast Guard Museum of the Northwest**, Pier 36, 1519 Alaskan Way South, 206-217-6993, www.uscg.mil/mlcpac/iscseattle; Coast Guard memorabilia, photographs, model ships and other nautical items are on display at this museum. Tours of Coast Guard cutters are available on weekends. Open Monday, Wednesday and Friday 9 a.m. to 3 p.m., Saturday and Sunday 1 p.m. to 5 p.m. No admission charged.
- **Experience Music Project (EMP)**, 325 5th Avenue North, 877-367-5483, www.emplive.com; Microsoft co-founder Paul Allen envisioned EMP as a place for music enthusiasts to explore and celebrate musical history and diversity. The 140,000-square-foot-building (either a masterpiece or an eyesore, depending on who you ask), is home to interactive exhibits, unique artifacts and performance spaces. Open Sunday-Thursday 10 a.m. to 6 p.m., Friday and Saturday 10 a.m. to 11 p.m. Admission is $19.95 for adults 18 to 64, $15.95 for teens 13 to 17, seniors, and members of the military, $14.95 for kids 7 to 12, and free for children 6 and under.
- **Museum of History and Industry**, McCurdy Park, 2700 24th Avenue East, 206-324-1126, www.seattlehistory.org; local Northwest history is presented in this museum near the University of Washington. A museum popular with children, exhibits include old-fashioned fire engines, model ships, and figureheads. History buffs will enjoy the large collection of archival photographs and the many artifacts of Seattle's fishing, lumber, and shipping industries. Hours are daily 10 a.m. to 5 p.m. Admission is $5.50 for adults, $3 for seniors and kids 6 to 12, $1 for kids 2 to 5, and free for children under 2.
- **Nordic Heritage Museum**, 3014 NW 67th Street, 206-789-5707, www.nordicmuseum.com; this museum chronicles the history of the Scandinavian immigrants who settled in the Ballard neighborhood and other areas of the Pacific Northwest. The museum offers Nordic dance and language classes, Scandinavian films and lectures. Hours are Tuesday-Saturday 10 a.m. to 4 p.m., and Sunday noon to 4 p.m. Admission ranges from $4 for adults to $2 for students K-12.

- **Seattle Metropolitan Police Museum**, 317 3rd Avenue South, 206-748-9991; located in Pioneer Square, the museum is the largest police museum in the western United States, combining historical displays with an interactive learning area for children and adults. The museum is open Tuesday-Saturday 11 a.m. to 4 p.m. Admission is $3 for adults and $1.50 for kids 11 and under.
- **Wing Luke Asian Museum**, 407 7th Avenue South, 206-623-5124, www.wingluke.org; housed in a converted garage in the historic International District, the nationally recognized Wing Luke Asian Museum showcases pan-Asian culture, history and art. Open Tuesday-Friday, 11 a.m. to 4:30 p.m., Saturday and Sunday, noon to 4 p.m. Admission is $4 for adults, $3 for students and seniors, and $2 for kids 5 to 12.

SCIENCE

- **Museum of Flight**, 9404 East Marginal Way South, 206-764-5700, www.museumofflight.org; located on the original site of the Boeing Company, the museum presents a complete history of flight and aviation technology. This is a great museum for kids and adults alike, with interactive exhibits, archival film footage, and colorful full-scale reproductions of some of Boeing's first airplanes, including early bi-planes and military jets, hanging from the ceiling. The Red Barn, which housed the first Boeing airplane factory, is also part of the exhibit. Open daily from 10 a.m. to 5 p.m., Thursdays until 9 p.m. General admission is $9.50, $8.50 for seniors, $5 for children ages 5 to 17, and free for those 4 and under.
- **Pacific Science Center**, Seattle Center, 206-443-2001, www.pacsci.org; not your traditional museum by any means, the Pacific Science Center has more than 200 interactive exhibits on science and nature. Children in particular enjoy the hands-on activities, which approach learning in fun and creative ways. During the school year, the Pacific Science Center is open Monday-Friday 10 a.m. to 5 p.m., weekends and holidays 10 a.m. to 6 p.m. In the summer, the center is open every day from 10 a.m. to 6 p.m. General admission ranges from $8 for adults to free admission for those under 3.

LITERARY LIFE

With its rainy days and coffee worship, Seattle is a great bookstore town, and area residents flock to fiction and poetry readings, and book-signings. Seattle is even home to that bookstore without any shelves, Amazon.com. While the city has chain stores like Barnes & Noble and Borders, many residents are fiercely loyal to Seattle's independent booksellers. See the *Seattle Weekly*, *Seattle Post-Intelligencer* and *The Seattle Times* for listings of upcoming readings and author signings, or contact your local bookstore for its calendar of events.

BOOKSTORES

GENERAL INTEREST

- **B. Dalton Bookseller**, Northgate Mall, 206-364-5810; Factoria Square, 425-746-2924; Southcenter, 206-246-4373
- **Bailey-Coy Books**, 414 Broadway East, 206-323-8842
- **Barnes & Noble Booksellers**, 2700 NE University Village, 206-517-4107; 600 Pine Street, 206-264-0156, www.barnesandnoble.com
- **Borders Books & Music**, 1505 4th Avenue, 206-622-4599, www.borders.com
- **City Books**, 1305 Madison Street, 206-682-4334
- **Elliott Bay Book Company**, 101 South Main Street, 206-624-6600, www.elliottbaybook.com
- **Fremont Place Book Company**, 621 North 35th Street, 206-547-5970
- **Island Books**, 3014 78th Avenue SE, Mercer Island, 206-232-6920
- **M. Coy Books & Espresso**, 117 Pine Street, 206-623-5354
- **Madison Park Books**, 4105 East Madison Street, 206-328-7323, www.madisonparkbooks.com
- **Magnolia's Book Store**, 3206 West McGraw Street, 206-283-1062
- **Queen Anne Avenue Books**, 1629 Queen Anne Avenue North, 206-283-5624, www.queenanneavebooks.com
- **Seattle University Book Store**, Seattle University, 1108 East Columbia Street, 206-296-5820, www.seattleu.edu
- **Second Story Books**, 1815 North 45th Street, 206-547-4605, www.secondstorybooks.com
- **Secret Garden Bookshop**, 2214 NW Market Street, 206-789-5006, www.secretgardenbooks.com
- **Square One Books**, 4724 42nd Avenue SW, 206-935-5764
- **Third Place Books**, 17171 Bothell Way NE, Lake Forest Park, 206-366-3333
- **Tower Books**, 550 106th Avenue NE, Bellevue, 425-451-2557
- **University Bookstore**, 4326 University Way NE, 206-634-3400; 1225 4th Avenue, 206-545-9230; 990 102nd Avenue NE, Bellevue, 425-462-4500; 1754 Pacific Avenue, Tacoma, 253-272-8080, www.bookstore.washington.edu
- **Wit's End Bookstore**, 770 North 34th Street, 206-547-2330, www.booksatoz.com/witsend

SPECIAL INTEREST

- **Armchair Sailor**, 2110 Westlake Avenue North, 206-283-0858
- **Aviation Book Company**, Boeing Field, 206-767-5232, www.aviation-book.com
- **Beyond the Closet Bookstore**, 518 East Pike Street, 206-322-4609, www.beyondthecloset.com
- **Cinema Books**, 4753 Roosevelt Way NE, 206-547-7667
- **East West Bookshop**, 6500 Roosevelt Way NE, 206-523-3726, 800-587-6002, www.ewbookshop.com
- **Flora & Fauna Books**, 121 1st Avenue South, 206-623-4727
- **Left Bank Books**, 92 Pike Street, 206-622-0195, www.leftbankbooks.com
- **Marco Polo**, 713 Broadway East, 206-860-3736
- **Mountaineers Bookstore**, 300 3rd Avenue West, 206-284-6310
- **Mystery Bookshop**, 117 Cherry Street, 206-587-5737
- **Open Books: A Poem Emporium**, 2414 North 45th Street, 206-633-0811, www.openpoetrybooks.com
- **Wide World Books & Maps**, 4411-A Wallingford Avenue North, 206-634-3453, www.travelbooksandmaps.com

USED BOOKSTORES

- **An Odd Volume Ltd.**, 1309 NE Ravenna Boulevard, 206-522-2137, www.abebooks.com
- **Couth Buzzard Used Books**, 7221 Greenwood Avenue North, 206-789-8965
- **Half Price Books**, 4709 Roosevelt Way NE, 206-547-7859, www.halfpricebooks.com
- **Twice Sold Tales**, 905 East John Street, 206-324-2421, 888-324-2421; 1311 NE 45th Street, 206-545-4226; 3504 Fremont Avenue North, 206-632-3759, www.twicesoldtales.com
- **University Used and Rare Books**, 4213 University Way NE, 206-632-3738, www.univ-used.com

LIBRARIES

In addition to the bookstores mentioned above, the Seattle area is fortunate to have two strong public library systems—Seattle Public and King County—an extensive university library network, and a handful of specialty collections. In 1998, Seattle voters approved a $196.4 million bond measure for use toward the construction of five new libraries, in Delridge, South

Park, the International District, Sand Point, and Northgate, to overhaul the Central Library, and to improve or replace the existing 22 branch libraries. Project completion is expected some time in 2007.

PUBLIC LIBRARIES

In Seattle, most residents borrow their books from the Seattle Public Library system, a network of 27 neighborhood branches, plus the Washington Talking Book and Braille Library and the central downtown branch. Temporarily housed in the Washington State Convention and Trade Center at 800 Pike Street, the Central Library is scheduled to move into its new, 355,000-square-foot digs at 1000 4th Avenue in June of 2003. For a public library branch near you, see the community resources listed at the end of each neighborhood profile.

The King County Library System (KCLS) complements the Seattle network. It is composed of 42 community branches from Kenmore to Muckleshoot and Vashon Island to North Bend. KCLS also offers TechLab, an innovative new service that allows trained library staff to visit senior centers, social service agencies, and recreation centers so that they may extend library services beyond the existing locales. For a list of neighborhood branches, visit www.kcls.org.

- **King County Library System**, 960 Newport Way NW, Issaquah, 425-369-3200, www.kcls.org
- **Seattle Public Library**, 800 Pike Street, 206-386-4636, www.spl.lib.wa.us
- **Washington Talking Book and Braille Library**, 2021 9th Avenue, 206-615-0400, TTY 206-615-0419, www.spl.lib.wa.us/wtbbl

SPECIALTY

- **Jewish Public Library**, 3502 NE 65th Street, 206-985-0702
- **Karpeles Manuscript Library**, Tacoma Museum, 407 South "G" Street, Tacoma, 206-383-2575, www.rain.org/~karpeles
- **The Mountaineers Library**, The Mountaineers Club, 300 3rd Avenue West, 206-284-6310, http://mountaineers.library.net
- **Railway Library**, Northwest Railway Museum, 38625 SE King Street, Snoqualmie, 425-888-3030, www.trainmuseum.org
- **Walter Johnson Memorial Library**, Nordic Heritage Museum, 3014 NW 67th Street, 206-789-5707, www.nordicmuseum.com
- **Seattle Metaphysical Library**, 1000 East Madison #B, 206-329-1794, www.seattlemetaphysical.net

UNIVERSITY OF WASHINGTON LIBRARIES

- **Architecture-Urban Planning Library**, 334 Gould Hall, 206-543-4067, www.lib.washington.edu/aup
- **Art Library**, 101 Stevens Way, 206-543-0648, www.lib.washington.edu/art
- **Miller Horticulture Library**, Isaacson Hall, 206-543-0415, http://depts.washington.edu/hortlib
- **Chemistry Library**, 60 Chemistry Library Building, 206-543-1603, www.lib.washington.edu/chemistry
- **Drama Library**, 145 Hutchinson-Stevens Way, 206-543-8512, www.lib.washington.edu/drama
- **East Asia Library**, 322 Gowen Hall, 206-543-4490, www.lib.washington.edu/east-asia
- **Engineering Library**, Engineering Building, 206-543-0740, www.lib.washington.edu/engineering
- **Fisheries-Oceanography Library**, 151 Oceanography Building, 206-543-4279, www.lib.washington.edu/fish
- **Forest Resources Library**, 60 Bloedel Hall, 206-543-2758, www.lib.washington.edu/forest
- **Foster Business Library**, Seafirst Executive Education Center, 206-616-6430, www.lib.washington.edu/business
- **Health Sciences Library**, T227 Health Sciences Building, 206-543-3390, http://healthlinks.washington.edu/hsl
- **Gallagher Law Library**, Condon Hall, 206-543-4086, http://lib.law.washington.edu
- **Mathematics Research Library**, C306 Padelford Hall, 206-543-7296, www.lib.washington.edu/math
- **Music Library**, 113 Music Building, 206-543-1168, www.lib.washington.edu/music
- **Odegaard Undergraduate Library**, 206-543-1947, www.lib.washington.edu/ougl
- **Physics-Astronomy Library**, C620 Physics/Astronomy Building, 206-543-2988, www.lib.washington.edu/physics
- **Suzzallo and Allen Libraries**, 206-543-0242, www.lib.washington.edu/Suzzallo

CULTURE FOR KIDS

In Seattle, there are so many cultural opportunities for kids they may grow up before they can see or do everything. Besides numerous musical and outdoor opportunities, there are museums, dance and theatre performances, and puppet shows all aimed at or comprised of children. Several print and online publications offer calendars of events for family and kids' events. In print, check the calendar listings in the Friday editions of *The Seattle Times*, www.seattletimes.com, and the *Seattle Post-Intelligencer*, www.seattle-pi.com. *Seattle* magazine publishes listings each month, and makes a sampling of them available on its web site at www.seattlemag.com. You may also want to pick up a copy of *The Lobster Kids' Guide to Exploring Seattle* by Shelley Arenas and Cheryl Murfin Bond. Online, visit the ParentCafe web site at www.parentcafe.org or Northwest Baby & Child at www.nwbaby.com for child-focused articles and listings of upcoming events. The Seattle Center, a popular family venue, hosts a variety of colorful festivals and cultural events throughout the year; www.seattlecenter.com.

The following child-oriented listing of events and places represents only a part of what the Emerald City has to offer. For more ideas on how to entertain the kids, including a cornucopia of family and holiday festivals, see **A Seattle Year**.

MUSIC

- **Columbia Choirs**, 425-486-1987, 866-486-1987, www.columbiachoirs.com; the Columbia Choirs program trains kindergarten through adult singers. The organization operates four choirs, including one each for boys, girls, youth, and women. Rehearsal facilities are located in downtown Kirkland and on the Sammamish Plateau.
- **Seattle Girls' Choir**, 433 Tog Road, Brinnon, WA 98320, www.seaweb.net/sgc; performances include an annual SGC concert series, collaborative events with the Seattle Opera and Seattle Symphony, and tours, festivals and competitions across the country. Students ages 6 to 18, from 35 communities around the Puget Sound, participate in seven different choirs, and receive instruction in vocal technique, music theory and composition.
- **Seattle Youth Symphony Orchestras (SYSO)**, 11065 5th Avenue NE, Suite A, 206-362-2300, www.syso.org; operates five full orchestras during the school year, three summer music festivals, and extensive outreach programs, including the Endangered Instruments Program. Each of the five orchestras performs three concerts during the academic year.

MUSEUMS

- **The Children's Museum**, Center House, Seattle Center, 206-441-1768, www.thechildrensmuseum.org; intended for children ages one to eight, this delightful interactive museum also presents special multi-cultural programs in the lower level of the Center House. Open Monday-Friday 10 a.m. to 5 p.m., Saturday and Sunday 10 a.m. to 6 p.m. Admission is $5.50.

- **Northwest Railway Museum**, 38625 SE King Street, Snoqualmie, 425-888-3030, www.trainmuseum.org; the Snoqualmie Depot, the center-piece of the Northwest Railway Museum, is on the National Register of Historic Places. The museum's collection includes steam locomotives, passenger and freight cars, and railway artifacts. Open Thursday-Monday, 10 a.m. to 5 p.m. No charge for admission

OUTDOOR

- **Point Defiance Zoo & Aquarium**, 5400 North Pearl Street, Tacoma, 253-591-5337, www.pdza.org; a favorite among residents south of Seattle, Point Defiance Zoo & Aquarium puts kids eye-to-eye with beluga whales, pachyderms, sharks and reptiles. Summer hours are 10 to 7 daily. The rest of the year, the zoo is open daily, 10 a.m. to 4 p.m. Admission is $5.50 for adults, $5 for seniors, $4.50 for kids 4 to 13, and free for kids under 3. Admission is higher for non-residents of Pierce County.
- **Seattle Aquarium**, Pier 59, 1483 Alaskan Way, 206-386-4300, www.seattleaquarium.org; the star attractions at the Seattle Aquarium are those adorable sea otters, but kids also love the jellyfish tank and the octopus exhibit. Open daily, 10 a.m. to 5 p.m. in the fall, winter, and spring; 9:30 a.m. to 7 p.m. in the summer. Admission is $9 for adults, $8 for seniors, $6.25 for kids 6 to 18, $4.25 for children three to five, and free for kids two and under.
- **Woodland Park Zoo**, 5500 Phinney Avenue North, 206-684-4800, www.zoo.org; in November 2000, the Woodland Park Zoo welcomed Hansa, a newborn Asian elephant. The toddler is now a zoo favorite, along with popular exhibits like the African Village and Butterflies & Blooms. Hours vary, depending on the season. Call for specifics. Admission is $8.50 for adults, $7.75 for seniors, $6.25 for kids 6 to 17, $4.25 for children 3 to 5, and free for kids 2 and under. Non-King County residents pay more.
- **Northwest Trek**, 11610 Trek Drive East, Eatonville, 360-832-6117, www.nwtrek.org; located in Eatonville, southeast of Seattle, the Northwest Trek wildlife park features up-close views of cougars, eagles, grizzly and black bears, and wolves, among others. Park hours vary depending on the time of year, so call or visit their web site before you visit. Admission is $8.75 for adults, $8.25 for seniors, $6 for kids 5 to 17, $4 for 3- and 4-year-olds, and free for kids 2 and under.

THEATER

- **Seattle Children's Theatre**, Charlotte Martin Theater, Seattle Center, 206-441-3322, www.sct.org, offers six productions each season, plus school matinees and two school touring productions. The season runs from September to June.
- **Youth Theatre Northwest**, 8805 SE 40th Street, Mercer Island, 206-232-4145, www.youththeatre.org, presents six productions, August through May.

I N SOME WAYS, SEATTLE IS ONE BIG COLLEGE TOWN. IT IS THE SITE OF the state's largest public university, the University of Washington, and home to many other well-known private and community colleges. You can become a doctor, a diver, a lawyer or a massage therapist without ever leaving the city limits. Educational programs abound outside the city limits as well.

The state's Direct Transfer Agreement makes it convenient for students to transfer from any Washington community college to one of the state's six four-year universities. The system works well for students who prefer to earn an Associate's degree before choosing a university, or who need to improve their grades a bit before applying to a four-year school.

In addition to traditional colleges, there are many special interest, vocational, and technical programs. Here is a partial list of schools located in the Seattle area.

SEATTLE

- **Antioch University**, 2326 6th Avenue, 206-441-5352, www.anti-ochsea.edu, is a five-campus system that emphasizes an inter-disci-plinary curriculum. In addition to undergraduate courses, the college offers graduate programs in environment and community, manage-ment, whole systems design, and organizational psychology.
- **Art Institute of Seattle**, 2323 Elliott Avenue, 206-448-0900, 800-275-2471, www.ais.edu; students here learn from artists and professionals in a hands-on environment. AIS offers either Associate of Applied Arts degrees or diploma certificates through the schools of design, fashion, culinary arts, and media arts.
- **Ashmead College**, 2111 North Northgate Way, 206-527-0807, www.ashmeadcollege.com, provides instruction in massage and fitness

training, as well as a new program for aromatherapy and spa treatments. Campuses are also located in Everett, Tacoma and Vancouver.

- **City University**, 2150 North 107th Street, 206-364-4228, www.cityu.edu, serves working adults who want to continue their education without interrupting their careers. CU offers more than 50 undergraduate and graduate programs, and has campuses in Everett, Renton, and Tacoma.
- **Cornish College of the Arts**, 710 East Roy Street, 206-726-5151, www.cornish.edu, offers Bachelor of Fine Arts and Bachelor of Music degrees in art, dance, design, music, theater, performance production, and humanities and sciences. Cornish College of the Arts is in the process of moving its campus into the Denny Triangle neighborhood.
- **North Seattle Community College**, 9600 College Way North, 206-527-3600, www.gonorth.org; located in a pleasant concrete building near Northgate Mall, NSCC is a versatile community college that offers day and evening classes for undergraduates and professionals. The school's continuing education program offers a variety of computer courses for all levels of users.
- **Seattle Central Community College**, 1701 Broadway, 206-587-3800, http://seattlecentral.org; a school of 10,000 students, SCCC is located in the Capitol Hill neighborhood, offering both undergraduate and professional education classes. In 2001, *TIME* magazine named SCCC as one of its four "Colleges of the Year" for its success in helping first-year students make the transition into college life.
- **Seattle Pacific University**, 3rd Avenue West and West Nickerson Street, 206-281-2000, www.spu.edu; located at the north end of Queen Anne, SPU is a private Christian university with a picturesque campus, offering degrees in liberal arts, fine arts, business and education, among others.
- **Seattle University**, 900 Broadway, 206-296-6000, www.seattleu.edu; an independent Jesuit university located on First Hill, SU offers courses in a wide variety of subjects, including graduate programs in law, nursing and software engineering, as well as undergraduate degrees in philosophy, theology, and the sciences.
- **South Seattle Community College**, 6000 16th Avenue SW, 206-764-5300, www.sccd.ctc.edu/south; located in West Seattle, SSCC offers both vocational and academic classes. The college's Duwamish Center provides apprentice-related training and first aid instruction. The Home and Family Life department is here as well.
- **University of Washington**, 17th Avenue NE and NE 45th Street, 206-543-2100, www.washington.edu; founded in 1861, the University of Washington is a public research university attended by about 35,000 students. Known internationally for its bio-medical research, the UW also

has outstanding masters programs in business and law, and is a respected undergraduate institution. The university hosts guest speakers, dance troupes, and musicians throughout the year. In the fall, the Husky Football team attracts alumni and sports fans from across the state.

EASTSIDE

- **Bellevue Community College**, 3000 Landerholm Circle SE, Bellevue, 425-564-1000, www.bcc.ctc.edu; one of western Washington's most popular two-year colleges, BCC offers A.A, A.S. and A.A.S. degrees in a variety of academic programs.
- **Lake Washington Technical College**, 11605 132nd Avenue NE, Kirkland, 425-739-8100, www.lwtc.ctc.edu, offers job-training and professional development programs, and serves as a community resource, featuring a job placement center, library, dental clinic, and arboretum.

NORTH

- **Cascadia Community College**, 18345 Campus Way NE, Bothell, 425-352-8000, www.cascadia.ctc.edu, is the state's newest community college, offering two-year degrees, certificate programs and continuing education.
- **Edmonds Community College**, 20000 68th Avenue West, Lynnwood, www.edcc.edu; ECC's 50-acre campus is located just 15 miles north of Seattle. The college allows students the opportunity to combine weekend, online and evening classes to fit busy schedules.
- **Everett Community College**, 2000 Tower Street, Everett, 425-388-9100, www.evcc.ctc.edu; in 1999, EvCC added a state-of-the-art instructional technology center to its campus, which also includes a fitness and sports center and an applied technology training center.
- **Shoreline Community College**, 16101 Greenwood Avenue North, Shoreline, 206-546-4101, http://oscar.ctc.edu/shoreline; boasts a gorgeous, 83-acre campus just 10 miles north of downtown Seattle. More than 12,000 full- and part-time students benefit from small classes and the surrounding recreational and cultural opportunities.
- **Western Washington University**, 516 High Street, Bellingham, 360-650-3000, www.wwu.edu; just 90 miles north of Seattle, WWU commands 200 acres in scenic Bellingham, a bayside city of 65,000. Specializing in the liberal arts, WWU consistently ranks high on *U.S. News & World Report's* list of regional public universities.

SOUTH

- **Evergreen State College**, 2700 Evergreen Parkway NW, Olympia, 360-866-6000, www.evergreen.edu; with a reputation as the state's most liberal and laid-back college, Evergreen State offers team-taught, multi-disciplinary programs that draw from many areas of study.
- **Green River Community College**, 12401 SE 320th Street, Auburn, 253-833-9111, www.greenriver.ctc.edu, offers AA degrees in a variety of disciplines, from accounting to wastewater technology.
- **Highline Community College**, 2400 South 240th Street, Des Moines, 206-878-3710, www.highline.ctc.edu; Highline's courses of study are divided into academic transfer, professional/technical, pre-college study, and extended learning.
- **Pacific Lutheran University**, Tacoma, 253-531-6900, www.plu.edu; located in Tacoma's suburban Parkland neighborhood, PLU includes a College of Arts and Sciences, professional schools of the arts, business, education, nursing and physical education, and both graduate and continuing education programs.
- **Tacoma Community College**, 6501 South 19th Street, 253-566-5000, www.tacoma.ctc.edu, offers a range of academic and occupational degrees, worker retraining programs, and continuing education classes.
- **University of Puget Sound**, 1500 North Warner Street, Tacoma, 253-879-3100, www.ups.edu; UPS is a private liberal arts college with less than 3,000 students, mostly undergraduates.

SEATTLE HAS MUCH TO OFFER IN THE WAY OF SPORTS AND REC-reation. For weekend warriors who enjoy playing games as much as they like watching them, there are plenty of indoor and outdoor activities available, from a recreational pick-up game at one of Seattle's many parks to participation in an organized league. For avid spectators, there is professional and college action galore.

Health clubs and sporting goods stores are listed at the end of this chapter.

These **sports publications** offer in-depth coverage of local sporting events and activities:

- *48 Degrees North*, 6327 Seaview Avenue NW, 206-789-7350, www.48north.com
- *Elevation Magazine*, 3131 Western Avenue, Suite 511, 206-272-9744, www.elevationmagazine.com
- *Fishing & Hunting News*, P.O. Box 19000, Seattle, WA 98109, 206-624-3845, www.fishingandhuntingnews.com
- *Northwest Runner*, 4831 NE 44th Street, 206-527-5301, www.nwrunner.com
- *Northwest Yachting Magazine*, 7342 15th Avenue NW, 206-789-8116, www.nwyachting.com
- *Sports Etc.*, 11715 Greenwood Avenue North, 206-418-0747, www.sportsetc.com

TICKETS

If you follow sports at all, you already know that Seattle has professional basketball, baseball, and football teams. What you may not realize until you live here is that fans in the Pacific Northwest tend to be of the fair-weather variety, both figuratively and literally. While that can be upsetting to the players, it is often good news for die-hard fans, because during mediocre seasons, tickets generally can be purchased without much advance notice.

In boom years, however, like the record-setting 2000-2001 Seattle Mariners' season, tickets are hard to come by.

Tickets for all Seattle professional sporting events can be purchased by phone or online at **Ticketmaster**, 206-628-0888, www.ticketmaster.com, or in person at Ticketmaster outlets at most Rite Aid stores. Or, you can visit the venue's box office. The Seattle Sonics and Storm play at Key Arena, and the Seattle Mariners play at Safeco Field. The Seattle Seahawks' play at the newly built Seahawks Stadium. See below under **Professional Sports** for web addresses and contact information for each team.

In recent years, high-profile sporting events like the American League Championship Series, the Major League Baseball All-Star Game, and the early rounds of the NCAA men's basketball tournament resulted in a bonanza for ticket brokers. These services can charge top dollar for tickets by operating outside the city, thereby skirting Seattle's anti-scalping ordinance. If you have your heart set on a sold-out event, brokers can usually provide a ticket, but expect to pay dearly for the opportunity. Look in the Yellow Pages under "Ticket Sales—Entertainment & Sports" for brokers.

PROFESSIONAL AND COLLEGE SPORTS

PROFESSIONAL SPORTS

BASEBALL

Seattle is home to the Seattle Mariners, which after many years of being a sub-500 team, now make their yearly mark in the play-offs, to the delight of area baseball fans. Also in the Seattle area, two minor league teams, the Tacoma Rainiers and the Everett AquaSox.

- The American League's **Seattle Mariners** play approximately 80 home games. They used to play in the covered Kingdome, but now they have one of the most highly touted ballparks in baseball, Safeco Field. Opened in the summer of 1999, the new facility offers improved amenities, including seating designed specifically for easy viewing of baseball, and a retractable roof for those notorious Seattle rain showers. Because of the Mariners' recent success, tickets are harder to come by than they were several years ago. You can order tickets by calling 206-622-HITS. For a Mariners schedule and more information, or to order tickets or merchandise online, go to http://mariners.mlb.com.
- The **Tacoma Rainiers** are a Triple-A club in the Pacific Coast league. A farm team for the Mariners, the Rainiers play during the spring and summer in Cheney Stadium. There are usually several fun theme nights throughout the season with extra entertainment and prizes. For a schedule or tickets call 253-752-7700, or visit www.tacomarainiers.com.

- The **Everett AquaSox** host their home games at Everett Memorial Stadium in downtown Everett. The AquaSox are a Single-A farm team for the Seattle Mariners, and offer many exciting games during the summer. Contact their office at 425-258-3673, or visit www.aquasox.com.

BASKETBALL

- The National Basketball Association's **Seattle SuperSonics** play their home games at the Key Arena, located at the Seattle Center. At one time, the Sonics were perennial NBA championship contenders, reaching the NBA finals in 1996. While they were NBA champions in 1979, the only professional team in Seattle to achieve such national recognition, in recent years the Sonics have not performed well. New owner and Starbucks CEO Howard Schultz hopes to turn things around, and games remain a popular attraction. For tickets, call 206-283-DUNK, or visit www.nba.com/sonics.
- The **Seattle Storm** joined the Women's National Basketball Association for the 2000 season. Like most expansion teams, the Storm struggled in their first season, but improved in their second. The team is expected to make further strides under the new ownership of Howard Schultz. The Storm share Key Arena with the Sonics and Seattle Thunderbirds hockey team. For tickets and information, call 206-217-WNBA or visit www.wnba.com/storm.

FOOTBALL

In 2002, the National Football League's **Seattle Seahawks** moved into their new, state-of-the-art Seahawks Stadium—and into a new division, the NFC West. The 67,000-seat stadium, located in Seattle at 800 South Occidental Avenue, was funded partly by public dollars, and partly by billionaire Paul Allen, who bought the team in 1998. Once considered the most difficult tickets to come by in Seattle, the struggling Seahawks made the playoffs only once in the 1990s, in the 1999-2000 season. For more about the Seahawks, go to www.seahawks.com. For tickets, call 888-NFL-HAWK.

HOCKEY

Key Arena is also home to the **Seattle Thunderbirds**, a Western Hockey League team. The Thunderbirds always draw a large and enthusiastic crowd for competitive games and the occasional brawl. Tickets and information are at 206-448-PUCK or www.seattle-thunderbirds.com.

HORSE RACING

Northwest thoroughbred racing enthusiasts trek to Auburn to catch the action at **Emerald Downs**. For more information call 253-288-7000 or visit www.emdowns.com.

SOCCER

The **Seattle Sounders** are Seattle's professional soccer team. Part of the USISL A-League, they play their home games at the Memorial Stadium in the Seattle Center. Though soccer is usually less popular than other major league sports in most US cities, the Sounders have a loyal following of boisterous fans. Call 800-796 KICK for tickets, or visit www.seattlesounders.net.

COLLEGE SPORTS

Many sports fans prefer college games to professional contests. For reasons of convenience, cost, or alum loyalty, it's true that the frenzied fans and the youthful energy found at college events make for an exciting experience. The area's largest draw for college sports is the University of Washington, which offers many first class sporting events. The ticket office is at 101 Graves Building on the UW campus. For more information about UW athletics see below or visit http://gohuskies.fansonly.com. To find out more about the sports programs of other nearby colleges or universities, call their information desk. (See **Higher Education** for a list of area schools.)

UW BASEBALL

The Huskies have a men's baseball team and a women's softball team. Both play at Husky Ballpark. Call 206-543-2200 or go to http://gohuskies.fansonly.com for more information.

UW BASKETBALL

The Husky Women's Basketball team is a frequent contender in the NCAA championship tournament, and the Husky Men's team made the NCAA championship tournament in 1998. Both play their home games at Bank of America Arena on the UW campus. Check http://gohuskies.fansonly.com on the web or call 206-543-2200 for tickets and information.

UW FOOTBALL

The University of Washington's Husky Football team has a long list of national championships. Games are played at Husky Stadium, which is one of the best college football venues in the nation. Not only does the stadium offer great seating for the game, it provides fans a panoramic view of Lake Washington and snow-capped Mount Rainier. Football games are popular with students, and many alumni are season ticket holders, so it's often difficult to get tickets. Call 206-543-2200 or go to http://gohuskies.fansonly.com for more information.

PARTICIPANT SPORTS AND ACTIVITIES

Ask residents what they love most about the Puget Sound area, and a common response will be the great selection of outdoor recreation opportunities. From watching the sunset over the Olympics in a nearby neighborhood park, to climbing to the summit of Mount Rainier, there are hundreds of activities for every level of athlete throughout the four seasons. Summer brings water skiers to Lake Washington; fall offers breathtaking autumn foliage and pleasant muddy hikes; winter provides snow covered mountains perfect for skiing, snowmobiling, and snow-shoeing; and in the spring cool mornings are nice for long bike rides, kayaking or rowing.

If you're looking for general information on local parks, kiddie pools, tennis courts or community programs start with the **Seattle Parks and Recreation Department**, 206-684-4075, www.cityofseattle.net/parks, or your local community center (listed after the neighborhood profiles). In addition to playgrounds, ball fields, swimming pools, and basketball and tennis courts, neighborhood community centers offer fitness classes, dance lessons, pottery and art classes, and other activities. **King County Parks** can be reached at 206-296-4232 or www.metrokc.gov/parks.

PARKS AND RECREATION DEPARTMENTS

- **Bainbridge Island**, 7666 NE High School Road, 206-842-2306, www.biparks.org
- **Bellevue**, 11511 Main Street, 425-452-6881, www.ci.bellevue.wa.us
- **Bothell**, 18305 101st Avenue NE, 425-486-7430, www.ci.bothell.wa.us
- **Burien**, 425 SW 144th Street, 206-988-3700, www.ci.burien.wa.us
- **Des Moines**, 21630 11th Avenue South, 206-878-4595, www.ci.des-moines.wa.us
- **Edmonds**, 700 Main Street, 425-771-0230, www.ci.edmonds.wa.us
- **Everett**, 805 Mukilteo Boulevard, 425-257-8300, www.ci.everett.wa.us

- **Federal Way**, 33901 9th Avenue South, 253-661-4050, www.ci.federal-way.wa.us
- **Issaquah**, 301 Rainier Boulevard South, 425-837-3300, www.ci.issaquah.wa.us
- **Kenmore**, 6700 NE 181st Street, 425-398-8900, www.cityofken-more.com
- **Kent**, 220 4th Avenue South, 253-856-5100, www.ci.kent.wa.us
- **Kirkland**, 123 5th Avenue, 425-828-1100, www.ci.kirkland.wa.us
- **Lake Forest Park**, 20150 45th Avenue NE, 206-368-5440, www.cityoflfp.com
- **Lynnwood**, 19000 44th Avenue West, 425-744-6475, www.ci.lynnwood.wa.us
- **Mercer Island**, 9611 SE 36th Street, 206-236-3545, www.ci.mercer-island.wa.us
- **Mountlake Terrace**, 23204 58th Avenue West, 425-776-9173, www.ci.mountlake-terrace.wa.us
- **Newcastle**, 13020 SE 72nd Place, 425-649-4444, www.ci.newcastle.wa.us
- **Redmond**, 15965 NE 85th Street, 425-556-2311, www.ci.redmond.wa.us
- **Renton**, 1715 Maple Valley Highway, 425-430-6700, www.ci.renton.wa.us
- **SeaTac**, 17900 International Boulevard, Suite 401, 206-241-9100, www.seatac.wa.gov
- **Seattle**, 100 Dexter Avenue North, 206-684-4075, www.cityofseattle.net/parks
- **Shoreline**, 17544 Midvale Avenue North, 206-546-5041, www.cityofshoreline.com
- **Tacoma**, 4702 South 19th Street, 253-305-1000, www.cityoftacoma.org
- **Tukwila**, 12424 42nd Avenue South, 206-767-2342, www.ci.tukwila.wa.us
- **Woodinville**, 17301 133rd Avenue NE, 425-489-2700, www.ci.woodinville.wa.us

BASEBALL/SOFTBALL

Every spring, as the cherry trees blossom, Seattle residents flock to local fields to play baseball or softball. Call one of the area parks and recreation departments listed above to reserve a field for a casual game between friends, or put together your own team and participate in a league. Most leagues are organized privately or through local community centers (listed after the neighborhood profiles). The following resources may also be helpful:

ADULT LEAGUES

- **Bellevue Baseball/Softball Athletic Association**, 425-746-4592
- **Puget Sound Senior Baseball League**, 425-401-9999, www.pssbl.com
- **Seattle Sport and Social Club**, 206-328-7772
- **United States Amateur Baseball Association**, 425-776-7130, www. usaba.com

YOUTH LEAGUES

- **Eastlake Little League**, Redmond, 425-868-1004
- **Highline E Little League**, SeaTac, 206-243-9229
- **Issaquah Little League**, Issaquah, 425-391-9747
- **Kenmore Little League**, Bothell, 425-485-6421
- **Kent Little League**, Kent, 253-872-3848
- **Maple Valley Youth Baseball**, Renton, 425-226-9408
- **North Kenmore Little League**, Bothell, 425-481-1618
- **Northshore Little League**, Bothell, 425-486-7333
- **Roosevelt-University-Greenlake Little League**, Seattle, 206-524-0784
- **Tahoma Little League**, Maple Valley, 425-433-1333
- **Woodinville West Little League**, 425-481-2846

If you're simply in the mood for an impromptu game with friends or for some casual batting practice, ball fields are available. To reserve a field, call the **Seattle Parks and Recreation Individual Field Reservation Line** at 206-684-4077. For parks in surrounding communities, contact the city parks and recreation departments listed previously in this chapter.

BASKETBALL

Considering Seattle's unpredictable weather, you might think that basketball would be near the bottom of the list as a favorite sport. That's definitely not the case. Lively pick-up games are common in Seattle's playgrounds and community centers, and there are many organized leagues at gyms and athletic clubs. If you're interested in league play or workshops, consider the health clubs listed later in this chapter, or call one of the area's parks and recreation departments (see above). For a casual but competitive pick-up game in Seattle call your local community center (see **Community Resources** following **Neighborhoods**) or call the Seattle Parks and Recreation Department at 206-684-4075.

BICYCLING

In Seattle, cycling is popular as both a sport and a means of transportation. Despite the unpredictable weather and hilly topography, many residents bike to work and school, and to do errands. Bicycle lanes have become more common on major thoroughfares throughout the city and its surrounding communities. (For more information on commuting by bike, see the **Transportation** chapter.)

Green Lake is a popular destination for recreational cyclists, as are many locations along the **Burke-Gilman Trail**. For a fun and scenic ride, bike the Burke-Gilman Trail from Gasworks Park on Lake Union to Matthews Beach on Lake Washington. This trail is also used as a shortcut for many UW students riding to school each morning.

Cascade Bicycle Club (CBC), the largest cycling club in the United States, is based in Seattle. With over 5,000 members, CBC sponsors several rides each day, for riders of all skill levels, as well as several annual events. Contact CBC at 206-522-BIKE, or check out their comprehensive web site at www.cascade.org. Those interested in track racing should contact the **Marymoor Velodrome Association** at 206-675-1424, or go to http://marymoor.velodrome.org. Racing events are held regularly at Marymoor Park in Redmond.

The following are a few of the most popular annual street rides in the Seattle area:

- The **Cannonball**, held in late June and organized by the **Redmond Cycling Club**, is a one-day trek from Seattle to Spokane along I-90. Call 425-739-8610 or visit www.redmondcyclingclub.org.
- **Chilly Hilly**, held in late February and sponsored by CBC, is a 28-mile bicycle tour around Bainbridge Island. It marks the official opening of bicycle season in the Pacific Northwest.
- The **Daffodil Classic**, an annual ride sponsored by the **Tacoma Wheelmen's Bicycle Club**, is held in mid-April. There are several routes, ranging from 20 to 100 miles. Call 253-759-2800 or visit www.twbc.org.
- The **Kitsap Color Classic**, a ride through Kitsap County on the Olympic Peninsula, is held in early October when the leaves begin to turn. CBC sponsors this ride.
- The **RAMROD (Ride Around Mount Rainier in One Day)** is sponsored by the Redmond Cycling Club and takes place in late July. It is a 150+ mile race around Mount Rainier, and is perhaps the most challenging in the area, with 10,000 feet of climbing during the race.
- **STP (Seattle-to-Portland)** is a two-day non-competitive bike ride from Seattle to Portland, sponsored by the CBC. Riders can choose to participate for one or two days; those riding for two days stay overnight midway. The STP takes place in mid-July and is the best-known bicycling event in the area.

Just as popular as traditional bicycling, mountain biking is a favorite recreational activity for many Seattle residents. Seattle's hills provide great practice routes, and there are several scenic and challenging mountain-bike trails just a short drive out of the city. An excellent resource for local mountain-biking information is the **Backcountry Bicycle Trails Club** at 206-283-2995 or www.bbtc.org. If you're new to the sport, the club offers a "boot camp" for first-time trail riders. For information on nearby trails, check out a copy of the *King Bicycling Guidemap,* available at King County Public Libraries, can be ordered by phone or online: 206-263-4700, www.metrokc.gov/kcdot/tp.

BIRD WATCHING

Though bird watching may not rank high on Seattle's list of popular pursuits, the region does include its fair share of birders. In Seattle, the **National Audubon Society** recommends Discovery and Green Lake parks, the Montlake Wetlands, Washington Park Arboretum, and in West Seattle, Alki Beach and Lincoln Park. To find bird watching spots in surrounding communities, visit http://wa.audubon.org.

- **East Lake Washington Audubon Society**, P.O. Box 3632, Bellevue, 425-451-3717, www.elwas.org
- **National Audubon of Washington**, 1063 Capitol Way South, Olympia, 360-786-8020, http://wa.audubon.org
- **Pilchuck Audubon Society**, 1803 Hewitt Avenue, #108, Everett, 425-252-0926, www.pilchuckaudubon.org
- **Seattle Audubon Society**, 8050 35th Avenue NE, 206-523-4483, www.seattleaudubon.org
- **Washington Ornithological Society**, P.O. Box 3178, Seattle, WA 98103, www.wos.org

BOATING

It's no surprise that Seattle residents love their watercraft. Even on cloudy days, you'll see several boats out on the lakes or in Puget Sound. Colorful spinnakers dot the Sound each weekend, as sailing races are held near Shilshole Bay. On sunny days, floatplanes arriving at Lake Union dodge the many sailboats that crowd the lake, and the early-morning calm of Lake Washington entices crowds of skiers.

ROWING, CANOEING, AND KAYAKING

- **Green Lake Small Craft Center**, 5900 West Green Lake Way North, 206-684-4074

- **Lake Washington Rowing Club**, 910 North Northlake Way, 206-547-1583, http://lakewashingtonrowing.com
- **Moss Bay Rowing & Kayaking Center**, 1001 Fairview Avenue North, 206-682-2031, www.mossbay.net
- **Mount Baker Rowing and Sailing Center**, 3800 Lake Washington Boulevard South, 206-386-1913, www.ci.seattle.wa.us/parks/boats
- **Northwest Legends Rowing**, P.O. Box 3301, Everett, WA 98203, 425-337-6614
- **Northwest Outdoor Center**, 2100 Westlake Avenue North, 206-281-9694
- **Pacific Water Sports**, 16055 Pacific Highway South, 206-246-9385
- **Sammamish Rowing Association**, 5022 West Lake Sammamish Parkway NE, Redmond, 425-653-2583, www.srarowing.com
- **Seattle Canoe and Kayak Club**, 5900 West Green Lake Way North, 206-684-4074
- **Washington Kayak Club**, P.O. Box 24264, Seattle, WA 98124, 206-433-1983, www.wakayakclub.com

SAILING AND SPEED BOATING

- **Elliott Bay Yachting Center**, 2601 West Marina Place, 206-285-9499, 800-422-2019, www.ebyc.com
- **Mount Baker Rowing and Sailing Center**, 3800 Lake Washington Boulevard South, 206-386-1913, www.ci.seattle.wa.us/parks/boats
- **Renton Sailing Club**, 425-235-0952, www.halcyon.com/rscsail
- **Seattle Sailing Club**, 7001 Seaview Avenue NW, 206-782-5100, www.seattlesailing.com
- **Wind Works Sailing Center**, 7001 Seaview Avenue NW, 206-784-9386

YACHT CLUBS

- **Corinthian Yacht Club of Seattle**, 7755 Seaview Avenue NW, 206-789-1919, http://cycseattle.org
- **Edmonds Yacht Club**, 456 Admiral Way, Edmonds, 425-778-5499, www.edmondsyachtclub.com
- **Meydenbauer Bay Yacht Club**, P.O. Box 863, Bellevue, WA 98009, 425-454-8880, www.mbycwa.org
- **Queen City Yacht Club**, 2608 Boyer Avenue East, 206-709-2000, www.queencity.org
- **Rainier Yacht Club**, 9094 Seward Avenue South, 206-722-9576
- **Seattle Yacht Club**, 1807 East Hamlin Street, 206-325-1000, www.seattleyachtclub.org

- **Tyee Yacht Club**, 3229 Fairview Avenue East, 206-324-0200, www.tyeeyachtclub.org
- **Washington Yacht Club**, University of Washington, 206-543-2219

OTHER BOATING RESOURCES

- **Boating Safety Classes**, 800-336-BOAT
- **Seattle Police Harbor Patrol Unit**, 206-684-4071
- **Seattle Boat Ramp Supervisor**, 206-684-7249
- **US Coast Guard 24-hour Emergency**, 800-982-8813

BOWLING

Bowling is most popular during Seattle's wet, gray winter months. The following bowling alleys organize leagues regularly, but also welcome amateur and first-time bowlers.

- **Imperial Lanes**, 2101 22nd Avenue South, 206-325-2525
- **Hi-Line Lanes**, 15733 Ambaum Boulevard SW, Burien, 206-244-2272
- **Leilani Lanes**, 10201 Greenwood Avenue North, 206-783-8010
- **Magic Lanes**, 10612 15th Avenue SW, 206-244-5060
- **Roxbury Lanes**, 2823 SW Roxbury Street, 206-935-7400
- **Sunset Bowl**, 1420 NW Market Street, 206-782-7310
- **West Seattle Bowl**, 4505 39th Avenue SW, 206-932-3731

CHESS

- **America's Foundation for Chess**, 720 North 35th Street, 206-675-0490, www.af4c.org
- **Seattle Chess Club**, 17517 15th Avenue NE, 206-417-5405, www.seattlechessclub.org

DANCE

- **Arthur Murray Dance Studios**, 530 Dexter Avenue North, 206-447-2701, www.washingtondancesport.com
- **Century Ballroom**, 915 East Pine Street, 206-324-7263, www.centuryballroom.com
- **DanceSport International**, 12535 Lake City Way NE, 206-361-8239, www.dancesportseattle.com
- **Fifth Avenue Dance Studios**, 2211 3rd Avenue, 206-621-9824
- **Sharon Ardelle's Dance Factory**, 327 NE 91st, 206-522-0575
- **Washington Dance Club**, 1017 Stewart Street, 206-628-8939

FISHING AND SHELLFISH GATHERING

The fishing and shellfishing opportunities in Washington are nothing short of amazing. Although the area is famous for salmon and Dungeness crab, you'll also find clams, mussels, oysters, trout, and steelhead. If you're gathering shellfish with a local, you may even get a glimpse of a geoduck. Geoduck, pronounced "gooey-duck," are huge razor clams indigenous to Washington's ocean beaches. Like clams, you'll need to dig for geoduck, although they're a lot tougher to catch (they're fast!) and you probably won't want to eat one anyway.

Several types of salmon and trout migrate through the waters of western Washington. Chinook are the largest of the Pacific salmon and spawn in the Columbia and Snake rivers, as well as other small rivers and streams. Coho or silver salmon are a popular sport fish in the Puget Sound, and can also be found in coastal tributaries. Sockeye salmon are a flavorful salmon, found in Lake Washington, Baker Lake, Quinault Lake, Ozette Lake, and Lake Wenatchee. Pink salmon, or humpback salmon, spawn only every other year, so they appear in Washington waters during odd-numbered years only. Chum salmon can be found in small coastal streams, but are not particularly tasty and so are not popular as a sport fish. Steelhead and cutthroat trout, named for the red markings just below the head of the fish, live in freshwater streams and Puget Sound bays. Although cutthroats are common throughout North America, those in Washington are the only ones that spend the warm summer months in saltwater.

Lakes and rivers in Washington yield an unusual catch of fish, including many non-native species. When settlers arrived here in the mid-1800s, they caught trout, char, whitefish and a few other small fish in the freshwater lakes and streams. As more people moved to the area and the trout population began to dwindle, additional species of fish were imported. While trout (including cutthroat, steelhead, brook and brown trout) are still the most popular fish in Washington's many rivers, the state's lakes and rivers are now stocked with a variety of fish, from sunfish and catfish, to perch and pike.

Favorite locations for trout fishing near the Puget Sound are the Skagit, Snoqualmie, Skykomish and Green rivers. Other plentiful rivers in the state include the Columbia, Cowlitz, Kalama and Hoh. Bottomfish such as halibut, cod, and rockfish are common in Neah Bay, the Hood Canal, and around the San Juan Islands. Lake Washington and the Puget Sound have limited numbers of sturgeon, which are more numerous in the Columbia and Snake Rivers. If you're looking for largemouth bass, try Moses Lake, Silver Lake, Long Lake, Sprague Lake or the Columbia River. Smallmouth bass are commonly found in the Columbia, Snake, and Yakima rivers, and in Lake Washington, Lake Sammamish, and Lake Stevens. You may catch yellow perch in Lake Washington, Lake Sammamish or Lake Stevens. You're more likely to find walleye in eastern Washington lakes such as Moses Lake, Lake Roosevelt or Soda Lake. If you're a fan of catfish, you'll find brown bullheads in Lake Washington, Moses Lake or Liberty Lake, and channel catfish in Fazon Lake and Sprague Lake. Tiger muskies (pike) are commonly found in Mayfield Lake in Lewis County, while northern pikes swim in Long Lake near Spokane.

The **Washington Department of Fish and Wildlife (WDFW)** regulates fishing and shellfish gathering throughout the state, acting as both conservation and licensing entity. The agency provides many helpful publications on a variety of fish and wildlife subjects, which can be ordered by phone or downloaded from the department's web site (see below). Recreational fishing licenses are required for all state residents over 15, and for all non-residents, regardless of age. Licenses are divided into three categories: freshwater, saltwater, and shellfish/seaweed. Licenses are valid for one year, and must be displayed at all times while fishing or gathering shellfish. Two-day licenses are also available at reduced prices. License fees and restrictions vary according to the fish or shellfish collected; fees range from $6.57 to $39.42 for residents. Licenses may be purchased from most sporting goods stores, or online at http://fishhunt.dfw.wa.gov.

- **Washington State Department of Fish and Wildlife**, 1111 Washington Street SE, Olympia, 360-902-2200, www.wa.gov/wdfw

FRISBEE

While many Seattle parks have adequate open spaces for a game of frisbee, a few parks are especially popular with enthusiasts. Gasworks Park, at the north end of Lake Union, combines a wide expanse of green lawn with pleasant breezes off the lake. Discovery Park in Magnolia has a good-sized grassy meadow in which to play, and Woodland Park near Green Lake offers a quiet shady expanse.

If ultimate frisbee is your game of choice, you may want to try one of several regular pick-up games in the area. Common locations are Volunteer Park on Sunday mornings, Lincoln Park in West Seattle on Wednesday evenings, and Marymoor Park in Redmond on Monday evenings. League play is organized privately or through the **Northwest Ultimate Association**, P.O. Box 85112, Seattle, WA 98145, 206-781-5840, www.discnw.org.

GOLF

Three public golf courses, run by the City of Seattle Parks and Recreation Department, are listed below, along with public courses in surrounding communities. In addition, the parks department offers a short course near Green Lake, the **Green Lake Pitch and Putt** (walk-ons only), and near Queen Anne, the **Interbay Family Golf Center**, with miniature golf course and driving range (reservations taken up to seven days in advance). While there are many other golf courses in the greater Seattle area, most are private or semi-private courses. Check the local Yellow Pages for more information.

- **Classic Country Club**, 4908 208th Street East, Spanaway, 253-847-4440
- **Green Lake Pitch and Putt**, 5701 West Green Lake Way North, 206-632-2280, www.cityofseattle.net
- **Harbour Pointe Golf Club**, 11817 Harbour Pointe Boulevard, Mukilteo, 206-355-6060, www.harbourpt.com
- **Interbay Family Golf Center**, 2501 15th Avenue West, 206-285-2200
- **Jackson Park Golf Club**, 1000 NE 135th Street, 206-363-4747, www.jacksonparkgolf.com
- **Jefferson Park Golf Club**, 4101 Beacon Avenue South, 206-762-4513, www.jeffersonparkgolf.com
- **Kayak Point Golf Course**, 15711 Marine Drive, Stanwood, 360-652-9676, www.kayakgolf.com
- **Meadow Park Golf Course**, 7108 Lakewood Drive, Tacoma, 253-473-3033, www.tacomaparks.com
- **Port Ludlow Golf Course**, 751 Highland Drive, Port Ludlow, 800-455-0272
- **West Seattle Golf Club**, 4470 35th Avenue SW, 206-935-5187, www.westseattlegolf.com

HIKING

If you like to hike, you'll love living in Seattle. Not only are there several short hikes in local parks, such as Discovery Park and Seward Park, but just outside of the city there are hundreds of trails for hikers of all fitness levels. Mountaineers Books publishes a series of useful books that describe nearly every trail in Washington. The following resources may be helpful when choosing a trail.

- **Mountaineers Books**, 1011 SW Klickitat Way, 800-553-4453, www.mountaineersbooks.org
- **National Park Service**, 909 1st Avenue, 206-220-4000, www.nps.gov
- **The Mountaineers Club**, 300 3rd Avenue West, 206-284-6310, www.mountaineers.org
- **WashingtonHikes.com**, www.washingtonhikes.com
- **Washington Trails Association**, 1305 4th Avenue, Suite 512, 206-625-1367, www.wta.org

HORSEBACK RIDING

Horseback rides and lessons are available in many of Seattle's surrounding rural communities. Check with the following, or look in the Yellow Pages under "Horse Rentals & Riding" for more listings.

- **Cedar Ridge Equestrian Center**, 22131 31st Avenue SE, Bothell, 425-398-8416
- **Elk Run Stable**, 45004 SE 161st Place, North Bend, 425-888-4341
- **Gold Creek Equestrian Center**, 16528 148th Avenue NE, Woodinville, 425-806-4653, www.gold-creek.com
- **Phoenix Farm**, 16630 Sunset Road, Bothell, 425-486-9395, www.phoenixfarm.com
- **Tiger Mountain Outfitters**, 24508 SE 133rd, Issaquah, 425-392-5090

ICE SKATING

Most bodies of water in Seattle never freeze, but there are plenty of ice skating opportunities available, albeit the indoor kind. Most rinks offer skate rentals, lessons, and open ice sessions. During the holiday season, an ice rink at **Seattle Center** is open to the public. Call 206-684-7200 for details. Year-round rinks include:

- **Castle Ice Arena**, 12620 164th SE, Renton, 425-254-8750, www.castleice.com
- **Highland Ice Area**, 18005 Aurora Avenue North, Shoreline, 206-546-2431, www.highlandice.com
- **Lynnwood's Sno-King Ice Arena**, 19803 68th Avenue West, Lynnwood, 425-775-7511
- **Olympic View Arena**, 22202 70th Avenue West, Mountlake Terrace, 425-672-9012, www.olyview.com

IN-LINE/ROLLER SKATING

In-line skating is a popular activity on Seattle's paved paths, particularly at Green Lake, Alki Beach, and on the Burke-Gilman Trail. Some skaters even turn vacant parking lots into impromptu rinks for trick skating or pick-up hockey games. Several sporting goods stores offer in-line skating rentals. **Gregg's Greenlake Cycle**, 7007 Woodlawn Avenue NE, 206-523-1822, www.greggscycles.com, and **Urban Surf**, 2100 North Northlake Way, 206-545-9463, www.urbansurf.com, offer easy access to a paved path.

For in-line skating lessons, try **Arena Sports**, Seattle: 4636 East Marginal Way, Building 3, 206-762-8606, 7400 Sand Point Way NE, 206-985-8990; Redmond: 9040 Willows Road, 425-885-4881; Tacoma: 2610 Bay Street East, 253-627-2255, www.arenasports.net.

RACQUET SPORTS

TENNIS

Outdoor public tennis courts dot the city and are generally open on a first-come, first-served basis, although reservations may be requested through the Seattle Parks and Recreation Department. The Seattle Tennis Center in the Mount Baker neighborhood, also run by the Seattle Parks and Recreation Department, offers lessons and indoor and outdoor courts. For tennis courts in surrounding communities, contact one of the parks and recreation departments listed previously in this chapter.

- **Seattle Parks and Recreation Department**, Outdoor Court Information/Reservations, 206-684-4077, www.cityofseattle.net
- **Seattle Tennis Center**, 2000 Martin Luther King Jr. Way South, 206-684-4764, www.cityofseattle.net

RACQUETBALL

A few racquetball courts in the greater Seattle area are open to the public:

- **Kent Commons**, 525 4th Avenue North, Kent, 253-856-5000, www.ci.kent.wa.us
- **Lynnwood Recreation Center**, 18900 44th Avenue West, Lynnwood, 425-771-4030
- **Mountlake Terrace Recreation Pavilion**, 5303 228th Street SW, Mountlake Terrace, 425-776-9173
- **White Center Park**, 1321 SW 102nd Street, Seattle, 206-296-4232, www.metrokc.gov

CLUBS

Private racquet clubs and health clubs offer lessons and court rentals for a variety of games, including tennis, racquetball, and squash. Call for details, as activities and services vary.

- **Central Park Tennis Club**, 12630 NE 59th, Kirkland, 425-822-2206, www.centralparktennisclub.com
- **Edge Brook Club**, 13454 SE Newport Way, Bellevue, 425-746-2786
- **Forest Crest Tennis Club**, 4901 238th Street SW, Mountlake Terrace, 425-774-0014
- **Gold Creek Tennis & Sports Club**, 15327 140th Place NE, Woodinville, 425-487-1090
- **Mercer Island Country Club**, 8700 SE 71st Street, Mercer Island, 206-232-5600

- **Olympic Athletic Club**, 5301 Leary Way NW, 206-789-5010, www.oac24hour.com
- **Seattle Tennis Club**, 922 McGilvra Boulevard East, 206-324-3200, www.seattletennisclub.org
- **Silver Lake Tennis & Fitness Club**, 505 128th Street SE, Everett, 425-745-1617, www.columbiaathletic.com

ROCK CLIMBING

Rock climbing is a popular sport in Washington, with several local climbing clubs and walls, as well as many nearby outdoor destinations. Closest perhaps is **Little Si**, near North Bend along I-90. **Leavenworth**, a Bavarian-style village on Highway 2, attracts a variety of climbers. If you're new to the sport, visit the Leavenworth area and start with the boulders near Icicle Creek; many of them have bars embedded in the rock for easy top-roping. More difficult climbs near Leavenworth can be found at Castle Rock and the Peshastin Pinnacles. **Near Stevens Pass**, the Index Town Wall provides challenging routes for climbers of all levels. Close to the town of **Vantage**, basalt columns near the Columbia River offer good climbing for experienced climbers only. Nearby, an area known as The Feathers is appropriate for beginners. In the **Olympics**, Flapjack Lakes Trail leads to challenging rock-climbing.

If you've never tried rock-climbing before, or if you're an experienced climber who wants to stay in practice without leaving the city, the following climbing walls and clubs offer a variety of rock-climbing experiences. Most of the clubs offer rock-climbing lessons, as do those organizations listed under "Lessons and Guide Resources" below.

CLIMBING WALLS

- **REI Pinnacle** (indoor), 222 Yale Avenue North, 206-223-1944, www.rei.com
- **University of Washington Climbing Rock** (outdoor), south of Husky Stadium on Montlake Avenue NE, 206-543-9433
- **Glacier** (outdoor), Camp Long, 5200 35th Avenue SW, 206-684-7434, www.ci.seattle.wa.us
- **Marymoor Climbing Structure** (outdoor), east end of Marymoor Park, Redmond, 206-296-2964

ROCK-CLIMBING CLUBS

- **Stone Gardens**, 2839 NW Market Street, 206-781-9828, www.stonegardens.com

- **Vertical World**, 2123 West Elmore Street, Seattle, 206-283-4497; 15036-B NE 95th Street, Redmond, 425-881-8826, www.verticalworld.com

LESSONS AND GUIDE RESOURCES

- **Cascade Alpine Guides & Adventures**, 24800 NE 8th Street, Sammamish, 425-602-0656, 800-981-0381, www.cascadealpine.com
- **Mountain Madness**, 4218 SW Alaska, Suite 206, 206-937-8389, www.mountainmadness.com
- **The Mountaineers**, 300 3rd Avenue West, 206-284-6310, www.mountaineers.org
- **REI**, 222 Yale Avenue North, 206-223-1944; 7500 166th Avenue NE, Redmond, 425-882-1158; 4200 194th Street SW, Lynnwood, 425-774-1300; 2565 South Gateway Center Place, Federal Way, 253-941-4994, www.rei.com
- **Wilderness Sports**, 14340 NE 20th Street, Bellevue, 425-746-0500

RUNNING

Considering the weather in Seattle, you might think that running wouldn't be a favorite sport in the city. For some reason, though, the rain just seems to make area runners more determined. The most popular running locations in Seattle are Green Lake (the inner loop is 2.8 miles, the outer loop is slightly over 3 miles), the Burke-Gilman Trail, Myrtle Edwards Park, and Alki Beach in West Seattle. Listed below are several running clubs in Seattle, which sponsor weekly club runs and annual events:

- **Eastside Runners**, P.O. Box 2616, Redmond, WA 98073, 877-570-8596, www.eastsiderunners.com
- **Seattle Frontrunners** (Gay/Lesbian), P.O. Box 31952, Seattle, WA 98103, 206-295-1811, www.seattlefrontrunners.org
- **Rain City Hash House Harriers**, 206-528-2050, www.cs.washington.edu
- **West Seattle Runners**, 3911 SW Portland Street, 206-938-2416, www.wsr.org

Many races are held annually throughout Seattle. Some of the most popular are the St. Patrick's Day Dash (4 miles) held in March, the Jingle Bell Run (5K) held in early December, and the Race for the Cure (5K) held in mid-October. The Torchlight Run (8K), held in August as part of the Seafair celebration, is both a run and a parade event, with prizes given for best costume and group theme. The Beat the Bridge Run (8K) is a favorite local run, so named because the object is to cross the University Bridge before the bridge goes up. Comedians and musicians entertain those runners who get stuck behind the bridge until the bridge is lowered again. The Seattle Marathon and Half-Marathon are held each year in November. The best option for getting information on upcoming races is to contact a local running club or running store. The following stores advertise races and also sponsor weekly group runs:

- **Fast Lady Sports**, 2710 NE University Village, 206-522-2113
- **Super Jock 'n Jill**, 7210 East Green Lake Drive North, 206-522-7711, www.superjocknjill.com; runners' hotline, 206-524-7876

SKIING AND SNOWBOARDING

The highways over the Cascade Mountains lead to several ski resorts that are not too far. Whistler, a few hours drive north of Vancouver, BC, is considered one of the best ski resorts in North America. Skiing and snowboarding are both popular activities at nearby resorts, which usually offer lessons for all levels of skiers. Call ahead for details and lodging reservations.

WASHINGTON STATE SKI AREAS

- **Crystal Mountain**, near Mount Rainier, 33 miles east of Enumclaw on Highway 410, 360-663-2265, www.crystalmt.com
- **Mission Ridge**, 12 miles east of Wenatchee on Highway 2, 509-663-6543, www.missionridge.com
- **Mount Baker**, 56 miles east of Bellingham on Highway 542, 360-734-6771, www.mtbakerskiarea.com
- **Stevens Pass**, 65 miles east of Everett on Highway 2, 206-812-4510, www.stevenspass.com
- **The Summit at Snoqualmie** (includes Alpental, Hyak, Ski Acres and Snoqualmie ski areas), 60 miles east of Seattle on I-90, 206-236-7277, snow-line, 206-236-1600, www.summit-at-snoqualmie.com
- **White Pass**, near Mount Rainier, 50 miles west of Yakima on Highway 12, 509-672-3101, snow-line, 509-672-3100, www.skiwhitepass.com

OUT OF STATE SKI AREAS

- **Mount Bachelor**, 22 miles southwest of Bend, OR, 541-382-2442 or 800-829-2442, www.mtbachelor.com
- **Mount Hood Meadows**, 80 miles east of Portland near Hood River, OR, 503-337-2222 or 800-SKI-HOOD, www.skihood.com
- **Mount Washington**, located 80 miles north of Nanaimo on Vancouver Island, BC, 888-231-1499, www.mtwashington.bc.ca
- **Silver Mountain**, located 70 miles east of Spokane in Kellogg, ID, 208-783-1111, www.silvermt.com

- **Schweitzer**, located 86 miles northeast of Spokane near Sandpoint, ID, 208-263-9555, 800-831-8810, www.schweitzer.com.
- **Whistler** (includes Whistler and Blackcomb ski areas), 75 miles north of Vancouver, BC, 800-766-0449, www.whistler-blackcomb.com

SNOWMOBILING

In Washington, snowmobiling is allowed on many forest and park trails. Snowmobiles are available for rent near most ski areas and in other wilderness areas throughout the state. Rentals generally include a short lesson that covers riding techniques and safety tips. The following resources may be helpful if you're planning a day of snowmobiling:

- **Washington State Parks and Recreation Commission**, 800-233-0321, www.parks.wa.gov
- **Washington State Snowmobile Association**, 1690 Winona Lane, Walla Walla, 800-783-9772, www.wssaonline.com

WASHINGTON STATE SNOWMOBILE SNO-PARK INFORMATION

- **Apple Country Snowmobile Club**, 509-884-6515
- **Blue Mountains**, 509-337-6323
- **Chelan Ranger District**, 509-682-2576
- **Cle Elum Ranger District**, 509-674-4411
- **Cowlitz Valley Ranger District**, 360-497-1100
- **Entiat Ranger District**, 509-784-1511
- **Lake Wenatchee Ranger District**, 509-763-3103
- **Mount Adams Ranger District**, 509-395-3400
- **Mount Baker Ranger District**, 360-856-5700
- **Mount St. Helens Ranger District**, 360-247-3900
- **Okanogan County**, 509-422-7319
- **Naches Ranger District**, 509-653-2205
- **Pomeroy Ranger District**, 509-843-1891
- **Spokane County Parks and Recreation**, 509-477-4730, www.spokanecounty.org/parks
- **White River Ranger District**, 360-825-6585

SNOWMOBILE RENTALS

- **Back-Country Adventure Corp.**, 902 Parkview, Chelan, 509-670-0877, www.back-country.com
- **Mountain Springs Lodge**, 19115 Chiwawa Loop Road, Leavenworth, 800-858-2276, www.mtsprings.com

- **Stampede Pass Snowmobile Rentals**, 3019 South 256th Street, Kent, 253-941-7425, www.nielsensenterprises.com/snomo

SOCCER

While a few high schools have teams, most children and adults play competitive soccer in private leagues. The following soccer resources are in the greater Seattle area:

- **Capitol Hill Soccer Club**, 3809 Corliss Avenue North, 206-675-0397, www.capitolhillsoccer.org
- **Co-Rec Soccer Association**, 206-329-1548
- **Eastside Youth Soccer Association**, 15600 NE 8th Street, Suite B1, Bellevue, 425-462-6616, www.eysa.org
- **Everett Youth Soccer League**, 2418 California Street, Everett, 425-259-5667, www.everettweb.com/sports/eysl
- **Greater Seattle Soccer League (GSSL)**, 9750 Greenwood Avenue North, 206-782-6831, www.gssl.org
- **LVR Youth Soccer Club** (Laurelhurst, View Ridge, Ravenna), P.O. Box 15923, Seattle, WA 98115, 206-525-6045, www.lvr-soccer.org
- **Lake Hills Youth Soccer Club**, P.O. Box 6744, Bellevue, WA 98008, 425-643-1029, www.eysa.org/lakehills
- **Lake Washington Youth Soccer Association**, 8141 161st Avenue NE, Redmond, 425-883-3009, www.lwysa.org
- **Magnolia Soccer Club**, 3213 West Wheeler Street, 206-835-5514, www.magnoliasoccerclub.com
- **Mount Baker/Lakewood Youth Soccer Club**, 206-725-2286
- **Queen Anne Soccer Club**, 206-281-9579
- **Seattle Youth Soccer Association**, 206-365-6146, www.sysa.org
- **Silver Lake Soccer Club**, Bothell, 425-481-2665
- **Washington State Soccer Association**, 7802 NE Bothell Way, Kenmore, 425-485-7855, www.wssa.org
- **Washington State Youth Soccer Association**, 33710 9th Avenue South, Federal Way, 253-4-SOCCER, www.wsysa.com
- **Woodinville Indoor Soccer Center**, 12728 NE 178th Street, Woodinville, 425-481-5099, www.woodinvilleindoor.com

SWIMMING

When hot weather hits Seattle, folks head in droves to the few swimming beaches in the city. Lifeguards are generally on duty at Seattle beaches 11 a.m. to 8 p.m., from June 20 through Labor Day (except in inclement weather). To find beaches in communities outside Seattle, contact one of the parks and recreation departments listed previously in this chapter. The following are

Seattle parks with swimming areas (call Seattle Parks and Recreation's general information line at 206-684-4075 for more information):
- **Green Lake Park**: 7201 East Green Lake Drive and 7312 West Green Lake Drive
- **Madison Park**, 1900 43rd Avenue East
- **Madrona Park**, 800 Lake Washington Boulevard South
- **Magnuson Park**, 7400 Sand Point Way NE
- **Matthews Beach Park**, 9300 51st Avenue NE
- **Mount Baker Park**, 2301 Lake Washington Boulevard South
- **Pritchard Beach**, 8400 56th Avenue South
- **Seward Park**, 5900 Lake Washington Boulevard South

Wading pools are open for the little ones in a few parks, playgrounds, and community centers in Seattle. Park wading pools are open daily (provided the temperature is over 70 degrees), from 11 a.m. to 8 p.m. Community center and playground wading pools are open weekdays only, and hours vary. Call the city's **Aquatic Information Hotline** at 206-684-7796 for more information. Here are the city's three biggest **wading pools**:
- **Green Lake Park**, 7312 West Green Lake Drive
- **Lincoln Park**, 8600 Fauntleroy Way SW
- **Volunteer Park**, 1400 East Galer Street

For those interested in year-round swimming, Seattle city pools offer a variety of open swim sessions, lessons and lap-swimming options. Many host swim club practices for Masters and all ages programs. To find pools in communities outside Seattle, contact one of the parks and recreation departments listed previously in this chapter.
- **Ballard Pool**, 1471 NW 67th Street, 206-684-4094
- **Colman Pool** (outdoor), 8603 Fauntleroy Way SW, 206-684-7494
- **Evans Pool**, 7201 East Green Lake Drive North, 206-684-4961
- **Madison Pool**, 13401 Meridian Avenue North, 206-684-4979
- **Meadowbrook Pool**, 10515 35th Avenue NE, 206-684-4989
- **Medgar Evers Pool**, 500 23rd Avenue, 206-684-4766
- **Mounger Pool** (outdoor), 2535 32nd Avenue West, 206-684-4708
- **Queen Anne Pool**, 1920 1st Avenue West, 206-386-4282
- **Rainier Beach Pool**, 8825 Rainier Avenue South, 206-386-1944
- **Southwest Pool**, 2801 SW Thistle Street, 206-684-7440

Several swim clubs hold regular practices at pools around Seattle, many offering a variety of practices for all levels of experience. Call for details, as prices and entrance requirements vary widely. An excellent resource for competitive swimming information in Washington is **Pacific Northwest Swimming (PNS)**, 402 South 333rd Street, Suite 103, Federal Way, 253-

661-7748. The organization maintains a comprehensive web site at www.pns.org. Several local swim clubs are listed below. Because many practice at multiple locations, business office addresses are given for some clubs.

- **Cascade Swim Club**, P.O. Box 77043, Seattle, 98177, 206-367-9069, www.cascadeswimclub.org
- **Chinook Aquatic Club**, P.O. Box 555, Bellevue, 98009, 206-230-5812, www.chinookaquaticclub.org
- **Husky Swim Club**, P.O. Box 66248, Seattle, 98166, 206-575-0808
- **Salmon Bay Aquatics**, 206-781-0827, www.salmonbay.org
- **Swim Seattle**, P.O. Box 51115, Seattle, 98115, 206-365-4907, www.swimseattle.org
- **West Seattle YMCA Dolphins Swim Team**, 4515 36th Avenue SW, Seattle, 206-935-6000

WATER-SKIING

During the summer, there are hundreds of people water-skiing on Lake Washington. Many skiers launch their boats early in the morning from Magnuson Park in Sand Point and head out to the middle of the lake. Other lakes in Washington popular with water-skiers are Lake Sammamish in Bellevue and Lake Chelan, north of Wenatchee. For equipment and supplies, try the following resources:

- **Active Water Sports Waterski Pro Shop**, 800-832-7547, www.aws-online.com
- **Adrenaline Water Sports**, 2021 130th Avenue NE, Bellevue, 425-885-3909
- **Extremely Board**, 1175 NW Gilman Boulevard, Suite B-7, Issaquah, 425-391-4572
- **Pro Tour Watersports**, 13131 NE 124th Street, Suite A, Kirkland, 425-814-1395, www.protourwatersports.com
- **Ski Masters Water Sports Warehouse**, Bothell, 425-481-2754
- **Straight-Line Water Sports**, 966 153rd Avenue NE, Redmond, 425-881-3377
- **Sturtevant's Sports**, 622 Bellevue Way NE, Bellevue, 425-454-6465 or 888-454-7669, www.sturtevants.com
- **Wiley's Ski Shop**, 1417 South Trenton Street, 206-762-1300

WIND-SURFING

While Green Lake, Lake Union, the Puget Sound, and Lake Washington are all popular destinations for windsurfing enthusiasts, the Columbia River Gorge is the ultimate thrill for experienced wind-surfers. Located on the southern border of Washington near Hood River, OR, the gorge is challenging and exciting for veteran surfers, but can be rough and even dangerous for beginners. The following resources provide information and lessons for both experienced wind-surfers and beginners:

- **Columbia Gorge Windsurfing Association**, 202 Oak Street, Suite 150, Hood River, OR, 541-386-9225, www.windsurf.gorge.net/cgwa
- **Urban Surf**, 2100 North Northlake Way, 206-545-9463, http://urbansurf.com

YOGA

Yoga has become enormously popular in Seattle, with studios popping up all over the city, and health clubs rushing to add classes. Here are a few Seattle yoga studios:

- **The Ashtanga Yoga School**, 1412 12th Avenue, 206-261-1711
- **Ballard Firehouse Yoga Studio**, 5429 Russell Avenue NW, Suite 300, 206-789-8099
- **Bikram's Yoga College of India**, 7900 East Green Lake Drive North, Suite 200, 206-547-0188
- **The Center for Yoga in Seattle**, 2261 NE 65th Street, 206-526-9642, www.yogaseattle.com
- **Hatha Yoga Center**, 4550 11th Avenue NE, 206-632-1706
- **Jai Ma Yoga Studio**, 323 Queen Anne Avenue North, 206-283-9393, www.jaimayoga.com
- **Kaya Yoga**, 5004 South Genesee Street, 206-760-1917, www.kayayogaseattle.com
- **The Moving Space**, 5340 Ballard Avenue NW, 206-706-0069
- **Santosha Yoga**, 2812 East Madison Street, 206-264-5034, www.yoga4everyone.com
- **Seattle Holistic Center**, 7700 Aurora Avenue North, 206-525-9035, www.seattleholisticcenter.com
- **Seattle Yoga Arts**, 109 15th Avenue East, 206-440-3191, www.seattleyogaarts.com
- **Soundyoga**, 5639 California Avenue SW, 206-938-8195, www.soundyoga.com
- **The Yoga Tree**, 3601 Fremont Avenue North, #315, 206-545-0316, www.yogatree.com

HEALTH CLUBS

Whether you're trying to stay in shape during the off-season, get in shape for spring break, or simply prefer group fitness or weight-lifting to outdoor sports, Seattle is full of health clubs and gyms. Most offer conditioning classes, as well as personal training programs. Some clubs also offer yoga, spinning, swimming workouts, and nutrition and health classes. Call or visit the club you're interested in to get details on their programs.

- **24 Hour Fitness**, 1827 Yale Avenue, 206-624-0651, www.24hourfitness.com
- **1201 Nautilus**, 1201 3rd Avenue, 4th Floor, 206-583-8848
- **Allstar Fitness**, 330 2nd Avenue West, 206-282-5901; 509 Olive Way, Suite 213, 206-292-0900; 2629 SW Andover Street, 206-932-9999, www.allstarfitness.com
- **Anderson's Nautilus Fitness Center**, 7203 Woodlawn Avenue NE, 206-524-7000, www.andersonsnautilus.com
- **Aqua Dive Swim & Fitness Club**, 12706 33rd Avenue NE, 206-364-2535, www.aquadive.net
- **Ballard Health Club**, 2208 NW Market Street, 206-706-4882
- **Bally Total Fitness**, 13201 Aurora Avenue North and other locations, 800-695-8111, www.ballyfitness.com
- **Cross Train Concepts Conditioning Studio**, 1446 NW 53rd Street, 206-782-2199
- **Every Body Health and Fitness**, 2609 South Jackson Street, 206-324-6062
- **Fitness for Women**, 5908 California Avenue SW, 206-937-7733
- **Gateway Athletic Club**, 700 5th Avenue, 206-343-4692
- **Gold's Gym**, 9701 Aurora Avenue North, 206-524-5543; 825 Pike Street, 206-583-0640
- **Living Well Lady Fitness Center**, 2656 NE University Village Mall, 206-522-9318
- **Magnolia Athletic Club**, 3320 West McGraw Street, 206-283-1490
- **Mieko's Fitness**, 2438 32nd Avenue West, 206-286-9070, 12015 31st Avenue NE, 206-417-4715
- **Olympic Athletic Club**, 5301 Leary Avenue NW, 206-789-5010, www.oac24hour.com
- **One on One**, 5007 3rd Avenue South, 206-764-1661
- **Pro-Robics**, 1530 Queen Anne Avenue North, 206-283-2303; 3811 NE 45th Street, 206-524-9246
- **Seattle Athletic Club**, 2020 Western Avenue, 206-443-1111; 333 NE 97th Street, 206-522-9400
- **Seattle Fitness Club**, 83 South King Street, 206-467-1800, www.seattle-fitness.com
- **Sound Mind & Body**, 437 North 34th Street; 3130 East Madison Street; 1165 Eastlake Avenue East; 206-547-3470, www.smbgym.com
- **The Vault**, 808 2nd Avenue, 206-224-9000
- **Washington Athletic Club**, 1325 6th Avenue, 206-622-7900, www.wac.net
- **Westlake Club**, 1275 Westlake Avenue North, 206-283-9320

- **XGYM**, 2505 2nd Avenue, Suite 100, 206-728-XGYM
- **YWCA Health & Fitness Center**, 1118 5th Avenue, 206-461-4868

SPORTING GOODS AND OUTDOOR WEAR STORES

Whether you're heading out of town for a rugged hike or spending an hour at the park with a Frisbee, you may need to go shopping first. Seattle residents take their sports and recreational activities seriously, so there are many places to find just the right equipment:

- **2nd Base** (used), 1101 East Pine Street, 206-325-2273
- **3 GI Sports**, 9000 Holman Road NW, 206-782-5860
- **Athletic Supply**, 224 Westlake Avenue North, 206-623-8972
- **Avanti Sports**, 3503 NE 45th Street, 206-527-8866
- **Avid Angler Fly Shoppe**, 11714 15th Avenue NE, 206-362-4030
- **Bicycle Center**, 4529 Sandpoint Way NE, 206-522-2196
- **Big 5 Sporting Goods**, 1101 Leary Way NW, 206-706-7531; 2500 SW Barton Street, 206-932-2212; 4315 University Way NE, 206-547-2445, www.big5sportinggoods.com
- **Chubby & Tubby**, 7906 Aurora Avenue North, 206-524-1810; 3333 Rainier Avenue South, 206 723-8800; 4110 A NE 4th Street, Renton, 206-762-9791
- **Discount Divers Supply**, 2710 Westlake Avenue North, 206-298-6998
- **Fast Lady Sports**, 2710 University Village NE, 206-522-2113; 4015 Stone Way North, 206-547-4854
- **Feathered Friends**, 119 Yale Avenue North, 206-292-2210, www.featheredfriends.com
- **Fiorini Sports**, 4720 University Village Place NE, 206-523-9610, www.fiorinisports.com
- **Footzone**, 919 East Pine Street, 206-329-1466, www.footzonecapitol-hill.com
- **Niketown**, 1500 6th Avenue, 206-447-6453, www.nike.com
- **NordicTrack**, 831 NE Northgate Way, 206-362-1694, www.nordic-track.com
- **Northwest Outdoor Center**, 2100 Westlake Avenue North, 206-281-9694
- **Olympic Sports**, 10700 5th Avenue NE, 206-363-3007
- **Outdoor Emporium**, 420 Pontius Avenue North, 206-624-6550
- **Outdoor & More**, 510 Westlake Avenue North, 206-340-0677, www.outmore.com
- **Patagonia**, 2100 1st Avenue, 206-622-9700, www.patagonia.com
- **Patrick's Fly Shop**, 2237 Eastlake Avenue East, 206-325-8988
- **Play It Again Sports** (new and used), 1304 Stewart Street, 206-264-9255

- **Puetz Golf Centers**, 11762 Aurora Avenue North, 206-362-2272, www.puetzgolf.com
- **REI (Recreational Equipment Inc.)**, 222 Yale Avenue North, 206-223-1944, www.rei.com
- **Seattle Athletic & Exercise**, 842 NE Northgate Way, 206-364-5890
- **Second Bounce** (new and used), 513 North 36th Street, 206-545-8810, www.secondbounce.com
- **Sound Sports**, 80 Madison Street, 206-624-6717
- **Sporthaus Schmetzer Inc.**, 12524 Lake City Way NE, 206-365-2161
- **The Sports Junction**, 4519 1/2 California Avenue SW, 206-938-2555
- **Sports Specialties**, 2319 2nd Avenue, 206-441-8412
- **Super Jock 'n Jill**, 7210 East Green Lake Drive North, 206-522-7711, www.superjocknjill.com
- **Urban Surf**, 2100 North Northlake Way, 206-545-9463, www.urbansurf.com
- **Velo Stores**, 1535 11th Avenue, 206-325-3292
- **Wiley's Water Ski Shop**, 1417 South Trenton Street, 206-762-1300, www.wileyski.com

SEATTLE'S LANDSCAPE IS THE RESULT OF VARIOUS GEOLOGIC FORCES; the hills and mountains created by shifting plates far beneath the earth's surface, the lakes and waterways carved out by a great system of glaciers and several ice ages. Add to this a rainy climate broken by bright sunlight, throw in lush indigenous evergreens and colorful rhododendrons, and it is no wonder that Seattle residents spend so much time outdoors. The city's park system, which includes many lakes, provides abundant opportunities for enjoying the area's natural beauty.

In 1903, J.C. Olmsted designed most of Seattle's park system. The Seattle park board hired Olmsted to design a boulevard system that would link much of the city's parkland, which had been purchased between 1897 and 1903. The result is impressive, with approximately 20 miles of winding parkway connecting many of Seattle's major green spaces. The following is a brief description of Seattle's most popular parks, although in addition to those listed here, many neighborhoods also have small parks, athletic fields and playgrounds. To get more information on any of the parks listed here, call the **Seattle Parks and Recreation Department** at 206-684-4075 or visit www.cityofseattle.net/parks.

LAKE WASHINGTON PARKS

These parks are located along the shores of Lake Washington, and are listed from south to north.

- **Seward Park**, in the southeast corner of Seattle, is located on the 277-acre Bailey Peninsula. In addition to a beach, the park has a system of nature trails perfect for solitary walks or bird-watching (bald eagles are occasionally sighted here). Also enticing, the 1920s bathhouse now serves as an artists' studio, offering a variety of ceramics classes for adults and children; call 206-722-6342 for class availability.

- **Mount Baker Park** is north of Seward Park, near the site of the Seafair hydroplane races that take place each August. The Mount Baker Rowing and Sailing Center hosts beginning rowing and sailing classes, and is home to both an adult and a high school crew team. Call the center at 206-386-1913 for details.
- **Madrona Park** provides stunning views of the lake from a sandy beach.
- **Madison Park** is located on Lake Washington at the far east end of Madison Street. Although not part of the Olmsted plan, it originated in the 1890s as the site of a summer amusement park. Today it is a popular sunny-day hangout, offering the perennial summer favorites of picnicking, swimming, and sunbathing.
- The **Washington Park Arboretum**, along Madison Avenue, picks up the Olmsted planned parkway in Madrona. The Arboretum is a 255-acre woodland managed by the University of Washington. Though it was a part of the Seattle park system as early as 1904, it was developed by the university as an arboretum in 1936. Originally filled with native Northwest plants and trees, today the Washington Park Arboretum is home to more than 5,500 flowers, trees and shrubs from all over the world. It includes the beautifully sculptured Japanese Tea Garden, designed in 1960 by Japanese architect Juki Iida. At the north end of the Arboretum, the Museum of History and Industry hosts fascinating exhibits of Seattle's industrial history and maritime heritage.
- **Magnuson Park** has softball fields and a boat launch to Lake Washington. It's also the entrance to the famous Soundgarden, a unique wind chime sculpture.
- **Matthews Beach Park**, on the Lake Washington waterfront near Sand Point, is a popular summer destination for sunbathers and swimmers, and is also a stop on the Burke-Gilman Trail.

INLAND PARKS

Located just north of downtown, these parks offer respite from the bustle of the city. They are listed from east to west.

- **Ravenna Park**, north of the University of Washington, follows a steep ravine northwest to **Cowen Park** and then Green Lake.
- **Green Lake** is perhaps Seattle's most popular public park. It is surrounded by almost three miles of paved walkway, attracting bicyclists, in-line skaters, runners and strolling couples. In Seattle, where locals are undaunted by drizzle and early winter darkness, Green Lake has become a year-round mecca for early-morning and late-evening walkers and joggers. During the summer, fields at the east side of the lake fill with volleyball teams, the basketball courts host informal but competi-

tive pick-up games, and in-line skaters can be found playing hockey in the drained kiddie pool. The Seattle Parks Department's Green Lake Small Craft Center, 206-684-4074, sponsors boating classes for novice sailors at the south end of the lake, and beginning wind-surfers set sail from the eastern shore. Another Seattle tradition, the annual Seafair Milk Carton Derby, launches from the shore each July, and there are many other events held on Green Lake throughout the year.

- **Woodland Park**, at the south end of Green Lake, offers tennis courts, lawn bowling and grassy picnic areas, as well as the Woodland Park Zoo, a seasonal favorite of adults and kids alike. One particularly popular program is the Bird of Prey program, where kids delight in watching trained raptors in flight. Small children enjoy the petting zoo and pony rides in the summer. The zoo is located in the Phinney Ridge neighborhood, at Phinney Avenue North and North 50th Street. Call 206-684-4800 for hours. Also worth a visit is the spectacular Rose Garden, just outside the zoo's south gate. Call 206-684-4863 for details and special events information.

PUGET SOUND VIEW PARKS

The following parks overlook the Puget Sound and offer beach access. They are listed from north to south.

- **Golden Gardens Park**, which is not a part of the Olmsted plan, is located at the north end of Ballard. The park features one of Seattle's few truly sandy beaches, luring swimmers, picnickers, and volleyball players through the summer months.
- **Discovery Park**, on the western point of Magnolia, is the largest of the Olmsted-designed parks. With over 500 acres of wooded trails and flowery meadows, towering sea cliffs and windy beaches, everyone can find something to do at this park. Visit in the evening to watch the sun set over the Olympics, or come during the day for a pleasant hike down to the beach. Clay cliffs overhang the rocky beach, providing hours of fun for kids. Nearby quiet meadows are great places for picnics or impromptu bird watching. You may see bald eagles, hawks, falcons or even an osprey. From the beach you may catch sight of migrating seabirds and views of the West Point Lighthouse. The Daybreak Star Cultural Center, in the center of the park, celebrates Native American culture with art exhibits and special programs. Call 206-285-4425 for details.
- **Alki Beach Park** in West Seattle is a great place to watch sunsets over the Olympics or enjoy a spectacular view of downtown Seattle. During the summer, in-line skaters, bicyclists and serious beach volleyball play-

ers flock to this park. The beach resort atmosphere adds to the charm of this narrow strip of land along the northwest shore of West Seattle.

DOWNTOWN PARKS

The parks listed here are close to downtown and offer spectacular views of either the city skyline or Lake Union. They are listed as they appear clockwise around Lake Union.

- **Gasworks Park,** at the north end of Lake Union, is built around the dramatic skeleton of the old gasworks factory and offers stunning views of the downtown skyline. The park attracts kite-flyers and Frisbee players, and is a starting point for the Burke-Gilman Trail, a paved walkway that heads east from Gasworks to Lake Washington, then along the lake shore to the Eastside. The giant sundial atop the park's central hill is always worth a visit. Gasworks Park hosts an annual Independence Day celebration, complete with a spectacular fireworks display over Lake Union, set to music by the Seattle Symphony.
- **Kerry Park,** on the southwest corner of Queen Anne Hill, overlooks Elliott Bay and the downtown skyline, providing a spectacular view of the city.
- **Volunteer Park,** on the northeast corner of Capitol Hill, also provides incredible views of downtown, as well as Puget Sound and the Olympic Mountains. For an even more dazzling view, climb to the top of the 75-foot water tower. In Volunteer Park you'll also find the Seattle Asian Art Museum, and a 1912 conservatory filled with orchids and other tropical plants. Just north of the park, the Lake View Cemetery contains the graves of several prominent Seattle citizens, including "Doc" Maynard and Bruce Lee.

SURROUNDING COMMUNITIES

Several Seattle area parks are owned or maintained by the King County Park System, a vast network of lakes and green spaces. In June of 2002, the King County parks system faced a critical budget shortage that may result in the closing or selling of some parks in Seattle's surrounding communities. A task force was considering several proposals to keep the parks open, but there was no consensus at press time. In the meantime, 20 parks remain closed year-round to save on maintenance costs, including eight on the Eastside. Visitors can still enter the parks, but may not be able to park in their lots, and will find upkeep services reduced. For current information, visit the Metropolitan Parks Task Force on the web at www.metrokc.gov/exec/mptf. To find a county park in your neck of the woods, call 206-296-4232 or visit www.metrokc.gov/parks.

MERCER ISLAND

- **Luther Burbank Park**, on the northeast end of Mercer Island, commands 77 acres and a three-quarters-of-a-mile stretch of Lake Washington waterfront. Nearly three miles of trails provide opportunities for walks and bird watching. Other amenities include tennis courts, a group picnic area, a grassy amphitheater and daily moorage. Luther Burbank's off-leash dog area offers pets the rare opportunity to swim legally in a public park. 206-296-4232, www.metrokc.gov/parks

BELLEVUE

- **Cougar Mountain Regional Wildland Park** is surrounded by the cities of Bellevue, Newcastle and Issaquah, just minutes from downtown Seattle. The park covers more than 3,000 acres, making it the largest park in the King County system. More than 36 miles of trails are for hikers, and 12 miles are devoted to equestrians. Fourteen creeks originate within the park, including three salmon-spawning creeks: Coal Creek, May Creek, and Tibbett's Creek. 206-296-4232, www.metrokc.gov/parks
- **Kelsey Creek Park** consists of 150 acres of wetland and forest habitat. The park boasts numerous hiking and jogging trails, including a gravel loop trail that circles picturesque barns and pastures. The highlight of the park is Kelsey Creek Farm, which is home to a variety of animals, and offers several children's programs. 425-452-6881, www.ci.bellevue.wa.us
- **Robinswood Community Park** is the setting for Robinswood House, one of the area's most popular wedding reception and private-party sites. For rental information, call 425-452-7850. The park also features four indoor and four outdoor tennis courts, a pond and playground, and a fully equipped baseball field with scoreboard. 425-452-6881, www.ci.bellevue.wa.us
- **Wilburton Hill Park**, which includes the Bellevue Botanical Garden, features ball fields, hiking trails, and a children's play area. The Botanical Garden contains 36 acres of lush flower gardens and landscaping. Guided tours of the grounds are available. 425-452-6881, www.ci.bellevue.wa.us

KIRKLAND

- **Juanita Bay Park** offers numerous opportunities to view a variety of wildlife, including songbirds, waterfowl, raptors, shorebirds, turtles, and beavers. The 144-acre park's paved trails and boardwalks make self-guided tours easy, but volunteer park rangers also offer interpretive tours on the first Sunday of the month at 1 p.m. 425-828-2237, www.ci.kirkland.wa.us

REDMOND

- **Marymoor Park** is the crown jewel of the King County Park System and one of the most popular parks in the entire Puget Sound region, particularly among dog-owners, soccer players, bicycle racers, rock climbers, and model-airplane enthusiasts. Covering 640 acres, the park is visited by more than a million people each year. Annual events at Marymoor include King County's Heritage Festival and WOMAD (a world-music celebration). Notable attractions at Marymoor include a 40-acre off-leash dog area, the Marymoor Velodrome, Willowmoor Farm, and the Marymoor Climbing Rock. 206-296-4232, www.metrokc.gov/parks

RENTON

- **Gene Coulon Memorial Beach Park** was originally named Lake Washington Beach Park because of its location on the southeast shore of the region's most popular recreational lake. The park consists of 53 acres, and encourages several aquatic activities, including swimming, boating, water skiing and windsurfing. A rarity at area parks, Gene Coulon is home to two commercial fast-food restaurants, Kidd Valley and Ivar's. 425-430-6700, www.ci.renton.wa.us/commserv/parks

TUKWILA

- **Fort Dent Park** is best known for its plentiful softball fields. The park hosts dozens of tournaments each year, including state and national competition. Fort Dent also features soccer fields and a kids' play area, along with a variety of birds and animals that flock to the park's wetlands. The 54-acre park is located adjacent to the Green River Trail, a regional pathway that winds 14 miles through South King County. 206-296-4232, www.metrokc.gov/parks

BURIEN

- **Seahurst Park** is popular with divers and beachcombers. The 185-acre park was owned by the King County Park System, until it was given to the new city of Burien in 1996. The park's main attraction is the 2,000-foot-long saltwater beach. Other highlights include picnic shelters and tables, a play area and numerous trails. 206-988-3700, www.ci.burien.wa.us

TACOMA

- **Point Defiance Park** is among the 20 largest urban parks in the United States, and is the setting for one of Tacoma's most popular destinations, the Point Defiance Zoo and Aquarium. About two million people visit the 698-acre park each year to stroll through gardens and old-growth forests, travel back in time at Fort Nisqually, ride behind an authentic locomotive at Camp 6 Logging Museum, or bike along Five Mile Drive. 253-305-1000, www.tacomaparks.com
- **Wright Park**, just north of Tacoma's city center, is one of the few Washington parks listed on the National Register of Historic Places. The park's centerpiece is the glass-domed W.W. Seymour Botanical Conservatory, which was built in 1908. The conservatory presents seasonal floral displays in addition to its permanent collection of exotic tropical plants. Other attractions include walking and jogging paths, a children's play area and wading pool, lawn bowling, horseshoes and a community center. 253-305-1000, www.tacomaparks.com

BAINBRIDGE ISLAND

- **Gazzam Lake Park and Wildlife Preserve**, on the southwest corner of the island, is Bainbridge's second-biggest area of undeveloped land. The 318-acre park includes 13 acres of freshwater wetlands, home to a variety of wildlife, including deer and birds. An interpretive center is planned for the park, as well as a trail to Puget Sound. 206-842-2306, www.biparks.org
- **Grand Forest** consists of 240 acres spread over three plots on central Bainbridge Island. The property includes second-growth forests plus wetlands and wildlife habitat. Thanks to the Eagle Scouts, the former Department of Natural Resources land now features trails and trail signs. 206-842-2306, www.biparks.org
- **Manzanita Park**, at the north end of Bainbridge Island, is popular with hikers and horseback riders because its 120 acres are ribboned with hiking and equestrian trails. 206-842-2306, www.biparks.org

MOUNTLAKE TERRACE

- **Terrace Creek Park** is Mountlake Terrace's largest park, occupying 60 acres in the center of the city. Amenities include barbecues, picnic areas, trails, play equipment, and playfields. 425-776-9173, www.ci. mountlake-terrace.wa.us/departments/parks

EDMONDS

- **Underwater Park** is located just north of the ferry dock, at the foot of Main Street in downtown Edmonds. One of the first underwater parks on the West Coast, Underwater Park is 27 acres of tide and bottom lands. Designated as a marine preserve and sanctuary in 1970, the park attracts scuba divers from across the state. 425-771-0230, www.ci.edmonds.wa.us/parks

STATE AND NATIONAL PARKS

If you're in the mood for something slightly more adventurous than a city outing, consider a trip to one of Washington's many state or national parks.
- **Mount Rainier National Park** activities include skiing, hiking, camping, and mountain climbing. Call 360-569-2211 for more information, or visit www.nps.gov/mora.
- **Olympic National Park** on the Olympic Peninsula (about two hours northwest of Seattle) also offers hiking, camping, and mountain-climbing opportunities. For an up-close look at the mountains without the hike, visit Hurricane Ridge near Port Angeles. You can drive to the ridge and view the mountains from the comfort of the visitors' center. Also worth a visit is Sol Duc Hot Springs, in the center of the park. For more information on the Olympic National Park, call 360-452-0330 or visit www.nps.gov/olym.
- **North Cascades National Park** offers stunning views, hundreds of hikes and an outstanding museum. 360-856-5700, www.nps.gov/noca.
- To receive information on any of Washington's 125 state parks, call the **Washington State Parks and Recreation Commission** at 360-902-8561 or 800-223-0321, or visit their web site at www.parks.wa.gov.

FORESTS

Surrounding Olympic National Park, on the Olympic Peninsula, is **Olympic National Forest**. Its 632,000 acres are shared by outdoor enthusiasts and wildlife, and are managed for timber, mining, grazing, oil and gas, watershed, and wilderness. Twenty campgrounds pepper the land, and 266 miles of trails wind through the area. For more information, call 360-956-2402 or visit www.fs.fed.us/r6/olympic.

ADDITIONAL RESOURCES

For comprehensive recreation information for the entire state, visit **Washington State Tourism** at www.tourism.wa.gov or call a state travel counselor, 360-725-5052, daily, from 7 a.m. to 7 p.m. If you're heading for one of the region's mountain passes, call the **Washington State Department of Transportation** highway information line at 206-368-HIWY, or check the pass report online at www.wsdot.wa.gov/traffic. For additional outdoor recreation ideas, read the **Quick Getaways** chapter of this book, or try these:

- **Adventure Charters**, Seattle, 206-789-8245
- **Alpine Adventures Wild & Scenic River Tours**, Seattle, 800-723-8386
- **Argosy Cruises**, Seattle, 206-623-1445, www.argosycruises.com
- **ATV Action Tours**, Seattle, 425-424-3451, 877-478-6455, www.atvactiontours.com
- **Cascade Canoe & Kayak Centers**, Eastside, 425-637-8838, www.canoe-kayak.com
- **Erickson Cycle Tours**, Seattle, 206-524-7731, 888-972-0140, www.ecycletours.com
- **First Descent Whitewater Expeditions**, Seattle, 206-418-0401, 888-525-3222, www.fdescent.com
- **Gray Line of Seattle Sightseeing**, Seattle, 206-624-5077, 800-544-0739, www.graylineofseattle.com
- **Lifestyle Winery Tours**, 206-526-LIFE, www.lifestyletours.net
- **Olympic Mountain Outdoors**, Port Townsend, 360-379-5336, www.olympicguides.com
- **Outdoor Odysseys**, Seattle, 206-361-0717, 800-647-4621, www.outdoorodysseys.com
- **Pacific Salmon Charters**, Ilwaco, 800-831-2695, www.pacificsalmoncharters.com
- **Seattle Seaplanes**, Seattle, 206-329-9638, 800-637-5553, www.seattleseaplanes.com
- **See Seattle Walking Tours & Events**, Seattle, 425-226-7641, www.see-seattle.com
- **Spirit of Washington Dinner Train**, Renton, 800-876-7245
- **Whidbey Tours**, Whidbey Island, 360-678-5641, 877-881-1203, www.whidbeytours.com

WEATHER AND CLIMATE

"THE BLUEST SKIES YOU'VE EVER SEEN ARE IN SEATTLE," SANG Perry Como, "and the hills the greenest green...." The late crooner was right. On a sunny summer day, the city is wrapped in aquamarine and the landscape glows green. Such brilliantly lush environs led in part to the city's nickname of the Emerald City. But, Como forgot to mention the rain, and the accompanying mudslides, the frequent windstorms, occasional earthquakes and, every now and then, a drought; such are some of the challenges that Gore-Tex-clad residents contend with every year.

In Seattle, jokes about the perpetual precipitation are as constant as the rain. One holds that residents of Seattle don't tan—they rust. Then there's the one about the woman who arrives in Seattle on a rainy day. She wakes up the next day and it's raining. It rains the day after that, the day after that, and the day after that. She goes to lunch and sees a kid sitting at a counter. Out of despair she asks him, "Hey, kid, does it ever stop raining around here?" The kid replies, "How should I know? I'm only six." While rainfall here isn't actually relentless, at times it does feel like Noah and his ark are about to sail into town.

The soggiest time in Seattle is November through February, with an average rainfall of nearly 22 inches during those four months. In 1996—a notorious year in the area's weather history—nearly 52 inches of rain fell in the region, close to the record 55 inches set in 1950. While waterlogged years like 1996 stand out because they are extraordinary, in general, Seattle is a soggy city throughout the winter, but stories of nine months of solid rain should be discounted.

When heavy rains do arrive, they are sometimes accompanied by damaging mudslides and floods. The same hills that offer residents spectacular views render homes, trees, and roads vulnerable in extreme weath-

293

er. In the aftermath of heavy rains and snowstorms in 1996 and 1997, residents faced mudslides and sinkholes that damaged houses, washed out roads and sank the tarmac of a gas station. In Shoreline, a 100-foot-wide section of street plunged into a steep ravine, hauling down a parked car, a utility pole and about 30,000 cubic yards of dirt. In Magnolia, six large mudslides forced the evacuation of more than 40 homes, and the Magnolia Bridge was closed for several months after some of its supports snapped. Tour guides still stop along the Magnolia Bluff to point out a wrecked house that toppled from the hillside to the beach.

New residents should keep such stories in mind when searching for a new home. Though **mudslides** certainly aren't an everyday occurrence during the rainy months, they happen often enough to cause concern. Geologists recommend that homeowners try to determine if they are at risk for a slide by understanding how water causes damage and what triggers slides. "Prevention is absolutely the best thing we can do," said geologist Dennis Hibbert in a *Seattle Times* article. According to experts, steep bluffs and hillsides where earth movement has occurred in the past or where the geology favors such movement, are most at risk. That includes the bluffs that encircle Puget Sound and parts of Lake Washington, like West and North Seattle, Magnolia and Bainbridge Island. With this in mind, folks should search a prospective property for signs of earth movement or signs that the property is getting a lot of water. Indicators include leaning or bent trees, and cracks in the yard, the foundation, driveway or patio. A property that is getting a lot of water may have spots on the lawn that stay greener or that are continually wet, and/or mossy. If you find potential problems, you may want to hire a civil or geo-technical engineer to analyze the drainage situation and make recommendations. Both can be found in the Yellow Pages.

Despite its proximity to both the Cascade and Olympic mountain ranges, Seattle is not a snowy city, receiving on average only 11.7 inches per year. Communities to the east, like Issaquah, North Bend and Snoqualmie, get a little more snowfall. Of course, there are exceptions, like the winter of 1999, when record snow levels were recorded in the Northwest and more than 300 inches piled up at the base of the Mount Baker Ski Area.

If you are looking for sun, you may have to drive to find it in abundance. According to the Western Regional Climate Center, Seattle enjoys only 58 days of clear skies. In comparison, Yakima, about two and a half hours east of the city, experiences 109 clear days. The WRCC defines a clear day as one that sees zero to 3/10 average cloud cover. The clearest months here are in July, with 10 days, August, with nine days, and September, with eight days. November and December average just two clear days per month.

Because sunshine is not a daily occurrence, and weeks can pass without a break in the clouds, about ten percent of the region's residents suffer from **Seasonal Affective Disorder**, according to David Avery, a professor of psychiatry and behavioral sciences at the University of Washington. The National Mental Health Association says that as the seasons change, a shift occurs in our internal biological clocks that can cause us to be out of step with our daily schedules. Symptoms include sadness, sluggishness, change in appetite, and excessive sleeping. If you are moving from a sunny state like California or Florida, you should be aware of possible seasonal depression. Many people affected by the disorder have found relief using portable light boxes, like the ones sold by The SunBox Company, www.sunbox.com.

Washington does occasionally experience drought conditions, which in turn set the stage for dangerous wildfires. During drought years, local governments usually ask resident to limit yard watering, and farming communities may impose rolling dry-outs to conserve irrigation water. Wildfires generally are confined to the eastern part of the state, though forested neighborhoods like those in southeast King County also can be at risk. The National Fire Protection Association offers tips on protecting your home from wildfire at its web site, www.firewise.org.

Though Seattle's weather picture can seem bleak, its bane—the rain—is also its blessing. If it weren't for the rain the hills wouldn't grow nearly as green and the deep blue skies wouldn't be so revered.

WEATHER STATISTICS

According to the **Western Regional Climate Center**, www.wrcc.dri.edu, the average maximum and minimum Fahrenheit temperatures at Sea-Tac Airport, from July 1931 to December 2000, are as follows:

Month	Maximum	Minimum
January	44.6°	34.7°
February	49.0°	36.7°
March	52.2°	38.0°
April	57.5°	41.2°
May	64.1°	46.4°
June	69.4°	51.3°
July	75.0°	54.5°
August	74.7°	54.8°
September	69.4°	51.3°
October	59.4°	45.3°
November	50.4°	39.5°
December	45.4°	35.8°
Annual	59.3°	44.1°

According to WRCC, The average total rainfall/snowfall in inches at Sea-Tac Airport is:

Month	Rain	Snow
January	5.70"	5.1"
February	4.21"	1.7"
March	3.75"	1.3"
April	2.51"	0.1"
May	1.69"	0.0"
June	1.44"	0.0"
July	0.78"	0.0"
August	1.09"	0.0"
September	1.78"	0.0"
October	3.47"	0.0"
November	6.00"	0.8"
December	5.85"	2.6"
Annual	38.27"	11.7"

And the average number of clear days each month at Sea-Tac Airport is (annually the number is 58):

Month	Average Clear Days
January	3
February	3
March	3
April	3
May	4
June	5
July	10
August	9
September	8
October	4
November	2
December	2

AIR POLLUTION

Most of Seattle's air quality problems are seasonal. In summer, the region's traffic congestion, and the emissions from gas engines on boats, jet skis and lawnmowers, create smog or ozone problems. In winter, particles associated with smoke from wood stoves and fireplaces build up. For the most part, however, Seattle meets national standards for clean air.

The **Puget Sound Clean Air Agency,** which is charged with enforcing federal, state and local air quality laws, provides current air quality reports and forecasts at its web site, www.pscleanair.org. You can also view images from its Seattle visibility camera and receive information about local burn bans. The agency recommends the following **tips for improving air quality during the winter:**
- Replace a pre-1988 uncertified wood stove with a clean-burning natural gas or propone stove or fireplace insert, or switch to a cleaner, more efficient EPA-certified pellet or wood stove.
- Burn manufactured logs or pellets.
- Dry firewood at least six months before using it.
- Give your fire lots of air for optimum heat and minimum smoke.
- Drive less.

During the summer:
- Drive less.
- Refuel during cooler evening hours.
- Make sure your gas cap seals properly.
- Wait until temperatures decrease and breezes pick up before mowing the lawn or using gas-powered garden equipment.
- Consider using non-gasoline powered equipment, like a sailboat instead of a motorboat or a manual push mower instead of a gas-powered lawn mower.

EARTHQUAKES

A federal study released in 2000 found that Washington is the nation's second-most-vulnerable state to costly damage from earthquakes. Seattle ranks seventh in the nation among major cities that could expect severe quake damage. Knowing this, it was nonetheless shocking when the 6.8-magnitude Nisqually Earthquake struck the Puget Sound region on February 28, 2001. It was the biggest quake to rattle the area in more than half a century. It caused 410 injuries, and damage statewide was estimated at $2 billion. Experts agree that Seattle was lucky. The quake was buried 32 miles deep, so its effects were muted. Experts also agree that the Nisqually Earthquake was not the "Big One" that the region can expect.

Aside from luck, the secret to surviving a major earthquake is found in the time-proven Boy Scout adage, "be prepared." There are dozens of good books about how to get ready for a seismic onslaught, and plenty of free information available from local, state and federal agencies. You should prepare to be on your own for three to seven days, as it may take that long for emergency crews to restore power, water and telephone service to affected areas.

The Red Cross of Seattle King County recommends a four-step plan to prepare your family for a disaster. First, research possible disasters (the most likely include poisoning, choking, and fire). Learn about your community's warning signals and find out about the disaster plans at your workplace, your children's school and other places where your family spends time. Second, create a disaster plan. Explain the dangers of home safety, fire, severe weather, and earthquakes to children. Pick two places to meet, one just outside your home and one outside your neighborhood. Plan how to take care of your pets and any elderly members of your family. Third, complete this checklist:

- Post emergency telephone numbers near phones (fire, police, ambulance, etc.).
- Teach children how and when to call 9-1-1 or your local emergency medical services number for emergency help.
- Show each family member how and when to turn off the water, gas and electricity at the main switches.
- Get training from the fire department on how to use the fire extinguisher; be sure all family members know how to use it and where it is kept.
- Install smoke detectors on each level of your home, especially near bedrooms.
- Conduct a home hazard hunt.
- Stock emergency supplies and assemble a disaster supplies kit.
- Take a Red Cross first aid and CPR class.
- Determine the best escape routes from your home. Find two ways out of each room.
- Find the safe places in your home for each type of disaster.
- Check your insurance plan for adequate coverage.

Finally, practice and maintain your plan. Keep the items that you would most likely need during an evacuation in an easy-to-carry container, like a large, covered bin with handles, a camping backpack or a duffel bag. The Red Cross of Seattle King County has assembled the following list for your **disaster supplies kit**:

WATER

- Store water in plastic containers such as soft drink bottles. Avoid using containers that will decompose or break, like milk cartons or glass bottles. Store one gallon of water per person per day. Keep at least a three-day supply of water per person.

FOOD

- Store at least a three-day supply of non-perishable food. Select foods that require no refrigeration, preparation or cooking, and little or no water. Recommended items include ready-to-eat canned meats, fruits and vegetables; canned juices; staples like salt, sugar, pepper and spices; high-energy foods; vitamins, food for infants; and comfort or stress foods.

FIRST AID SUPPLIES

- Sterile adhesive bandages in assorted sizes
- Assorted safety pins
- Cleansing agent/soap
- Non-latex gloves (2 pairs)
- Sunscreen
- 2- and 4-inch sterile gauze pads (4 to 6 of each)
- Triangular bandages (3)
- Non-prescription drugs: aspirin or non-aspirin pain reliever, anti-diarrhea medication, antacid, syrup of Ipecac, laxative, activated charcoal (use if advised by the Poison Control Center)
- 2- and 3-inch sterile roller bandages (3 rolls each)
- Scissors
- Tweezers
- Needle
- Moistened towelettes
- Antiseptic
- Thermometer
- Tongue blades (2)
- Tube of petroleum jelly or other lubricant

TOOLS AND SUPPLIES

- Mess kits, or paper plates and cups, and plastic utensils
- Emergency preparedness manual
- Battery-operated radio and extra batteries
- Flashlight and extra batteries
- Cash or traveler's checks, and change
- Non-electric can opener
- Utility knife
- Fire extinguisher
- Tube tent
- Pliers
- Tape
- Compass
- Matches in a waterproof container
- Aluminum foil

- Plastic storage containers
- Signal flare
- Paper, pencil
- Needles and thread
- Medicine dropper
- Shut-off wrench, to turn off household gas and water
- Whistle
- Plastic sheeting
- Map of the area (for locating shelters)
- Sanitation: toilet paper or towelettes, soap or liquid detergent, feminine supplies, personal hygiene items, plastic garbage bags and ties, plastic bucket with tight lid, disinfectant, household chlorine bleach

CLOTHING AND BEDDING

- At least one complete change of clothing and footwear per person
- Sturdy shoes or work boots
- Rain gear
- Blankets or sleeping bags
- Hat and gloves
- Thermal underwear
- Sunglasses

Here are a few additional resources for earthquake preparedness:

- **American Red Cross**, Seattle King County Chapter, 206-323-2345, www.seattleredcross.org
- **City of Seattle Earthquake Information**, www.cityofseattle. net/html/citizen
- **Seattle Emergency Management**, 206-233-5076, www.cityofseat-tle.net/emergency_mgt
- **US Geological Survey Pacific Northwest Earthquake Hazards Program**, http://geohazards.cr.usgs.gov/pacnw
- **Federal Emergency Management Agency**, 202-646-4600, www.fema.gov

One final note: be sure to purchase a homeowner's insurance policy that covers quake damage. Generally, earthquake coverage is not part of a standard policy. See **Finding a Place to Live** for a list of area insurers.

CHOOSING A PLACE OF WORSHIP

FINDING A PLACE OF WORSHIP CAN BE AS SIMPLE AS SOLICITING THE suggestion of a co-worker or neighbor, or as intensely personal and complex as choosing a spouse. If you belong to a congregation in your old hometown, your religious leader might be able to refer you to a kindred congregation in Seattle. If you don't have a referral, pick up a copy of the Saturday edition of *The Seattle Times*, which publishes a "Religion Digest" in the local section. Or check the Yellow Pages under "Churches" and "Synagogues." The phone book listings are arranged by denomination and include sections for nondenominational, interdenominational, and independent churches, as well as metaphysical centers.

These interfaith agencies, representing congregations working together to address hunger, homelessness, and other urban problems, might be able to refer you to a congregation:

- **The Church Council of Greater Seattle**, 4759 15th Avenue NE, 206-525-1213, www.churchcouncilseattle.org
- **The Interfaith Council of Washington**, P.O. Box 53122, Bellevue, 425-455-0706, www.interfaithcouncil.com
- **Washington Association of Churches**, 419 Occidental Avenue South, 206-625-9790,www.thewac.org

Online directories— generally limited to Christian denominations— include **Net Ministries**, http://netministries.org, **Churches Dot Net**, http://churches.net, and **for Ministry**, www.forministry.com. Synagogues serving all branches of Judaism are listed at Jewish Community Online, www.jewish.com.

BUDDHISM

The non-sectarian **Northwest Dharma Association** publishes the *Northwest Dharma News* and organizes multi-tradition events. The organization's web site provides a calendar of Buddhist retreats, classes and events, and links to other Buddhist sites. For more information visit their office at 158 Thomas Street #17, 206-441-6811, or visit www.nwdharma.org.

The **Seattle Buddhist Center**, 3315 Beacon Avenue South, is affiliated with the international movement known as the Friends of the Western Buddhist Order. The center offers shrine rooms for meditation, Dharma book sales and merchandise, a lending library, and conversation areas. Call 206-726-0051 or visit http://members.aol.com/sttlfwbo.

- **Dharmadhatu Buddhist Meditation Center**, 919 East Pike Street, 206-860-4060, www.shambhala.org
- **Rissho Kosei-Kai**, 5511 Martin Luther King Jr. Way South, 206-725-4268
- **Seattle Buddhist Temple**, 1427 South Main Street, 206-329-0800

CHRISTIANITY

If you are looking for a church that is convenient to where you live, start your search at the **Seattle Area Churches and Places of Worship** web site, www.halcyon.com/churches/Seattle, which provides links to area churches, organized by location. The **National Council of the Churches of Christ in the USA**, 212-870-2227, www.ncccusa.org, publishes the *Yearbook of American & Canadian Churches,* a directory that lists thousands of Christian churches in North America. Order one for $40 at 888-870-3325 or browse the directory links at www.electronicchurch.org.

The list of churches below is a sampling of places of worship in Seattle. For a more thorough selection, check the Yellow Pages under "Churches."

HISTORIC AND NOTABLE CHURCHES

- **First African Methodist Episcopal Church**, 1522 14th Avenue, 206-324-3664, www.fameseattle.org; First AME Church Seattle is the oldest congregation in the Pacific Northwest to be established by African-Americans. Founded in 1886, the church is an historical landmark. In August 2001, the church welcomed Bishop Vashti McKenzie, the first woman ever appointed bishop in the AME Church.
- **Mount Zion Baptist Church**, 1634 19th Avenue, 206-322-6500, www.mountzion.net; founded in 1890, Mount Zion Baptist Church is one of the city's oldest continuously active places of worship. It is perhaps best known to those outside its congregation for its annual Martin Luther King Jr. celebration. The church is also active in community out-

reach, and serves as a meeting place for a variety of local organizations and committees.

- **St. James Cathedral**, 804 9th Avenue, 206-622-3559, www.stjames-cathedral.org; recently restored, St. James is the cathedral for the Catholic Archdiocese of Seattle, as well as an active parish church for the Capitol Hill community. Check the schedule for outstanding classical musical events throughout the year, including a popular New Year's Eve gala.
- **Seattle First United Methodist Church**, 811 5th Avenue, 206-622-7278, www.firstchurchseattle.org; recognizable for its terra cotta dome, the First United Methodist Church is a downtown sanctuary that seats approximately 1,000 worshippers, though the current congregation numbers only about 300. The church houses emergency shelters and lends its rooms for various rehearsals and support groups. Look for it in the shadow of the 76-story Bank of America Tower.
- **Temple of The Church of Jesus Christ of Latter-day Saints**, 2808 148th SE, Bellevue, 425-643-5144; the 110,000-square-foot temple attracted its share of controversy when it was built in the late 1970s, from environmentalists who balked at its size and location, to women's rights activists who opposed the church's stand on the Equal Rights Amendment. Today, the temple's lofty gold leaf statue of the angel Moroni is a familiar local beacon.

CATHOLIC

BYZANTINE CATHOLIC

- **St. John Chrysostom Byzantine Catholic Church**, 1305 South Lander Street, 206-329-9219

ROMAN CATHOLIC

The **Archdiocese of Seattle** encompasses all of western Washington, and includes more than 160 parishes and missions that serve over half a million Catholics. In addition to managing more than 60 ministries and programs that serve the Catholic community, the Archdiocese runs a library/media center and publishes the *Catholic Northwest Progress*. The Archdiocese offices are located at 910 Marion Street. For more information, call 206-382-4560, 800-869-7027, or visit www.seattlearch.org.

- **Holy Family Church**, 9622 20th SW, 206-767-6220
- **Our Lady of Fatima Church**, 3218 West Barrett Street, 206-283-1456
- **Our Lady of Guadalupe Church**, 7000 35th Avenue SW, 206-935-0358
- **St. James Cathedral**, 804 9th Avenue, 206-622-3559, www.stjames-cathedral.org

- **St. Margaret's Church**, 3221 14th Avenue West, 206-282-1804
- **St. Peter Catholic Church**, 2807 15th Avenue South, 206-324-2290

EASTERN ORTHODOX

- **Russian Orthodox Cathedral of St. Nicholas**, 1714 13th Avenue, 206-322-9387
- **St. Demetrios Greek Orthodox Church**, 2100 Boyer Avenue East, 206-325-4347, www.saintdemetrios.com
- **St. Nectarios American Orthodox Church**, 10300 Ashworth Avenue North, 206-522-4471

PROTESTANT

AFRICAN METHODIST EPISCOPAL

- **First AME Church**, 1522 14th Avenue, 206-324-3664
- **Primm Tabernacle AME Church**, 4455 South Brandon Street, 206-723-2142
- **Walker Chapel AME Church**, 800 28th Avenue South, 206-325-8468

AFRICAN METHODIST EPISCOPAL ZION

- **Catherine Memorial AME Zion Church**, 5943 Martin Luther King Jr. Way South, 206-723-7973
- **Ebenezer AME Zion Church**, 1716 23rd Avenue, 206-322-6620

ANGLICAN

- **St. Barnabas Anglican Church**, 2340 North 155th Street, Shoreline, 206-365-6565
- **St. Paul Anglican Church**, 1040 NE 95th Street, 206-526-9020

APOSTOLIC

- **The Apostolic Faith**, 7420 9th Avenue NE, 206-522-1350
- **Bethel Christian Church of the Apostolic Faith**, 200 24th Avenue South, 206-324-2141
- **Grace Apostolic Temple**, 6718 Martin Luther King Jr. Way South, 206-723-5433
- **Jesus the Rock**, 555 16th Avenue, 206-325-4358

ASSEMBLIES OF GOD

- **Ballard Assembly of God**, 2051 NW 61st Street, 206-784-2064, www.ballard-aog.org
- **Calvary Temple Seattle**, 6810 8th Avenue NE, 206-525-7473, www.ctseattle.com
- **Latin American Assemblies of God Temple El Redentor**, 5500 17th Avenue South, 206-768-1868
- **North Seattle Christian Fellowship**, 12345 8th Avenue NE, 206-367-6500, www.nseacf.com
- **Queen Anne Christian Center**, 1716 2nd Avenue North, 206-283-6944
- **Seattle Outreach Ministries of the Assemblies of God**, 4402 South Graham Street, 206-722-3319
- **Westwood Christian Assembly**, 9252 16th Avenue SW, 206-763-0585

BAPTIST

- **Fellowship Baptist Church**, 817 South 3rd Street, 206-227-0781
- **Queen Anne Baptist Church**, 2011 1st Avenue North, 206-282-7744, www.qabc.org
- **Rosehill Missionary Baptist Church**, 7550 Martin Luther King Jr. Way South, 206-721-0426

BAPTIST AMERICAN

- **Chinese Baptist Church**, 5801 Beacon Avenue South, 206-725-6363, www.geocities.com/Athens/2052/cbcindex
- **Damascus Baptist Church**, 5237 Rainier Avenue South, 206-725-9310
- **Fremont Baptist Church**, 717 North 36th Street, 206-632-7994, www.fremontbaptist.org
- **Wedgwood Community Church**, 8201 30th Avenue NE, 206-522-5778

BAPTIST, GENERAL CONFERENCE

- **Ballard Baptist Church**, 2004 NW 63rd Street, 206-784-1554
- **Dunlap Baptist Church**, 8445 Rainier Avenue South, 206-723-2676
- **Haller Lake Baptist Church**, 14054 Wallingford Avenue North, 206-364-1811

CHRISTIAN SCIENCE

- **First Church of Christ-Scientist**, 16th Avenue East and East Denny Way, 206-324-3020
- **Third Church of Christ-Scientist**, 1707 NE 50th Street, 206-522-5755
- **Sixth Church of Christ-Scientist**, 2656 42nd Avenue SW, 206-932-6004
- **Seventh Church of Christ-Scientist**, 2555 8th Avenue West, 206-282-9255
- **Thirteenth Church of Christ-Scientist**, 3500 NE 125th Street, 206-362-7646

CHURCH OF CHRIST

- **Church of Christ Iglesia Ni Cristo**, 6020 Rainier Avenue South, 206-723-0346
- **Church of Christ North Seattle**, 13315 20th Avenue NE, 206-367-9232
- **Church of Christ West Seattle**, 4220 SW 100th Street, 206-938-0212
- **Holgate Street Church of Christ**, 2600 South Holgate Street, 206-324-5530
- **Madison Park Church of Christ**, 1115 19th Avenue, 206-324-6775

CHURCH OF GOD IN CHRIST

- **Berean Church of God in Christ**, 3417 Rainier Avenue South, 206-725-0745
- **Greater Glory Church of God in Christ**, 6419 Martin Luther King Jr. Way South, 206-723-6419, www.gcogic.org
- **Madison Temple Church of God in Christ**, 2239 East Madison Street, 206-323-4900
- **Survival Church of God in Christ**, 8459 50th Avenue South, 206-725-9366

CHURCH OF JESUS CHRIST OF LATTER-DAY SAINTS (MORMON)

- **Greenwood Ward**, 102 North 132nd Street, 206-364-1420
- **Seattle First Ward**, 2415 31st Avenue West, 206-285-9744
- **Seattle University Second Ward**, 3925 15th Avenue NE, 206-633-2955

COVENANT

- **Interbay Covenant Church**, 3233 15th Avenue West, 206-283-9660

EPISCOPAL

- **Downtown Trinity Episcopal Church**, 609 8th Avenue, 206-624-5337
- **St. Andrew's Episcopal Church**, 111 NE 80th Street, 206-523-7476
- **St. John the Baptist Episcopal Church**, 3050 California Avenue SW, 206-937-4545
- **St. Mark's Episcopal Cathedral**, 1245 10th Avenue East, 206-323-0300
- **St. Stephen's Episcopal Church**, 4805 NE 45th Street, 206-522-7144, www.st.stephens-seattle.org

EVANGELICAL

- **Evangelical Chinese Church**, 651 NW 81st Street, 206-789-6380
- **Maple Leaf Evangelical Church**, 1059 NE 96th Street, 206-525-3707
- **Medhane-Alem Evangelical Church** (Ethiopian), 1300 East Olive Way, 206-720-0181

FRIENDS (QUAKERS)

- **Friends Memorial Church**, 7740 24th Avenue NE, 206-525-8800
- **University Friends Meeting**, 4001 9th Avenue NE, 206-547-6449

INTERDENOMINATIONAL

- **Church of Mary Magdalene**, 811 5th Avenue, 206-621-8474
- **Metro Christian Church**, 153 14th Avenue, 206-720-1629

JEHOVAH'S WITNESSES

- **Central and Spanish Congregation**, 333 19th Avenue East, 206-325-4192
- **Ballard and North Park Congregation**, 9240 6th Avenue NW, 206-783-9940
- **Queen Anne Congregation**, 3626 34th Avenue West, 206-285-7986
- **Rainier Congregation**, 5933 39th Avenue South, 206-722-1250
- **Southwest Cambridge and White Center Congregation**, 2121 SW Cambridge Street, 206-762-5486

LUTHERAN

ELCA
- **Bethel Chinese Lutheran Church**, 6553 40th Avenue NE, 206-524-7631
- **Central Lutheran Church of the Holy Trinity**, 1710 11th Avenue, 206-322-7500
- **Crown Lutheran Church**, 1501 NW 90th Street, 206-784-1930
- **Gethsemane Lutheran Church**, 911 Stewart Street, 206-682-3620, www.urbanfaith.org
- **Luther Memorial Church**, 13047 Greenwood Avenue North, 206-364-2510
- **Queen Anne Evangelical Lutheran Church**, 2400 8th Avenue West, 206-284-1960, www.qaelc.org
- **University Lutheran Church**, 1604 NE 50th Street, 206-525-7074

MISSOURI SYNOD
- **Beacon Lutheran Church**, 1720 South Forest Street, 206-322-0251
- **Hope Lutheran Church**, 4456 42nd Avenue SW, 206-937-9330
- **Messiah Lutheran Church**, 7050 35th Avenue NE, 206-524-0024, www.messiahseattle.org
- **Zion Evangelical Lutheran Church**, 7109 Aurora Avenue North, 782-6734

WELS
- **Grace Lutheran Church**, 11501 Phinney Avenue North, 206-363-8551

METHODIST

CHRISTIAN METHODIST EPISCOPAL
- **Curry Temple**, 172 23rd Avenue, 206-325-9344

FREE METHODIST
- **Ballard Free Methodist Church**, 1460 NW 73rd Street, 206-784-6111
- **First Free Methodist Church**, 3200 3rd Avenue West, 206-281-2240, www.ffmc.org
- **Rainier Avenue Free Methodist Church**, 5900 Rainier Avenue South, 206-722-5616

UNITED METHODIST
- **Beacon United Methodist Church**, 7301 Beacon Avenue South, 206-722-5042

- **Green Lake United Methodist Church**, 6415 1st Avenue NE, 206-526-2900
- **Haller Lake United Methodist Church**, 13055 1st Avenue NE, 206-362-5383, www.hallerlakeumc.org
- **Magnolia United Methodist Church**, 2836 34th Avenue West, 206-282-3266
- **Seaview United Methodist Church**, 4620 SW Graham Street, 206-932-7609
- **Trinity United Methodist Church**, 6512 23rd Avenue NW, 206-784-2227, www.gbgm-umc.org/trinityumcseattle

NAZARENE

- **Ballard Church of the Nazarene**, 6541 Jones Avenue NW, 206-784-1418
- **Beacon Hill Church of the Nazarene**, 4352 15th Avenue South, 206-762-2136, www.raycast.com/users/gerald/beaconhill
- **North Seattle Church of the Nazarene**, 13130 5th Avenue NE, 206-367-5955
- **Seattle First Church of the Nazarene**, 4401 2nd Avenue NE, 206-632-4560
- **West Seattle Church of the Nazarene**, 4201 SW Juneau Street, 206-932-4581

NON-DENOMINATIONAL

- **Faith Bible Church**, 128 18th Avenue, 206-322-8044, www.fbcseattle.org
- **Mars Hill Fellowship**, 7758 Earl Avenue NW, 206-706-6641, www.marshill.fm
- **Vineyard Christian Fellowship of Seattle**, 4142 Brooklyn Avenue NE, 206-547-4354, www.seattlevineyard.org
- **Westside Church**, 2601 NW Market Street, Ballard, 206-781-5154, www.westsidechurch.com

PENTECOSTAL

- **Bethany Temple Church**, 1122 26th Avenue South, 206-328-1816
- **Full Gospel Pentecostal Federated Church**, 5071 Delridge Way SW, 206-935-1511
- **Holy Ground Pentecostal Temple**, 4515 Rainier Avenue South, 206-723-5260

PRESBYTERIAN

- **Beacon Hill Presbyterian Church**, 1625 South Columbian Way, 206-762-0870
- **Bethany Presbyterian Church**, 1818 Queen Anne Avenue North, 206-284-2222
- **Bethel Presbyterian Church**, 11002 Greenwood Avenue North, 206-362-3600
- **Japanese Presbyterian Church**, 1801 24th Avenue South, 206-323-5990
- **Korean Community Presbyterian Church**, 3902 Woodland Park North, 206-547-7005, www.seattlenewlife.org
- **Northminster Presbyterian Church**, 7706 25th NW, 206-783-3402, www.northwestminsterpres.org
- **Seattle First Presbyterian Church**, 1013 8th Avenue, 206-624-0644, www.firstpres.org
- **West Side Presbyterian Church**, 3601 California Avenue SW, 206-935-4477, www.wspc.org

SEVENTH-DAY ADVENTIST

- **Ballard Seventh-day Adventist Church**, 2054 NW 61st Street, 206-783-1661, www.tagnet.org/ballardsda
- **Green Lake Seventh-day Adventist Church**, 6350 East Green Lake Way North, 206-522-1330
- **Seward Park English and Japanese Seventh-day Adventist Church**, 5200 South Orcas Street, 206-725-5253
- **West Seattle Seventh-day Adventist Church**, 7901 35th Avenue SW, 206-932-4211

UNITARIAN UNIVERSALIST

- **University Unitarian Church**, 6556 35th Avenue NE, 206-525-8400, www.uuchurch.org

UNITED CHURCH OF CHRIST

- **Admiral Congregational United Church of Christ**, 4320 SW Hill Street, 206-932-2928
- **Broadview Community United Church of Christ**, 325 North 125th Street, 206-363-8060
- **Prospect United Church of Christ**, 1919 East Prospect Street, 206-322-6030

UNITY

* **Seattle Unity Church**, 200 8th Avenue North, 206-622-8475, www.seattleunity.org

WESLEYAN

* **Crown Hill Wesleyan Church**, 9204 11th Avenue NW, 206-783-6400

HINDUISM

The **Vedanta Society of Western Washington** is a branch of the Ramakrishna Order of India, which was established by Swami Vivekananda in 1894. The main temple and bookshop are located at 2716 Broadway East, on Capitol Hill, and the Tapovan Retreat is at 23217 27th Avenue NE, in Arlington, north of Seattle. On Sundays at 11 a.m., the society presents a lecture on the Vedanta philosophy and religion. A second class is conducted Tuesdays at 7:30 p.m. For more information, call 206-323-1228 or visit www.vedanta-seattle.org.

ISLAM

The **Islamic Educational Center** of Seattle is located near the University of Washington at 1315 40th Street North. Membership in the non-profit organization, which serves Puget Sound-area Muslims, is $30 per year. For details, call 206-547-1990 or visit www.ershad.org.
* **Islamic (Idriss) Mosque**, 1420 NE Northgate Way, 206-363-3013
* **Jamaatul Ikhlas**, 1350 East Fir Street, 206-322-6246
* **Southwest Seattle Islamic Center**, 1022 SW Henderson, 206-763-2239

JUDAISM

The **Jewish Federation of Greater Seattle**, 2031 3rd Avenue, which coordinates and funds Jewish projects, provides leadership, and supports educational programs, is a substantial resource for the Jewish community. The organization's comprehensive web site, www.jewishInseattle.org, provides links to Jewish resources, lists holidays and Shabbat candle-lighting occasions, and offers reprints of the *Guide to Jewish Washington*, which is published each year by Seattle's only Jewish newspaper, the *Jewish Transcript*. For more information, call 206-443-5400.

The **Samuel and Althea Stroum Jewish Community Center of Greater Seattle** promotes intergenerational Jewish events, informal education programs and activities, and social services, including a childcare center and senior adult programs. The JCC's primary facility on Mercer Island, 3801 East Mercer Way, features a state-of-the-art fitness center. The Center also has facilities at 8606 35th Avenue NE, at the Seattle Hebrew Academy, 1617 Interlaken Drive NE, and at 15749 NE 4th Street in Bellevue. Call 206-232-7115 or visit www.sjcc.org.

REFORM

- **Temple Beth Am**, 2632 NE 80th Street, 206-525-0915
- **Temple de Hirsch Sinai**, 1511 East Pike Street, 206-323-8486, http://tdhs-nw.org
- **Temple B'nai Torah** 15727 NE 4th Street, Bellevue, 425-603-9677, www.templebnaitorah.org, is a newly constructed synagogue of contemporary design. The temple has over 900 households in attendance, and over 650 children enrolled in its religious school. Temple B'nai Torah hosts special events for prospective members.

CONSERVATIVE

- **Congregation Beth Shalom**, 6800 35th Avenue NE, 206-524-0075

ORTHODOX

- **Bikur Cholim-Machzikay Hadath**, 5145 South Morgan Street, 206-721-0970, www.ou.org/network/shuls/bikurcholim
- **Chabad-Lubavitch Chabad House**, 4541 19th Avenue NE, 206-527-1411
- **Congregation Ezra Bessaroth**, 5217 South Brandon Street, 206-722-5500, www.ezrabessaroth.org
- **Emanuel Congregation** (Modern Orthodox), 3412 NE 65th Street, 206-525-1055

GAY & LESBIAN

Here is a sampling of gay-friendly Seattle area congregations:

CHRISTIAN

- **Broadview United Church of Christ**, 325 North 125th Street, 206-363-8060, www.religion-research.org/broadview
- **Central Lutheran Church**, 1710 11th Avenue, 206-322-7500

- **Dignity Seattle**, 206-325-7314, www.dignityusa.org, is the country's largest and most progressive organization of gay, lesbian, bisexual and transgender Catholics.
- **Gethsemane Lutheran Church**, 911 Stewart Street, 206-682-3620, www.urbanfaith.org
- **Grace Gospel Chapel**, 2052 NW 64th Street, 206-784-8495
- **Keystone Congregational Church**, 5019 Keystone Place North, 206-632-6021
- **St. Joseph Catholic Church**, 700 18th Avenue East, 206-324-2522
- **St. Patrick's Catholic Church**, 2702 Broadway East, 206-329-2960, http://stpats.kendra.com
- **St. Mark's Episcopal Cathedral**, 1245 10th Avenue East, 206-323-0300, www.saintmarks.org
- **Seattle First Baptist Church**, 1111 Harvard Avenue, 206-325-6051, www.seattlefirstbaptist.org
- **Ravenna United Methodist Church**, 5751 33rd Avenue NE, 206-525-7988, www.gbgm-umc.org/ravenna
- **Trinity United Methodist Church**, 6512 23rd Avenue NW, 206-784-2227, www.gbgm-umc.org/trinityumcseattle
- **University Baptist Church**, 4554 12th Avenue NE, 206-632-5188

JEWISH

- **Congregation Tikvah Chadashah**, P.O. Box 2731, 206-329-2590

RELIGIOUS STUDIES

The following colleges and universities offer graduate degree programs in religious studies:
- **Seattle University**, Theology and Ministry, 206-296-5900, www.seattleu.edu
- **University of Washington**, Jackson School of International Studies, Comparative Religion Program, 206-543-7320, www.washington.edu
- **Western Reformed Seminaries**, Pastoral Studies, 253-272-0417, www.wrs.edu

WHEN YOU'RE NEW IN TOWN, VOLUNTEERING MAY PROVIDE the perfect opportunity to get acquainted with the community and to make new friends in the process. In addition to meeting people with similar interests, you'll be helping organizations that are often short on cash and resources. Seattle has many charitable and philanthropic organizations that offer a variety of services, from the basics of food and clothing, to counseling, to funding education or medical research.

VOLUNTEER PLACEMENT

If you're not sure where to begin, the following volunteer placement services can point you in the right direction:

- **Seattle Works**, 2123 East Union Street, 206-324-0808, www.seattleworks.org
- **United Way of King County**, 107 Cherry Street, 206-461-3655, www.uwkc.org
- **Volunteers of America**, 6559 35th Avenue NE, 206-523-3565, www.volunteersofamerica.org

ORGANIZATIONS

Volunteer opportunities also can be found in the Yellow Pages and in newspaper advertisements. The following is a sample of possibilities, listed by category:

AIDS

- **Bailey-Boushay House**, 2720 East Madison Street, 206-322-5300, www.virginiamason.org/dbbailey-boushay
- **Lifelong AIDS Alliance**, 1002 East Seneca, 206-329-6923, www.lifelongaidsalliance.org

- **People of Color Against AIDS Network**, 607 19th Avenue East, 206-322-7061, www.pocaan.org

ALCOHOL AND DRUG DEPENDENCY

- **Salvation Army Adult Rehabilitation Center**, 1000 4th Avenue South, 206-587-0503, www.nwarmy.org
- **Stonewall Recovery Services**, 430 Broadway East, 206-461-4546, www.stonewallrecovery.org

ANIMALS

- **The Humane Society for Seattle/King County**, 13212 SE Eastgate Way, Bellevue, 425-641-0080, www.seattlehumane.org
- **Progressive Animal Welfare Society (PAWS)**, 15305 44th Avenue West, Lynnwood, 425-787-2500, www.paws.org
- **Seattle Animal Control**, 2061 15th Avenue West, 206-386-PETS, www.ci.seattle.wa.us/rca/animal

CHILDREN

- **Big Brothers Big Sisters of King County**, 1600 South Graham Street, 206-763-9060, 877-700-2447, www.bigsandlittles.org
- **Big Brothers Big Sisters of Pierce County**, 1501 Pacific Avenue, Tacoma, 253-396-9630, www.bigsandlittles.org
- **Boys and Girls Clubs of King County**, 107 Cherry Street #200, 206-461-3890, www.positiveplace.org
- **Catholic Community Services**, 100 23rd Avenue South, 206-325-5162, www.ccsww.org
- **Childhaven**, 316 Broadway, 206-624-6477, www.childhaven.org
- **Children's Home Society of Washington**, 3300 NE 65th Street, 206-695-3200, www.chs-wa.org

CRIME PREVENTION

- **Seattle Police Department Volunteer Alliance**, 206-625-5011, www.cityofseattle.net/police

CULTURAL IDENTITY

- **Chinese Information and Service Center**, 409 Maynard Avenue South Suite 203, 206-624-5633, www.cisc-seattle.org

- **El Centro de la Raza**, 2524 16th Avenue South, 206-329-9442, www.elcentrodelaraza.com
- **Filipino Youth Activities**, 810 18th Avenue, Room 108, 206-461-4870, www.fya-pinoy.org
- **Japanese American Citizens League**, 316 Maynard Avenue South, 206-622-4098, www.jaclseattle.org
- **Jewish Family Service**, 1601 16th Avenue, 206-461-3240; 606 110th NE, Bellevue, 425-451-8512
- **Jewish Federation of Greater Seattle**, 2031 3rd Avenue, 206-443-5400, www.jewishinseattle.org
- **Korean Community Counseling Center**, 302 North 78th Street, 206-784-5691
- **Seattle Indian Center**, 611 12th Avenue South, 206-329-8700
- **Seattle Samoan Center**, 12629 16th Avenue South, 206-835-9440
- **Society of African Americans USA**, 1218 East Cherry Street, 206-860-0531
- **United Indians of All Tribes Foundation**, Daybreak Star Art & Cultural Center, Discovery Park, 206-285-4425, www.unitedindians.com
- **Urban League of Metropolitan Seattle**, 105 14th Avenue, 206-461-3792, www.urbanleague.org

CULTURE AND THE ARTS

- **Business Volunteers for the Arts**, 1301 5th Avenue, Suite 2400, 206-389-7272, www.bvaseattle.org

DISABILITY ASSISTANCE

- **Catholic Community Services**, 100 23rd Avenue South, 206-325-5162, www.ccsww.org
- **Community Services for the Blind and Partially Sighted**, 9709 3rd Avenue NE, 206-525-5556, www.csbps.com
- **Deaf-Blind Service Center**, 2366 Eastlake Avenue East, 206-323-9178, http://mytown.koz.com/community/dbsc
- **Easter Seal Society of Washington**, 521 2nd Avenue West, 800-678-5708, www.seals.org

ENVIRONMENT

- **Cascadia Quest**, 7400 Sand Point Way NE, Building 30, 206-322-9296, www.cascadiaquest.org
- **Earth Ministry**, 6512 23rd Avenue NW, Suite 317, 206-632-2426, www.earthministry.org

- **Earth Share of Washington**, 1402 3rd Avenue, 206-622-9840, www.esw.org
- **Friends of the Earth**, 6512 23rd Avenue NW, Suite 320, 206-297-9460, www.foe.org
- **Greenpeace**, 4649 Sunnyside Avenue North, 206-632-4326, www.greenpeaceusa.org
- **Seattle Audubon Society**, 8050 35th Avenue NE, 206-523-8243, www.seattleaudubon.org
- **Sierra Club, Cascade Chapter**, 8511 15th Avenue, NE, 206-523-2147, www.cascadechapter.org

FOOD DISTRIBUTION

- **Beacon Avenue Food Bank**, 6230 Beacon Avenue South, 206-722-5105
- **Bothell Food Bank**, 18220 96th Avenue NE, Bothell, 425-485-6521
- **Des Moines Area Food Bank**, 22225 9th Avenue South, Des Moines, 206-878-2660, www.ci.tukwila.wa.us
- **Downtown Food Bank**, 1531 Western Avenue, 206-626-6462, www.pikeplacemarket.org/learn/foundation/foodbank
- **Edmonds Food Bank**, 828 Caspers Street, Edmonds, 425-778-5833
- **Federal Way Food Bank**, 1200 South 336th Street, Federal Way, 253-838-6810
- **Food Lifeline**, 1702 NE 150th Street, Shoreline, 800-404-7543, www.foodlifeline.org
- **Highline Food Bank**, 18300 4th Avenue South, 206-433-9900
- **Issaquah Food Bank**, 179 1st Avenue SE, Issaquah, 425-392-4123, www.scn.org/civic/ivfcb
- **Kent Community Service Center Food Bank**, 525 North 4th, Kent, 253-856-5180
- **Kirkland Multi-Service Center**, 302 1st Street, Kirkland, 425-889-7880
- **Lynnwood Food Bank**, 5326 176th Street SW, Lynnwood, 425-745-1635
- **Northwest Harvest**, 711 Cherry Street, 206-625-0755, www.northwestharvest.org
- **Redmond Food Bank**, 16225 NE 87th Street, Redmond, 425-882-0241
- **University District Food Bank**, 4731 15th Avenue NE, 206-523-7060, www.scn.org/civic/udfb
- **West Seattle Food Bank**, 3518 SW Genesee Street, 206-932-9023, www.scn.org/civic/westseattlefoodbank

GAY AND LESBIAN

- **Freedom Day Committee**, 1122 East Pike Street #969, 206-324-0405, www.seattlepride.org

- **Lambert House**, 1818 15th Avenue, 206-322-0415, www.lamberthouse.org
- **Lesbian Resource Center**, 2214 South Jackson, 206-322-3953, www.lrc.net
- **The Pride Foundation**, 1801 12th Avenue, 206-323-3318
- **Stonewall Recovery Services**, 430 Broadway East, 206-461-4546, www.stonewallrecovery.org

HEALTH AND HOSPITALS

Most hospitals welcome volunteers—just give the nearest one a call. For specific health issues, contact one of the following organizations:

- **Alzheimer's Association**, Western and Central Washington State Chapter, 12721 30th Avenue NE Suite 101, 206-363-5500, www.alzwa.org
- **American Cancer Society**, 2120 1st Avenue North, 206-283-1152; 1001 North Broadway, Everett, 425-339-4141, www.cancer.org
- **American Heart Association**, 4414 Woodland Park Avenue North, 206-562-6718, www.americanheart.org/northwest
- **American Lung Association**, 2625 3rd Avenue, 206-441-5100, www.alaw.org
- **March of Dimes Birth Defects Foundation**, 1904 3rd Avenue, Suite 230, 206-624-1373, www.modimes.org
- **National Multiple Sclerosis Society**, Greater Washington Chapter, 192 Nickerson Street Suite 100, 206-284-4236, www.nmsswas.org

HOMELESS SERVICES

- **Family Services**, 615 2nd Avenue, Suite 150, 206-461-3883
- **Jubilee Women's Center**, 620 18th Avenue East, 206-324-1244, www.jwcenter.org
- **Millionair Club**, 2515 Western Avenue, 206-728-5600, www.millionairclub.org
- **Sacred Heart Shelter**, 232 Warren Avenue North, 206-285-7489, http://sacredheart.catholiccharitiesseattlearch.org
- **Salvation Army**, 811 Maynard Avenue South, 206-621-0145, www.nwarmy.org
- **Strand Helpers**, 5747 Martin Luther King Jr. Way South, 206-723-6082
- **Union Gospel Mission**, Men's Shelter, 318 2nd Avenue Extension South, 206-622-5177; Women and Family Shelter, 520 South King Street, 206-628-2008; Youth Reach Out Center, 3800 South Othello, 206-725-2432, www.ugm.org

HUMAN SERVICES

- **American Red Cross**, 1900 25th Avenue South, 206-323-2345, www.seattleredcross.org
- **Catholic Community Services**, 100 23rd Avenue South, 206-325-5162, www.ccsww.org
- **Emergency Feeding Program**, 4620 South Findlay Street, 206-723-0647; 2650 148th Avenue SE, Bellevue, 425-562-0698
- **Habitat for Humanity**, 306 Westlake Avenue North, 206-292-5240, www.seattle-habitat.org
- **Salvation Army**, 1101 Pike Street, 206-442-9944, www.nwarmy.org
- **Seattle Goodwill**, 1400 South Lane Street, 206-329-1000, www.seattlegoodwill.org

LEGAL AID

- **American Civil Liberties Union of Washington**, 705 2nd Avenue, 206-624-2180, www.aclu-wa.org
- **Catholic Community Services**, 100 23rd Avenue South, 206-325-5162; 14044 NE 8th Street, Bellevue, 800-872-3204, www.ccsww.org
- **Volunteer Legal Services**, 900 4th Avenue, 206-623-0281
- **Washington State Bar Association**, 2101 4th Avenue, 800-945-WSBA, 206-443-WSBA

LITERACY

- **King County Library System**, 960 Newport Way NW, Issaquah, 425-369-3200, www.kcls.org
- **Literacy Action Center**, 8016 Greenwood Avenue North, 206-782-2050
- **Literacy Council of Seattle**, 811 5th Avenue, 206-233-9720
- **Washington Literacy**, 220 Nickerson Street, 206-284-4399, 800-323-2550, www.waliteracy.org

MEN'S SERVICES

- **Dads Against Discrimination**, 1106 NE 198th, 206-623-DADS, www.dadsusa.com

POLITICS—ELECTORAL

- **Freedom Socialist Party**, Bush Asia Center, 409 Maynard Avenue South, #201, 206-682-0990, www.socialism.com
- **International Socialist Organization**, 206-292-8809, www.internationalsocialist.org
- **King County Democratic Central Committee**, 616 1st Avenue Suite 350, 206-622-9157, www.kcdems.org
- **Labor Party**, 206-382-5712, www.igc.org/lpa
- **League of Women Voters of Washington**, 1402 18th Avenue, 206-329-4848, www.scn.org/civic/lwvseattle
- **Libertarian Party of Washington State**, 10115 Greenwood Avenue North #297, 206-329-5669, www.lpws.org
- **King County Republican Party**, 1305 Republican Street, 206-467-1996, www.kcgop.org

POLITICS—SOCIAL

- **American Veterans Association**, 915 2nd Avenue, 206-220-6244, www.amvets.org
- **Blacks in Government**, 810 3rd Avenue, 206-624-4870
- **Peace & Justice Alliance**, 5828 Roosevelt Way NE, 206-527-8050, www.peaceaction.gen.wa.us

REFUGEE ASSISTANCE

- **Lutheran Refugee Program**, 4130 University Way NE, 206-547-5306
- **Refugee Women's Alliance**, 3004 South Alaska Street, 206-721-0243, www.rewa.org

SENIOR SERVICES

- **Catholic Community Services**, 100 23rd Avenue South, 206-325-5162, www.ccsww.org
- **Central Area Senior Center**, 500 30th Avenue South, 206-726-4926
- **Federal Way Senior Center**, 4016 South 352nd, Auburn, 253-838-3604
- **Greenwood Senior Center**, 525 North 85th Street, 206-297-0875
- **Highline Senior Center**, 1210 SW 136th Street, Burien, 206-244-3686
- **Issaquah Valley Senior Center**, 105 2nd Avenue NE, Issaquah, 425-392-2381

- **Lynnwood Senior Center**, 5800 198th Street SW, Suite K, Lynnwood, 425-670-6401
- **Northshore Senior Center**, 10201 East Riverside Drive, Bothell, 425-487-2441
- **Northwest Senior Activity Center**, 5429 32nd Avenue NW, 206-461-7811
- **Pike Market Senior Center**, 1931 1st Avenue, 206-728-2773
- **Senior Center of West Seattle**, 4217 SW Oregon Street, 206-932-4044
- **Senior Services of Seattle/King County**, 1601 2nd Avenue, Suite 800, 206-448-5757, www.seniorservices.org
- **Shoreline Senior Activity Center**, 18560 1stAvenue NE, 206-365-1536
- **Southeast Seattle Senior Center**, 4655 South Holly Street, 206-722-0317

WOMEN'S SERVICES

- **Center for the Prevention of Sexual and Domestic Violence**, 2400 North 45th Street, #10, 206-634-1903, www.cpsdv.org
- **Catherine Booth House**, Salvation Army Shelter for Abused Women, 206-324-9943, www.nwarmy.org
- **Junior League of Seattle**, 4119 East Madison Street, 206-324-3638, http://jrleagueseattle.org
- **New Beginnings for Battered Women and Their Children**, 206-783-4520
- **Refugee Women's Alliance**, 3004 South Alaska Street, 206-721-0243, www.rewa.org

YOUTH

- **Central Area Youth Association**, 119 23rd Avenue, 206-322-6640, www.seattle-caya.org
- **Central Youth and Family Services**, 1901 Martin Luther King Jr. Way South, 206-322-7676
- **Southwest Youth and Family Services**, 8808 Delridge Way SW, 206-764-1933, www.bulldogbeach.com/swyfs
- **University District Youth Center**, 4516 15th Avenue NE, 206-526-2992

GETTING AROUND BY CAR

DESPITE EFFORTS BY THE CITY AND KING COUNTY TO REDUCE THE number of single-occupancy vehicles on the road, I-5 and both bridges to the Eastside are always crowded during rush hour. According to the 2000 census, the number of people in the state of Washington commuting an hour or more to work increased 73% from 1990 to 2000! Despite this knowledge, many Seattle residents still drive everywhere—to work, to church, to the grocery store. There *are* alternatives. Buses, carpools and ride-sharing programs are viable options for many residents. The city offers incentives to businesses that encourage their employees to share the commute, walk or bicycle to work—something you may want to investigate at your office. If you must drive, here are a few tips for making your commute a little easier.

- **Metered ramps** are freeway on-ramps equipped with traffic lights to control the flow of traffic. Most in-city ramps to I-5 are now metered, although the lights operate only during high-volume hours. Metered ramps usually have an H.O.V. (high occupancy vehicle) on-ramp lane, which allows carpool vehicles on without stopping.

- **Traffic reports** are available on all major radio stations during rush hour, and on news radio station KIRO 710 AM every 10 minutes weekday mornings and afternoons. These reports can be invaluable once you've identified a few routes to your usual destinations. Or call the **Washington State Department of Transportation (WSDOT)** traffic line at 206-DOT-HIWY (206-368-4499) to get information on current traffic conditions, including traffic flow statistics and accident and construction reports; or check local freeways at www.wsdot.wa.gov/PugetSoundTraffic. Site features include traffic flow maps and live camera shots of area freeways. Transportation trouble spots are listed on the

Seattle Post-Intelligencer's web site at http://seattlep-i.nwsource.com/transportation. This is also the site to visit for more information about local transportation issues and concerns, including a question/answer section called "Getting There."

MAJOR EXPRESSWAYS

As you get to know Seattle, you'll establish alternatives to the major freeways, highways and thoroughfares. Until then, here are some of the **main arteries**:

- The main north-south freeway is **Interstate 5**. Running smack through the middle of the city, this freeway is both a blessing and a curse for those living near it. If you're running errands, and if I-5 is moving at all, it is usually the quickest way to other neighborhoods in the city. However, if you're more than ten minutes from the freeway, it's often quicker to take local streets across town.
- Another north-south thoroughfare in the city is **Highway 99** (Aurora Avenue), which parallels I-5 as far as the Seattle Center, then cuts under the city and follows the waterfront. The section of Highway 99 along the waterfront is a stacked freeway known as "the viaduct." North of the Green Lake area, Highway 99 can be fairly slow because of the traffic lights. South of the lake and through the downtown area Highway 99 is a reliable alternative to I-5, especially for those coming from the Greenwood, Phinney Ridge, Fremont or Wallingford neighborhoods. If you travel to the airport often from any of these neighborhoods, there is a shortcut to the airport, which includes Highway 99, Highway 509, and then Highway 518. This can save you 30 minutes during rush hour.
- The main east-west freeway is **Interstate 90**. The I-90 bridge is usually the best of the two Lake Washington bridges, because it has several lanes in each direction as well as a reversible H.O.V. lane. Because it begins near Safeco Field and the new football stadium, I-90 does back up before and after Mariners and Seahawks games, so give yourself extra time when traveling on those days.
- The other east-west thoroughfare, **Highway 520**, runs from I-5 just north of Capitol Hill to the Eastside. The 520 Bridge is one of the worst stretches of road during rush hour. Even if there is no accident on the bridge, the amazing view of the lake and Mount Rainier, as well as bright sunlight, slows traffic on the bridge decks. The "high rises" (the high portions of the bridge) at the west end also cause traffic backups because drivers have to slow for the curves and accelerate for the incline. If you can't use I-90 as your regular route over the lake, set up a carpool and take advantage of the H.O.V. lanes or try to use an on-ramp as close to the bridge as possible.

- Another route from Seattle to the Eastside is **Interstate 405**, which generally runs north-south on the east side of Lake Washington. Interstate 405 goes through Renton, Bellevue, Kirkland, and Bothell, connecting with I-5 south of Seattle near Southcenter Mall, and north of Seattle in Lynnwood. Depending on your destination and the time of day, an I-5 to I-405 route might be the quickest way around the lake.
- The **West Seattle Freeway** starts at I-5 near Beacon Hill and heads west to the West Seattle peninsula, crossing Highway 99 on the way. This is the main thoroughfare in and out of the north end of West Seattle.

CARPOOLING

High Occupancy Vehicle lanes or "diamond lanes" are located on Interstates 5, 405 and 90. These lanes are reserved for carpools (minimum two or three passengers, depending on the lane), buses and motorcycles. If you must travel over one of the Lake Washington bridges (I-90 or Highway 520) during rush hour, these lanes are the way to go. You'll be able to pass the rest of the traffic and cut to the front of the line at the bridge deck. For information on carpool parking permits, which can be used for discounted or free parking in downtown Seattle, call the city's **Carpool Parking/Permits** line at 206-684-0816.

If you don't have a carpool partner, Metro Transit offers **Ridematch**, a regional ride-sharing program that matches commuters with carpools. Visit www.rideshareonline.com to find a commuting partner in just minutes. Another option available through Metro is a vanpool. **Vanpools** require 6 to 14 passengers and monthly fares range from $26 to $160 per person. The advantages are that Metro provides the van, insurance, and gasoline. In addition, the carpool parking permit is free for vanpools.For more information on both the Ridematch and vanpool programs, call 206-625-4500 or 800-427-8249, or visit Metro's web site, http://transit.metrokc.gov.

PARK & RIDES

Many drive to Park & Ride lots and then commute by bus to Seattle.

BELLEVUE
- **Bellevue Christian Reformed Church,** 1221 148th Avenue NE
- **Bellevue Church of Christ,** 1212 104th Avenue SE
- **Bellevue Foursquare Church,** 2015 Richards Road
- **Bellevue Transit Center,** 108th Avenue NE and NE 6th Street
- **Bellevue Transfer Point,** 106th Avenue NE and NE 6th Street
- **Eastgate Park & Ride,** SE Eastgate Way and 141st Avenue SE
- **Grace Lutheran Church,** NE 8th Street and 96th Avenue NE

- **Newport Covenant Church**, SE Newport Way and Coal Creek Parkway SE
- **Newport Community Church**, 119th Avenue SE and SE 58th Street
- **Newport Hills Park & Ride**, I-405 and 112th Place SE
- **South Bellevue Park & Ride**, Bellevue Way SE and 112th Avenue SE
- **St. Andrew's Lutheran Church**, 2650 148th Avenue SE
- **St. Luke's Lutheran Church**, Bellevue Way NE and NE 30th Place
- **St. Margaret's Episcopal Church**, 4228 Factoria Boulevard
- **Wilburton Park & Ride**, I-405 and SE 8th Street

BURIEN

- **Burien Transit Center**, SW 150th Street and 4th Avenue SW
- **Normandy Park Congregational Church**, 19247 1st Avenue South

BOTHELL

- **Bothell Park & Ride**, Woodinville Drive and Kaysner Way
- **Brickyard Road**, I-405 and NE 160th Street

DUVALL

- **Duvall Park & Ride**, State Route 203 and Woodinville-Duvall Road

FEDERAL WAY

- **Federal Way Transit Center**, 23rd Avenue South and South 323rd Street
- **Our Saviour's Baptist Church**, South 320th Street and 8th Avenue South
- **South Federal Way Park & Ride**, 9th Avenue South and South 348th Street
- **St. Luke's Lutheran Church**, 515 South 312th Street
- **Sunrise United Methodist Church**, 150 South 356th Street
- **Twin Lakes Park & Ride**, 21st Avenue SW and SW 344th Street

ISSAQUAH

- **Issaquah Park & Ride**, State Route 900 and Newport Way
- **Klahanie Park & Ride**, SE Klahanie Boulevard and 244th Place SE
- **Sammamish Hills Lutheran Church**, SE 8th Street and 228th Avenue SE
- **Tibbitt's Valley Park**, 12th NW and Newport Way

KENMORE

- **Kenmore Park & Ride**, Bothell Way NE and 73rd Avenue NE

KIRKLAND

- **Holy Spirit Lutheran Church**, NE 124th Street and 100th Avenue NE
- **Houghton Park & Ride**, I-405 and NE 70th Place
- **Kingsgate Park & Ride**, I-405 and NE 132nd Street
- **Kirkland Transit Center**, 3rd Street and Park Lane
- **Lake Washington Christian Church**, 13225 116th Avenue NE

- **Northup Park & Ride**, Northup Way and Lake Washington Boulevard
- **Rosehill Presbyterian Church**, NE 90th Street and 122nd Avenue NE
- **South Kirkland Park & Ride**, 108th Avenue NE and NE 38th Place
- **SR-908/Kirkland Way Park & Ride**, NE 85th Street and Kirkland Way

KENT
- **Kent Covenant Church**, 12010 SE 240th Street
- **Kent-Des Moines Park & Ride**, I-5 and Kent-Des Moines Road
- **Kent Transit Center**, North Lincoln Avenue and West James Street
- **Kent United Methodist Church**, SE 248th Street and 110th Avenue SE
- **Kent Valley View Christian Church**, 124th Avenue SE and SE 256th Street
- **Lake Meridian Park & Ride**, 132nd Avenue SE and SE 272nd Street
- **St. Columba's Episcopal Church**, 26715 Military Road South
- **Star Lake Park & Ride**, I-5 and 272nd Street

MEDINA
- **Evergreen Point Bridge**, State Route 520 and Evergreen Point Road
- **St. Thomas Episcopal Church**, 84th Avenue NE and NE 121st Street

MERCER ISLAND
- **Mercer Island Presbyterian Church**, 84th Avenue SE and SE 39th Street
- **Mercer Island United Methodist Church**, SE 24th Street and 70th Avenue SE
- **Mercer Island Park & Ride**, 80th Avenue SE and North Mercer Way
- **QFC Village**, SE 68th Street and 84th Avenue SE

REDMOND
- **Bear Creek Park & Ride**, 178th Place NE and NE Union Hill Road
- **Overlake Park & Ride**, 152nd Avenue NE and NE 24th Street
- **Overlake Park Presbyterian Church**, 1856 156th Avenue NE
- **Redmond Park & Ride**, 161st Avenue NE and NE 83rd Street
- **Sammamish Hills Lutheran Church**, SE 8th Street and 228th Avenue SE

RENTON
- **Fairwood Assembly of God**, 131st Avenue SE and SE 192nd Street
- **First Baptist Church**, Hardie Avenue SW and SW Langston Road
- **Fred Meyer**, 365 Renton Center Way
- **Kennydale United Methodist Church**, Park Avenue North and North 30th Street
- **King of Glory**, Renton Avenue Extension and Hardie Avenue NW
- **Nativity Lutheran Church**, 140th Avenue SE and SE 177th Street
- **Renton Assembly of God**, 15025 SE Renton-Maple Valley Road
- **Renton Boeing Lot 3**, North 8th Street and Park Avenue North

- **Renton Highlands Park & Ride**, NE 16th Street and Edmonds Avenue NE
- **Renton Park & Ride**, 232 Burnett Avenue South
- **Renton Transit Center**, South 2nd Street and Burnett Avenue South
- **South Renton Park & Ride**, South Grady Way and Shattuck Avenue South

SEATTLE—CENTRAL
- **Calvary Temple**, NE 68th Street and 8th Avenue NE
- **Green Lake Park & Ride**, I-5 and NE 65th Street

SEATTLE—NORTH
- **South Jackson Park Park & Ride**, 5th Avenue NE and NE 133rd Street
- **North Jackson Park Park & Ride**, 5th Avenue NE and NE 145th Street
- **North Seattle Park & Ride**, 1st Avenue NE and NE 100th Street
- **Northgate Transit Center**, NE 103rd Street and 1st Avenue NE
- **Northgate Park & Ride**, NE 112th Street and 5th Avenue NE
- **Our Savior Lutheran Church**, NE 125th Street and 25th Avenue NE
- **Prince of Peace Lutheran Church**, 14514 20th Avenue NE

SEATTLE—SOUTH
- **Airport and Spokane Park & Ride**, Airport Way South and South Spokane Street
- **Church by the Side of the Road**, South 148th Street and Pacific Highway South
- **Holy Family Church**, SW Roxbury Street and 20th Avenue SW
- **Lutheran Social Services**, South 188th Street and 42nd Avenue South
- **Olson Place and Myers Way Park & Ride**, Olson Place SW and SW Myers Way
- **Skyway Marketplace**, South 116th Street and 68th Avenue South
- **Southwest Spokane Street Park & Ride**, 26th Avenue SW and SW Spokane Street

SHORELINE
- **Aurora Church of the Nazarene**, 175th Street and Meridian Avenue North
- **Aurora Village Transit Center**, North 200th Street and Ashworth Avenue North
- **Bethany Baptist Church**, NE 181st and 62nd Avenue NE
- **Bethel Lutheran Church**, NE 175th Street and 10th Avenue NE
- **Korean Zion Presbyterian Church**, 17920 Meridian Avenue North
- **Northshore Park & Ride**, 68th Avenue NE and NE 182nd Street
- **Shoreline United Methodist Church**, NE 145th Street and 25th Avenue NE
- **Shoreline Park & Ride**, Aurora Avenue North and North 192nd Street

TUKWILA
- **Tukwila Park & Ride**, Interurban Avenue South and 52nd Avenue South

WOODINVILLE
- **Woodinville Park & Ride**, 140th Avenue NE and NE 179th Street
- **Woodinville Seventh-Day Adventist**, NE Woodinville-Duvall Road and Avondale Road NE

FLEXCAR

Seattle and Eastside residents now have a car sharing option, good for out of the way errands or appointments. Called Flexcar, this car-sharing service offers the freedom of driving a car without the expense of owning one. Drivers pay for the time they use the car, and the company pays for gas, insurance, and maintenance. Flexcar members determine their monthly driving needs and then choose one of five plans, which range from $35 for five hours' time to $525 for 100 hours. For more information, call 206-323-FLEX, or visit www.flexcar.com.

CAR RENTAL

Those who need a weekend rental should reserve at least a week in advance.
- **Advantage**, 800-574-6000, www.easyreservations.com
- **Alamo**, 800-GO-ALAMO, www.alamo.com
- **Avis**, 800-831-2847, www.avis.com
- **Budget**, 800-527-7000, www.budget.com
- **Dollar**, 800-800-4000, www.dollar.com
- **Enterprise**, 800-RENT-A-CAR, www.enterprise.com
- **Hertz**, 800-654-3131, www.hertz.com
- **National**, 800-CAR-RENT, www.nationalcar.com
- **Thrifty**, 800-THRIFTY, www.thrifty.com

TAXIS

Unless you are downtown, on Capitol Hill, or at the airport, you'll probably need to call ahead to arrange for a taxi. A few of Seattle's many taxicab companies are listed here; others can be found in the Yellow Pages.
- **Emerald City Taxi**, 206-433-1788
- **Farwest Taxi**, 206-622-1717
- **Orange Cab**, 206-522-8800
- **Yellow and Graytop Cab**, 206-622-6500, www.whatrain.com/psd/yellow

BY BIKE

Despite the hilly terrain and the wet, chilly fall and winter weather, a surprisingly large number of Seattle residents use bikes for recreation or transportation. The city estimates that the number of people commuting each day ranges between 4,000 and 8,000. To assist bicycle commuters, the **Seattle Transportation Bicycle Program** has created about 28 miles of bike trails and paths, 14 miles of on-street, striped bike lanes, and 90 miles of signed bike routes.

During the summer months, Seattle's Lake Washington Boulevard becomes a long, winding playground for the city's bike enthusiasts. On Bicycle Saturdays and Sundays, between 10 a.m. and 6 p.m., the city shuts down the lakeside thoroughfare to automobile traffic. For more information about the Seattle Bicycle & Pedestrian Program or to order a free Seattle bicycling guide map, call 206-684-7583 or visit www.ci.seattle.wa.us/td.

Bicyclists can "bike and ride" at no extra cost, thanks to a Metro Transit program that allows riders to load their bikes onto racks installed on Metro buses. For details on the **Bike & Ride Program**, visit Metro's web site at http://transit.metrokc.gov or call 206-553-3000.

Though helmets are not required for bicyclists, they are recommended. According to a study by the Harborview Injury Prevention and Research Center, helmets that meet ANSI or Snell standards can cut the risk of head injuries by 85%. For more information on helmets, visit the **Bicycle Helmet Safety Institute** web site, www.helmets.org.

BY PUBLIC TRANSPORTATION

Traffic and public transportation issues have snarled recent legislative sessions in the state, and have taken center stage in local elections for many years. Unfortunately, lawmakers and residents continue to struggle with some of the worst traffic in the country. According to *The Seattle Times*, the cost of fixing the major congestion hot spots between Tacoma and Everett, and building a regional mass-transit system, could top $30 billion. Major state transportation issues include widening part of I-5 near Vancouver and through Centralia, completing a 297-mile system of car-pool lanes, widening I-405, connecting Highway 509 to I-5, and creating some type of regional transit.

In 1996, state voters passed a 21-mile light-rail package for service from SeaTac to the University District, but the plan has since been hampered by controversy, cost increases, congressional scrutiny, and mismanagement. In spring of 2000, Sound Transit, the agency in charge of the project, scaled back the plan, and now proposes a 14-mile route from downtown Seattle to Tukwila. However, in June of 2002, Tukwila rejected the proposed route, endangering Sound Transit's ability to obtain federal funds for the project. At the time of this publication, it was unclear whether Sound Transit would proceed with the light rail plan.

In the meantime, a group called the Elevated Transportation Company (ETC) developed a plan for a 14-mile monorail system that would run from Ballard through downtown Seattle to West Seattle. The proposed Green Line, which would cost $1.2 billion, would consist of 19 stations and transport an estimated 68,000 riders a day. Proposed financing of the system would come from an annual car tax. At press time, the proposal was scheduled for a vote in November of 2002.

For the time being, and until light rail or the Green Line comes to town, buses are the primary means of mass transit in Seattle.

BUSES

Metro Transit provides buses that are generally clean and on time, although they make frequent, time-consuming stops as they traverse the city. Express buses are much faster but go to fewer destinations. Crosstown buses are limited and transfers are often necessary when travelling between neighborhoods. The good news is that the bus fares are reasonable: adult fares are $1.25/off-peak, $1.50/one-zone peak, $2/ two-zone peak; youth fares are $.50; seniors and persons with disabilities are $.25/off-peak and $.50/peak. In addition, most of downtown is part of a ride-free zone, meaning that passengers can use the bus for free in the downtown area as long as they disembark before crossing Denny Way or Yesler Way—most bus drivers announce the end of the ride-free zone. The ride-free area in downtown is possible since fares are collected at the beginning of the ride if you're traveling toward downtown, or at the end of the ride if you're traveling away from downtown. A sign at the front of the bus will let you know when to pay your fare.

Bus passes and ticket books are available and can save a lot of money for regular passengers. Some employers, institutions and community organizations provide free or discounted passes for employees and members, as part of the Employer Commute Services sponsored by King County Metro. Bus passes are available at over 100 locations in the city, including some drug stores and cash machines, or you can call Metro at 206-624-PASS or visit http://transit.metrokc.gov, and purchase with a credit or debit card.

Bus schedules are posted at all bus stops (but only for the buses that use that route), or you can call Metro's Automated Schedule Information Line at 206-BUS-TIME. Metro's 24-hour Rider Information Line at 206-553-3000 connects you to a Metro employee who can assist you with schedule and route information, as long as you can provide your starting point and destination. Metro Transit also has an informative and comprehensive web site at http://transit.metrokc.gov.

In addition to buses, Metro runs two unique public transportation systems. A relic of the Seattle World's Fair, the **Monorail** runs between Westlake Center in the downtown shopping district and the Seattle Center. The **Waterfront Trolley** uses an old railroad track to travel from the International District to the north end of the Waterfront, making several stops along the way.

Despite the problems Sound Transit has encountered with light rail, the agency has successfully initiated much of the service approved by voters in 1996, including **ST Express** bus service linking Seattle, Bellevue, Tacoma, and Everett. The buses operate on a three-zone fare system. The cost depends on the number of fare zones you traverse and your fare type (youth, adult or senior/disabled). Fares range from $1.25 to $2.50 for adults, $.75 to $2 for youth, and $.50 to $1.25 for senior/disabled passengers. For more information, call 800-201-4900 or visit www.soundtransit.org.

Outside Seattle, Community Transit covers most of Seattle's neighboring communities; Everett Transit covers the greater Everett area north of Seattle; Pierce Transit provides bus service in Tacoma.

- **Community Transit**, 425-353-RIDE or 800-562-1375, www.comm-trans.org
- **Everett Transit**, 425-257-8803, www.ci.everett.wa.us
- **Pierce Transit**, 253-581-8000, 800-562-8109, www.ptbus.pierce.wa.us

COMMUTER TRAINS

The **Sounder** commuter trains offer rail service between Tacoma and downtown Seattle, with stops in Puyallup, Sumner, Auburn, Kent and Tukwila. Service between Lakewood and Tacoma is scheduled to begin in late 2002, with service between Everett and Seattle slated for 2003. Once in full operation, 18 trains will serve the Lakewood-Tacoma-Seattle segment, and 12 trains will serve the Seattle-Everett leg. King Street Station, in Seattle, and the Tacoma Dome currently serve as the Seattle-Tacoma segment's final destination points. For more information about Sounder trains, call 800-201-4900 or visit www.soundtransit.org.

FERRIES

Because there are no bridges connecting Seattle with the Olympic Peninsula, many area residents commute to and from work by ferry. The **Washington State Ferries** system is the largest in the United States and includes 10 routes that serve the Puget Sound area. To commute to the city, residents ride the **Seattle-Bremerton, Seattle-Bainbridge Island** and **Seattle-Vashon Island** routes, which dock at the Seattle waterfront terminal. The **Fauntleroy-Vashon-Southworth** route serves West Seattle, Vashon Island and the Olympic Peninsula, and the **Edmonds-Kingston** route departs from a terminal in Edmonds, 20 minutes north of Seattle. The **Anacortes-San Juan Islands** and **Anacortes-Sidney, BC** routes, originate in Anacortes, about an hour north of Seattle.

Those routes used for commuting to Seattle can be very busy in the morning and evening hours. If you're walking on, you probably won't have any problem, even if you arrive just a few minutes before departure. If you're driving, however, you'll need to arrive early or be prepared to take a later ferry. This is also true for weekends or holidays. The wait time for those who want to ferry their vehicles on the San Juan Islands routes can be several hours on summer holiday weekends.

Fares vary according to season and route. Passenger only round-trip fares are about $4.50 (usually collected at the eastern terminal of the ferry route only). Vehicle and driver one-way fares are $8 to $10 on most routes, and are always collected in both directions. Additional fees may be charged for oversized vehicles. Discounts are available for frequent passengers, children, disabled persons, and senior citizens.

Schedules vary by season and route. Ferry information pamphlets are available at all ferry terminals, as well as at some transit information booths in the city. For more information, call the Washington State Ferries' information line at 206-464-6400 or 800-84-FERRY or visit www.wsdot.wa.gov/ferries.

REGIONAL/NATIONAL TRANSPORT

AMTRAK

King Street Station, which serves as Seattle's **Amtrak** station, borders the historic International District and Pioneer Square, near the new football stadium at the south end of downtown. The station is served by the Cascades (Eugene, Portland, Seattle, Vancouver, BC), Coast Starlight (Seattle, Portland, Oakland, Los Angeles), and Empire Builder (Chicago, Seattle or Portland) trains.

- **Amtrak National Route Information**, 800-USA-RAIL, www.amtrak.com
- **Amtrak Seattle Station**, 303 South Jackson Street, 206-382-4125

BUSES

The **Greyhound Lines** bus terminal is located at 8th Avenue and Stewart Street in downtown Seattle. For reservation information call the terminal directly at 206-628-5526, Greyhound's national reservation number at 800-

231-2222, or visit www.greyhound.com. Another option for bus trips to some eastern Washington cities is **Northwestern Stage Lines**. Call 800-366-3830 for reservations and information, or visit www.nwadv.com/northw.

AIRPORTS/AIRLINES

The **Seattle-Tacoma International Airport**, known locally as Sea-Tac, is located south of Seattle at 17801 Pacific Highway South. For parking rates and information, airport weather conditions and general information, call 206-431-4444 or visit www.portseattle.org/seatac.

Construction woes seem never-ending at Sea-Tac, and can affect everything from parking, to drop-off, to pick-up—even the location of your gate. And, as a result of September 11, increased security has added to the confusion. The airport has added express security lines at two of its concourses, C/D and North Satellite, for the following passengers: those in wheelchairs, passengers with no carry-on luggage, passengers on Horizon Air's Portland Shuttle, Alaska Airlines MVP Gold Cardholders, American Airlines Executive Platinum Cardholders, TWA Platinum Cardholders, and United Airlines 1K Cardholders.

Curbside check-in is available on the upper airport drive, but stopping your car is allowed only for picking up or dropping off passengers, and loading or unloading luggage. Passengers are not permitted to leave their cars while they check their bags curbside. Vehicles left unattended are ticketed even if the driver is nearby. At Sea-Tac, the upper drive is for departures, and baggage claim and pick-up are located on the lower drive. Note: when the upper drive is congested, passengers with few or no bags should consider being dropped-off on the lower drive.

Finally, a word about delays. According to the US Transportation Department, Sea-Tac Airport is notorious for delays. In fact, from January through May of 2001 over 31% of flights at Sea-Tac were late. Rain and fog are often to blame, reducing visibility so drastically that only one of the airport's two closely positioned runways can be used. Capacity is also a problem, but should be cleared up in 2006, when a third runway is scheduled to open. Be sure to call your airline before you head to the airport.

These major airlines serve passengers at Sea-Tac:

- **Aeroflot**, 206-464-1005, www.aeroflot.org
- **Air Canada**, 800-247-2262, www.aircanada.ca
- **Alaska Airlines**, 800-426-0333, www.alaska-air.com
- **America West**, 800-235-9292, www.americawest.com
- **American Airlines**, 800-433-7300, www.im.aa.com
- **British Airways**, 800-247-9297, www.british-airways.com
- **Continental Airlines**, 800-525-0280, www.continental.com
- **Delta Airlines**, 800-221-1212, www.delta.com

- **Hawaiian Airlines**, 800-367-5320, www.hawaiianair.com
- **Horizon Air**, 800-547-9308, www.horizonair.com
- **Japan Airlines**, 800-5253663, www.japanair.com
- **Northwest Airlines**, 800-225-2525, www.nwa.com
- **Southwest Airlines**, 800-435-9792, www.iflyswa.com
- **Trans World Airlines**, 800-221-2000, www.twa.com
- **United Airlines**, 800-241-6522, www.ual.com
- **US Airways**, 800-428-4322, www.usair.com

TRAVELING TO SEA-TAC AIRPORT BY CAR

When traveling to the airport by car, use the following directions: from Seattle take I-5 south to the Southcenter/Sea-Tac Airport exit and follow the signs to get on Highway 518. From Highway 518 take the Sea-Tac Airport exit and stay to the left as you exit. This will put you on the main road into the airport, which is clearly marked with signs to baggage claim, airline counters and parking.

Alternate directions from downtown Seattle, Ballard, Phinney Ridge, Greenwood, Fremont, and Broadview (these are just a little faster during rush hour): take Highway 99 south until it forces you left onto 1st Avenue South. Stay in the right lane and follow directions to the 1st Avenue South Bridge (only a few blocks). After you cross the bridge, the road you are on becomes Highway 509. Stay on Highway 509 to the Sea-Tac Airport and Highway 518 exit. Take Highway 518 east then, from Highway 518, take the Sea-Tac exit. This exit puts you on the main road into the airport.

The parking garage at Sea-Tac is connected to the main terminal by skybridges on the 4th floor. The following **parking options** are available:

- Short-term parking, for people who plan to spend less than two hours at the airport: $2 up to 30 minutes, $4 for 30 minutes to an hour, $6 for 1 to 2 hours.
- General parking, available on the top five floors of the garage: $2 up to 30 minutes, $4 for 30 minutes to an hour, $6 for 1 to 2 hours, $8 for 2 to 4 hours, $13 for 4 to 8 hours, $16 for 8 to 12 hours, and $20 for 12 to 24 hours.
- Disabled parking: about 70 stalls are located on the 4th floor of the airport garage; general parking rates apply. In addition, 14 stalls are located on the short-term parking floor; short-term parking rates apply.
- Monthly parking: pre-paid monthly parking is available for unlimited use. Call 206-248-6887 for more information.
- Valet parking: $20 for up to 4 hours, $30 for 4 to 24 hours.

Sea-Tac recently introduced an automated parking payment system to help travelers get out of the airport quickly. Automated pay kiosks on the 4th floor of the garage allow visitors to pay for both long- and short-term parking before they reach their cars. Simply take a ticket as you enter the parking garage, and keep it with you. When you're ready to retrieve your car, you can pay at the kiosks with either cash or a credit card. For additional parking details, call 206-431-4444 or visit the Port of Seattle's web site at www.portseattle.org/seatac.

TRAVELING TO SEA-TAC AIRPORT BY BUS & SHUTTLE VAN

The following **public transportation bus routes** provide airport service to and from Seattle and surrounding communities. Buses arrive at and leave from the baggage claim area, near Door 6. Departure times are posted at the bus stop.

- **Metro Route 140**: daily service to and from Southcenter, Renton and Burien, with departures every 20 to 30 minutes Monday through Friday and every 60 minutes Saturday and Sunday. Travel time is 60 minutes.
- **Metro Route 174**: daily service to and from downtown Seattle and to and from Federal Way, with departures every 30 minutes. Travel time is 45 minutes. Also, daily early-morning service to and from downtown Seattle, with departures from downtown at 2:15 and 3:30 a.m. and from Sea-Tac at 1:28 and 2:43 a.m. Travel time is 30 minutes.
- **Metro Route 194**: daily service to and from downtown Seattle and Federal Way, with departures every 30 minutes. Travel time is 30 minutes.
- **Sound Transit Route 560**: daily service to and from Bellevue and Renton, with departures every 30 minutes on weekdays and every 60 minutes on Saturday and Sunday. Travel time is 45 minutes to and from Bellevue and 15 minutes to and from Renton.
- **Sound Transit Route 570**: service to and from the International District, West Seattle, White Center and Burien, with departures every 30 minutes during peak hours and every 60 minutes during off-peak hours. Travel time is 60 minutes to and from downtown Seattle.
- **Sound Transit Route 574**: daily service to and from Lakewood, Tacoma and Sea-Tac Airport, with departures every 30 minutes during peak hours and every 60 minutes during off-peak hours Saturday and Sunday.

Shuttle van or **bus**: most downtown hotels offer shuttle service to the airport; call ahead for times and costs (it may be free if you are a hotel guest). For door-to-door shuttle service, try one of the following:
- **Airport Express by Gray Line**, 206-626-6088, 800-426-7505, www.graylineofseattle.com; service to major downtown hotels
- **Airporter Shuttle**, 360-380-8800, 800-235-5247; service to the Alaska Ferry Terminal, Anacortes, Anacortes Ferry to San Juan Islands, Bellingham, Blaine, Ferndale, LaConner, Marysville, Mt. Vernon, Oak Harbor, and Stanwood

- **Bremerton-Kitsap Airporter**, 360-876-1737; service to Bangor Submarine Base, Bremerton, Gig Harbor, Gorst, Port Orchard, Poulsbo, Puget Sound Naval Shipyard, Purdy, Silverdale, and northwest Tacoma
- **Capital Aeroporter**, 253-838-7431, 800-962-3579, www.capair.com; service to Centralia, Chehalis, Federal Way, Fife, Hoodsport, Lacey, Lakewood, Olympia, Parkland, Puyallup/Sumner, Shelton, Tacoma, Tumwater, and Union
- **Centralia Sea-Tac Airporter**, 800-773-9490; service to Centralia, Chehalis, Lacey, Olympia, and Tumwater
- **Olympic Van Tours**, 360-452-3858; service to Port Angeles and Sequim, reservations necessary.
- **Shuttle Express**, 425-981-7000, 800-487-7433, www.shuttleexpress. com; service to Auburn, Bellevue, Bothell, Everett, Federal Way, Fife, Issaquah, Kent, Kirkland, Lakewood, Mercer Island, Puyallup, Redmond, Renton, Seattle, Steilacoom, Tacoma, Totem Lake, and Woodinville
- **Quick Shuttle**, 604-940-4428, 800-665-2122; service to Vancouver, BC

There are two other airports in the Seattle area, but both are restricted to charter, corporate, and recreational aircraft. **Renton Municipal Airport**, 425-430-7471, www.ci.renton.wa.us/pw, owned by the City of Renton, is located about 25 miles south of downtown Seattle. The airport is used primarily by single and twin-engine planes, a few corporate jets, and some private flying clubs. There is no commercial flight activity. **King County International Airport**, also known as Boeing Field, serves air cargo companies, recreational fliers, charter services, flight schools and emergency services. The airport is also a major center for Boeing operations. For more information, visit www.metrokc.gov/airport.

TRAVEL RESOURCES

There are a number of online travel sites where you can sometimes find good deals. They include, among others, **Travelocity.com, Expedia.com, Orbitz.com, Lowestfare.com** and **Cheaptickets.com**. If cost far outweighs convenience, check **Priceline**, www.priceline.com, where you may be able to pin down an inexpensive fare at inconvenient hours (often in the middle of the night). Their motto, "Name Your Price and Save" says it all. **Hotwire.com** advises consumers of the best offer between six major airlines: American, Continental, Delta, Northwest, United and US Airways. **Sidestep.com** also offers comparison shopping—listing comparable routes, services, and prices.

Many airlines post last-minute seats at reduced rates, usually on Wednesdays. In fact, booking with the airline of your choice, either online or by phone, often proves less expensive than booking with some so-called discount travel sites.

To **register a complaint against an airline**, the Department of Transportation is the place to call or write: 202-366-2220, Aviation Consumer Protection Division, C-75 Room 4107, 400 7th Street SW, Washington, DC 20590.

Information about airport conditions, including weather and air traffic congestion, which could create flight delays can be checked online at www.fly.faa.gov.

I
F YOU NEED TEMPORARY QUARTERS WHILE YOU ARE LOOKING FOR A
place to live, Seattle offers a variety of options. Those planning on staying in temporary housing for more than a couple of weeks, should consider a sublet or short-term lease. Apartment sublets are often advertised in
classifieds, particularly during the spring and summer when college students head out of town. The apartment search firms listed in the **Finding a
Place to Live** chapter can assist you with finding a short-term lease, or see
below under the **Short Term Leases and Residence Hotels** and **Summer
Only** sections. For additional lodging options, and to get a packet of information on accommodations in Seattle or surrounding communities, try
Seattle-King County Convention and Visitors Bureau, 520 Pike Street,
206-461-5800, 206-461-5840 (TDD), www.seeseattle.org, or **Washington
State Department of Tourism**, 360-725-5052, www.tourism.wa.gov.

HOTELS AND MOTELS

As a port city, business hub, and tourist destination, Seattle has a large
number of hotels and motels offering various levels of service and facilities.
In general, the least expensive motels are those along Aurora Avenue North
(Highway 99) north of downtown. These lodgings come with the security
risks inherent to the high crime area of Aurora. They generally are not suitable for children or for adults uncomfortable with fast-paced urban set-
tings, and for that reason are not listed here.

The following list of hotels and motels is by no means complete. For a
more comprehensive listing, check the Yellow Pages under "Hotels and
Other Accommodations." For up-to-the-minute room availability in Bellevue,
Kent, Lynnwood, Renton, and Seattle, call **Seattle Hotel Reservations** at
866-234-9330 or visit www.seattle-hotel-reservation.com. **Seattle Hotel
Hotline** is another local reservation service. Call 800-361-1029 or visit

http://seattle.hotel-hotline.com. **AAA** travel guides are a good source for hotel and motel recommendations. Free to members, their listings are useful because AAA weeds out those hotels that are not up to their standards. **Quikbook** is a national, discount room-reservation service that costs nothing to join. It offers reduced room rates for many hotels. For a list of cities and hotels, and information about them, call 800-789-9887 or visit www.quikbook.com. Other companies include **Hotels.com**, 800-715-7666, and **Central Reservation Services**, 800-555-7555, both at www.hotels.com.

Hotel prices fluctuate, based on the season, special events, and vacancy rates. Call ahead for reservations, and be sure to ask about special discounts or business rates. Often, hotels will offer a special "internet only" rate, so be sure to check web sites before you book.

LUXURY LODGINGS

A room at one of the following hotels costs $200 or more per night.

SEATTLE
- **Alexis Hotel**, 1007 1st Avenue, 206-624-4844, 800-264-8482, www.alexishotel.com
- **Crowne Plaza**, 1113 6th Avenue, 206-464-1980, 800-227-6963, www.crowneplaza.com
- **Four Seasons Hotel Seattle**, 411 University Street, 206-621-1700, 800-819-5053, www.fourseasons.com
- **Hotel Monaco**, 1101 4th Avenue, 206-621-1770, 800-715-6513, www.monaco-seattle.com
- **Hotel Vintage Park**, 1100 5th Avenue, 206-624-8000, 800-853-3914, www.hotelvintagepark.com
- **The Sorrento Hotel**, 900 Madison Street, 206-622-6400, 800-426-1265, www.hotelsorrento.com
- **W Hotel Seattle**, 1112 4th Avenue, 206-624-6000, 877-WHOTELS, www.whotels.com
- **WestCoast Grand Hotel on Fifth Avenue**, 1415 5th Avenue, 206-971-8000 or 800-325-4000, www.westcoasthotels.com

MIDDLE RANGE LODGINGS

These hotels charge between $100 and $200 per night.

BELLEVUE
- **Courtyard by Marriott**, 14615 NE 29th Place, 425-869-5300, 800-321-2211, www.courtyard.com

- **Hyatt Regency Bellevue**, 900 Bellevue Way NE, 425-462-1234, 800-233-1234, www.hyatt.com

ISSAQUAH
- **Holiday Inn of Issaquah**, 1801 12th NW, 425-392-6421, 800-HOLIDAY, www.holiday-inn.com

KIRKLAND
- **Clarion Inn at Totem Lake**, 12233 NE Totem Lake Way, 425-821-2202, 800-CLARION, www.clarioninn.com

REDMOND
- **Redmond Inn**, 17601 Redmond Way, 425-883-4900, 800-634-8080, www.redmondinn.com
- **Residence Inn by Marriott**, 7575 164th Avenue NE, 425-497-9226, 800-331-3131, www.residenceinn.com

RENTON
- **Holiday Inn Renton**, 800 Rainier Avenue South, 425-226-7700, 800-521-1412, www.holiday-inn.com

SEATTLE
- **Best Western Executive Inn**, 200 Taylor Avenue North, 206-448-9444, 800-351-9444, www.bestwestern.com
- **Days Inn Downtown Seattle**, 2205 7th Avenue, 206-448-3434, 800-329-7466, www.daysinn.com
- **Elliott Grand Hyatt**, 721 Pine Street, 206-774-1234, www.hyatt.com
- **Hotel Edgewater**, 2411 Alaskan Way, 206-728-7000, www.edgewaterhotel.com
- **The Inn at the Market**, 86 Pine Street, 206-443-3600, 800-446-4484, www.innatthemarket.com
- **The Inn at Virginia Mason**, 1006 Spring Street, 206-583-6453, 800-283-6453
- **Mayflower Park Hotel**, 4th Avenue and Olive Way, 206-623-8700, 800-426-5100, www.mayflowerpark.com
- **Ramada Inn Downtown**, 2200 5th Avenue, 206-441-9785, 888-298-2054, www.ramada.com
- **Renaissance Madison Hotel**, 515 Madison Street, 206-583-0300, 800-278-4159, www.renaissancehotels.com
- **Sheraton Seattle Hotel & Towers**, 1400 6th Avenue, 206-621-9000, 800-325-3535, www.sheraton.com/seattle
- **Silver Cloud Inn Lake Union**, 1150 Fairview Avenue North, 206-447-9500, 800-551-7207, www.scinns.com

- **Silver Cloud Inn University District**, 5036 25th Avenue NE, 206-526-5200, 800-205-6940, www.scinns.com
- **WestCoast Vance Hotel**, 620 Stewart Street, 206-441-4200, 800-325-4000
- **The Westin Seattle**, 1900 5th Avenue, 206-728-1000, www.starwood.com/westin

TUKWILA
- **Embassy Suites**, 15920 West Valley Highway, 425-227-8844, 800-EMBASSY, www.embassysuites.com

BUDGET STAYS

You can stay at one of these hotels for less than $100.

BELLEVUE
- **Best Western Bellevue Inn**, 11211 Main Street, 425-455-5240, 800-528-1234, www.bestwestern.com
- **Doubletree Hotel**, 818 112th NE, 425-455-1515, 800-222-8733, www.doubletree.com

BOTHELL
- **Comfort Inn & Suites**, 1414 228th Street SE, 425-402-0900, www.comfortinn.com

EVERETT
- **Holiday Inn Everett**, 101 128th SE, 425-337-2900, 800-HOLIDAY, www.holiday-inn.com
- **Howard Johnson Plaza Hotel**, 3105 Pine Street, 425-339-3333, 800-406-1411, www.the.hojo.com

FEDERAL WAY
- **Best Western Federal Way Execultel**, 31611 20th South, 253-941-6000, 800-528-1234, www.bestwestern.com
- **Comfort Inn**, 31622 Pacific Highway South, 253-529-0101, www.comfortinn.com

KENT
- **Best Western Plaza by the Green**, 24415 Russell Road, 253-854-8767, 800-648-3311, www.bestwestern.com
- **Comfort Inn**, 22311 84th South, 253-872-2211, www.comfortinn.com

KIRKLAND
- **Best Western Kirkland Inn**, 12223 NE 116th, 425-822-2300, 800-332-4200, www.bestwestern.com

LYNNWOOD
- **Courtyard by Marriott**, 4220 Alderwood Mall Boulevard, 425-670-0500, 800-321-2211, www.courtyard.com
- **Hampton Inn & Suites**, 19324 Alderwood Mall Parkway, 425-771-1888, www.hamptonseattlenorth.com

SEATTLE
- **Ace Hotel**, 2423 1st Avenue, 206-448-4721, www.theacehotel.com
- **Best Western Loyal Inn**, 2301 8th Avenue, 206-682-0200, 800-351-9444, www.bestwestern.com
- **Camlin Hotel**, 1619 9th Avenue, 206-682-0100
- **Commodore Hotel**, 2013 2nd Avenue, 206-448-8868, 800-714-8868, www.commodorehotel.com
- **Hotel Seattle**, 315 Seneca Street, 206-623-5110
- **St. Regis Hotel**, 116 Stewart Street, 206-448-6366, www.saintregis.com
- **Travelodge**, 2213 8th Avenue, 206-624-6300, 888-515-6375, www.travelodge.com
- **Travelodge by the Space Needle**, 200 6th Avenue North, 206-441-7878, 888-515-6375, www.travelodge.com
- **Travelodge University**, 4725 25th Avenue NE, 206-525-4612, 888-515-6375, www.travelodge.com
- **University Inn**, 4140 Roosevelt Way NE, 206-632-5055, 800-733-3855, www.universityinnseattle.com

TUKWILA
- **Best Western at Southcenter**, 15901 West Valley Highway, 425-226-1812, 800-544-9863, www.bestwestern.com

SHORT-TERM LEASES AND RESIDENCE HOTELS

The following hotels and leasing companies offer full suites for rent by the day, week or month. Rooms include a kitchen or kitchenette, living room, and bedroom. Often maid service and other amenities are available.
- **Accommodations Plus**, 425-455-2773, www.aplusnw.com
- **Alternative Suites International**, 206-860-1616, 888-900-4050, www.asuites.com
- **Executive Extended Stay**, 300 10th Avenue, 206-223-9300, www.executiveextendedstay.com

- **Executive Residence Inc.**, 206-329-8000, 800-428-3867, www.executiveresidence.com
- **Home-Pac Inc.**, 253-922-1177, 800-272-1461, www.homepacor.com
- **Inn at Queen Anne**, 505 1st Avenue North, 206-282-7357, www.innatqueenanne.com
- **Oakwood Corporate Housing**, 425-861-1175, www.oakwood.com
- **Pacific Guest Suites**, 425-454-7888, 800-962-6620
- **Summerfield Suites**, 1011 Pike Street, 206-682-8282, www.wyndham.com/summerfield

BED & BREAKFASTS

If you're in the mood for quaint or cozy, consider a bed and breakfast. Most of Seattle's B&Bs are outside the downtown area, so this may also be a good way to check out prospective neighborhoods. You may contact the inn directly (listed below), or try one of the local or national bed and breakfast registries. Locally, call **Seattle Bed & Breakfast Association**, 206-547-1020, 800-348-5630, www.seattlebandbs.com; **Bed & Breakfast Association of Suburban Seattle**, www.seattlebestbandb.com; or **Pacific Reservation Service**, 206-439-7677, 800-684-2932, www.seattlebedandbreakfast.com. Other sites include **InnSite**, www.innsite.com, and the **Inn and Travel Network**, www.innandtravel.com.

- **Amaranth Inn**, 1451 South Main Street, 206-720-7161, 800-720-7161, www.amaranthinn.com, $70-$160
- **Bacon Mansion**, 959 Broadway East, 206-329-1864, 800-240-1864, www.baconmansion.com, $99-$174
- **Capitol Hill Inn**, 1713 Belmont Avenue, 206-323-1955, www.capitolhillinn.com, $85-$165
- **Chambered Nautilus Bed & Breakfast**, 5005 22nd Avenue NE, 206-522-2536, 800-545-8459, www.chamberednautilus.com, $99-$144
- **Chelsea Station on the Park**, 4915 Linden Avenue North, 206-547-6077, 800-400-6077, www.bandbseattle.com, $100-$185
- **Gaslight Inn**, 1727 15th Avenue, 206-325-3654, www.gaslight-inn.com, $78-$178
- **Green Gables Guesthouse**, 1503 2nd Avenue West, 206-282-6863, 800-400-1503, www.greengablesseattle.com, $69-$159
- **Hill House Bed & Breakfast**, 1113 East John Street, 206-720-7161, 800-720-7161, www.foxinternet.net/business/hillhouse, $75-$165
- **Mildred's Bed & Breakfast**, 1202 15th Avenue East, 206-325-6072, 800-327-9692, www.mildredsbnb.com, $90-$160
- **Salisbury House**, 750 16th Avenue East, 206-328-8682, www.salisburyhouse.com, $119-$155

- **Villa Heidelberg Bed & Breakfast**, 4845 45th Avenue SW, 206-938-3658, 800-671-2942, www.villaheidelberg.com, $90-$150
- **Wildwood Bed & Breakfast**, 4518 SW Wildwood Place, 206-819-9075, 800-840-8410, www.wildwoodseattle.com, $65-$110

ALTERNATIVE LODGINGS

HOSTELS

Hostels offer basic accommodations at low prices, but there are a few restrictions. Generally, you should expect to sleep in a shared room and use a common bathroom and shower, although some have private rooms at a higher price. Some hostels require membership in an international hostelling association, some restrict the number of nights you can stay or limit the time that you can be in the hostel during the day. The wisest course is to call in advance to make sure that you qualify (and that you'll be happy with the house rules).

- **Backpackers Garden Apartments**, 1525 2nd Avenue, 206-340-1222
- **Green Tortoise Backpackers Guesthouse**, 1525 2nd Avenue, 206-340-1222, 888-424-6783, www.greentortoise.net
- **Hostelling International**, 84 Union Street, 206-622-5443, www.hiseattle.org

WASHINGTON ATHLETIC CLUB

The Inn at the Washington Athletic Club offers hotel rooms for members of reciprocal clubs across the country, and their guests. Member rates range from $123 to $474, and guest rates from $137 to $521. For more information, or a list of reciprocal clubs visit www.wac.net.

YWCA

- **YWCA Downtown**, 1118 5th Avenue, 206-461-4888, www.ywcaworks.org; hotel accommodations for women only; rates range from $33 to $80 per night.

SUMMER ONLY

Summer housing on Seattle-area campuses is restricted to students, visiting conference attendees, and special-interest groups. If you're looking for an apartment or rental house in which to spend the summer (which *is* the best time of year in Seattle), concentrate your efforts in university neighborhoods where students vacate from June to September. The University District, adjacent to the University of Washington is a good place to start. Also consider the Fremont area near Seattle Pacific University. Short-term and seasonal housing opportunities are listed in the classifieds section of *The Seattle Times*, www.seattletimes.com, and *Seattle Post-Intelligencer*, www.seattle-pi.com, under "Vacation/Seasonal Rentals" and in the *Seattle Weekly*, www.seattleweekly.com, under "Short Term Housing."

A FTER YOU'VE FOUND A HOME AND HAVE SETTLED IN A BIT, YOU'LL probably want to explore outside Seattle. The communities of the Puget Sound area and western Washington are wonderful places to visit. Just a short drive away (five hours at most) you'll discover mountain peaks, lush valleys, azure lakes and streams, delightful fields of flowers, and picturesque farms. For general travel information, and a tourism packet, call the **Washington State Tourism Office** at 360-725-5052 or visit www.tourism.wa.gov.

Most of the locations listed in this chapter offer a variety of activities, lodgings and other attractions. For information on outdoor sports like hiking, fishing, and skiing, read the **Sports and Recreation** chapter of this book. See also **Outdoor Guides** in **A Seattle Reading List**.

VASHON ISLAND, WHIDBEY ISLAND, SAN JUAN ISLANDS

Vashon Island is located in the Puget Sound just southwest of West Seattle. Small and green, with a quaint shopping district and an annual strawberry festival, Vashon Island is a great day trip or weekend destination. A ferry ride from downtown Seattle or West Seattle will take you to the island. Although there is bus service on the island, you'll probably want a car once you're there.

Whidbey Island, northwest of Seattle, is one of the two longest islands in the United States (Long Island and Whidbey Island trade the honor back and forth as their measurements change with erosion). Whidbey Island is most easily reached by ferry from Mukilteo, but a longer route through Mount Vernon and Anacortes can save you the ferry fare. Whidbey has several picturesque towns, such as **Coupeville** and **Oak Harbor**. While visiting, make sure you try some mussels in a local seafood restaurant, and take the time to drive to **Deception Pass**, at the north end of the island. The view from the bridge is stunning, though not recommended for those afraid of heights. For a free **Island County Discovery Guide** and other tourist information, call 888-747-7777, or visit www.islandweb.org.

The **San Juan Islands** are reached by ferry, either from Anacortes or Bellingham, and are worth the trip. If possible, give yourself a long weekend or several days; the wait for the ferry can take several hours, especially on a holiday or summer weekend. There are several islands in the San Juans worth visiting, each with breathtaking views. Stay in a quaint bed and breakfast or hotel, or check for vacation rentals on the internet or in Seattle newspapers. You'll find secluded beaches, cozy coffee shops and charming towns. If possible, take your bike or kayak, and tour the islands that way. Ferry rides between islands, especially if you're walking or taking a bicycle, are inexpensive, but you'll want to make sure that the dock is close enough to town, or you might be in for a long haul. For more information, contact the **Orcas Island Chamber of Commerce** at 360-376-2273 or www.orcasisland.org, **Tourist Information and Island Reservations** at 360-378-6977 or www.interisland.net/tourist, or visit the San Juan web site at www.sanjuanweb.com.

SKAGIT VALLEY

Skagit Valley, located only a couple hours north of Seattle, is famous for its tulips, producing more tulips than the Netherlands. During the spring and summer, thousands of visitors come to the valley to see the colorful tulip fields. In addition to viewing acres of waving tulips, be sure to visit nearby **La Conner** or **Mount Vernon**. La Conner is a captivating village, with intimate cafes, homemade ice cream and candy shops, and scrumptious bakeries. A few antique malls on the edges of town attract Seattle collectors as well. Mount Vernon offers several antique malls, delicious eateries, and a local brewpub with excellent food. For more information, call the **Skagit Valley Tulip Festival Office** at 360-428-5959, or visit www.tulipfestival.org.

VICTORIA, VANCOUVER AND HARRISON HOT SPRINGS, B.C.

Located on the southern tip of Vancouver Island, **Victoria, B.C.** is a direct ferry ride from the Seattle Waterfront on the Victoria Clipper. It's a small but appealing city, with a lively waterfront and beautiful gardens. The **Butchart Gardens** in particular are worth a visit. Bus tours leave for the gardens several times a day from the waterfront. Children will enjoy the wax museum with its replicas of famous and historical figures. A trip to Victoria isn't complete without high tea at the Empress Hotel, which presides over the waterfront. For visitor information call Tourism Victoria at 250-953-2033 or visit www.tourismvictoria.com.

A three-hour drive north of Seattle on I-5, **Vancouver, B.C.** is a cosmopolitan port city offering great shopping, including an extensive underground mall and Robson Street, which is lined with fashionable clothing boutiques, trendy cosmetics stores, and unique beauty and bath shops. Visit **Granville Island** for a bustling farmers' market during the day or live music and dancing at night. Rent bicycles and pack a picnic lunch to ride through beautiful **Stanley Park**, which overlooks the shipping activity in the bay. Music concerts and live theater performances draw many Seattle residents to Vancouver, since many tours stop at only one of the two cities. For more information, visit www.tourismvancouver.com

If you're in the mood to relax and get away from the big city pace, consider a trip to the sleepy resort town of **Harrison Hot Springs, B.C.** From any point in this small town, you'll have a spectacular view of Harrison Lake and surrounding mountains. During spring and summer, you can charter a fishing boat, take a cruise on the lake, play golf, go parasailing, play tennis, swim in the lake or the public hot springs, hike, water ski, windsurf, or go horseback riding. Harrison Hot Springs is just a little more than four hours away from Seattle. A stay at the Harrison Hot Springs Resort offers a soak in private hot springs pools and complimentary high tea. While you're in town, stop by Sweet Martha Bakery and Coffee Shop for a slice of homemade pie with real whipped cream. For additional information on the town and neighboring communities call the **Harrison Hot Springs Chamber of Commerce** at 604-796-3425 or visit www3.telus.net/harrisonhotsprings.

EAST OF THE CASCADES

Washington's own Bavarian village, **Leavenworth** is located on Highway 2 on the east side of the Cascade Mountains and attracts many visitors. During the summer, the town is a destination for novice rock climbers, who scale boulders along Icicle Creek. In the fall, Leavenworth presents the music and beer-soaked Oktoberfest celebration. In winter, the village offers nearby skiing at Steven's Pass, as well as Christmas festivals and concerts. For more information, contact the **Leavenworth Chamber of Commerce** at 509-548-5807 or visit www.leavenworth.org.

Also east of the Cascades, **Lake Chelan** is a favorite among sun-seekers and water enthusiasts. In the past, Lake Chelan was best known as the state playground of recent high school grads and college students, but in recent years the area has become a favorite family destination as well. At the southern tip of the lake, the town of Lake Chelan offers crowded bars, casual restaurants and sporting goods shops. Condominiums and motels line the lakeshore, and there is public camping at nearby parks. Call ahead for reservations, though, because the area is usually packed during the summer months. For additional tourist information call 800-4-CHELAN or go to www.lakechelan.com.

OLYMPIC PENINSULA AND MOUNTAINS

A short ferry ride across Puget Sound, the **Olympic Peninsula** has something for everyone. **Poulsbo** is a small Scandinavian style village located 30 minutes east of the Bainbridge ferry terminal. Stop in for a fabulous donut at the Poulsbo Bakery, home of the original recipe for Poulsbo Bread. Just outside of town, the Thomas Kemper microbrewery offers daily tours and a tasty pub menu. **Port Townsend,** where "An Officer and A Gentleman" was filmed, has historic buildings, antique stores, unusual boutiques and kite shops. You can also catch a ferry to Whidbey Island from downtown Port Townsend. **Port Angeles,** at the northern tip of the peninsula, offers ferry service to Victoria, B.C. **Hurricane Ridge,** located only 15 minutes away from Port Angeles, is always worth a visit. The mountaintop views from the ridge are sensational, even if you only drive to the parking lot and visitors' center. Nestled in the Olympic National Park, **Sol Duc Hot Springs,** 360-327-3583, www.northolympic.com/solduc, has cabins and a campground for visitors. Soak in the beautiful outdoor pools, take a short hike to the Sol Duc waterfall, or arrange for a massage from on-site massage therapists.

Another short drive takes you to secluded **Ruby Beach,** one of the nicest sandy beaches on the Washington Coast. For more information on the Olympic Peninsula, visit the **North Olympic Peninsula Visitor and Convention Bureau** at www.olympicpeninsula.org or call 800-942-4042.

If you are interested in hiking or mountain climbing, get a copy of one of the many hiking guides to the Olympics. (See the **Literary Life** section of the **Cultural Life** chapter for a list of area bookstores.) If you enjoy mountain climbing, two mountains on the Peninsula are especially challenging: The Brothers is the twin-peaked mountain that is easily visible from Seattle, and Mount Olympus, while it cannot be seen from the city, is the tallest mountain in the Olympic range. To climb to the summit of either of these peaks, contact a local mountain climbing club or guide service (see the **Sports and Recreation** chapter for listings). Happily, there are many more hikes in the Olympics that are manageable for the average person. For information on **Olympic National Park,** call 360-452-4501 or visit www.nps.gov/olym.

THE COAST

In the mood for a picturesque beach resort town and spectacular ocean view? Try either the southwest Washington coast or northern Oregon coast. **Long Beach,** at the far southwest tip of Washington, is said to be the world's longest beach. Several annual events are held in Long Beach, such as a state kite-flying festival, regional stunt kite competition, sand sculpture contest and Fourth of July fireworks celebration. Contact the **Long Beach**

Peninsula Visitor's Bureau at 360-642-2400 or 800-451-2542, or visit www.funbeach.com. Across the mouth of the Columbia, the Oregon coast offers a stretch of beautiful beaches and ocean surf. **Seaside** is the best known destination, with affordable beach cottages and hotels and access to an expanse of white sandy beach. Other nearby towns attract fewer visitors, a plus for those in search of a private stretch of beach or a romantic getaway. If that's your preference, rent a cottage in **Gearhart** or reserve a room overlooking the ocean in **Cannon Beach**. For more information on these and other Oregon destinations, call the **Oregon Tourism Commission** at 503-986-0000 or visit www.traveloregon.com. The drive to Long Beach from Seattle is about four hours; Seattle to Seaside takes four to five hours, even in Friday rush hour traffic. If possible, give yourself a long weekend, but expect more crowds if it's a holiday.

MOUNT RAINIER

Majestic **Mount Rainier** will be a familiar sight soon after you move here, and definitely worth a visit. During the winter, **Crystal Mountain Ski Resort** bustles with activity while the rest of the mountain is deserted. In early spring however, the roads begin to re-open and visitors flock to the area to hike, mountain climb and camp. Mount Rainier is a challenging hiking or climbing destination even for experienced climbers. Some short hikes near the base of the mountain are suitable for the average recreational hiker; look in a good hiking book or trail guide for details. For anything other than a day hike on a well-marked trail be sure to research your route carefully and take an experienced outdoorsman or guide with you. If you're interested in climbing to the summit, contact a local mountain climbing club or guide service (several are listed in the **Sports and Recreation** chapter). Don't let the beauty of the Cascades and Olympics fool you; people get lost and some die every year climbing mountains in Washington. For more information, call Mount Rainier National Park at 360-569-2211 or visit the National Park Service's Mount Rainier web site at www.nps.gov/mora.

S PEND A YEAR IN SEATTLE AND THE DELIGHTFUL MIX OF EVENTS THAT take place here will amaze you. Residents embrace the few months of sunshine and the long, wet winter months with a variety of music, food, and arts festivals, and sporting events. Below is a list of annual highlights you won't want to miss. Unless otherwise noted, all events are held in Seattle. To find events in communities outside of Seattle, check your local newspaper or visit www.festivals.com.

JANUARY

- **Keeping the Dream Alive: Martin Luther King, Jr. Celebration**—Seattle Center, 206-684-7200, www.seattlecenter.com; this annual celebration features a unity march, motivational speakers, music and entertainment.
- **Seattle Boat Show**—Stadium Exhibition Center, 206-634-0911, www.seattleboatshow.com; the Northwest Marine Trade Association sponsors this annual event for boat enthusiasts and prospective buyers.
- **Vietnamese Lunar New Year Celebration**—Seattle Center, 206-706-2658, www.tetinseattle.org; the Vietnamese community celebrates Tet, its most important festival of the year.

FEBRUARY

- **Chinese New Year**—International District, 206-382-1197, www.internationaldistrict.org; this traditional Chinese festival includes a colorful parade.
- **Festival Sundiata**—Seattle Center, 206-684-7200, www.seattlecenter.com; this annual celebration commemorates African and African-American culture, history, and art, with exhibits and live performances.

- **Mardi Gras**—Pioneer Square, 206-622-2563; Seattle's very own Fat Tuesday celebration takes place in bars throughout the city's historic district.
- **Northwest Flower and Garden Show**—Washington State Convention Center, 206-789-5333, www.gardenshow.com; a gardener's paradise, featuring seminars, displays, workshops, and vendors.
- **Seattle Home Show**—Stadium Exhibition Center, 206-284-0960, www.seattlehomeshow.com; homeowners find thousands of ideas for improving their homes inside and out.
- **Seattle International Sportsmen's Expo**—Stadium Exhibition Center, 800-545-6100, www.sportsexpos.com; fans of hunting, fishing, camping and outdoor travel flock to this annual event.
- **Wintergrass Bluegrass Festival**—Sheraton Tacoma Hotel and Convention Center, Tacoma, 253-428-8056, www.wintergrass.com; this midwinter festival is filled with music, workshops and music.

MARCH

- **Board This**—the Summit at Snoqualmie, www.1077theend.com; local alternative rock station KNDD "The End" sponsors this annual snowboarding and punk rock extravaganza. In addition to loud music and exuberant fans, the event features a pro-invitational snowboard competition, and related demos and products.
- **Daffodils in Bloom Celebration**—La Conner, 888-642-9287, www.laconnerchamber.com; fields ablaze with yellow blossoms are found just a short drive from Seattle.
- **Irish Week Festival**—Seattle Center, 206-684-7200, www.seattlecenter.com; this family festival celebrates St. Patrick's Day by presenting Irish films, history, dancing, language workshops, and a festive parade through downtown Seattle.
- **Seattle International Bicycle Expo**—Stadium Exhibition Center, 206-522-3222, www.cascade.org/expo; cycling enthusiasts enjoy exhibits, demonstrations, and presentations on all aspects of the sport.
- **Seattle Women's Show**—Stadium Exhibition Center, 425-485-0285, www.nwwomenshow.com; fashion, fitness, and food combine to make this event a local favorite.
- **St. Patrick's Day Parade**—Bainbridge Island, 206-842-2982, www.bainbridgechamber.com; the island community of Bainbridge hosts a kids' parade to celebrate the Irish in everyone.
- **Whirligig**—Seattle Center, 206-684-7200, www.seattlecenter.com; the Seattle Center presents an educational and fun-filled family event, with activities for children.

APRIL

- **Earth Day Puget Sound**—206-781-7888; www.earthdayseattle.org; a variety of events are held throughout the region in recognition of Earth Day, including exhibits, activities, and music along Seattle's waterfront.
- **Seattle Cherry Blossom Festival**—Seattle Center, 206-993-3999, www.seattlecenter.org; this annual festival celebrates both contemporary and traditional aspects of Japanese culture with artists, stage performances, children's entertainment, and exhibits.
- **Seattle Jewish Festival**—Seattle Center, 206-684-7200, www.seattlecenter.com, seattlejewishfestival.org; celebrate the culture and traditions of Judaism with food, entertainment, and art.
- **Skagit Valley Tulip Festival**—Mount Vernon, 360-428-5959, www.tulipfestival.org; for two weeks in April, the Skagit Valley hosts the annual Tulip Festival, featuring tours of brilliantly colored fields of silky tulips, set against a backdrop of Mount Baker and the Cascade Mountains. Enjoy local art exhibits and special events, dine in local restaurants, visit nearby antique malls in La Conner or Mount Vernon, or send bulbs in your favorite colors to loved ones.
- **Take Our Daughters to Work Day**—206-684-4537, http://takeourdaughterstowork.org; the City of Seattle promotes the national celebration by encouraging teachers and employers to participate.

MAY

- **Bike to Work Day**—206-684-5420; Seattle joins the national promotion of the two-wheeled commute.
- **MS Walk**—206-284-4236, www.nmsswas.org; the MS Walk supports national research and local programs for more than 6,500 people living with Multiple Sclerosis in Western and Central Washington.
- **Northwest Folklife Festival**—Seattle Center, 206-684-7200, www.nwfolklife.org; held every Memorial Day weekend, the Folklife Festival celebrates the folk arts communities of the Northwest. This free event offers a blend of world music and dance performance, arts and crafts exhibits, musical and artistic workshops, and films and demonstrations focusing on ethnic and folk heritage from the Northwest. There's always an abundance of fragrant and delicious foods, but sunshine can be in short supply.
- **Opening Day**—206-325-1000, www.seattleyachtclub.org; on the first Saturday of May, the Seattle Yacht Club sponsors the Opening Day celebration, which marks the first official day of the summer boating sea-

son, a Seattle tradition since 1909. Hundreds of gaudily decorated pleasure boats parade through the Montlake Cut and then tie up to one another in Lake Washington to watch the Windermere Cup rowing race. Even if you don't own a boat, you can enjoy the spectacle from the Montlake Bridge or from the sloping sides of the cut.

- **Pike Place Market Festival**—Pike Place Market, 206-587-0351, www.seattlepublicmarket.com; held each Memorial Day weekend to celebrate the arrival of summer, this event features music stages, Northwest food and craft vendors, and beer and coffee gardens.
- **Seattle International Children's Festival**—Seattle Center, 206-684-7338, www.seattleinternational.com; this annual event—one of the largest of its kind in the United States—features appearances by performing troupes from around the world.
- **Seattle International Film Festival**—206-324-9996, www.seattlefilm.com; the Seattle International Film Festival (SIFF) hosts new, independent and restored films in Seattle theaters for three weeks of May and June. SIFF is known internationally and often debuts new films, or shows independently produced films well before their scheduled release dates. The filmmakers or screenwriters attend some showings, and audience members can ask questions or offer comments.
- **Syttende Mai**—Ballard, 206-784-9705, www.ballardchamber.com; this annual Scandinavian festival is held in the Ballard neighborhood to commemorate Norwegian Independence Day.
- **University District Street Fair**—University District, 206-547-4417; several blocks of University Way are closed to traffic for this fair, which features arts and crafts kiosks, music and dance performances, and lots of great food.

JUNE

- **Chinese Culture and Arts Festival**—Seattle Center, 206-684-7200, www.seattlecenter.com; the Seattle Center hosts two days of Chinese opera, dance, visual arts, ancient crafts and children's activities.
- **Edmonds Arts Festival**—Frances Anderson Center, Edmonds, 425-771-6412, www.edfest.com; this festival 20 miles north of Seattle attracts more than 75,000 spectators over Father's Day weekend.
- **Lake Union Wooden Boat Festival**—the Center for Wooden Boats, 206-382-2628, www.cwb.org; maritime experts and wooden boats gather at the south end of Lake Union.
- **Out to Lunch Concert Series**—206-623-0340, www.downtownseattle.com; held at venues in downtown Seattle, this intimate concert series produced by the Downtown Seattle Association attracts many popular musicians.

- **Seattle Pride**—Capitol Hill, 206-324-0405, www.seattlepride.org; the Seattle Pride march, parade and celebration are boisterous events that take place on the last weekend in June. The sidewalks along the Broadway route are jammed with animated onlookers. Parade participants range from politicians to "dykes on bikes."
- **Pagdiriwang**—Seattle Center, 206-684-7200, www.seattlecenter.com; a celebration of Philippine culture, this festival includes music, dance and dramatic performances.
- **Solstice Parade**—Fremont, 206-547-7440, www.fremontartscouncil.org; a festival that sometimes features nude bicyclists and unusually costumed participants, this event celebrates the summer solstice with a boisterous parade.

JULY

- **Arab Festival**—Seattle Center, 206-684-7200; a tribute to the more than 5,000 Arab people who live in Washington, the Arab Festival features folk dancing, a traditional bazaar, food, and cultural and educational booths.
- **AT&T Family Fourth**—Gasworks Park, Lake Union, 206-281-7788, www.familyfourth.org; the annual fireworks spectacular sponsored by AT&T takes place above Lake Union near downtown. The Seattle Symphony accompanies the brilliant display from Gasworks Park, which is always crowded with people. Other viewpoints along the lake are usually full of onlookers as well. If you know anyone with a boat, convince them to head out to Lake Union to watch the fireworks from the water—truly a memorable experience.
- **AT&T Summer Nights at the Pier**—Seattle Waterfront, 206-628-0888; www.summernights.org; throughout the summer months, a series of concerts is held on Piers 62 and 63. Perhaps the most intimate live music venue in Seattle, this location is also breathtakingly beautiful, with the sun setting over the Olympic Mountains, sailboats floating in the Puget Sound, and the moon rising slowly over the city skyline. The lineup of musicians is equally inspiring, with folk, jazz and blues bands predominating. Arrive early and have a glass of wine while watching the boats in Elliott Bay.
- **Bellevue Art Museum Fair**—Bellevue, 425-519-0770, www.bellevueart.org; artists from across the country exhibit their work at the most successful art festival in the Pacific Northwest.
- **Bite of Seattle**—Seattle Center, 206-684-7200, www.biteofseattle.com; "The Bite" showcases local restaurants, microbreweries, wineries, and coffee houses. Local merchants and artisans open small booths to display

NEWCOMER'S HANDBOOK FOR SEATTLE

358

and sell their wares, and musicians, jugglers and other performers provide outdoor entertainment.

- **Chinatown/International District Summer Festival**—International District, 206-382-1197, www.internationaldistrict.org; Chinatown celebrates summer with cultural entertainment, ethnic foods, arts and crafts, and community booths.
- **Fourth of Jul-Ivars**—206-587-6500, www.ivars.net; a fantastic show of fireworks over Elliott Bay, this Independence Day event is enjoyed from the Seattle Waterfront and Myrtle Edwards Park.
- **King County Fair**—King County Fairgrounds, Enumclaw, 800-325-6165, www.metrokc.gov/parks/fair; Washington's oldest county fair includes nationally known entertainers, a professional rodeo and all the usual fair fixin's.
- **Seafair**—206-728-0123, www.seafair.com; the Seafair festival begins in mid-July but lasts well into August, and offers something for everyone. The Milk Carton Derby at Green Lake, which usually kicks off Seafair, is a race of homemade boats kept afloat (or not) by milk cartons. A true community celebration, Seafair consists of numerous neighborhood festivals, kids' parades and sidewalk sales. Athletic events include a sprint-distance triathlon and the Torchlight Run. Other events include the Annual Torchlight Parade, a performance by the Blue Angels, and the arrival of the Seafair Fleet, Naval and Coast Guard ships that can be toured on the Seattle Waterfront. The grand finale of this event is the Seafair hydroplane race (and qualifying races), which takes place on Lake Washington. During the races, Seward Park is packed, and everyone with access to a boat takes to the water to watch the excitement.
- **Seattle to Portland Bicycle Classic**—206-522-3222, www.seattletoportland.com; this annual Cascade Bicycle Club event runs more than 200 miles between Seattle and Portland.
- **WOMAD**—Marymoor Park, Redmond, www.womad.org/usa; inspired by musician Peter Gabriel, WOMAD celebrates world music, arts and dance with three days of back-to-back performances.

AUGUST

- **BrasilFest**—Seattle Center, 206-684-7200; www.seattlecenter.com; this sultry celebration of South American soul and Brazilian style features performances, children's activities, workshops, and food.
- **Danskin Triathlon**—800-452-9526, www.danskin.com/triathlon; more than 3,000 women compete each August in the largest and longest-running triathlon series in multi-sport history. The annual event consists of a half-mile swim, 12-mile bike, and 3.1-mile run in and along Lake Washington.

- **Evergreen State Fair**—Monroe, 360-805-6700, www.evergreenfair.org; concerts, exhibits, plus carnival and rodeo events pack twelve days in late August and early September.
- **Hempfest**—Myrtle Edwards Park, 206-781-5734, www.seattle-hempfest.com; attendees rally in support of legalized marijuana at the north end of the Seattle Waterfront.
- **Night Out Against Crime**—206-684-7555; Seattle joins the rest of the country in promoting crime and drug prevention awareness. Residents turn on their porch lights and gather outdoors to strengthen neighborhood spirit and safety.
- **TibetFest**—Seattle Center, 206-684-7200, www.seattlecenter.com; this festival showcases Tibetan and Himalayan cultural arts, folk music, and dance.

SEPTEMBER

- **Bark in the Park**—Gasworks Park, 425-787-2500, www.barkinthepark.com; this festival for dogs and the people who love them includes a fundraising walk for the PAWS animal shelter, off-leash areas, contests and canine-inspired artwork.
- **Bumbershoot**—Seattle Center, 206-281-7788, www.bumbershoot.org; named after a slang term for umbrella, Bumbershoot is a Labor Day weekend event that has been a Seattle tradition since 1971. The festival that *Rolling Stone* magazine called "The Mother of All Arts Festivals" showcases more than 2,500 artists from all over the world. In addition to arts and crafts booths and dance performances, you'll find fortunetellers, street musicians, delicacies from local restaurants, and non-stop music concerts in multiple venues. The ticket price covers admittance to all of the exhibits and performances, but you'll need to stand in line to get seats for the headlining acts.
- **Commencement Bay Maritime Fest**—Tacoma, http://maritimefest.org; dragon-boat races and a two-day boat-building contest highlight this celebration of Tacoma's working waterfront.
- **Fiestas Patrias**—Seattle Center, 206-684-7200, www.seattlecenter.com; this Latin American cultural festival features traditional food, music and dance performances.
- **Italian Festival**—Seattle Center, 206-684-7200, www.seattlecenter.com; this celebration showcases Italian food, music, art, and dance, including a bocce tournament and film festival.
- **Komen Seattle Race for the Cure**—SAFECO Field, 206-667-6700, www.komenseattle.org; proceeds from this popular 5K run fund research efforts and local breast health and breast cancer outreach efforts.

- **Northwest AIDS Walk & Fun Run**—Seattle Center International Fountain, 206-323-9255, www.nwaidswalk.org; the state's largest single-day fundraising event supports people living with AIDS and HIV in King County.
- **The Puyallup Fair**—Puyallup Fairgrounds, 253-841-5045, www. thefair.com; also known as the Western Washington Fair, this event has been held in Puyallup (PYEW-al-lup) since 1900. If you decide to "do the Puyallup," give yourself a whole day. You'll want to sample a famous onion burger, tour a cattle barn, ride the roller coaster, watch a concert and savor fresh corn on the cob. Or perhaps you'll decide to try your hand at bungee jumping, marvel at the hypnotist's skill, visit the prize-winning vegetable exhibit, and have several hot buttery scones. Don't assume this is a little country affair, or you'll miss out on one of the best events of the year. Puyallup is near Tacoma, about an hour and a half drive from Seattle. The fair lasts for 2-3 weeks in September.
- **Salmon Homecoming Celebration**—The Seattle Aquarium, Piers 62/63, Waterfront Park, 206-386-4300, www.salmonhomecoming.org; The Seattle Aquarium, Northwest Indian Fisheries Commission and the Muckleshoot Tribe together host this celebration that aims to build bridges between tribal and non-tribal communities.
- **Seattle Fringe Theatre Festival**—206-342-9172, www.seattlefringe.org; emerging writers, actors and directors hone their craft at venues throughout the city.

OCTOBER

- **Issaquah Salmon Days Festival**—Issaquah, 206-270-2532, www.salmondays.org; Issaquah celebrates the return of salmon to its lakes, streams and downtown hatchery.
- **Northwest Bookfest**—Stadium Exhibition Center, 206-378-1883, http://nwbookfest.org; the largest literary festival in the Pacific Northwest attracts more than 30,000 bibliophiles each year.
- **Seattle Home Show 2**—Stadium Exhibition Center, 206-284-0960, www.seattlehomeshow.com; the popular spring event is duplicated in the fall, with tips on winterizing your home.

NOVEMBER

- **Apple Cup**—206-543-2200, http://gohuskies.fansonly.com; the state football rivalry of the season pits the University of Washington Huskies against the Washington State University Cougars. The venue alternates between Husky Stadium in Seattle and Martin Stadium in Pullman, east of the Cascades.

- **Green Lake Frostbite Regatta**—206-684-4074, www.ci.seattle. wa.us/parks/boats; just as the weather gets a little too cold and the wind picks up the bite of winter, two annual rowing events are held in Seattle. The Frostbite Regatta is a series of fairly short races, easily watched from the side of the lake with a hot cup of coffee in hand.
- **Head of the Lake Race**—206-547-1583, http://lakewashingtonrowing.com; the Head of the Lake Race, which is held on a course that includes parts of both Lake Union and Lake Washington, is a three-mile race that tests the endurance of both rowers and spectators.
- **Hmong New Year Celebration**—Seattle Center, 206-684-7200, www.seattlecenter.com; this Laotian Hmong festival celebrates the lunar new year with art exhibits and dance performances.
- **Seattle International Auto Show**—Stadium Exhibition Center, 206-623-2034, www.seattleautoshow.com; Valvoline and Wells Fargo present 700 new cars, trucks, SUVs and minivans, plus rare "super-cars" and concept vehicles.
- **Seattle Marathon**—206-729-3660, www.seattlemarathon.org; this annual athletic event features a rolling course with scenic views, and a reputation for cold and rainy weather. The event also offers a marathon walk, half-marathon run and walk, and kids' marathon.
- **Winterfest**—Seattle Center, 206-684-7200, www.king5.com/winterfest; an annual holiday event, this festival features school choirs, a public ice rink and a model train display. The five-week festival is a family favorite.
- **Yulefest**—Nordic Heritage Museum, Ballard, 206-789-5707, www.nordicmuseum.com; Ballard celebrates the holidays and its Scandinavian heritage the weekend before Thanksgiving.

DECEMBER

- **Christmas Ship Festival**—206-623-1445, www.argosycruises.com; boaters in Seattle celebrate the holiday season with a festive parade of lighted boats that tour Puget Sound, Lake Washington and Lake Union during the weeks before Christmas.
- **New Year's Eve at the Space Needle**—Space Needle, 800-937-9582, www.spaceneedle.com; for the past several years, the Space Needle has been the site of the liveliest New Year's celebration in Seattle. From the formal dinner dance at the revolving restaurant level to the casual party at the base of the needle, it has become a destination for New Year's revelers. Even if you decide to spend a quiet New Year's Eve at home, consider driving (or walking) to one of the many parks overlooking the Space Needle just before midnight. The fireworks display, which is set off from the top and sides of the structure, is spectacular.

- **The Nutcracker**—Seattle Center Opera House, 206-441-9411, www.pnb.org; no Christmas in Seattle would be complete without the annual production of The Nutcracker by Pacific Northwest Ballet. With marvelous sets by Maurice Sendak, this unique production is popular with all age groups.
- **Zoolights**—Point Defiance Zoo and Aquarium, Tacoma, 253-591-5337, www.pdza.org; more than half a million lights shimmer in the shapes of animals, nursery rhymes, and local landmarks.

AGING

- **American Association of Retired Persons (AARP)**, 206-517-9348, 800-424-3410, 206-517-9344 (TTY), www.aarp.org
- **King County Aging Program**, 206-296-5216, www.metrokc.gov
- **Senior Information and Assistance Program**, 206-448-3110
- **Senior Services of Seattle/King County**, 206-448-5757, 206-448-5025 (TDD), www.seniorservices.org

ALCOHOL AND DRUG ABUSE

- **Adult Children of Alcoholics/Adult Children Anonymous**, 206-783-3722, 800-562-1240
- **The Al-Anon & Alateen Information Service**, 206-625-0000
- **Alcohol/Drug 24-Hour Help Line**, 206-722-3700, 800-562-1240, www.adhl.org
- **Alcohol Drug Teen Help Line**, 206-722-4222, 800-562-1240, www.theteenline.org
- **Alcoholics Anonymous**, 206-587-2838; Bellevue, 425-454-9192; Edmonds, 425-672-0987, www.alcoholics-anonymous.org
- **Cocaine Anonymous**, 206-365-8029, www.ca.org
- **Highline Recovery Services**, 206-242-2260
- **King County Alcoholism and Substance Abuse Services & Information**, 206-296-5213, www.metrokc.gov
- **King County Chemical Dependency Civil Commitment**, 206-296-7612
- **Nicotine Anonymous**, www.nicotine-anonymous.org

- Salvation Army Adult Rehabilitation Center, 206-587-0503, www.nwarmy.org
- Valley Medical Recovery Center, 425-228-3450, www.valleymed.org
- Women's Recovery Center, 206-547-1955

ANIMALS

- Animal Bites, 911
- City of Seattle Animal Control, 206-386-4254, www.ci.seattle. wa.us/rca/animal
- City of Seattle Pet Licenses, 206-386-4262, www.ci.seattle. wa.us/rca/animal
- Humane Society for Seattle/King County, 425-641-0080, www.seattlehumane.org
- The Humane Society of the United States, 206-526-0949, www.hsus.org

THE ARTS

- King County Arts Commission, 206-296-7580, www.metrokc. gov/exec/culture/arts
- Seattle Arts Commission, 206-684-7171, www.cityofseattle.net/arts
- Washington State Arts Commission, 360-753-3860, www.wa.gov/art
- Washington Commission for the Humanities, 206-682-1770, www.humanities.org

AUTOMOBILES

- American Automobile Association (AAA) of Washington, 206-448-5353; Bellevue, 425-455-3933; Everett, 425-353-7222; Lynnwood, 425-775-3571; Renton, 425-251-6040; www.aaawa.com
- City of Seattle—Abandoned Automobiles/Public Areas, 206-684-8763, www.ci.seattle.wa.us
- City of Seattle—Illegally Parked Vehicles, 206-625-5011, www.ci.seattle.wa.us
- City of Seattle—Inoperative Automobiles/Private Property, 206-684-7899, www.ci.seattle.wa.us
- Department of Ecology, 800-272-3780, www.ecy.wa.gov
- King County Vehicle/Vessel License Information, 206-296-4000, 206-296-2709 (TTY), www.metrokc.gov/lars/autoboat
- Municipal Court of Seattle (parking tickets/traffic violations), 206-684-5600, 206-684-5210 (TTY), www.ci.seattle.wa.us/courts
- Seattle Police Department Auto Impound, 206-684-5444, www.cityofseattle.net/police

- **Washington State Department of Licensing**, 360-902-3600, www.wa.gov/dol

BIRTH AND DEATH RECORDS

- **King County Vital Statistics**, 206-296-4769, www.metrokc.gov
- **State of Washington Department of Health Center for Health Statistics**, Birth/Death/Marriage/Divorce Certificates, 360-236-4300, www.doh.wa.gov

CHAMBERS OF COMMERCE

SEATTLE
- **Ballard Chamber of Commerce**, 206-784-9705, www.ballardchamber.com
- **Beacon Hill Chamber of Commerce**, 206-326-2479
- **Greater Seattle Chamber of Commerce**, 206-389-7200, www.seattlechamber.com
- **Greater University Chamber of Commerce**, 206-547-4417, www.gucc.org
- **Lake City Chamber of Commerce**, 206-363-3287
- **Magnolia Chamber of Commerce**, 206-284-5836
- **Southwest King County Chamber of Commerce**, 206-575-1633, www.swkcc.org
- **Wallingford Chamber of Commerce**, 206-632-0645, www.wallingford.org/chamber
- **West Seattle Chamber of Commerce**, 206-932-5685, www.wschamber.com
- **White Center Chamber of Commerce**, 206-763-4196

EASTSIDE
- **Bellevue Chamber of Commerce**, 425-454-2464, www.bellevuechamber.org
- **Greater Issaquah Chamber of Commerce**, 425-392-7024, www.issaquahchamber.com
- **Greater Kirkland Chamber of Commerce**, 425-822-7066, www.kirklandchamber.org
- **Mercer Island Chamber of Commerce**, 206-232-3404, www.mercerislandchamber.org
- **Redmond Chamber of Commerce**, 425-885-4014, www.redmondchamber.org
- **Woodinville Chamber of Commerce**, 425-481-8300, www.woodinvillechamber.org

WEST
- **Bainbridge Island Chamber of Commerce**, 206-842-3700, www.bainbridgechamber.org

NORTH
- **Everett Area Chamber of Commerce**, 425-252-5181, www.snobiz.org
- **Greater Edmonds Chamber of Commerce**, 425-670-1496, www.edmondswa.com
- **Northshore Chamber of Commerce**, 425-486-1245, www.northshorecc.org
- **Shoreline Chamber of Commerce**, 206-361-2260
- **South Snohomish County Chamber of Commerce**, 425-774-0507, www.sscchamber.org

SOUTH
- **Greater Federal Way Chamber of Commerce**, 253-838-2605, www.federalwaychamber.com
- **Greater Des Moines Chamber of Commerce**, 206-878-7000
- **Greater Renton Chamber of Commerce**, 425-226-4560, www.renton.net
- **Kent Chamber of Commerce**, 253-854-1770, www.kentchamber.com
- **Tacoma Pierce County Chamber of Commerce**, 253-627-2175, www.tacomachamber.org

CITY GOVERNMENTS

SEATTLE
- **Citizens Service Bureau** (complaints and information), 206-684-8811, 206-615-0476, www.cityofseattle.net/don/csb
- **City Attorney**, 206-684-8200, 206-233-7206 (TTY), www.cityofseattle.net/law
- **City Auditor**, 206-233-3801, www.cityofseattle.net/audit
- **City Council**, 206-684-8888, 206-233-0025 (TTY), www.cityofseattle.net/council
- **City Information**, 206-386-1234, 206-615-0476 (TTY), www.cityofseattle.net
- **Crime Prevention**, 206-684-7555, www.cityofseattle.net/police
- **Office for Civil Rights**, 206-684-4500, www.cityofseattle.net/civilrights
- **Mayor's Office**, 206-684-4000, www.cityofseattle.net/mayor
- **Neighborhoods**, 206-684-0464, www.cityofseattle.net/don
- **Seattle Chamber of Commerce**, 206-389-7200, www.seattlechamber.com

EASTSIDE

- **Bellevue**, 425-452-6800, www.ci.bellevue.wa.us
- **Duvall**, 425-788-1185, www.cityofduvall.com
- **Issaquah**, 425-837-3020, www.ci.issaquah.wa.us
- **Kirkland**, 425-828-1100, 425-828-2245 (TTY/TTD), www.ci.kirkland.wa.us
- **Mercer Island**, 206-236-5300, www.ci.mercer-island.wa.us
- **Newcastle**, 425-649-4444, www.ci.newcastle.wa.us
- **Redmond**, 425-556-2900, www.ci.redmond.wa.us
- **Snoqualmie**, 425-888-1555, www.ci.snoqualmie.wa.us
- **Woodinville**, 425-489-2700, www.ci.woodinville.wa.us

WEST

- **Bainbridge Island**, 206-842-2545, www.ci.bainbridge-isl.wa.us

NORTH

- **Bothell**, 425-486-3256, www.ci.bothell.wa.us
- **Edmonds**, 425-775-2525, www.ci.edmonds.wa.us
- **Everett**, 425-257-8700, www.everettwa.org
- **Kenmore**, 425-398-8900, www.cityofkenmore.com
- **Lake Forest Park**, 206-368-5440, www.cityoflfp.com
- **Lynnwood**, 425-775-1971, www.ci.lynnwood.wa.us
- **Mountlake Terrace**, 425-776-1161, www.ci.mountlake-terrace.wa.us
- **Shoreline**, 206-546-1700, 206-546-0457 (TTY), www.cityofshoreline.com

SOUTH

- **Burien**, 206-241-4647, 206-248-5538 (TTY), www.ci.burien.wa.us
- **Des Moines**, 206-878-4595, www.ci.des-moines.wa.us
- **Federal Way**, 253-661-4013, www.ci.federal-way.wa.us
- **Kent**, 253-856-5200, www.ci.kent.wa.us
- **Normandy Park**, 206-248-7603, www.ci.normandy-park.wa.us
- **Renton**, 425-430-6400, www.ci.renton.wa.us
- **SeaTac**, 206-241-9100, www.seatac.wa.gov
- **Tacoma**, 253-591-5000, www.cityoftacoma.org
- **Tukwila**, 206-433-1800, www.ci.tukwila.wa.us

CONSUMER COMPLAINTS AND SERVICES

- **Better Business Bureau of Oregon and Western Washington**, 206-431-2222, www.thebbb.org
- **Citizens Service Bureau**, 206-684-8811, 206-615-0476, www.cityof-seattle.net/don

- **US Consumer Product Safety Commission**, 800-638-2772, 800-638-8270 (TTY), www.cpsc.gov
- **Federal Trade Commission Northwest Regional Office**, 206-220-6363, www.ftc.gov
- **State of Washington Attorney General's Office**, 206-464-7744, 800-276-9883 (announcement line), www.wa.gov/ago
- **State of Washington Consumer Protection Complaints and Inquiries**, 206-464-6684, 800-551-4636, www.wa.gov/ago/consumer
- **State of Washington, Office of Insurance Commissioner**, 360-753-7300, 800-562-6900, www.insurance.wa.gov

COUNTY GOVERNMENTS

KING

- **King County Executive**, 206-296-4040, 206-296-0200 (TTY), www.metrokc.gov/exec
- **King County Department of Development and Environmental Services**, 206-296-6600, 206-296-7217 (TTY), www.metrokc.gov/ddes
- **King County Health Services**, 206-296-4600, www.metrokc.gov/health
- **Metropolitan King County Council**, 206-296-1000, 206-296-1024 (TTY/TDD), www.metrokc.gov/mkcc

PIERCE

- **Pierce County Council**, 253-798-7777, 253-798-4018 (TDD), www.co.pierce.wa.us
- **Pierce County Executive**, 253-798-7477, www.co.pierce.wa.us
- **Tacoma-Pierce County Health Department**, 253-798-6500, 800-992-2456, www.healthdept.co.pierce.wa.us
- **Pierce County Planning and Land Services Department**, 253-798-7210, www.co.pierce.wa.us

SNOHOMISH

- **Snohomish County Executive**, 425-388-3460, www.co.snohomish.wa.us/executiv
- **Snohomish County Council**, 425-388-3494, www.co.snohomish.wa.us/council
- **Snohomish Health District**, 425-258-4227, www.snohd.org
- **Snohomish County Planning and Development Services**, 425-388-3311, www.co.snohomish.wa.us/pds

CRIME

- **Crime in Progress,** 911
- **City of Seattle Crime Prevention,** 206-684-7555, www.cityofseattle. net/police

CRISIS LINES

CHILD ABUSE AND NEGLECT
- **New Beginnings for Battered Women and their Children,** (TTY/Voice) 206-522-9472
- **State of Washington Department of Social and Health Services— Child Abuse Reporting,** (24-hours) 206-721-6500, (weekdays), 425-649-4110; East King County, 425-649-4110. 800-952-0073; South King County, 253-872-2665, 800-422-7880; North Seattle, 206-721-6500, 800-379-3395; South Seattle, 206-721-6500, 800-379-4139; www.dshs.wa.gov
- **State of Washington Domestic Violence Hotline,** 800-562-6025, www.courts.wa.gov/dv

CRISIS HOTLINE
- **Crisis Clinic 24-hour Crisis Line,** 206-461-3222, 206-461-3219 (TDD)

DOMESTIC ABUSE
- **Domestic Abuse Women's Network,** 425-656-7867, www.dawnonline.org
- **King County Domestic Violence Automated Information Service,** 206-205-5555, www.metrokc.gov/dvinfo
- **National Domestic Violence Hotline,** 800-799-SAFE, 800-787-3224 (TTY), www.ndvh.org
- **New Beginnings for Battered Women and their Children,** (TTY/Voice) 206-522-9472
- **Northwest Family Life Skills,** 206-363-9601
- **State of Washington Adult Protective Services,** 206-341-7660, 800-346-9257, www.aasa.dshs.wa.gov
- **State of Washington Domestic Violence Hotline,** 800-562-6025, www.courts.wa.gov/dv

RAPE AND SEXUAL ASSAULT
- **Harborview Center for Sexual Assault and Traumatic Stress,** 206-521-1800, www.washington.edu/medical
- **King County Sexual Assault Resource Center,** 425-226-7273, 800-825-7273, www.kcsarc.org

DISABLED, SERVICES FOR THE

See the **Helpful Services** chapter

DISCRIMINATION

- **City of Seattle Office for Civil Rights**, 206-684-4500, 206-684-4503 (TTY), www.cityofseattle.net/civilrights
- **City of Seattle Office for Civil Rights**, Hate Crimes Hotline, 206-233-1080, www.cityofseattle.net/civilrights
- **State of Washington Human Rights Commission**, (Voice/TTY) 206-464-6500, www.wa.gov/hrc

EMERGENCY

- **Fire, Police, Medical**, 911
- **Federal Emergency Management Agency**, 425-487-4600, 800-525-0321, www.fema.gov

FEDERAL OFFICES/CENTERS

- **Centers for Disease Control and Prevention**, 404-639-3311, www.cdc.gov
- **Consumer Product Safety Commission**, 800-638-2772, 800-638-8270 (TTY), www.cpsc.gov
- **Federal Consumer Information Center**, 888-878-3256, www.pueblo.gsa.gov
- **Federal Emergency Management Agency**, 425-487-4600, 800-525-0321, www.fema.gov
- **Federal Information Center**, 800-688-9889, 800-326-2996 (TTY), http://fic.info.gov
- **Health Care Information**, 800-358-9295, 800-586-6340 (TTY)
- **Small Business Administration**, 206-553-7310, 206-553-7349 (TTY), www.sbaonline.sba.gov
- **Social Security Administration**, 800-772-1213, 800-325-0778 (TTY), www.ssa.gov
- **US Attorney, Western District of Washington**, 206-553-7970, www.usdoj.gov
- **US Census Bureau**, 206-553-5837, www.census.gov
- **US Government Bookstore**, 206-553-4270

GARBAGE

- **Seattle Public Utilities Household Hazardous Waste**, 206-296-4692, www.cityofseattle.net
- **Seattle Public Utilities Recycling and Disposal Station Information Line**, 684-8400, www.cityofseattle.net
- **Seattle Public Utilities Solid Waste Services**, Missed Collection Hotline, 206-684-7600, 206-233-7241 (TTY), www.cityofseattle.net

HEALTH AND MEDICAL CARE

STATE OF WASHINGTON
- **Washington State Healthcare Authority**, 800-826-2444, www.wa.gov/hca
- **Healthy Mothers, Healthy Babies**, 800-322-2588, www.hmhbwa.org
- **State of Washington Department of Social and Health Services**, 360-902-8400, 800-737-0617, www.dshs.wa.gov

SEATTLE
- **Children's Hospital & Medical Center Resource Line**, 206-526-2500, 877-526-2500, www.seattlechildrens.org
- **Columbia Public Health Center**, 206-296-4650, www.metrokc.gov/health
- **Community Health Access Program**, 206-284-0331
- **Downtown Public Health Center**, 206-296-4755, www.metrokc.gov/health
- **Family Planning Information and Referral Line**, 800-770-4334
- **Harborview Medical Center Sexually Transmitted Disease Program**, 206-731-3590, www.washington.edu/medical/hmc
- **King County Communicable Disease 24-Hour Report Line**, 206-296-4782, www.metrokc.gov/health
- **King County Health Services**, (TTY/Voice) 206-296-4600, www.metrokc.gov/health
- **King County HIV/STD Hotline**, 206-205-7837, www.metrokc.gov/health
- **King County HIV/AIDS Program**, 206-296-4649, www.metrokc.gov/health
- **King County Immunization Program Information**, 206-296-4774, www.metrokc.gov/health
- **King County Medical Society**, 206-621-9393, www.kcmsociety.org
- **North Seattle Public Health Center**, 206-296-4765, www.metrokc.gov/health

- **Northwest Hospital MED-INFO Physician Referral Line**, 206-633-4636, 206-368-1571 (TDD), www.nwhospital.org
- **Seattle Indian Health Board**, 206-324-9360, 800-367-5978, www.sihb.org

SURROUNDING COMMUNITIES
- **Eastgate Public Health Center**, 206-296-4920, www.metrokc.gov/health
- **Federal Way Public Health Center**, 253-838-4557, www.metrokc.gov/health
- **Highline Community Hospital 24-NURSE Information Line**, 206-246-8773, www.hchnet.org
- **Kent Public Health Center**, 206-296-4500, www.metrokc.gov/health
- **Northshore Public Health Center**, 206-296-9787, www.metrokc.gov/health
- **Renton Public Health Center**, 206-296-4700, www.metrokc.gov/health
- **White Center Public Health Center**, 206-296-4646, www.metrokc.gov/health

HOUSING

- **Central Area Motivation Program**, 206-812-4940, www.cityofseattle.net
- **King County Housing Authority**, 206-574-1100, 206-574-1108 (TDD)
- **King County Housing Rehabilitation Programs & Repair Hotline**, 206-296-7640, www.metrokc.gov/dchs/csd/Housing
- **Seattle Housing Authority**, 206-615-3300, www.sea-pha.org
- **Seattle Office for Civil Rights Housing Discrimination**, 206-684-4500, www.cityofseattle.net/civilrights
- **Tenants Union**, 206-723-0500, www.tenantsunion.org
- **Urban League of Metropolitan Seattle**, 206-461-3792, www.urban-league.org
- **Department of Housing and Urban Development**, 206-220-5204, www.hud.gov

LEGAL REFERRAL

- **City of Seattle Attorney**, 206-684-8200, 206-233-7206 (TTY), www.cityofseattle.net/law
- **King County Bar Association**, Lawyer Referral and Information Service, 206-623-2551, www.kcba.org
- **King County Prosecuting Attorney's Protection Order Advocacy Program**, 206-296-9547, www.metrokc.gov/proatty

- **Legal Action Center**, 206-324-6890, www.lac.org
- **Northwest Women's Law Center**, 206-621-7691, www.nwwlc.org
- **Unemployment Law Project**, 206-441-9178, www.unemploymentlawproject.org
- **Volunteer Legal Services**, 206-623-0281

LIBRARIES

See the **Neighborhoods** chapter for branch libraries.

- **Everett Public Library**, 425-257-8000, www.epls.org
- **King County Library System**, 425-369-3200, 800-462-9600, www.kcls.org
- **Pierce County Library System**, 253-536-6500, www.pcl.lib.wa.us
- **Seattle Public Library**, 206-386-4636, www.spl.lib.wa.us
- **Sno-Isle Regional Library System**, 425-778-2148, www.sno-isle.org
- **Tacoma Public Library**, 253-591-5666, www.tpl.lib.wa.us

MARRIAGE LICENSES

- **King County Marriage Licenses**, 206-296-3933, www.metrokc.gov/lars/marriage
- **Pierce County Marriage Licenses**, 253-798-7030, www.co.pierce.wa.us
- **Snohomish County Marriage Licenses**, 425-388-3627, www.co.snohomish.wa.us

PARKS

See the **Neighborhoods** chapter for community center locations, or the **Sports and Recreation** or **Lakes and Parkways** chapters for individual parks.

SEATTLE AND KING COUNTY
- **King County Parks and Recreation Department**, 206-296-4232, 206-296-4245 (TTY), www.metrokc.gov/parks
- **Seattle Parks and Recreation Department**, 206-684-4075, 206-684-4950 (TTY), www.pan.ci.seattle.wa.us/seattle/parks

EASTSIDE
- **Bellevue Parks and Community Services Department**, 425-452-6881, www.ci.bellevue.wa.us/Parks
- **Issaquah Parks and Recreation Department**, 425-837-3300, www.ci.issaquah.wa.us

- **Kirkland Department of Parks & Community Services**, 425-828-1100, www.ci.kirkland.wa.us
- **Mercer Island Parks and Recreation**, 206-236-3545, www.ci.mercer-island.wa.us
- **Newcastle Parks Department**, 425-649-4444, www.ci.newcastle.wa.us/parks
- **Redmond Parks and Recreation**, 425-556-2311, www.ci.redmond.wa.us
- **Snoqualmie Community Development**, 425-888-5337, www.ci.snoqualmie.wa.us
- **Woodinville Recreation and Parks**, 425-398-9327, www.ci.woodinville.wa.us

WEST
- **Bainbridge Island Park and Recreation District**, 206-842-2302, www.biparks.org

NORTH
- **Bothell Parks and Recreation**, 425-486-7430, www.ci.bothell.wa.us/departments/publicworks
- **Edmonds Parks, Recreation & Cultural Services**, 425-771-0230, www.ci.edmonds.wa.us
- **Everett Parks and Recreation**, 425-257-8300, www.everettwa.org/parks
- **Kenmore Parks**, 425-398-8900, www.cityofkenmore.com/local
- **Lake Forest Park Parks**, 206-368-5440, www.cityoflfp.com
- **Lynnwood Parks, Recreation and Cultural Arts Department**, 425-744-6475, www.ci.lynnwood.wa.us
- **Mountlake Terrace Recreation and Parks**, 425-776-9173, www.ci.mountlake-terrace.wa.us/departments/parks
- **Shoreline Parks**, 206-546-6517, www.cityofshoreline.com

SOUTH
- **Burien Parks, Recreation and Cultural Services**, 206-988-3700, www.ci.burien.wa.us
- **Des Moines Parks**, 206-878-4595, www.ci.des-moines.wa.us/parks
- **Kent Parks, Recreation and Community Services**, 253-856-5100, www.ci.kent.wa.us/ParksRecreation
- **Renton Community Services**, 425-430-6600, www.ci.renton.wa.us
- **SeaTac Parks and Recreation**, 206-241-9100, www.seatac.wa.gov
- **Tacoma Metropolitan Park District**, 253-305-1000, www.tacomaparks.com

- **Tukwila Parks and Recreation Department**, 206-767-2342, www.ci.tukwila.wa.us

POLICE

STATE OF WASHINGTON
- **Emergency**, 911
- **Washington State Patrol Non-Emergency**, 425-649-4370, 425-649-4367 (TTY), www.wa.gov/wsp

SEATTLE AND KING COUNTY
- **Emergency**, 911
- **King County Sheriff's Office Non-Emergency**, 206-296-3311, www.metrokc.gov/sheriff
- **Seattle Police Department Non-Emergency**, 206-625-5011, www.cityofseattle.net/police
- **Seattle Police Department East Precinct**, 206-684-4300, www.cityofseattle.net/police
- **Seattle Police Department North Precinct**, 206-684-0850, www.cityofseattle.net/police
- **Seattle Police Department South Precinct**, 206-386-1850, www.cityofseattle.net/police
- **Seattle Police Department West Precinct**, 206-684-8917, www.cityofseattle.net/police

EASTSIDE
- **Bellevue Police Department**, 425-452-6917, 877-881-2731, www.ci.bellevue.wa.us/police
- **Issaquah Police Department**, 425-837-3200, www.ci.issaquah.wa.us/police
- **Kirkland Police Department**, 425-828-1183, 425-822-1244 (TDD), www.ci.kirkland.wa.us
- **Mercer Island Police Division**, 206-236-3500, www.ci.mercer-island.wa.us
- **Newcastle Police Department**, 425-649-4444, www.ci.newcastle.wa.us
- **Redmond Police Department**, 425-556-2500, www.ci.redmond.wa.us
- **Snoqualmie Police Division**, 425-888-3333, www.ci.snoqualmie.wa.us

NORTH

- **Bothell Police Department**, 425-486-1254, www.ci.bothell. wa.us/departments/bpd
- **Edmonds Police Department**, 425-771-0200, www.ci.edmonds. wa.us/PoliceWeb
- **Everett Police Department**, 425-257-8400, www.everettwa.org/city-hall/citydepts
- **Lake Forest Park Police Department**, 206-364-8216, www.cityoflfp. com/city
- **Lynnwood Police Department**, 425-744-6900, www.ci.lynnwood. wa.us/depts/dept/Police
- **Mountlake Terrace Police Department**, 425-670-8260, www.ci. mountlake-terrace.wa.us
- **Shoreline Police Department**, 206-546-6730, www.cityofshoreline. com/cityhall

SOUTH

- **Kent Police Department**, 253-856-5800, www.ci.kent.wa.us/Police
- **Renton Police Department**, 425-430-7500, www.ci.renton.wa.us
- **SeaTac Police Services**, 206-241-9100, www.seatac.wa.gov
- **Tacoma Police Department**, 253-5915905, www.tacomapolice.org
- **Tukwila Police Department**, 206-433-1808, www.ci.tukwila.wa.us

POST OFFICE

See the **Neighborhoods** chapter for branch stations.
- **US Postal Service**, 800-275-8777, www.usps.com

ROAD CONDITION INFORMATION

- **Washington State Department of Transportation Highway Information Line**, 206-368-HIWY, 800-695-7623, www.wsdot.wa.gov

RECYCLING

- **City of Seattle Recycling Information**, 206-684-3000
- **State of Washington Recycling Information**, 800-732-9253

SCHOOLS

GREATER SEATTLE
- **Bellevue School District**, 425-456-4111, 425-456-4211 (TTY), http://belnet.bellevue.k12.wa.us

- **Edmonds School District**, 425-670-7000, www.edmonds.wednet.edu
- **Federal Way Public Schools**, 253-945-2000, www.fwsd.wednet.edu
- **Highline School District**, 206-433-0111, www.hsd401.org
- **Issaquah School District**, 425-837-7000, www.issaquah.wednet.edu
- **Kent School District**, 253-373-7000, www.kent.wednet.edu
- **Lake Washington School District**, 425-702-3200, www.lkwash.wednet.edu
- **Mercer Island School District**, 206-236-3330, www.misd.wednet.edu
- **Northshore School District**, 425-489-6000, www.nsd.org
- **Renton School District**, 425-204-2300, www.renton.wednet.edu
- **Shoreline School District**, 206-367-6111, www.shorelineschools.org
- **Tukwila School District**, 206-901-8000, www.tukwila.wednet.edu

SEATTLE PUBLIC
- **Administrative Center**, 206-252-0000, www.seattleschools.org
- **Automated Enrollment Services Line**, 206-252-0410
- **Bilingual Family Center**, 206-252-7750
- **Central Enrollment Service Center**, 206-720-3533
- **Customer Service Center**, 206-252-0010
- **Highly Capable Services**, 206-252-0130
- **North Enrollment Service Center**, 206-252-0765
- **School Board**, 206-252-0040
- **South Enrollment Service Center**, 206-252-7732
- **Superintendent's Office**, 206-252-0100
- **Special Education Services**, 206-252-0055
- **Transportation Services**, 206-252-0900
- **Wait List Automated Info Line**, 206-252-0212
- **West Seattle Enrollment Service Center**, 206-252-8660

SHIPPING SERVICES

- **Airborne Express**, 800-247-2676, www.airborne.com
- **DHL Worldwide Express**, 800-225-5345, www.dhl-usa.com
- **FedEx**, 800-238-5355, www.fedex.com/us
- **FedEx Ground**, (formerly RPS), 800-238-5355, www.fedex.com/us
- **United Parcel Service (UPS)**, 800-742-5877, www.ups.com
- **US Postal Service Express Mail**, 800-222-1811, www.usps.com

SOCIAL SECURITY

- **Social Security Administration**, 800-772-1213, 800-325-0778 (TTY), www.ssa.gov

SPORTS

- **Everett Aqua Sox** (Northwest League Baseball), 425-258-3673, 800-GO-FROGS, www.aquasox.com
- **Seattle Mariners** (Major League Baseball), 206-346-4000, 206-322-HITS (tickets), http://mariners.mlb.com
- **Seattle Seahawks** (National Football League), 800-300-9540, 206-515-4791 (tickets), www.seahawks.com
- **Seattle Sounders** (A-League Soccer), 206-622-3415, 800-796-5425, www.seattlesounders.net
- **Seattle Sonics** (National Basketball Association), 206-283-DUNK, www.nba.com/sonics
- **Seattle Storm** (Women's National Basketball Association), 206-217-WNBA, www.wnba.com/storm
- **Seattle Thunderbirds** (Western Hockey League), 206-448-PUCK, www.seattle-thunderbirds.com
- **Tacoma Rainiers** (Pacific Coast League Baseball), 800-281-3834, www.tacomarainiers.com
- **University of Washington Huskies** (all teams), 206-543-2200, http://gohuskies.fansonly.com

STATE OF WASHINGTON

- **Attorney General's Office**, 206-464-7744, 800-276-9883 (TTY), www.wa.gov/ago
- **General Information**, 800-321-2808, www.wa.gov
- **Governor's Office**, 360-753-6780, 360-753-6466 (TTY), www.governor.wa.gov
- **Legislative Hotline**, 800-562-6000
- **Secretary of State**, General Information and Elections, 360-902-4151, 800-422-8683 (TTY), www.secstate.wa.gov

STREET MAINTENANCE

- **City of Seattle Street Repairs**, 206-386-1218 (asphalt and concrete), 206-386-1206 (emergency signs and signals), www.cityofseattle.net
- **King County Transportation Department Road Services Division**, 206-296-8100, 800-527-6237, 206-296-0933 (TTY), www.metrokc.gov/tran
- **State of Washington Department of Transportation**, 206-440-4000; Emergency Maintenance, 206-440-4490; Maintenance Administration, 206-440-4650, www.wsdot.wa.gov

TAXES

CITY
- **City of Seattle Finance Office**, 206-684-8300; City Business Tax, 206-684-8484, www.cityofseattle.net/financedepartment

COUNTY
- **King County Assessor's Office**, 206-296-7300, 206-296-7888 (TTY), www.metrokc.gov/assessor
- **King County Personal Property Tax Line**, 206-296-4290, 206-296-4184 (TTY), www.metrokc.gov/taxes
- **King County Property Tax Advisor**, 206-196-5202, www.metrokc.gov/taxes
- **King County Real Estate Tax Information**, 206-296-0923 (automated), 206-296-3850, www.metrokc.gov/taxes

FEDERAL
- **Internal Revenue Service**, Federal Tax Questions, 800-829-1040, 800-829-4059 (TTY); 24-hour Recorded Tax Help, 800-829-4477; www.irs.ustreas.gov
- **Internal Revenue Service Local Taxpayer Advocate**, 206-220-6037, outside Seattle, 877-777-4778

STATE (NO INCOME TAX)
- **Washington State Department of Revenue**, 425-277-7300, 800-647-7706, http://dor.wa.gov

TAXIS

- **Emerald City Taxi**, 206-433-1788
- **Farwest Taxi**, 206-622-1717
- **Orange Cab**, 206-522-8800
- **Yellow and Graytop Cab**, 206-622-6500, www.whatrain.com/psd/yellow

TIME OF DAY/CURRENT TEMPERATURE, 206-361-TIME (8463)

TOURISM

- **Canada, British Columbia**, 800-663-6000
- **City of Seattle Tourism and Sightseeing Links**, www.ci.seattle.wa.us
- **National Park Service**, 202-208-6843; Pacific West Region, 510-817-1300, www.nps.gov

- **National Park Service Campground Reservations**, 800-365-2267, www.nps.gov
- **Seattle-King County Convention and Visitors Bureau**, 206-461-5800, 206-461-5840 (TDD), www.seeseattle.org
- **State of Idaho**, 800-635-7820, www.visitid.org
- **State of Oregon**, 800-547-7842, www.traveloregon.com
- **Washington State Department of Tourism**, 800-890-5493, 360-725-5052, www.tourism.wa.gov

TRANSPORTATION

AIRPORTS
- **Seattle-Tacoma International Airport**, 206-431-4444, www.portseattle.org/seatac
- **King County International Airport** (Boeing Field), 206-296-7380, www.metrokc.gov/airport
- **Renton Municipal Airport**, 425-430-7471, www.ci.renton.wa.us/pw

BUSES
- **Community Transit**, 425-353-RIDE or 800-562-1375, www.commtrans.org
- **Everett Transit**, 425-257-8803, www.ci.everett.wa.us
- **Pierce Transit**, 253-581-8000, 800-562-8109, www.ptbus.pierce.wa.us
- **Greyhound Bus Lines**, 800-231-2222, www.greyhound.com
- **Metro Transit**, 206-553-3000, http://transit.metrokc.gov
- **Seattle Personal Transit**, (TTY/Voice) 206-860-8000
- **Senior Services Volunteer Transportation**, 206-448-5740, www.seniorservices.org
- **ST Express**, 800-201-4900, www.soundtransit.org

TRAINS
- **Amtrak National Route Information**, 800-USA-RAIL, www.amtrak.com
- **Amtrak Seattle Station**, 206-382-4125
- **Sounder Commuter Trains**, 800-201-4900, www.soundtransit.org

FERRIES
- **Washington State Ferries**, 206-464-6400, 800-84-FERRY, www.wsdot.wa.gov/ferries

RIDE SHARING PROGRAMS
- **Metro Transit Ridematch and Vanpool**, 206-625-4500, 800-427-8249, www.rideshareonline.com

UTILITY EMERGENCIES

- **Puget Sound Energy**, 888-225-5773, 800-962-9498 (TTY), www.pse.com
- **Seattle City Light**, 206-684-3000, 206-223-0025 (TTY), www.ci.seattle.wa.us/light
- **Seattle City Light 24-Hour Power Outage Hotline**, 206-684-7400
- **Seattle City Light 24-Hour Electrical Emergency**, 206-706-0051
- **Seattle Public Utilities**, 206-684-3000, 206-233-7241 (TTY), www.cityofseattle.net/util
- **Seattle Public Utilities Emergency Resource Center** (activated during major emergencies), 206-684-3355
- **Seattle Public Utilities Missed Collection Hotline**, 206-684-7600
- **Seattle Public Utilities Sewer or Surface Drainage Emergencies**, 206-386-1800
- **Snohomish County Public Utility District**, 425-783-1000, www.snopud.com
- **Tacoma Power**, 253-502-8602, www.tacomapower.com.

VOTING

- **King County Voter Registration**, 206-296-8683, www.metrokc.gov
- **Washington State Voting and Elections Information**, vote.wa.gov
- **Washington State Voter Registration Information**, 800-448-4881

WASHINGTON STATE LOTTERY

- Seattle Regional Office, 206-764-6455
- Winning Numbers, 800-545-7510, www.wa.gov/lot/home

WEATHER

- **National Weather Service Forecast Office**, 206-526-6087, www.seawfo.noaa.gov
- *Seattle Times* **Information Line**, 206-464-2000, www.seatimes.com

ZIP CODES

- **US Postal Service**, 800-275-8777, www.usps.com

ARCHITECTURE

- *Common Place: Toward Neighborhood and Regional Design* edited by Doug Kelbaugh, applies design concepts to urban issues like housing, transportation, and sprawl, and explores how architecture can improve our lives.
- *Shaping Seattle Architecture: A Historical Guide to the Architects* by Jeffrey Karl Ochsner, traces the history of Seattle's architecture through biographies of the area's best known architects. Many famous Seattle buildings and houses are profiled in this book.

ART

- *A Field Guide to Seattle's Public Art* edited by Steven Huss, contains five self-guided tours of Seattle's best-known public artworks, as well as essays by artists, writers, and historians.
- *Seattle: The Time Has Come* *Seattle Times* columnist Erik Lacitis introduces this breathtaking photo essay.

EMPLOYMENT

- *How to Find a Good Job in Seattle* by Linda Carlson; this regional best seller lists thousands of Northwest employers, professional and alumni associations, and job lines. The author offers seminars based on the book at local community colleges.

FAMILY AND PETS

- *Best Hikes with Children in Western Washington and the Cascades* by Joan Burton; an essential hiking guide for parents, this book describes day hikes and overnighters suitable for the entire family.
- *The Dog Lovers' Companion to Seattle: The Inside Scoop on Where To Take Your Dog in the Seattle Area, Including Victoria and Vancouver* by Steve Giordano; the author and his four-legged friends rate the dog-friendliest parks, hotels and businesses in the Northwest.
- *Out and About Seattle with Kids: The Ultimate Family Guide for Fun and Learning* by Ann Bergman and Stephanie Dunnewind; this handbook can help families who are new to Seattle become acquainted with the city and its child-friendly diversions.

FICTION

- *Deception Pass* by Earl W. Emerson; one of several mysteries by this author that take place in or around Seattle and feature private eye Thomas Black. Also check out *Catfish Café, The Rainy City, Poverty Bay,* and *The Million-Dollar Tattoo.*
- *Indian Killer* by Sherman Alexie; a compelling novel by the author of *The Lone Ranger and Tonto, Fistfight in Heaven,* and *Reservation Blues.*
- *Middle of Nowhere* by Ridley Pearson; the 2001 thriller featuring Seattle detective Lou Boldt. Earlier titles set in the Emerald City include *The Angel Maker, No Witnesses,* and *The First Victim.*
- *More Perfect Union* by J.A. Jance; one in a series of mysteries featuring fictional Seattle detective J.P. Beaumont. Others include *Dismissed with Prejudice, Payment in Kind, Trial by Fury,* and *Improbable Cause.*
- *Skeleton Dance* by Aaron Elkins; one of many mystery novels by local author Elkins. Other titles include *Make No Bones, Loot, Old Bones,* and *Twenty Blue Devils.*
- *Snow Falling on Cedars* by David Guterson; the author of this award-winning mystery set in the Puget Sound area hails from Bainbridge Island. His other books include *East of the Mountains* and *The Country Ahead of Us, the Country Behind.*

FOOD & DINING

- *The Food Lover's Guide to Seattle* by Katy Calcott; a guide book to the city's freshest greens, best baguettes, and surliest fishmongers.
- *Simply Classic: A Collection of Recipes to Celebrate the Northwest* by Junior League of Seattle; an essential guide to Northwest cooking.

- *Tom Douglas' Seattle Kitchen* by Tom Douglas; Seattle's favorite chef and owner of Dahlia Lounge, Etta's Seafood and Palace Kitchen shares some of his inspired recipes.
- *Zagat Survey: Seattle/Portland Restaurants;* the annual edition of this indispensable survey will help you find the right restaurant for every occasion.

HISTORY

- *Answering Chief Seattle* by Albert Furtwangler; a comprehensive historical analysis of Chief Sealth's famous speech.
- *Loser: The Real Seattle Music Story* by Clark Humphrey and Art Chantry; a history of Seattle music from the 1960s to the mid 1990s.
- *Rites of Passage: A Memoir of the Sixties in Seattle* by Walt Crowley; this book blends the author's personal experiences in Seattle with an exploration of the major political events of the 1960s.
- *Seattle Past to Present* by Roger Sale; an excellent book that traces the history of Seattle while providing unique insight into many important decisions made by local politicians and citizens.
- *Skid Road* by Murray Morgan; the now-famous account of early Seattle, from which the phrase "skid row" was coined.

OUTDOOR GUIDES

- *100 Hikes in the Inland Northwest* by Rich Landers; the "100 Hikes" series published by Mountaineers Books also includes *100 Hikes in Washington's Alpine Lakes* by Vicky Spring, *100 Hikes in Washington's Glacier Peak Region, 100 Hikes in Washington's North Cascades National Park Region,* and *100 Hikes in Washington's South Cascades and Olympics* by Ira Spring.
- *Don't Jump!; The Northwest Winter Blues Survival Guide* by Novella Carpenter and Traci Vogel; some silly—and some serious—tips to help Northwesterners through the winter doldrums.
- *Bicycling the Backroads Around Puget Sound* by Bill and Erin Woods; the authors lead readers through 54 scenic tours covering more than 2,000 miles.
- *Nature Walks in and Around Seattle* by Cathy McDonald, Stephen Whitney and James Hendrickson; the updated version of this local guide includes more Eastside hikes. Entries include details about trail distances, nature highlights, terrain, facilities, wheelchair accessibility, and dog prohibitions.

- *Seattle's Lakes, Bays & Waterways (Including the Eastside)* by Marge and Ted Mueller; the "Afoot & Afloat" series from Mountaineers Books also includes Middle Puget Sound & Hood Canal, North Puget Sound, South Puget Sound and The San Juan Islands.

REAL ESTATE

- *Seattle Homes: Real Estate Around the Sound* by Jim Stacey; a quirky must-have for those looking to buy; provides detailed information about the sticky process of finding and buying a house in the Seattle area.

SPORTS

- *Baseball Is Just Baseball: The Understated Ichiro* by David Shields; a collection of quotes from the Japanese baseball star who took Seattle by storm in 2001. Nuggets include, "It was a fly ball. I caught it."
- *Seattle Slew* by Dan Mearns; a biography of the city's most famous thoroughbred, from his Triple Crown glory to the illness that nearly took his life.

MONICA FISCHER grew up in a suburb south of Seattle and couldn't move to the city fast enough after graduating from college. She lived in the First Hill, West Seattle and Wallingford neighborhoods before discovering Magnolia, where she currently lives with her husband, dog and cat. A freelance writer and editor, she has contributed to a variety of newspapers, magazines, and web sites since earning a journalism degree in 1991. While writing this, her first book, she trained for and participated in her first triathlon.

AMY BELLAMY was born in Seattle. She has lived in the Ballard, Eastlake, University District, Fremont, and Capitol Hill neighborhoods. In 1991, she received a BA from the University of Washington with a major in English. Currently she works as a supervisor and technical writer for a telecommunications company.

We would appreciate your comments regarding this second edition of the *Newcomer's Handbook® for Moving to and Living in Seattle.* If you've found any mistakes or omissions or if you would just like to express your opinion about the guide, please let us know. We will consider any suggestions for possible inclusion in our next edition, and if we use your comments, we'll send you a *free* copy of our next edition. Please send this response form to:

Reader Response Department
First Books
6750 SW Franklin, Suite A
Portland, OR 97223 USA

Comments:

_____

_____

_____

_____

_____

_____

Name: _____

Address _____

_____

_____

Telephone (   ) _____

E-mail ____ _____

6750 SW Franklin, Suite A
Portland, OR 97223
503-968-6777
www.firstbooks.com

FIRST BOOKS

THE ORIGINAL, ALWAYS UPDATED, ABSOLUTELY INVALUABLE GUIDES FOR PEOPLE MOVING TO A CITY!

Find out about neigborhoods, apartment and house hunting, money matters, deposits/leases, getting settled, helpful services, shopping for the home, places of worship, cultural life, sports/recreation, volunteering, green space, schools and education, transportation, temporary lodgings and useful telephone numbers!

	# COPIES	TOTAL
Newcomer's Handbook® for Atlanta	_____ x $17.95	$_____
Newcomer's Handbook® for Boston	_____ x $20.95	$_____
Newcomer's Handbook® for Chicago	_____ x $18.95	$_____
Newcomer's Handbook® for London	_____ x $20.95	$_____
Newcomer's Handbook® for Los Angeles	_____ x $17.95	$_____
Newcomer's Handbook® for Minneapolis-St. Paul	_____ x $20.95	$_____
Newcomer's Handbook® for New York City	_____ x $19.95	$_____
Newcomer's Handbook® for San Francisco	_____ x $20.95	$_____
Newcomer's Handbook® for Seattle	_____ x $21.95	$_____
Newcomer's Handbook® for Washington D.C.	_____ x $21.95	$_____
	SUBTOTAL	$_____
POSTAGE & HANDLING (*$7.00 first book, $1.00 each add'l.*)		$_____
	TOTAL	$_____

SHIP TO:

Name _____

Title _____

Company _____

Address _____

City _____ State _____ Zip _____

Phone Number (   ) _____

E-mail _____

Send this order form and a check or money order payable to:
First Books

First Books, Mail Order Department
6750 SW Franklin, Suite A, Portland, OR 97223
Allow 1-2 weeks for delivery

FIRST BOOKS

Visit our web site at

www.firstbooks.com

for a sample of all our books.

THE NEWCOMER'S HANDBOOK® SERIES

Newcomer's Handbook® for Atlanta

Newcomer's Handbook® for Boston

Newcomer's Handbook® for Chicago

Newcomer's Handbook® for Moving to London

Newcomer's Handbook® for Los Angeles

Newcomer's Handbook® for Minneapolis-St. Paul

Newcomer's Handbook® for Moving to New York City

Newcomer's Handbook® for Moving to San Francisco and the Bay Area

Newcomer's Handbook® for Moving to Seattle

Newcomer's Handbook® for Moving to Washington D.C.

NOTES

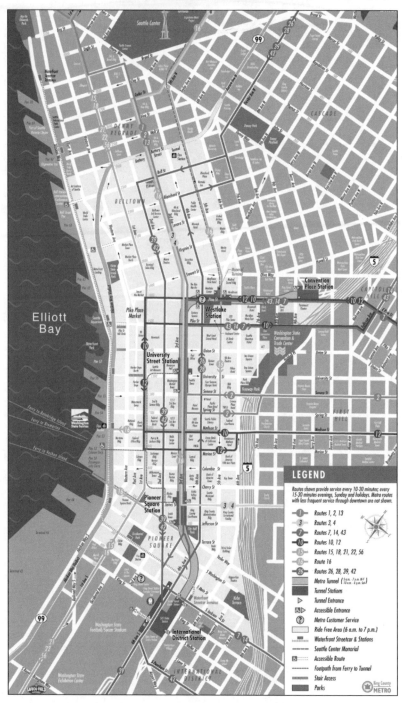

METRO TRANSIT DOWNTOWN ROUTES